The Devil's Mariner

ALSO BY ANTON GILL

NON-FICTION
Martin Allen is Missing
The Journey Back From Hell
Berlin to Bucharest
A Dance Between Flames
An Honourable Defeat

FICTION
The Egyptian Trilogy:
City of the Horizon
City of Dreams
City of the Dead

THE DEVIL'S MARINER

A Life of William Dampier,
Pirate and Explorer,
1651–1715

ANTON GILL

MICHAEL JOSEPH
LONDON

MICHAEL JOSEPH

Published by the Penguin Group
27 Wrights Lane, London w8 5tz
Viking Penguin Inc., 375 Hudson Street, New York, New York 10014, USA
Penguin Books Australia Ltd, Ringwood, Victoria, Australia
Penguin Books Canada Ltd, 10 Alcorn Avenue, Toronto, Ontario, Canada m4v 3b2
Penguin Books (NZ) Ltd, 182–190 Wairau Road, Auckland 10, New Zealand

Penguin Books Ltd, Registered Offices: Harmondsworth, Middlesex, England

First published in Great Britain 1997
Copyright © Anton Gill, 1997
1 3 5 7 9 10 8 6 4 2

Set in 11.75/14.5pt Monotype Van Dijck
Typeset by Rowland Phototypesetting Ltd, Bury St Edmunds, Suffolk
Printed in England by Clays Ltd, St Ives plc

A CIP catalogue record for this book is available from the British Library

ISBN 0718I 4114 8

The moral right of the author has been asserted

To the memory of my parents,
George and Nikki Gill,
who died in February 1995

CONTENTS

LIST OF ILLUSTRATIONS

Text Illustrations

ACKNOWLEDGEMENTS

Many people have helped me with the research for this book, and others have shown either kind interest, great support, or both, during the time I have spent on it.

I especially want to thank: Joel H. Baer, Karin Barton, Richard Barton, Richard Beswick, Elizabeth Cockburn, Flora Duley, Louise Haines, Simon Heneage, Timothy Heneage, the Reverend David Hunt, Richard Johnson, Mark Lucas, William Monteith, Judy Parker and Richard Timmis. My late mother, Nikki Gill, helped with the initial stages of the research, and at the latter end of the work I was grateful to have the assistance of Sophia Wickham.

I must also thank the staffs of the following institutions: the British Library; the Manuscript Students' Room at the British Library; the Map Library at the British Library; the Institute of Historical Research; the National Maritime Museum; the National Portrait Gallery; the Public Record Office; the Library of the Royal Naval College; the Senate House Library; Somerset House, and Somerset Record Office.

The final eighteen months' work on this book coincided with a difficult time for me personally, and it is appropriate to thank the following people for their friendship. Truthfully, without them this book might not have been written: Marji Campi, Peter Ewence, the late Moira de Fries, Nicola S. Gill, Barbara Hastings, David and Sally Neville, and Peter and Sophia Wickham.

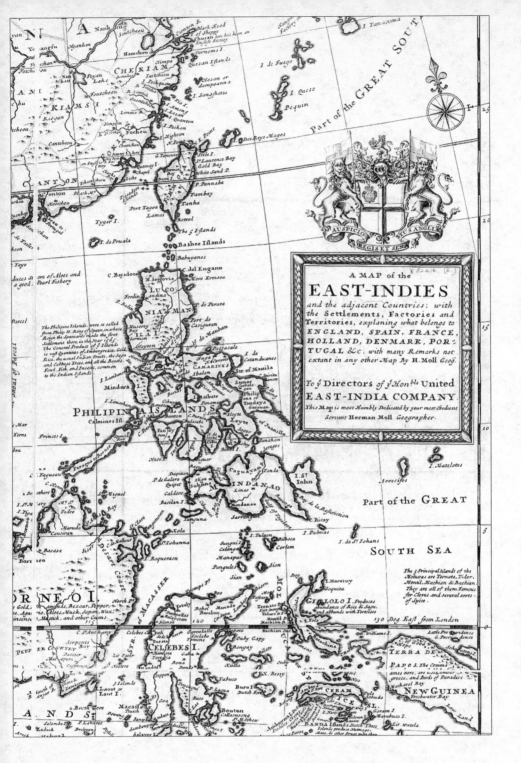

Detail from a map of the East Indies, 1710, by Herman Moll

xii

Detail from a map of the West Indies from 'Atlas Royal', *c.* 1710, by Herman Moll

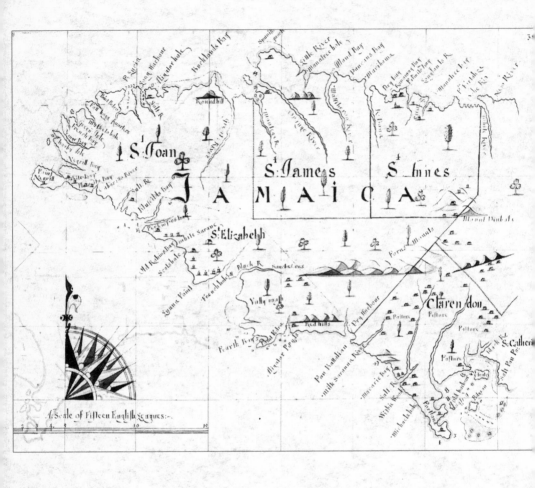

Jamaica from 'A Description of Coasts, Islands and Co. in the North Sea of America . . .',
c. 1690, by William Hack

xiv

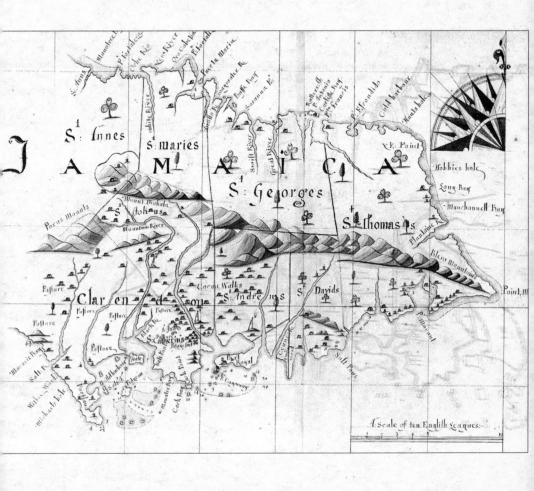

FOREWORD

In the Preface to his *New Voyage round the World*, William Dampier wrote:

> As to my style, it cannot be expected that a seaman should affect politeness; for were I able to do it, yet I think I should be little solicitous about it, in a work of this nature. I have frequently indeed divested myself of sea-phrases, to gratify the land reader, for which the seamen will hardly forgive me . . . I have not been curious as to the spelling of the names of places, plants, fruits, animals, & c. which in any of these remoter parts are given at the pleasure of travellers, and vary according to their different humours. Neither have I confined myself to such names as are given by learned authors, or so much as enquired after many of them. I write for my countrymen, and have, therefore, for the most part, used such names as are familiar to our English seamen, and those of our colonies abroad, yet without neglecting others that occurred.

Before I embark, I should explain how I have dealt with the vagaries of seventeenth-century English spelling, particularly in connection with the writing of seafaring men. Many mariners were literate, but their adhesion to standard orthography was slight. It is true that the reader often encounters good words which have fallen from common usage – like *gashly* for *ghastly* – but if you take the word for the primitive firearm for which the *Oxford English Dictionary* gives two possible modern spellings: *arquebus* and *harquebus*, you enter a minefield. William Swan Stallybrass, a modern editor of John Esquemeling's *The Buccaneers of America*, opts for harquebus, but points out that 'other early spellings are: arkebusshe, ha(c)quebute, hargubush, harquebuz(e), herquebuze, hagabus, etc.!'

Faced with this, I have usually standardized spelling to conform with modern usage. Where no exact modern equivalent can be found I have retained the original and, where necessary, explained what the word means in brackets immediately following. An example is *fuzee* – a light musket. The *OED* does offer *fusil* as the modern version, but it seems to me that even such a word may need explanation for most of us. I have tried to keep such interruptions to a minimum: often it is clear from the context what is meant. All such explanations within a quoted passage are within square brackets, as are interpolated words or phrases which clarify or expand the sense. Round brackets in such a passage belong to it.

I have brought punctuation and grammar into line with modern usage, and this has sometimes meant dividing one sentence into several. The advantage is that the modern reader will be able to follow the seventeenth-century thought with greater ease and clarity.

Proper names suffer from a variety of spellings. This is especially true of the names of Indian chiefs, written down phonetically, but there is also confusion about Europeans' names. John Esquemeling, the author mentioned above, may have been called that by the English, but his original name was Alexander Olivier Exquemelin, or perhaps even Hendrik Smeeks. The notorious and successful pirate Henry Avery (or Every) was also known as John Every (or Avery), Long Ben, and as Captain Bridgeman. At least his nationality – British – was not in doubt. Exquemelin may have been Dutch or French – though there is reason nowadays to believe that he was born at Harfleur.

The problem is compounded by the frequency with which some names crop up. There are three Captain Cooks in the account which follows (none of whom is, or is related to, the famous one): Edmund or Edmond, John and Edward. Their surnames are variously spelt Cook and Cooke. I have tried to resolve all this by sticking to the spelling most commonly encountered in my reading. Even so, a good deal of concentration is sometimes demanded of the reader in keeping track of who is who!

Names of places can differ very widely from their modern equivalents. Though some remain the same, many of the ports, towns, islands and countries visited by Dampier have changed colonial hands, and hence their names, several times since, or have gained their independence. In the text, I have usually used the names Dampier called them by, but I have given a general list of modern equivalents at the end of the book.

The problem of the names of ships has been easier to resolve. In most cases the names remain as they were. Because I like them, I have not modernized the name of *The Batchelor's Delight*, nor that of the *Dutchess*. The galleon taken by Woodes Rogers and renamed the *Batchelor* remains unchanged, since it was named after a Bristol linen draper and alderman, John Batchelor, who was one of the venture's principal backers. Most people who have written on the subject before have modernized *Marquiss* – the renamed prize *Havre de Grâce* – as *Marquis*. The modern English equivalent would be *Marquess*, but I have stayed with *Marquiss*. Captain Swan's ship, often written down in contemporary accounts as the *Signett*, becomes the *Cygnet*. I was tempted to leave the name in its older form, but too many accounts, some contemporary and all later ones, adopt the latter spelling for me to stand out from them – though in Dampier's *manuscript* account the spelling is *Signett*.

There remains the question of the calendar. In 1582, Pope Gregory XIII reformed the Julian Calendar by suppressing ten days (5th October 1582 became the 15th), and introducing the leap year together with an extra day in every centennial year divisible by four. The reform was adopted by most Roman Catholic countries immediately, but Great Britain did not adopt the Gregorian Calendar until 1752, when eleven days were docked from the year to bring the country into line (eleven days, because 1700 had been a leap-centennial year). From then on, the Julian Calendar was known as Old Style and the Gregorian as New Style. The year would henceforward begin on 1st January. As the legal year before 1752 began on 25th March, 1751 is notionally minus January, February and twenty-four days of March, while 1752 loses 3rd–13th September inclusive. Hence the customary usage in contemporary documents was to differentiate between the start of the legal and the start of the historical year – i.e., 1st January. Thus, for example, in Dampier's manuscript, he mentions falling in with Captain Eaton on 25th January 1683/84: 1684 is the historical year. Years given in the text are historical years, but for simplicity's sake I have used Dampier's dates for days of the month.

The edition of Dampier's works which I have chiefly used is that of

John Masefield (1906), which is the only complete modern edition, sadly limited to a printing of 1,000 copies, though in 1994 the Folio Society brought out an abridged edition, by Gerald Norris. For Basil Ringrose's account, apart from his manuscript, I have chiefly used the version which forms Part IV of *The Buccaneers of America*, edited by William Swan Stallybrass (1923), already referred to. Lionel Wafer's account is taken mainly from the edition of 1934 by L. E. Elliott-Joyce for the Hakluyt Society.

There have not been many biographies of Dampier. The last, a short one by Christopher Lloyd, was published in 1966; William Bonner's biography of 1934 concentrates on Dampier's literary influence – on Defoe and Swift in particular. The fullest all-round account to date is that of Clennell Wilkinson (1929).

All other principal sources, and a select bibliography, including other biographies, are to be found at the back of this book.

AG
11.3.97

PART ONE

Seaman, Lumberjack, Merchant, Buccaneer

CHAPTER ONE

William Dampier in his Time

I first came across William Dampier in autumn 1988. I was in the British Library reading a biography of Captain Cook. Someone had suggested that I write a biography, and as I had always been interested in nautical exploration I decided to start with one of the most obvious candidates. I was a little alarmed at the number of biographies of Cook which already existed, and I was beginning to wonder what I might be able to add to them, when a footnote caught my eye.

The footnote made reference – luckily for me, pretty full reference – to someone called William Dampier. Apart from the initial and irrational attraction of such a nice name, there was enough information here to intrigue me, and I couldn't have been in a better place for following up leads. An hour or so later, I had had two biographies of the man himself delivered to my desk – one very old, the other very short – and a superb limited-edition two-volume copy of the works of the man himself, edited by none other than John Masefield, and bearing a publication date of 1906. One of the jewels in my own library today is another copy – only 1,000 were produced – bought at great expense and even more difficulty. I wonder how many of the original thousand are still in existence?

Over the next few days I read the biographies and Dampier's own writings. My fascination grew fast. Here was a man born with few advantages, whose single-minded determination to see the world bore all before it. Here was an important and all-but-unsung major English nautical explorer who stood midway between Ralegh and Cook. Here was a man who, though he worked and lived as a pirate and a privateer, was able to show his contemporaries then-unknown parts of the world

3

for the first time, in vividly descriptive prose, yet without exaggeration or elaboration. This was the man who first described such exotic creatures as tapirs and manatees for us, who told us for the first time about plantains, bananas and breadfruit, and whose navigational research inspired and informed many generations of seafarers and explorers who came after him – among them Horatio Nelson, and the great James Cook himself.

William stands not only head and shoulders above his contemporary mariners: he is alone in reviving the great tradition of marine exploration started by Drake and Ralegh. He pioneered seaways which opened the oceans to the major expeditions of the eighteenth century, which in turn would be instrumental in laying the foundations of the British Empire.

I am an armchair explorer, but it seemed incredible to me that this man, however lauded his work was in his day and throughout the first half of the eighteenth century, should have received so little recognition in our own time: there are half a dozen short Victorian memoirs of him, and only one major biography, which was published seventy years ago and leaves a lot unsaid. Why? Because William was a pirate? Because his brief career in the Royal Navy ended in disgrace? Because later in life he seems to have lost much of his enthusiasm, his bearings, and even his grip? Because he died in obscurity not twenty years after the zenith of his career?

Perhaps the reasons do not matter. The most important thing, it seemed to me, was to redress the balance, and introduce to a wider world this astonishing and seminal English hero. There were times during the course of my research when I was sidetracked. Other important work came between him and me, and I was to complete three major books on subjects totally unrelated to the nautical world of the late seventeenth century before I was able to come back to him. But I never lost my deep interest in him, and whenever I had time I would return to the British Library to mine the rich lodes in the Reading Room and the Manuscript Room. My rewards included the thrill of holding in my own hands a manuscript atlas of South America captured by one of Dampier's pirate commanders and brought back to present to Charles II, as well as the salt-stained memoirs, in brown ink on thick vellum, of many a seafarer of the savage and unknown oceans of 300 years ago. A few manuscript letters in Dampier's hand still exist, and to hold these, as I sat in the brightly lit and austere surroundings of the Public Record Office and the Somerset Record Office in Taunton, gave me intense pleasure.

The more information I got, the more fascinated I became, and sometimes this was a mystery because Dampier's private character is very elusive. He is secretive about his personal life, and very few contemporary accounts survive to help us fill in the many gaps. I hate fanciful speculation that has no basis in fact; but if I had wanted to present a man of singular attractiveness, I would have been disappointed, for many of the traits of William's character that are exposed to view turn out to be unpleasant. But overriding all this is his wonderful thirst for knowledge and for new experiences, which, once acquired, he faithfully and patiently shares with us, writing his journals – which are now lost – in conditions which were appallingly difficult.

Dampier's enthusiasm is what communicates itself, and that, together with a life of unparalleled adventure, is what also makes him, despite his defects and the impossibility of getting close to the private man, such an attractive, and for me, irresistible subject. Dampier lived at a time when there were still unknown horizons to cross, when a voyage over the Pacific was less certain than sending a rocket to Jupiter is now. When the peoples of the world knew nothing of one another, and when the all-pervading pollution of tourism, satellite television and the cola-drink culture was unknown. In short, when there was still a really undiscovered country out there.

A likeness exists of William Dampier. It is in the collection of the English National Portrait Gallery. It is the only incontestably genuine portrait of a British pirate that there is.

The painting is by Thomas Murray, and it was made at the end of the seventeenth century, probably in 1697, the year which saw the publication of Dampier's first book, *A New Voyage round the World*. Dampier holds a copy of it rather self-consciously in his right hand, the spine directed towards the observer. The book, the first great travel book, apart from anthologies, in the English language, was an instant success and earned its author fame, if not fortune.

Murray was almost certainly commissioned to do Dampier's portrait by Sir Hans Sloane, one of the many members of the London elite who befriended and adopted the blunt-mannered sailor, as the importance of his book became apparent. Dampier had just spent twelve years in a circumnavigation of the globe. What he had found out about the world in that time was not only brand new, but illuminating, because the man had an unusually sensitive and scientific eye.

People were prepared to gloss over the way he had made his living during those years.

The portrait isn't one of Murray's best: it is a dutiful work, and the sitter is as stiff and uncomfortable before the artist as people unhappy or unfamiliar with cameras are before the lens.

He would have been about forty-six when it was done. He wears his own hair – still dark brown and thick, without a hint of grey – to the shoulders. He has a plain brown jacket on, with a richer, red waistcoat beneath into which a plain white stock is tucked. The face is nervous, bluff, belligerent and resolute.

Looking at it in more detail, there are contradictions: below the long, fleshy nose, the set of the mouth is determined. But isn't there a little weakness about the chin? And isn't there a hint of defensiveness, even apology, in the bright, dark-brown eyes? One wonders if this is a man whom it would be easy to get on with.

When one examines his life, the contradictions suggested in the face become even more apparent. The title on the frame once read: *William Dampier – Pirate and Hydrographer*.

Early in his *New Voyage round the World* he wrote:

My friends did not originally design me for the sea, but bred me at school till I came to years fit for a trade. But upon the death of my father and mother, they who had the disposal of me took other measures: and having removed me from the Latin school to learn writing and arithmetic, they soon after placed me with a master of a ship at Weymouth, complying with the inclinations I had very early of seeing the world. With him I made a short voyage to France; and returning thence, went to Newfoundland, being then about eighteen years of age. In this voyage I spent one summer; but so pinched with the rigour of that cold climate that upon my return

I was absolutely against going to those parts of the world, but went home again to my friends. Yet going up a while after to London, the offer of a warm voyage and a long one, both which I always desired, soon carried me to sea again.

This kind of writing is rare, coming from William Dampier's pen. He rarely describes his own feelings, or his personal life. In fact, he was born into an age which perfectly suited his disposition.

Dampier was to become one of Britain's greatest maritime explorers in an age of intense curiosity.

There had been great explorers before – the Cabots, Columbus, Drake, Magellan, Ralegh, had all sailed dauntlessly into the unknown long before William Dampier was born. Similarly, the spirit of scientific and philosophical inquiry had been alive – though for long periods as glowing, even dying embers rather than a blaze – since the days of ancient Greece. But in western Europe, notwithstanding the Renaissance, we can mark the beginnings of recognizably modern approaches and thinking from approximately the middle of the seventeenth century.

It isn't the purpose of this book to define why, but the core of the reason, I think, is that during this period inquiry became truly and consistently scientific. It was an age that saw a prodigious number of great minds come to prominence. Among William Dampier's close contemporaries are Joseph Addison, Aphra Behn, Robert Boyle, Daniel Defoe, John Dryden, John Evelyn, Edmond Halley, Robert Hooke, Andrew Marvell, Isaac Newton, Samuel Pepys, Alexander Pope, Hans Sloane, Richard Steele, Jonathan Swift and Christopher Wren. The Royal Society was incorporated under the patronage of King Charles II in 1662, and the *Philosophical Transactions* began to appear in 1665. Ten years later, John Ogilby produced his *Britannia*, the first comprehensive survey of the country's roads, done at the express desire of the king. This was an age of extreme curiosity, but it was also still an age of splendour, when kings were kings. When she married Charles II, Catherine of Braganza's dowry was £800,000 in cash, plus Bombay and Tangier. (Charles II handed Bombay over to the East India Company in 1668.)

It was also an age of brutality, cruel punishment, lingering superstition, fumbling medicine and social unfairness. There had been a prison on the site of London's most famous gaol, Newgate, since the twelfth century, and conditions there 500 years later were as terrible as ever. In Dampier's day, Newgate was so full that prisoners slept three to a bed, and so verminous that lice 'crunched underfoot like shells on a beach'. The smell was such that visitors had to hold bunches of violets or pomanders to their nostrils in order to withstand it. Prisoners were bathed in vinegar before making an appearance in court. It's interesting for English late-twentieth-century society to note that Newgate was run as a private business at the time; inmates were made to pay rent for their cells and the warders charged fees for their services.

London was the capital and principal port, and contained about 10 per cent of the country's population in Dampier's day. It was the biggest and probably the liveliest city in Europe. Hundreds of thousands of people lived there. The nation's second city and second port, Bristol, had fewer than 30,000 inhabitants; but the burgeoning slave trade was beginning to make the fortunes of merchant venturers, who were busily buying up real estate there.

Dampier started out on his travels 100 years before James Cook set out on his famous series of voyages of exploration; and Cook's achievements should be regarded as the apotheosis of the work of scientific exploration begun by Dampier.

By Cook's time, no one seriously believed in sea monsters. The men of Dampier's generation were just beginning to liberate themselves from such fears. Fifty years before Dampier's birth, a mariner who saw a giant squid might have believed that he was in the presence of a supernatural being. By the time Dampier was sailing the world, such creatures had begun to be viewed not as sea monsters, but instead as monsters of the sea: hitherto undiscovered animals, whose size and behaviour were due to scientifically explicable causes.

William Dampier himself, a largely self-taught geographer, hydrographer and navigator, was also a keen natural historian. He made observations rather than drawing conclusions, because his was pioneering work, a laying of cornerstones on which men like Cook, with the advantages of a technology unthought of in Dampier's day, would build. Cook was in charge of a series of professional expeditions, and sailing with him were experts. Though a thoroughly professional seaman and navigator, Dampier in the field of the natural sciences was essentially an amateur: he made his way round the world at first by hitching lifts on pirate ships, always following his instincts and, above all, his demanding, imperious curiosity. But he was aware of his status, and if he was confident about the importance of his discoveries, he was also modest about them.

Dampier may have worked alone, but he was not alone. Although English exploration had been in abeyance since the days of Drake and Ralegh, the Dutchman Abel Tasman had made his voyages of discovery to Terra Australis Incognita in the 1640s. The end of the seventeenth century saw a vogue for travel literature, as curiosity about the rest of the world became current, and people began to look outwards, in a confident and optimistic spirit. Sir Hans Sloane may have been the prince of collectors of 'oddities', but he was by no means the only great collector. Without film and television to record fauna and flora, elements of the real thing had to be collected, dried, stuffed, pressed between the leaves of books, or preserved in alcohol, and brought home, to give an impression of what the original had been like. Artefacts of every kind were collected and shipped to England. Freaks were eagerly sought, and, where necessary, faked in order to supply demand. As superstition was by no means wholly conquered in people's minds, an awe of the supernatural added to the impressiveness of the unfamiliar objects offered to view.

Cartography and ship design improved, and so did navigational skills and navigation technology. Dying in 1715, William Dampier benefited little from any of this, but he had made his contribution, particularly in the field of navigation. The Board of Longitude began its sittings in 1713, and in the same year offered three prizes for the discovery of an accurate method of determining longitude. By 1726 the 33-year-old John Harrison had built a timepiece whose mechanism was able to correct erroneous readings caused by variations in the climate. Forty years later, he had perfected his instrument – the chronometer – and won the first prize. It was just in time for James Cook to make use of.

Dampier's navigational instruments were similar to ones used in the

Middle Ages. The estimation of lines of longitude in his day was a complicated, vexed and inaccurate business. And yet as early as 1726 – fewer than forty years after Dampier had completed his first, epic circumnavigation, Daniel Defoe wrote with blasé offhandedness:

> I do not . . . lessen the merit of those gentlemen who have made such a long voyage as that round the globe; but I must be allowed to say, as the way is now a common road . . . so the world has done wondering at it . . . and he that can carry a ship to Lisbon, may with the same ease carry it round the world.

Most exploration from Europe at that time had been by sea, not by land. Routes to the Far East via Cape Horn and via the Cape of Good Hope had been established long since, though the English had scarcely been seen on the Pacific coast of America since the days of Hawkins and Drake, and the Pacific itself, or South Sea, lay uncharted and empty, except for the annual Manila ship that plied, with its fabled cargo of Indian and Chinese riches, between the Philippines and Acapulco.

Exploration was inspired by military and economic considerations: war and trade. All Europe knew of the vast possessions Spain laid claim to in America, and all Europe knew how ill-equipped Spain was to protect them. The mounting of major military expeditions at such a great distance was beyond the powers of Europe, however, and so for centuries a series of small depredations was made, often freelance, by English, French and Dutch traders and pirates; while at home the same nations and Spain participated, especially in the period which concerns us, in a series of wars.

It is not possible in this context to pass absolute judgement on the quality of William Dampier's own voyages; but he is also one of the very first explorers to be interested in discovery for its own sake – this is clear from the record of his first and most important long voyage round the world. A difficult man: a robber and a scientist; a pirate and an explorer; a materialist and a visionary.

To understand William Dampier better, it is worth looking at the world in which he lived. Although there were many ships at sea, the number relative to our times was still small, and anyone setting out on a voyage of exploration was going into the unknown, especially when sailing in the Pacific Ocean, where Dampier pioneered, developing what was for the time a unique knowledge of that huge sea.

Voyages to the north of Cancer and south of Capricorn were equally adventurous. Though they might have had a notion of what their ultimate goal was, nautical explorers of 300 years ago often had no more than a rough idea of the distances they had to cover, and of what they might find *en route*. They met with the natives of remote lands with no preconceptions whatsoever, no visual images of the landscapes, people, animals and plants they would encounter at all. Dampier's writing is phlegmatic, scientific, restrained: one occasionally wishes that a greater note of excitement would creep into it. But understatement, and calm observation of what he saw, is his great strength. It is just that sometimes such a style gets in the way of our ability to imagine the precise *novelty* of what he saw.

But his style does reflect the age, and although there is little doubt that his work is not ghosted by a professional writer, he has been encouraged to polish his prose for the printed page. There is nothing wrong with that, and his first major work, *A New Voyage round the World*, was an immediate bestseller, because it satisfied the voracious intellectual appetite of the time. Because his descriptions were so detailed, the knowledge he was sharing was also of great mercantile and military use, and there is no doubt that Dampier, and all his colleagues and contemporaries, had these applications in mind when they collected their information. But where many are fanciful, Dampier is always factual.

The bullishness of the second half of the seventeenth century, coupled with the new markets that were opening up in the world at large, led to sharper trade rivalry between neighbouring west-European nations, and thence to wars.

Relations with the Dutch had been difficult since the beginning of the century. Between 1600 and 1650 English trade had grown significantly, since England had remained neutral during the Thirty Years War, and had profited from the city of Dover's role as the principal port linking the nations at war. Already long-standing sources of friction between

England and Holland – the cloth trade, the carriage trade, and disputes over fishing rights – were added to after the English Revolution. William II of Orange was a son-in-law and a supporter of King Charles I. Marauding Dutch and French privateers made life difficult for English merchant ships, and the Depression which followed the Civil War increased fears of Dutch domination of trade, especially with America and the East Indies. The English wanted to nip any threat of Dutch trade dominance in the bud; the Dutch sought to protect themselves by destroying the English Navy.

In December 1651, the year of Dampier's birth, the Dutch government sent a delegation to London to ask that the current Navigation Act be repealed. The Act, one of a series of similar type, forbade the importing of goods to England from Europe except in ships owned by Englishmen, or in ships belonging to the exporting country. Goods from beyond Europe might not be carried in ships other than British ones or those belonging to Britain's colonies.

The situation was tense, and while negotiations were still under way a Dutch fleet commanded by Martin Harpertzoon Tromp met an English force under Robert Blake. This clash, in May 1652, in which two Dutch ships were lost, led to a formal declaration of war. When Oliver Cromwell became Lord Protector in December 1653, however, he was more interested in a Protestant Alliance than in promoting the interests of British merchant venturers. The war ended in April 1654. The terms of the peace treaty were mild, given the trouncing the Dutch had received; but through it Cromwell was able to reduce continental support for the exiled Stuarts.

In 1655 Cromwell turned his attention towards Spain, declaring war and sending a major expedition to the West Indies, partly to uphold a revived Elizabethan claim that the English should be free to trade with the Spanish in the colonies, and partly to stake an English claim in the Caribbean. The aim of the expedition, led by Admiral William Penn (the father of the famous Quaker) and General Robert Venables, was to take the island of Hispaniola. In this it failed, but it succeeded in taking the less well-defended and at the time much less important island of Jamaica. English possession of the island was to have a profound effect on the balance of power in the Caribbean in the years to come, but at the time the taking of Jamaica was not regarded as a major achievement. Cromwell was furious, and sent Venables and Penn to the Tower for a month when they returned. A number of grovelling letters from the imprisoned Venables to the Lord Protector survive, as does his rather apologetic account of the campaign.

The Parliament troops who remained in occupation on the island were left in the lurch, as is borne out by a dispatch from Colonel John Humphrey ('the son of him who carried the sword before President Bradshaw at the trial of Charles I') to the commander-in-chief 'of all his Highness' forces in America', Sir Edward D'Oyley, dated 4th July 1655:

> Whereas we are every day importuned both by the officers and soldiers of the army, representing the sadness of their condition, and discouraged by their great mortality and continual distress of late, utterly disabling them from either performing any public service for the Commonwealth, or to plant for their subsistence here. That we would commiserate their condition and use some speedy means for their removal hence, that so the handful of men yet remaining may be serviceable to his Highness the Lord Protector and the Commonwealth of England. We therefore from the sense of great duty that lieth upon us, both towards God and our own several charges, have made bold to make these our humble addresses to you, that you would be pleased to represent them effectually to the Admiral and Commissioner Sedgewick, that speedy course may be taken effectively for their relief.

Action was taken for this within a fortnight, but it is unlikely that it *was* effective. A sad note dated 13th February 1656, states that 'Whereas by reason of the great mortality it has pleased God to visit this army withal, almost all the chaplains and ministers are dead.' Venables and Penn had commanded a force of 8,000, partly made up of 3,500 former so-called indentured servants, virtual slaves, looking to escape their bonds, and recruited at Barbados (though the island was a Royalist enclave). Many of these men would never return home, and many would swell the ranks of the buccaneers, pirates and privateers who were soon to throng the Caribbean seas, some still wearing the now-faded red uniforms of the New Model Army.

The war with Spain lasted until 1659, when it ended in stalemate; but from the English point of view it had achieved its aims. There was now an English toehold in the Caribbean, and the Commonwealth had driven a Protestant wedge between France and Spain, the two powers most likely to oppose it. Moreover, the Navy, developed by the Republic under such men as Robert Blake, had become so powerful that there was now a squadron in the Baltic to protect nautical supplies – hemp, masts and tar – from the Danes and the Dutch, in their passage through the Sound. There was another squadron in the Mediterranean, protecting the ships of the Levant Company from Spanish privateers and Barbary corsairs. Yet the cost of the operation had been high. Money for the fleet and the army was now short, and the prospect of borrowing was dim, since the City began to feel the growing burden on trade. Between 1,200 and 2,000 English merchant vessels were taken by Spanish privateers during these years.

An additional problem was that trade rivalry between England and Holland had not disappeared, and another war began between the two countries in 1665, though hostilities had already broken out unofficially in 1664. In the struggle for dominance of the Channel and the North Sea, the English enjoyed some early success under the Duke of York, but a later attack on Dutch merchantmen sheltering in Bergen, led by the Earl of Sandwich, ended disastrously, and squabbles between commanding officers seriously hampered the campaign. The result of this was that in 1666 joint command of the fleet was passed to Prince Rupert (James I's grandson) and the Duke of Albemarle. The fortunes of war failed to go with either country, though each side scored victories and for a time the Dutch under de Ruyter managed to blockade the mouth of the Thames. It was later in this same war that de Ruyter famously sailed up the Thames itself. The Dutch set fire to Sheerness, and went up the Medway to burn or carry off some of England's largest ships, including the eighty-six-gun *Royal Charles*, which was displayed as a trophy in Rotterdam for years afterwards.

In the venture, de Ruyter enjoyed the assistance of English pilots. The war had been costing England dear, and sailors had been receiving 'treasury tickets' in lieu of pay. These tickets, or promises to pay, were the final insult to English seamen, who had fought hard and long in appalling conditions. Now, without money, many died of starvation; others managed to sell their tickets to speculators at a fraction of their face value; a few were paid in the end. But the simplest solution was to desert to the Dutch, who rewarded the sailors' nautical expertise with dollars. From the decks of the Dutch ships these men would shout to their former messmates: 'We did heretofore fight for tickets; now we fight for dollars!' It was a shameful reflection on Charles II's attitude to his Navy, and the people of London especially, already demoralized by the Great Plague and the Great Fire, heard the roar of de Ruyter's cannon with dismay. Samuel Pepys had begun work with the Navy Office in 1660. Now it took all his organizational flair to maintain the service, for his budget was tiny. He had to cajole merchants into supplying goods on credit, and it is a tribute both to his skill and their patriotism that many did so and went on doing so until lack of payment brought about their ruin. There is an example of one supplier of canvas still chasing a debt of £70,000 – a huge sum in those days – ten years after delivery. Charles was not a man to put money into the Navy, and it was left to his brother James, Duke of York and Lord High Admiral, to pull the service into shape after a further period of neglect between 1678 and 1684.

The second Dutch War ended with the Treaty of Breda, signed on 31st July 1667. The Dutch kept Surinam and Pulo Run, but New Amsterdam was surrendered to the English, who also kept Cape Coast Castle in Guinea, which established another strong toehold – this time in the African trades of gold, ivory and slaves.

The following year, in response to Louis XIV's designs on the Spanish Netherlands, the defensive Triple Alliance was formed between England, Holland and Sweden. This had the effect of checking the French king's ambitions, but Charles II, half-French himself and harbouring strong Roman Catholic sympathies, was soon negotiating secretly with Louis, which negotiations resulted in the Treaty of Dover of 1670. By its terms the two powers would attack and overwhelm Holland, dividing the spoils but leaving a small Dutch 'kingdom', to be ruled by the young William of Orange, cast in the role of vassal to Louis. A further secret treaty promised French soldiers and money to Charles, who would use them to back his own public conversion to Catholicism. Thereafter the plan was to promote Catholics to positions of power in England.

Much depended on a speedy victory over the Dutch, but England and France, whose alliance was in any case a cool one, had reckoned without the tenacity of the Dutch and the courage of William. The dykes were breached, bringing the French invading army to a standstill, and the Dutch fleet under de Ruyter discharged itself well at the battles of Solebay and Texel. Running out of money once again, Charles negotiated a separate peace with Holland and the Treaty of Westminster was signed on 19th February 1674.

For the remainder of the century and up until the Treaty of Utrecht in 1713, there was a series of wars and alliances, which essentially saw Protestant countries drawn up on one side, and Catholics on the other. Louis XIV, who married Maria Theresa, daughter of Philip IV of Spain, did not give up his ambitions in the Spanish Netherlands, and he sought to increase France's power and influence by promoting his grandson, Philip of Anjou, as heir to the Spanish throne following the death of the childless Carlos II in 1700. He also had an eye to Spanish possessions in America.

In 1701–2, Louis sent soldiers to occupy fortresses in the Spanish Netherlands, and at the same time recognized James II's son – the thirteen-year-old James Edward – as the rightful King of England. War with England broke out as a result, though James II died, in exile, in 1701 and William III of England, exhausted by the demands of his reign, in 1702. His successor was Anne, James II's second daughter.

The War of the Spanish Succession, which saw Marlborough's famous defence of the Spanish Netherlands, lasted until 1713. Anne died the following year, having outlived all her seventeen children. To ensure a Protestant succession, the crown passed to George of Hanover, a great-grandson of James I.

The Treaty of Utrecht established the Archduke Charles as Emperor of the Austrian dominions, and of Spanish possessions, now ceded to him, in Italy and the Netherlands. Philip V kept Spain and its colonies intact, but he also had to promise not to transfer to France any land held by Spain in America. Gibraltar and Menorca were ceded to England. France acknowledged the legitimacy of the English succession, and ceded to England St Kitts, Newfoundland and Nova Scotia. At the same time a mutually beneficial trade agreement was signed. The Treaty ushered in a new age of peace and stability. The Royal Navy was cut back drastically and thousands of seamen faced unemployment. The Golden Age of piracy was about to begin.

CHAPTER TWO

Natural Curiosity

Edward Barlow, a fellow seaman who once met Dampier when their voyages crossed, wrote in 1671:

> They are said here upon the Malabar coast, in some places, to worship the Devil for their God, and every Friday to offer one of their children to him. Taking notice two Fridays that we stayed there and at Tannanore that we saw a great fire about two or three miles up in the country, one day towards night, when the fire was almost out and it began to be dark, it presently began to rain and blow and thunder and lighten most horribly, and all the day before was as fair and clear a day as could possibly be, which made me think that then they were offering up as a sacrifice one of their sons or daughters to their God, the Devil, and that the Hellish Fiend, being offended at something, caused him to raise such a horrible tempest so suddenly, it continuing no longer than about an hour.

Barlow was born in 1642 at Prestwick, near Manchester. He was the son of a poor farmer. From his description it is possible to see something new for the time: a literate member of the working class taking a natural interest in scientific observation. This little descriptive passage also shows a transition in progress: Barlow was trying to observe local customs and draw inferences from them, but his interpretation is still clouded by superstition. Barlow's period was one in which ordinary men were beginning to wean themselves off superstitious beliefs and on to the explicable meanings behind them. Proper observation was beginning to beat a path towards comprehension and conclusion. Those who travelled had a duty to describe in detail what they saw: it could be of intense economic and military importance to their own countries, and of value to their own standing and business interests. Europe was becoming increasingly aware of what was out there for the taking – of the riches of the East and West which had for too long been the monopolies of Portugal and Spain, and of what yet remained to be discovered, known only by sketchy maps, or by vague reports and rumours, but definitely known to be there.

Barlow was a good draughtsman: his *Journal* is well illustrated with detailed views of elevated coastlines. There is no evidence to show that William Dampier could draw at all well, but his eye, allied to his pen rather than his brush, more than made up for that. Writing with exhaustive attention to detail of a prolonged visit to the East Indies in 1689, he launches into a description of Sumatra and its north-western islands which reveals that from an early age his gifts for observation and deduction were well established:

The mold [soil] of this continent [country] is different according to the natural position of it. The mountains are rocky, especially those towards the west coast, yet most that I have seen seems to have a superficial covering of earth, naturally producing shrubs, small trees, or pretty good grass. The small hills are most of them clothed with woods, the trees whereof seem by their growth to spring from a fruitful soil: the champion [level and open] land, such as I have seen, is some black, some grey, some reddish, and all of a deep mold. But to be very particular in these things, especially in all my travels, is no more than I can pretend to: though it may be I took as much notice of the difference of soil as I met with it, as most travellers have done, having been bred in my youth in Somersetshire, at a place called East Coker near Yeovil or Evil: in which parish there is as great variety of soil, as I have ordinarily met with anywhere, viz. black, red, yellow, sandy, stony, clay, morass or swampy, &c. I had the more reason to take notice of this, because this village in great measure is let out in small leases for lives of 20, 30, 40, or 50 pound per an. under Col. Helyar, the Lord of the Manor: and most, if not all these tenants had their own land scattering in small pieces, up and down several sorts of land in the parish: so that every one had some piece of every sort of land; his black ground, his sandy, clay, & c., some of 20, 30, or 40 shillings an acre, for some uses, and others not worth 10 groats an acre. My mother being possessed of one of these leases, and having of all these sorts of land, I became acquainted with them all, and knew what each sort would produce, (viz.) wheat, barley, maslin [a mixture of wheat and rye], rice [a misprint for 'rye'?], beans, peas, oats, vetches, flax, or hemp: in all which I had a more than usual knowledge for one so young; taking a particular delight in observing it.

William was born in East Coker, in the then Royalist county of Somerset, shortly before 5th September 1651, when his baptism was recorded in the parish register, together with the names of his parents, George and Ann. Both had died before he reached his mid-teens.

The name Dampier is not uncommon in the West Country and has been known in England since the thirteenth century. It is a corruption through French of Dominus Petrus – Saint Peter, who becomes Dom. Pierre. By tradition the descendants of one Guy de Dampierre, whose French successors were counts of Flanders in the thirteenth and fourteenth centuries, by the mid sixteenth century English Dampiers were settled in several Somerset parishes – Lovington, Marston Magna, Rimpton, Weston Bampfyld and Lymington – all in the same part of the county, though no blood link connects all of them.

William was a commonly used name among them, and as on the same page of the parish register there is an entry for the baptism of *another* William Dampier, on 8th June 1652, this William has sometimes been taken to be our mariner. Perhaps because his entry is more legible and more striking on the page, which is not organized in any way neatly, his earlier namesake has been passed over. However, this second Dampier, the son of William and Joan, is not our man, but a cousin.

The difficulties are understandable. Quite apart from the plethora of Williams, the incumbent vicar of East Coker, Richard Gore, had been replaced during the Revolution by one Henry Cackney. Gore's handwriting was neat and tidy. Cackney's was large and undisciplined, and the pages in which his entries are written are much harder to read. Then there is a problem with Dampier's immediate antecedents. Between 8th June and 10th September 1645, the Plague struck East Coker, and seventy people were buried. Of the Dampiers struck down, the following concern us:

1645	BURIALS
July 24	Dampeerie William s. of William Junr.
Aug 2	Dampeeire Elizabeth w. of William Junr.
Aug 4	Dampeeire Margaret & Elizabeth, ds. of William Junr.

In time of plague, people remarried quickly, and a little later the register notes the marriage of William Dampier junior to 'Joane Mudford'. These two are the William and Joan who were the parents of the William Dampier baptized in 1652. However, *that* William had no brothers (he had two half-brothers, who both died in infancy), only an older sister, Elizabeth.

In the register for births on 7th January 1646 there is noted: 'Dampier. Ann d. of George and Ann.'

This is the first mention of George and Ann; their daughter, who sadly only lived for a week, was the first of six children: George, born in 1648; William, in 1651; Thomasina, in 1652; Theophilus, in 1653; and Josias, the date of whose birth is not known, but who may be the same person as the Josias Dampier, mariner, of HMS *Swiftsure*, whose will was proven in 1691. Theophilus died in infancy.

Dampier makes reference to his brother George, who survived him and farmed locally all his life. The connection is reinforced by the fact that in 1698, through the influence of his by then famous brother, George was able to publish in *Philosophical Transactions* an account of a cure for 'the bitings of mad creatures', the recipe for which he inherited from his uncle William. The impression is one of a well-established and relatively well-to-do farming family.

Dampier's father, George, died in 1658, aged forty, and his will was proven in London on 20th July of that year. In it he 'did declare his will and mind to be to the effect following viz. that George his eldest son should have the living and tenement wherein he dwelt after the decease of his wife hereafter named and that William his son should have his land purchased of beer and so much in money to make up the said land worth one hundred pounds.' George Dampier senior's own father was still living at the time and provision is made for his welfare. Our William's mother remained at his farm until her own death on 1st October 1665, and it is probable that William's brother George began to take over the management of the farm thereafter, though in the father's will George senior 'did appoint Anthony Tassell, John Giles, Peter Templeman and Michael Dodge to be his overseers'. It is interesting that the 1664–5 Somerset Hearth Tax lists Ann Dampier's family as the only one of that name in the county, with three hearths, and only one more Dampier is recorded in the East Coker parish records after that date through to 1713. George Dampier probably looked after the land William inherited from his father, though we do not hear of it again.

Whoever had charge of him – and it is likely from what later occurred that the local Lord of the Manor, Colonel William Helyar, took a close interest – William's education was not neglected, because of the potential for learning and the natural curiosity he was already showing. Though removed from the Latin school before his education was complete, he retained enough of the language to be able to converse with a French missionary in Latin years later in Tonquin, and his later good application of his knowledge of 'writing and arithmetic' is evident. It is not known for sure where he went to school, but Crewkerne and Yeovil had grammar schools at the time, and Chard and the King's School, Bruton, are other candidates.

We have already learnt that his guardians did not intend him for a life at sea, but we also know from his own pen that that was what he wanted, and he must have persuaded them to change their minds and apprentice him to the shipmaster at Weymouth. It wouldn't have been unusual for a second son to go to sea. The West Country was proud of its maritime heritage; its geographical position and its coastline made it a natural cradle for seafarers, and it is no accident that so many of England's great maritime heroes and villains come from there.

Dampier was eighteen years old when he first set sail. His first voyage was a short one across to France, but soon afterwards he crossed the Atlantic to Newfoundland, where a great fishery had been established. William so disliked the cold he encountered there that ever afterwards he avoided extreme latitudes.

Once qualified as an able seaman, William set out for London. He was keen to expand his horizons, and London was nothing for him but a stepping stone to further travel. 'The offer of a warm voyage and a long one, which I always desired, soon carried me to sea again. For hearing of an outward-bound East-Indiaman, the *John and Martha* of London, Captain Earning Commander, I entered myself aboard.'

They sailed for Bantam, in Java, touching at St Iago in the Cape Verde Islands on the way out, and staying at their final destination two months. On the way home they stopped at Ascension Island. The entire trip took a year. The *John and Martha* was a big ship, perhaps 500 tons, and well armed and crewed. She would have sailed alone, and would have been able to defend herself not only against pirates, but in conflicts arising from trade rivalry, especially with the Dutch and the French. Dampier tells us nothing of events on the voyage, but in his *Discourse of Winds*, written over twenty years later, he makes this comment, indicating that he had begun to record his journeyings from the very beginning:

When we go from England, and are bound to the East or West Indies, or to Guinea, we commonly find these winds in the lat. of 30 d., sometimes sooner, as in the latitudes of 32 or 35. And it may so happen that we may meet with an easterly wind in 40 d., or go out of our channel with a north-east wind, which sometimes also fails us not till we come into a true trade-wind; but this is only accidental, therefore it is not the wind that I speak of; but between 32 and 28 I did never know nor hear that the true trade-wind failed.

If in coming from England, we have a north-easterly wind that brings us hither [i.e., into the true trade-wind] it sometimes stays at north-east, especially if we keep near the African shore, as Guinea ships do, till we are near the Tropic of Cancer, and then comes to the ENE [East-North-East] where it settles; but commonly it settles there in 28 d. if we are so far off shore as to receive the true Trade. When the wind is thus settled, we commonly have fair weather, and a clear sky, especially if the sun is in any southern sign; but if in a northern sign, the weather is usually cloudy.

On the contrary, when we are in south lat. in the Atlantic, if the sun is in northern signs, the sky is clear, but if in southern signs, the sky is cloudy. This I once experienced to my sorrow, in my return from Bantam, in the year 1671. We had cloudy weather and brisk winds while we were crossing the East India Ocean, and had a very good passage also about the Cape of Good Hope; where we had fair clear weather; and steering from thence for the Island of St Helena, where we thought to water and refresh, as all our English East-India ships do, we missed it for want of an observation. For before we came to the Tropic of Capricorn, the sky was again clouded, so that we seldom saw the sun or stars, till we were quite past the island. However we found the Isle of Ascension, where we struck two turtle, (for this was not the laying time, but the beginning of the cooting, or engendering, season; therefore some few only were drawn hither.) This was the latter end of November. From the time that we thought ourselves to the west of St Helena, we had our water measured out to us, two pints a man per day, till we came into our channel. This was the first time that I began to know the value of fresh water; for we took in none in all our way home from Bantam.

This is dry reading to anyone but a mariner. I have quoted at length to give an indication of how sharply developed Dampier's powers of observation were. In the absence of an accurate method of measuring longitude, Dampier's notes became essential reading for his peers, and even later, more technically advanced generations of navigators took Dampier's works along with them.

The *John and Martha* returned just before the outbreak of the third Dutch War: 'We arrived at Plymouth about two months before Sir Robert Holmes went out to fall upon the Dutch Smyrna fleet.' This was a pre-emptive action which led to the official outbreak of war, but Dampier did not immediately take part. Instead, he retired home to his brother's property in Somerset.

It was not long, however, before he grew 'weary of staying ashore', and enlisted on board the *Royal Prince*, commanded by Sir Edward Spragge. As a youthful volunteer, Dampier would have been in the minority. For all the bravery with which they undeniably fought, the majority of the crews were pressed men. Spragge himself was a former supporter of the Royalist cause, who had achieved his first captaincy in 1661 and was knighted in 1665. He became Admiral of the Blue Squadron in 1672, after the battle of Solebay. Pepys, who met him at a dinner given by Sir William Penn, described him as a 'merry man that sang a pleasant song pleasantly', and Dryden described him in *Annus Mirabilis* 'as bountiful as brave,/Whom his high courage to command had brought . . .'

Though not the ablest commander, he was one of the most popular. The 21-year-old Dampier saw action with him against de Ruyter in the engagements of 28th May and 4th June 1673. In the second encounter, de Ruyter sufficiently damaged the English fleet to oblige it to withdraw to refit. The two navies did not engage again until 11th August, at what was to be called the battle of Texel. But Dampier did not take part. A day or two earlier, he had been taken ill – he does not tell us how, but it must have been serious. He was transferred to a hospital ship, and watched the conflict from there.

Spragge's squadron engaged the Dutch Admiral Cornelis Tromp, an old adversary. Seeing Tromp approach, Spragge hove to – an action for which he was later criticized, because the rest of the English fleet sailed ahead to engage de Ruyter, and the force was thus split and weakened. Spragge and Tromp fought it out until ten in the morning, by which time both the *Royal Prince* and Tromp's *Golden Lion* were severely battered. Then both the main and mizzen masts of the *Royal Prince* were brought down and, she being completely disabled, Spragge transferred his flag to the *St George*. The battle continued all day, during which time Spragge changed ship twice more. It was during the last shift of the flag that he was killed, as the Dutch opened fire on the launch which was taking him from the *Michael* to the *Royal Charles*.

Dampier watched the battle with more relief than frustration. Transferred with the rest of the sick and wounded to Harwich soon afterwards, he 'languished a great while' before he was well enough to return once again home to his brother George, who at about this time moved from East Coker to a farm at Porton, near Bridport, where he still was at the time of Dampier's death. It may be that George had been able to buy his own land.

★

Dampier didn't stay at Porton long, but the war was over before 'with my health, I recovered my old inclination for the sea'. The Royal Navy did not beckon him again, but an offer came from Colonel William Helyar to go to a plantation of his in Jamaica. Helyar had kept a fatherly eye on the young man, and it is possible that George had put in a good word for his younger brother. Perhaps both Helyar and George thought that if William could not settle down at home, he might do so in the West Indies. Helyar had a long association with that part of the world, and black servants from there formed part of his establishment at home.

The terms of Dampier's employment were not clear cut. In his published work, Dampier, as he always does when dealing with awkward personal situations, describes matters as briefly and as coolly as possible. But he states that he was being sent out as Helyar's manager. Whether he really believed that is not so certain, for he did not trust Helyar's representatives in London. And any suspicions he may have harboured before embarking proved well founded when he reached Jamaica.

CHAPTER THREE

Jamaica

The estate in question had belonged to Helyar's brother, Cary. Cary had gone out to the West Indies in 1664, writing of his opportunistic decision in a letter home from Tenerife, 'because here is a ship bound for Jamaica, upon which we intend to embark and there settle'. Cary Helyar had made considerable profits from trading in cocoa, logwood, slaves and sugar, and bought his estate, Bybrook, in the district of Sixteen Mile Walk, with the money he had made. He worked hard and the estate flourished: he even devised a way of making the place more accessible, which Dampier describes admiringly:

> The way to Sixteen Mile Walk was formerly a great deal about, round a large mountain; till Mr Cary Helyar, the Colonel's brother, found out this way. For being desirous of making a shorter cut, he and some others coasted along the river, till they found it run between a rock that stood up perpendicularly steep on each side, and with much difficulty they climbed over it. But a dog that belonged to them, finding a hole to creep through the rock, suggested to them that there was a hollow passage, and he cleared it by blowing up the rock with gunpowder, till he had made a way through it broad enough for a horse with a pack, and high enough for a man to ride through . . . he was a very ingenious gentleman, and doubtless had he lived he would have propagated some very advantageous arts on that island.

But Cary died on 5th July 1672, leaving the estate equally to his brother William and to his manager, William Whaley, who had been with him since the previous year, 'on condition he pays £500 within twelve months to my dearly beloved wife Priscilla Helyar, and also £200 to Sir Thomas Modyford Bart. being patent money due to him'. Cary was newly married when he died. He added in his will, drawn up on 30th June 1672, a few days before his death: 'To my dearly beloved wife Mrs Priscilla Helyar my house and yard in the town of St. Jago.' The repetition of 'dearly beloved' in so short a space is very touching. I hope Mrs Helyar survived her loss well.

In a letter from Jamaica of 6th July to Colonel William Helyar, his cousin John gives details of the estate, which was valued at a total of £1133 15s 6d – a modest estimate, according to Cary's executors, Sir Thomas Modyford and Hender Molesworth, both senior officials on the island. It encompassed 836 acres of land, '35 planted in canes, two stills, two worms [a tube at the head of a still where vapour is condensed]', a watermill 'near finished', and among other property were '26 Negro men, 21 women, 3 children', valued at £904.

William Whaley, still a relatively young man and not yet married, had no capital to back him and so he sold his share of all this back to William Helyar on the understanding that he would remain as manager and take half the profits. It is understandable that Helyar would want to send a representative out to make sure that Whaley was not cheating him, but no evidence has come to light that he formally appointed Dampier as his representative; nor did the 22-year-old mariner have any qualifications for the job. From court rolls it even appears that both his grandfather and his brother had been in trouble for mismanaging their farms.

It seems most likely that Helyar intended Dampier to go out and learn the sugar trade under Whaley, while at the same time keeping an eye out for Helyar's interests, especially when it came to the accounts. It was hardly a situation which would make for harmony.

In his own published account, Dampier simply describes leaving London and the voyage out to Jamaica, which was uneventful apart from the meanness of some merchant fellow-travellers which prevented the ship from putting in at Barbados, which the captain was willing to do provided his passengers clubbed together for the port charges.

Always eager to share any information he had acquired, Dampier describes the last surviving Carib Indians, and relates the story of Captain Warner, the son of an English governor and an Indian mother. Captain Warner was brought up as an Englishman, but later lived with his mother's people, and was subsequently treacherously murdered by his half-brother, the governor's fully-English son. Whether the murder was politically motivated or whether it is a rare early example of racial prejudice is uncertain.

William mentions that he took care that Captain John Kent of the *Content*, the ship in which he was travelling, should take him on officially as a seaman and so discharge him at Jamaica. The reason for this was that Dampier knew how many poor Englishmen were inveigled into service in the colonies by so-called 'spirits' or 'crimps' – men who made a living by collecting people under the guise of offering them the possibility of employment, only to sell them into servitude. Indentured servants, as they were called, were bound to serve for a fixed term of years in return for their free passage, and the conditions in which they were held were strict at best, cruel at worst.

It is likely that Dampier suspected Colonel Helyar's agents in London – Thomas Hillyard, a Quaker merchant, and one Rex Rock – of being men of this kind; there is little evidence to suggest that they were in this instance, though there are hints in the letters that indicate that they knew all about that trade, and that Rex Rock was engaged in it. In fact, Dampier was one of a group of people legitimately sent out to Bybrook by previous arrangement with Whaley: Whaley wrote warmly to Helyar in October 1673: 'I shall be very glad of his [Dampier's] company for I am all alone and therefore should be very glad of his company.' Dampier was to be accompanied by a doctor, his assistant, who was called Charles Wentworth, a carpenter and a stonemason called Richard Dodge.

Whaley, though he does not emerge as sympathetic, never appears knowingly dishonest or treacherous. He was a godson of Helyar's and seems to have been a conscientious and dutiful young man. He had a lot to put up with after Dampier arrived and his tune was soon to change. Rivalry, not only for control of the estate, but for Helyar's favours, also played a part in the disagreements which followed.

The problem for Thomas Hillyard and Rex Rock was that Dampier and his fellow-travellers were under no indenture to serve at Bybrook, though they had been supplied with goods by Helyar for their journey and for setting themselves up in Jamaica. It seems likely that the agents saw themselves as responsible for ensuring that their charges did not abscond with what they had been given. They may have been right to be cautious. For the first time we see another side to Dampier. Before long, Hillyard was complaining to Helyar that the young man was demanding extra supplies: a pound of soap, needles and thread, scissors, a pair of shoes, a grater, nutmeg and two pounds of sugar – these last presumably to flavour the punch which Dampier must have developed a taste for in his earlier voyages.

I can only guess, given the problems of seventeenth-century spelling, at the unusual closeness of the names Hillyard and Helyar. Might Thomas Hillyard in fact have been another member of the Helyar clan?

The *Content* sailed from Gravesend, not before Dampier had provided himself there with paper, ink and quills, on about 6th April 1674, fortunately with all aboard. On 11th April Thomas Hillyard was writing a catalogue of horrors to Helyar, which are best told in his own words. One or two points are worth noting first: Rex (or 'Recks') Rock goes to no end of trouble to bring two further servants aboard – a tailor by the name of William Hayes and a joiner called John Gilstrop. It can only be deduced from what follows that if the servants sent to Whaley were of Helyar's own choosing, he must have been either a poor, eccentric or original judge of character:

London the 11th of the 2d Month
Called April 1674.

Col. Helyar and esteemed friend,

The occasion of my not desiring to write was . . . by . . . reason of some disturbance which happened aboard the *Content* by the servants there. The doctor being much dissatisfied because he was kept on board and was not suffered to go ashore, and William *Dampier* – he would hardly be persuaded to go. [I] was forced to supply him with more things otherwise he would not have gone; and Dodge and the other man, the carpenter, they were very quarrelsome.

None of them having indentures, complains Hillyard, the agents were forced to send one 'Ct. Hekes' to:

> testify to the searchers [customs officers] that they were servants belonging to Col. Helyar: and Hekes brought them more brandy and a joint of fresh meat and supplied them with what they would have. I did not understand but that there should have been indentures made between you here, otherwise they should have been bound [formally, not physically] before they had gone aboard of ship, which would have saved this extraordinary charge [extra expense].

But worse was to come:

> . . . one thing more has happened, which is that the person that went by the name of Charles Wentworth that was supposed to be the doctor's boy, was discovered to be a young woman who [*sic*] I suppose the said doctor married formerly. So the searchers examined her, she appearing in man's apparel, [whether] she was a man or a woman, she said, a man, and stood much in it, so they had her into the cabin and would have searched her, and she still stood in it till they found her otherwise, then they said it was of dangerous consequence, and thought that she might have done some murder, so Thomas Yoakley pacified them for the present and afterwards ordered her to go ashore in woman's apparel, and so went to the searchers, and as to their questions she gave this answer, that her husband had contracted with Col. Helyar to go to Jamaica and, that [as] the colonel would not accept of any women as servants, made her appear as a man for the love of her husband. In the meantime Rex and another made [forged] a certificate that they were lawfully married at Harwich . . . The searchers seeing the evidence so plain said, what love is this, and said, God forbid that we should part man and wife . . .

One can imagine the splendid drama – unless of course the customs officers had been bribed.

Once that deception passed on the authorities was confessed, Hillyard went on to describe Rex Rock's carrying of the two extra servants –

Hayes and Gilstrop – across to the ship, which had already sailed. It took two days of rowing to catch up with the *Content*, a sixty-mile trip fuelled by prodigious muscle and a quart of brandy. At least the two artisans thus delivered were properly indentured to the estate. Helyar, however, was billed for the women's clothes that had to be provided for 'Charles Wentworth', and the other extra expenses. It is a pity that we do not have his replies either to this letter or those that follow. They might explain a lot. But it's also possible that the colonel found it better to remain aloof from the squabbles of his underlings. There is nothing to suggest, however, that he did not settle his bills.

As to that, Hillyard continues:

> *William Dampier* hath been very extravagant. Methinks I shall prevent this extraordinary charge [on] the next servants, for the want of bindings [indentures] made them [cost] higher . . . but I hope if they get well to Jamaica they will answer this charge. John Kent went through the Downs last Wednesday with a very fresh gale, and I hope per this they are got out clear of Land's End.

How soon it was before William Whaley became disenchanted with the young sailor and the doctor and his 'wife' who had been sent by his partner and godfather in England to help him is not clear, but any cordiality cannot have lasted long. Whaley would not have liked the rivalry that Dampier's presence suggested, and as he was an intelligent man, he would have deduced the real reason why Dampier was there. That there was, even on an ordinary, basic, human level a conflict of personalities is obvious. It is also evident that the doctor and his lady and Dampier were on one side, and Whaley on the other.

It was a wretched situation, and one that seemed insoluble. They stuck it out for six months before Dampier exploded – at least in print. The letter we have which he wrote to Helyar on 13th January 1675 shows the same fury that was to appear in a pamphlet he wrote thirty years later, vindicating himself for his leadership of a failed privateering venture.

> Honoured Sir,
>   When I writ my first letter to you, being within a short while after my arrivance in this country, I thought my critical years had

been past, and began to persuade myself into a belief of a future fortune by my present condition which then seemed very happy by reason of the fair promises you made me in England which I thought had been already verified or at least not to be doubted because according to your order I was so well received by Mr Whaley, so welcome to him, so gracious in his eyes that I thought myself most happy; but this was too sweet to hold forever. I was nipped in the bud, and before I was well awake out of this pleasant dream I found myself like one led by an ignis fatuus – just ready to enter into his house in his thoughts when the false light leaves him either in a great pond of water or falling down some deep precipice ready to break his neck. Sir, I am sorry I should have to make a recital of my adventures here, but seeing I was so credulous to believe your words, and came out on your account, I [thought] myself bound to give you some relation of what has passed betwixt Mr Whaley and myself. After I had been some four months in the island, I was urged by Mr Whaley to agree with him by the year [sign an indenture], which I was very willing to do; but he saw into what a condition I was reduced, [and] proffered me so little that I was ashamed of myself; but at last he brought me to 12 li [£12] per annum which will scarce buy clothes in this country. He told me the plantation yet needed none to keep accounts but himself, and he had done it heretofore and was still able to do it; but I know how things are carried on at home, when he is a week at a time at town, sometimes in business and sometimes for his pleasure; but so soon as he thought he had got me under his lash he thought on nothing but how to abuse me, for either his jealousy, seeing me so diligent, or some other [thing] so ill affected his jealous pate that I came over to oversee his actions; but I will venture anyone that comes over hither to know any thing of either of your concerns for he does all things here in his own name.

Sir, I wish he may prove honest to you, but I assure you he has an ill name here, and I have both seen and found it experienced on myself. But, sir, it is neither my business nor intent to strive to set you two at variance; only to let you see how he strives to abuse me and those that you seem to have a particular respect for. After several abuses I received from him, and being not able longer to live in thraldom, which I always hated, I desired a discharge from him. He soon granted me that favour, but thought I would not have taken him at his word, as imagining I could not live elsewhere; but when he found his thoughts deceived him, he began to flatter me, and seeing that availed not, he began to reproach me in all places where he came, telling me I could not write nor cast account, or hindered me of several good places that I might have had. Thus you see, sir, how I have been abused for my credulity. A whole twelve months is spent in coming over and in your service I have got but 30 shillings for the first four or five months . . . I confess he is saving enough at home, but how he is abroad I know not; but great charges and expenses that man is at that lies from home, which he does very often, and it would be more commendable to keep a better house at home and lessen his expenses abroad. Sir, although I have little hopes to better my fortune here, the respect I owe you engages me to stay and know your pleasure before I return for England. I am willing to serve you, but not to be a slave. Therefore if you think it convenient that I should serve you here you must not forget to send me over a larger commission than I brought with me, otherwise your expectations will be vain; or if you send any other in my place to act anything for you, you must be sure to let him have as good a commission to act here in your name as Mr Whaley does in his. But I question, if you come yourself, whether or not you can put your business into so good an order as you might expect, seeing Mr Whaley buys and sells and does all in his name . . . When I parted from Mr Whaley he imagined I would have gone for England, and strived all that he could to stop me here. I know not his meaning in it, but I shrewdly guess he meant no good towards you. If he dies I know not who will look after your concerns, yet he told me he could trust enough with it; but I . . . wish humbly your son were capable of undertaking your business here, and I think you will be forced to send him sooner than you thought, for your own security. You have no better lease of life than other men, and if you should die before your son is settled here (which God forbid), your children will not be much the better

for anything here. So, wishing you may live to find the fruits of
your labours and laying-out here with the enjoyment of your health
and prosperity in all your domestic and foreign affairs I beg your
worship's favour to subscribe myself

   Your humble servant
     Willi Dampyer

None of this troubled Whaley, who comes out of the altercation with
more dignity than Dampier. His note, which accompanies this letter,
merely states:

Sir,
   I might easily have intercepted this letter, but thought it not
worth my trouble, there being nothing in it but a parcel of story
and lies, and any man may see that it savours more of spite than
reality, and had it been intercepted it might have caused worse
thought of me, and therefore to let you see that I am not at all
inclined that way that he would figure to you, I here enclosed it.

Even so, Whaley felt the nagging need to justify himself – perhaps
because he was a conscientious man who was disinclined to be upstaged
by a rebel who, for all he knew, was a favourite of his senior partner.
His letter, despite its obviously vested interest and its occasionally
rambling and anxious nature, is far from wheedling. It also takes the
story of the doctor and his mistress a stage further, and throws better
light upon all the characters involved, especially Dampier's, than any
paraphrase could:

Honoured Sir,
   As for the people you sent me over lately I could wish you had
kept one half of them at home, to wit the doctor and his boy and
amongst the rest *Mr Dampier*, for they have been nothing but a
plague to me ever since they came, for in all my days I never saw
such a company of wasteful people in my life, and for my part I
believe they came here to do nothing. For the doctor's part, he is
a man that might get money here, and had to my knowledge got
near £30 since he came, and to be sure if he has anything that is
better than other it does not belong to our people if they have

occasion for it, but is for better patients, about which the doctor and I have had some words, as also about his whore which he brought with him, which is the nastiest wasting slut as ever came into a house, and one that is fit to do nothing at all.

There is more in this vein before Whaley turns to the main object of his ire:

As for Wm. Dampier, he and I have had some words about several things which belong to the plantation. As I had formerly writ you, I do not know what you promised him in England, but he hath not stuck [hesitated] to say that you promised great things but perform little. As for my part, I know not what he would have, but do suppose he would have money for doing of nothing; but I am sure he cannot better his wages in any place of the island; but in short he is a self-conceited young man and one that understands little or nothing, and one that has been given to rambling, and therefore cannot settle himself to stay long in any place, and to tell you the truth we are parted, for he hath been gone this month.

From this, at least, we learn that Dampier had left the estate, unable to endure either the work or Whaley's company any longer. Whaley continues:

Not, sir, that I turned him away or would have him gone, for I would fain have had him to stay. Nay, I did myself use all the arguments that possibly I could to persuade him to stay, but could not by no fair means, so when I saw that I could by no means persuade him, I told him that I could force him to stay by reason of the agreement that I had made with him for a year. He told me I might, if I thought convenient, but told me that he could not nor would not do me any good, so I told him, when I saw he was resolved by bent to be gone, that it would be his best way to stay till he heard from you ... He made me answer that he was not resolved to go off the island but did question to light on a place where he might have better wages, and live better, for he could not nor would not slave it ... So, two days after Christmas he comes up and tells me, as I before have writ you, that he must be gone.

Neither have I seen him but once since, neither do I know whether he intends home per this ship [i.e., the one carrying Whaley's letter] or not, but I am informed by one in town [that] he was hiring himself to be an overseer at North Side, which he [is] not at all fit for, nor indeed for anything in a plantation, because he is not willing to do anything, for had he been anything ingenious he might have been a good boiler, but he thought it an undervaluing to him to handle a skimmer or ladle . . . And now, sir, I will tell you the first thing wherein *Wm.* did serve me basely, and indeed I there told him I should think of it when he had forgotten it, but he told me that neither he did not care for it. You must understand that the doctor and he were mighty great cronies, and the doctor could not tell which way to know how I liked of his bringing a woman instead of a boy, but set *Wm.* to do it. So, as *Wm.* and I were walking in the plantation we fell in discourse about the doctor, and he was wishing he had never brought her with him, and I told him what I thought of her and how I did not approve of it, and withal that I thought she had been some whore or other, and that I thought she had the pox, by reason of several blotches which she had about her. What does he do as soon as I came home and was out of the way, but tell the doctor of it – and indeed I look upon it as a dirty trick; but we had several other words which I could not well approve of . . . he told me he was as good a man as myself, at which I was slightly vexed, and asked him in what. [He said] he 'did not know but that in everything.' 'And that shall be tried presently,' said I . . . There was nobody in the house but he and I, so I shut the door and stepped to him and gave him a good box or two, and he returned me the like, but we quickly ended the fray, and I for my part ne'er thought of it more, but he, it seemed, did, and left me at Christmas, which was some three months after, besides several other things wherein he did not do as he should have done; but I am not at all sorry he is gone: only in one respect, and that is, if he comes to England per this ship he may be some hindrance to us in sending over servants. But as for the business of the plantation, you need not doubt it, for I do not question but to do it now as well as I have formerly . . . But perhaps you will say that *William* would have been able to have given you a note how business would go, and been able to manage the plantation if I should die; but I do assure you, sir, he would never have been fit for that business, for he knew nothing of keeping a book; but something he understands of sailing, which I think his mind hankers after still; but since he is gone I am not at all troubled at it, and shall never desire his return again, for I do assure you it will go shrewdly against my will that he would ever come to the plantation again.

Elsewhere, Whaley accuses Dampier of further crimes – of managing to get through fifty pounds of pork (together with the doctor and his lady) in the course of a week when Whaley was absent from the estate, and of going into town and getting drunk with the doctor. Both accusations are interesting. Whatever his faults, Dampier seems to have been an abstemious man – at least to begin with. Later accusations of drunkenness are based on gossip, though it is clear that Dampier became more of a drinker than he gave himself out to be. It's worth pointing out that the periods when he appears to have been drinking were those when he was least happy and least sure of himself. Allowing for prejudice, Whaley still paints an unattractive portrait of Dampier: arrogant, two-faced and pugnacious. It's hard to square these qualities with the measured observer who wrote *A New Voyage round the World*, but in his later travels, especially as commander, William seems to have shown precisely these traits again.

A few months later, Whaley writes again to Helyar, 'As for *Will Dampier* I know not what is become of him', and goes on to recommend one Edward Acherly as Helyar's representative on the plantation. Ironically, Acherly later cheated Helyar, though Whaley seems to have had no part in the deception. Helyar died on 2nd July 1677, and Whaley was dead by 10th July of the same year.

What became of the doctor and his wife is not known. Perhaps they were able to set up in St Jago or Port Royal. Even halfway decent doctors would have found employment on the island.

What happened to Dampier he tells us himself, very laconically:

I lived with Mr Whaley at 16 Mile-Walk for almost six months, and then entered myself into the service of one Captain Heming [Richard Hemmings], to manage his plantation at St Ann's, on the north side of the island, and accordingly rode from St. Jago de la Vega toward St Ann's.

This road has but sorry accommodation for travellers. The first night I lay at a poor hunter's hut, at the foot of Mount Diabolo, on the south side of it, where for want of clothes to cover me in the night I was very cold when the land wind sprang up.

This mountain is part of the great ridge that runs the length of the island from east to west; to the east 'tis called the Blue Mountain, which is higher than this. The next day crossing Mount Diabolo, I got a hard lodging at the foot of it on the north side; and the third day arrived at Captain Heming's plantation.

However, something went wrong here too. Dampier doesn't tell us what, but it's likely that another row blew up, for he continues:

I was clearly out of my element there, and therefore as soon as Captain Heming came thither I disengaged myself from him and took my passage on board a sloop to Port Royal, with one Mr Statham, who used to trade round the island, and touched there at that time.

Dampier had certainly been out of his element: he had been suffocating on land. But now he embarked on a few months of sailing with coastal traders around Jamaica, and there are no more reports of fallings-out. After leaving Statham at Port Royal, he signed on with a Captain Fishook. During the next six months, he did what he loved most: acquainting himself with all the bays and inlets, and logging them, together with the winds the ships used to get around.

Then he decided to leave the coastal trade. About the beginning of August 1675, he signed on with Captain Hudsel, who was setting off in consort with Captains Wren and Johnson to load logwood in the Bay of Campeachy, in the southern part of the Gulf of Mexico. There's no doubt that what led him to this decision was the opportunity the new voyage offered him of seeing a little more of the world. He could feel the wind in his face again.

CHAPTER FOUR

Trading

Logwood-cutting was a precarious and tough business, though it could be very lucrative.

Logwood is *Haematoxylon campechianum*. It is well described by Admiral Smyth in his early biography of Dampier:

> The trees resemble a large white thorn, and run from two to six feet in circumference; the wood is of great specific gravity, burns with a strong, clear and lasting fire, and is so saturated with its dye, that it turns water in which it is left as black as ink. It grows best on low swampy lands, whence the dwellings of the cutters were necessarily in comfortless situations . . .

At first it was traded merely as a fuel; it was specially favoured for tempering steel. If an English privateer took a Spanish ship laden with it, he generally sank the Spaniard, or turned him adrift. On one occasion a party of French buccaneers celebrated a victory by burning about £42,000 worth of it on what must have been the most expensive bonfire in history. They could all have lived on such a sum like kings for the rest of their lives.

The discovery of the wood's real and valuable quality is attributed to a certain Captain James, and though no date is given for this, logwood-cutting was well established on the Bay of Campeachy (Campeche) by the time Dampier arrived there. The wood yielded a red dye, much in demand in Europe for textiles, and the rate of pay at home for the raw material quickly rose to an extraordinary £110 per ton. Even more expensive was bloodwood, a similar tree found in the Gulf of Nicaragua.

English army and navy uniforms were red at the time – a colour adopted to conceal spilt blood; so armed forces represented a lucrative market.

The logwood tree grows best in low-lying, marshy ground, and among scrubwood. The mangrove swamps where the tree is found, especially around Terminos Lagoon, are plagued by mosquitoes (the area is also known as the Mosquito Coast), and to make matters worse the best time to cut is during the rainy season. Dampier does not describe malaria, but it is hard to believe that he never encountered it. It may be that local diseases did not attract his attention. For all the detail of his accounts, sickness is an area he seldom mentions. He does not seem to have caught malaria himself, for then he would almost certainly have told us.

It is the dense red heart of the tree which yields the dye; the spongy outer rings are discarded. The trade was carried on in Dampier's day by about 300 Britons, who had originally been buccaneers, or privateers put out of that work by the Treaty of America of 1670 between England and Spain. They did not wholly abandon their former occupation, however, and, forming themselves into small troops of anything between four and fourteen men, would occasionally launch attacks on neighbouring Indian villages. The men they would send off to be sold as slaves in Jamaica, the women they would take back to their encampments to serve them as cooks, cleaners, menders and bedmates. The more prosperous among them had European women, purchased in Port Royal for £30 each; others had African girls, bought or captured as slaves.

The encampments were composed of primitive wooden shacks, well thatched with palm leaves to protect them from sun and rain alike, and built as closely as possible to where the trees grew. They were constructed so as to be open to the sea breezes. Their beds were built up on stilts three feet or so above the level of the swamp, and protected by canvas awnings from the worst ravages of the mosquitoes. Their living and cooking quarters were raised likewise; though their kitchens were simply frames covered with packed earth. They built all their furniture – beds, tables and chairs – from local wood, and all were of the most basic type. Some of the men used hammocks, a convenient way of sleeping learnt from the Caribbean Indians.

Apart from the mosquitoes, their neighbours were alligators, biting ants and snakes. No wonder, when a supply ship came in, that the principal commodity they sought was rum. Along with the drink, they bought flour, bread and any other luxuries from the ships that came from Jamaica to bargain with them for logwood. Given the harshness of the life they led, the arrival of such ships was the signal for general celebration among the logwood lumberjacks, and a lot of hard drinking. Trading ketches were expected to provide free drinks on arrival. If the lumberjacks encountered a mean captain, they would 'pay him with their worst wood' – a load of hollow logs filled with earth, with their ends plugged with wood and neatly sawn off to disguise them properly. But a 'true twopenny' would find the lumberjacks generous with their money.

It wasn't unusual for them to spend four days at a stretch firing their guns and indulging in a drunken binge at such times, spending £40 – a huge sum – at a sitting, though in such a climate the effect on their health, let alone their mortality, of such indulgence was severe. What is worth noting is that these men had the same manner of squandering what they had earned as pirates: no sooner had, than spent. Generally, true privateers were not so susceptible. There was perhaps a kind of nihilism among the community: a short, hard life in the course of which what was gained was spent as harshly as it had been got. One could either view this as romantic or brutal.

They were free men, and it was the freedom of their way of living, not the way they lived, that appealed to Dampier. Despite this, it was not an anarchic society: the logwooders had their laws, as did the pirates. Among them, however, there was no capital punishment – probably because most of the men involved came from a tier of society which was at the sharp end of such usage under law at home.

In the rainy season the lumberjacks would get out of bed in the morning to step into two feet of water, and would continue so all day at their work. The men's hands and forearms were stained red from the dye of the wood, and they stank of the strong, sweet smell of the yellow flowers of the tree. For five or six days a week they hewed the trees and hauled them into piles near the shore, working in high humidity under a hot sun. On their days off, they hunted the wild cattle in the vicinity.

Apart from their tough physical surroundings, they had to contend with the Spaniards. The Campeachy coast was part of the Main, and viewed by Spain as its property. Not only were the logwooders squatters, but they were also a thorn in the side of the Spanish Empire, since every so often they would leave off their trade and embark upon opportunistic raids against Spanish ships and settlements. Additionally, Spain had been angered to find that in the treaty it had signed with England in 1670, there was a clause which empowered those already settled to remain where they were. Through allowing this *ubi posseditis*, Spain had legalized the position of the logwooders in Campeachy Bay. Stung, the Spanish made life for the English there as hard as they could. It was a complicated situation. Spain was not heavily involved in the logwood trade, and so adopted a dog-in-the-manger attitude to it. Through the treaty, Spain no longer claimed exclusive right to the whole of the Caribbean trade. In practice, however, she blocked foreign intervention wherever she could. It was on account of this that the logwooders had moved away from Spanish settlements and established themselves in the area surrounding the remote Terminos Lagoon.

If taken by Spanish forces, logwooders could expect a life of slavery. Lionel Wafer, a contemporary of Dampier, as well as being his comrade and a fellow-writer, relates the doleful story of Captain Buckenham. Wafer had sailed to Jamaica with Buckenham, who left him there and went on to Campeachy to fetch logwood, where he was captured by the Spaniards, and 'carried prisoner to Mexico, where one Russel saw him, who was then also a prisoner there, and after made his escape. He told me he saw Captain Buckenham, with a log chained to his leg, and a basket at his back, crying bread about the streets for a baker his master . . .' Russel crops up again later in Dampier's writings: he was an old logwooder who was himself captured by the Spaniards and sent to Mexico City. After his escape he turned buccaneer and took his revenge fully, capturing Vera Cruz 'about the year 1685'. Dampier relates a lighter anecdote concerning one 'Captain Jack': Jack was one of a small group of seamen landed by canoe from their privateer and ambushed by a Spanish force of forty soldiers:

The Spaniards carried them in triumph to the fort, and then demanded which was the captain. Upon this they all stood mute, for the captain was not among them; and they were afraid to tell the Spaniards so, for fear of being all hanged as stragglers; neither did any one of them dare to assume that title, because they had no commission with them, nor the copy of it; for the captains don't go ashore without a copy at least of their commission, which is wont to secure both themselves and their men. At last one John Hullock cocked up his little cropt hat, and told them he was the captain; and the Spaniards demanding his commission, he said it was aboard; for that he came ashore only to hunt, not thinking to have met any enemy. The Spaniards were well satisfied with this answer, and afterwards respected him as the captain, and served him with better provision and lodging than the rest; and . . . Capt Hullock had a horse to ride on, while the rest went on foot . . . and was frequently regaled with chocolate, & c. . . . At last, I know not how, they all got their liberties, and Hullock was ever after called Captain Jack.

It was foolish of the Spanish to hound the logwooders as they did, driving them back to buccaneering. Dampier himself points out what ought to have been obvious: 'It is not my business to determine how far we might have a right of cutting wood there, but this I can say, that the Spaniards never received less damage from the persons who generally follow that trade than when they are employed upon that work.' As we have seen, the whole trade, as Dampier says himself, 'had its rise from the decay of privateering', which the English authorities at that time were just as eager to stop as the Spanish – at least on a diplomatic level.

The voyage Dampier undertook with Captain Hudsel took about a fortnight from Port Royal in Jamaica, and they dropped anchor at 'Trist Island in the Bay of Campeachy, which is the only place they go to'. On his way, Dampier made his usual notes. He misses nothing: the coastline, the wildlife, the vegetation, the availability of local commodities, are all described with such minuteness as to appear, especially where his technical navigational observations are concerned, tedious at times to the modern reader; but one must remember that he was describing these things for the first time. His obsessive sense of detail is all the more extraordinary when one considers the difficult circumstances in which he wrote. It's worth remembering, though, that at the same time he was recording what he saw with a view to publishing it later. Such new information was of great value at home. Dampier's works are packed with long descriptions. He is always conscientious, being as exact as he can, and he avoids exaggeration. When he is uncertain, he admits it, and resorts to other authorities for clarification. It's worth stressing this aspect of his work again because it reinforces the impression Dampier gives of a man eager to establish scientific truth. It is a pity, though, that we do not have the notes he made at the time, from which the polished descriptions we read in his published work derive.

He does not forget to mention the effect of the European presence on local Indians, with a degree of sympathy not shared by many of his contemporaries:

> Since the privateers and the logwood-ships have sailed this way, these fishermen are very shy, having been often snapped by them. So that now when they are out at sea, if they see a sail, they presently sink their canoes even with the edge of the water; for the canoes when they are full of water will sink no lower, and they themselves lie just with their heads above water, till the ship which they saw is passed by . . . I have seen them under sail, and they have thus vanished on a sudden.

Trist Island provided the only anchorage for large ships: smaller vessels were able to make their way further across the lagoon to a place called One Bush Key. Dampier describes their arrival amongst the logwooders thus:

> One Bush Key is about a mile from the shore; and just against the island is a small creek that runs a mile farther, and then opens into another wide lagoon; and through this creek the logwood is brought to the ships riding at the Key. Between the oyster banks that lie about the island and the Main, there is good riding in about 12 foot water. The bottom is very soft ooze, insomuch that we are forced to show our anchors to make them hold . . .
>
> Our cargo to purchase logwood was rum and sugar; a very good commodity for logwood lumberjacks . . . Neither was it long before we had these merchants come aboard to visit us; we were but six

men and a boy in the ship, and all little enough to entertain them; for besides what rum we sold by the gallon or firkin, we sold it made into punch, wherewith they grew frolicsome.

They let off volleys of small-arms fire to accompany the toasts that were given, a custom which led to a great waste of powder, and in the midst of the drinking the business was done – commodities were exchanged for logwood at the rate of £5 per ton. It isn't hard to see by this that despite the potential they had for making money, most logwooders never did more than sqaunder their opportunities.

Dampier himself made two or three trips to the lumberjacks' huts, and there he and his companions found themselves always hospitably regaled with 'pig and pork, and pease, or beef and doughboys [a kind of dumpling]'. And he adds, 'As long as the liquor lasted, which they bought of us, we were treated with it, either in drams or punch.' Later on, Dampier was to remark rather stiffly that 'I did ever abhor drunkenness'. This does not seem to have been the case at this stage in his career.

He must have realized how hard the conditions were, but he was attracted to the life. Tough it may have been, but it allowed him the independence he cherished, and it offered the chance of making money, if he was sensible. 'I saw a great prospect of getting money here,' he writes enthusiastically, 'if men would be but diligent and frugal.' All his life he was attracted to money-making schemes. Apparently he had already decided to return to the Bay of Campeachy as soon as he had made the necessary preparations and arrangements at Jamaica.

They left the Bay for the return journey towards the end of September 1675. Dampier had just turned twenty-four.

The voyage from Trist to Jamaica was to last thirteen weeks, since the winds were contrary and the ship they were on, now fully loaded, was a 'sluggish sailer'; though Dampier hadn't criticized the vessel in this respect on the outward trip. On board with them were four passengers – Will Wooders and three others – who had lately escaped after several months of Spanish captivity. It was just as well they were aboard, for owing to Wooders's quick-wittedness the ship was given enough warning to escape two Spanish vessels which bore down on her shortly after leaving Trist. Battling against the trade wind, they had only reached Rio de la Gartos after a fortnight, and provisions were beginning to run low. A north wind helped them for a while, but did not last. Finding themselves off the fishing grounds of Yucatán, they decided to replenish their supplies, and had some success.

It was there that a horrible accident fell Captain Hudsel:

> after he had haled in a good fish, being eager at his sport, and throwing out his line a little too hastily, the hook hitched in the palm of his hand, and the weight of the lead that was thrown with a jerk, and hung about six feet from the hook, forced the beard [barb] quite through, that it appeared at the back of his hand.

They continued to flounder about in the hope of a favourable wind. Then, one evening, when Dampier was at the tiller (ship's wheels were only just beginning to make their appearance on smaller vessels), he noticed that the water had become smooth. Around him, all the men and the captain lay sleeping on the deck, no one believing any land to be nearer than thirty leagues away. Dampier scarcely had time to react to the change in the water than he was knocked off his feet as the ship struck a rock and the tiller was thrown against him. By luck, she did not stick on the rocks, for then they might have been wrecked: they had fallen foul of the notorious Alacran Reefs. Dampier gives a vivid description of them, together with the land and sea life on and around them:

> The Alcranes are 5 or 6 low sandy islands, lying in the lat. of about 23 d North, and distant from the coast of Jucatan about 25 leagues: the biggest is not above a mile or two in circuit. They are distant from one another 2 or 3 miles, not lying in a line, but scattering here and there, with good channels of 20 or 30 fathom water, for a ship to pass between. All of them have good anchoring on the west sides, where you may ride in what depths you please, from 10 to 2 fathom water, clean sandy ground. On some there are a few low bushes of burton-wood, but they are mostly barren and sandy, bearing nothing but only a little chicken-weed; neither have they any fresh water. Their land animals are only large rats, which are

in great plenty; and of fowls, boobies in vast abundance, with men-of-war and egg birds. These inhabit only some of the northern-most of them, not promiscuously one among another, but each sort within their own precincts, (viz.) the boobies and the other two sorts each a-part by themselves; and thus two or three of the islands are wholly taken up. The boobies being most numerous, have the greatest portion of land. The egg birds [a tern: *Hydrochelidon fulginosum*] though they are many, yet being but small, take up little room to the rest: yet in that little part which they inhabit, they are sole masters, and not disturbed by their neighbours. All three sorts are very tame, especially the boobies, and so thick settled, that a man cannot pass through their quarters, without coming within reach of their bills, with which they continually peck at us. I took notice that they sat in pairs; and therefore at first thought them to be cock and hen; but upon striking at them, one flew away from each place, and that which was left behind seemed as malicious as the other that was gone. I admired at the boldness of those that did not fly away, and used some sort of violence to force them, but in vain; for indeed these were young ones, and had not yet learned the use of their wings, though they were as big and as well feathered as their dams, only their feathers were somewhat whiter and fresher. I took notice that an old one, either the cock or hen, always sat with the young to secure them; for otherwise these fowls would prey on each other, the strong on the weak, at least those of a different kind would make bold with their neighbours. The men-of-war birds [frigate birds] as well as the boobies left guardians to the young, when they went off to sea, lest they should be starved by their neighbours; for there were a great many old and lame men-of-war birds that could not fly off to sea to seek their own food. These did not inhabit among their consorts, but were either expelled the community, or else chose to lie out at some distance from the rest, and that not altogether; but scattering here and there, where they could rob securest: I saw near 20 of them on one of the islands, which sometimes would sally into the camp to seek for booty, but presently retreated again, whether they got anything or nothing. If one of these lame birds found a young booby not guarded, it presently gave him a good poult [blow] on the back with his bill to make him disgorge, which they will do with one stroke, and it may be cast up a fish or two as big as a man's wrist; this they swallow in a trice, and march off, and look out for another prize. The sound men-of-war will sometimes serve the old boobies so off at sea. I have seen a man-of-war fly directly at a booby, and give it one blow, which has caused it to cast up a large fish, and the man-of-war flying directly down after it, has taken it in the air, before it reached the water.

There are abundance of fish at some distance from these islands, by which the fowls inhabiting here are daily supplied.

The fish near the island are sharks, swordfishes and nurses [nurse-sharks]; all three sorts delighting to be near sandy bays; those that I saw here were but of a small size, the swordfish not above a foot-and-a-half, or two foot long; neither were the sharks much longer, and the nurses about the same length. The nurse is just like a shark, only its skin is rougher, and is used for making the finest rasps. Here are many seals: they come up to sun themselves only on two or three of the islands, I don't know whether exactly of the same kind with those of colder climates, but . . . they always live where there is plenty of fish.

At the islands, they were able to replenish their supplies, though improvidently they did not salt any, or use the fresh food to preserve their stock on board. Dampier disapproved strongly: he dreaded their running out of food before the end of the voyage, and saw that this was a risk they did not need to run. He made his opinion clear, and, knowing that he was right, did not bother to express it tactfully. Dampier was never a man to compromise his views in order to make himself popular.

They sailed on, touching at Grand Cayman and the Isle of Pines, off Cuba, but avoiding the strait between it and the larger island on account of a Spanish garrison based at Cape Corrientes. The Island of Pines itself was not without its dangers:

Here are also a great many alligators and crocodiles that haunt about . . . and are said to be the most daring in all the West Indies. I have heard of many of their tricks; as that they have followed a canoe, and put their noses in over the gunwale, with their jaws wide open, as if ready to devour the men in it: and that when they have been ashore in the night near the sea, the crocodiles have boldly come in among them, and made them run away from their fire, and taken away their meat from them. Therefore when privateers are hunting on this island, they always keep sentinels out to watch for these ravenous creatures, as duly as they do in other places for fear of enemies, for fear of being devoured in their sleep.

Food was available here too, in the form of pigs and cattle. But they had ill success with their hunting, and almost lost two of their men. Not long afterwards, their remaining supply of food ran out. There was then a disagreement about what to do next: Dampier was for making directly for Jamaica; the others, unconvinced that they would find winds to carry them there, wanted to sail towards the South Keys in search of food. Dampier managed to persuade some over to his view, but not enough to sway the decision away from the South Keys. 'I was so much dissatisfied, that I turned into my cabin, and told them we should all be starved.'

He could not sleep for worrying about the consequences of their action. They had two barrels of beef, originally destined for sale to the logwooders; but it had gone so bad they hadn't taken it. They subsisted on these foul provisions, cut into small pieces and boiled twice over in water with flour. A few days later, their lookout sighted land, and to their joy they found they were off Blewfields Hill, on the south-west coast of Jamaica. Soon afterwards they anchored at South Negril Point. 'In these rambles,' Dampier comments, 'we got as much experience as if we had been sent out on a design.' One more encounter awaited them:

As soon as we came to anchor, we sent our boat ashore to buy provisions, and to regale ourselves, after our long fatigue and fasting, and were very busy going to drink a bowl of punch: when unexpectedly Capt Rawlins, commander of a small New England vessel that we had left at Trist, and one Mr John Hooker, who had been in the Bay a twelvemonth cutting logwood, and was now coming up to Jamaica to sell it, came aboard, and were invited into the cabin to drink with us; the bowl had not yet been touched (I think there might be six quarts in it), but Mr Hooker being drunk to by Capt Rawlins, who pledged Capt Hudsel, and having the bowl in his hand, said that he was under an oath to drink but three draughts of strong liquor a day, and putting the bowl to his head, turned it off at one draught, and so making himself drunk, disappointed us of our expectations, till we made another bowl.

The following day they took advantage of a brisk north-westerly wind, attractively known as a Chocolatto North, which took them home to Port Royal, presumably not in company with the heroic drinker of the day before, who must have been nursing a hangover correspondent to the size of the drink. 'And so ended this troublesome voyage.'

CHAPTER FIVE

The Logwood Cutter

As soon as he was back in Jamaica and had been paid off by Captain Hudsel (who was probably glad to see the back of the cocky young man who'd questioned his decisions, and, worse, been right to do so), Dampier set about buying the equipment he needed to start himself off as a logwood cutter. He doesn't tell us how he financed all this, but he may have raised enough capital from trading, or he may have negotiated a loan.

He collected hatchets, axes, machetes, saws, wedges, 'a pavilion to sleep in', a gun with powder and shot, and so on – he would have made a careful note of what was needed when he had been in Campeachy Bay, and probably discussed the matter with the cutters already there. It is likely that he had already found himself a place with a group of them before he left, in the west creek of the West Lagoon. As Captain Johnson was returning to the Bay, Dampier took passage with him and they sailed in mid February 1676.

Dampier gives a description of the area in which he was now to live, from all points of view – historical, geographical, commercial and zoological. His descriptions of the fauna are sympathetic and vivid:

The squash [muskrat or musquash, *Fiber zibethicus*] is a four-footed beast, bigger than a cat: its head is much like a fox's, with short ears and a long nose. It has pretty short legs, and sharp claws, by which it will run up trees like a cat. The skin is covered with short fine yellowish hair. The flesh of it is good, sweet, wholesome meat. We commonly skin and roast it; and then we call it pig; and I think it eats as well. It feeds on nothing but good fruit; therefore we find them most among the sapadillo trees; this creature never rambles very far: and being taken young, will become as tame as a dog, and be as roguish as a monkey.

The monkeys that are in these parts are the ugliest I ever saw. They are much bigger than a hare, and have great tails about two foot and a half long. The underside of their tail is all bare, with a black hard skin; but the upper-side, and all the body, is covered with coarse, long, black, staring hair. These creatures keep together 20 or 30 in a company, and ramble over the woods; leaping from tree to tree. If they meet with a single person they will threaten to devour him.

It's clear that Dampier felt seriously threatened: as with the crocodiles in the last chapter, wild animals had not yet learnt to fear man.

When I have been alone I have been afraid to shoot them, especially the first time I met them. They were a great company dancing from tree to tree, over my head; chattering and making a terrible noise; and a great many grim faces, and showing antic gestures. Some broke down dry sticks and threw at me; others scattered their urine and dung about my ears; at last one bigger than the rest, came to a small limb just over my head; and leaping directly at me, made me start back; but the monkey caught hold of the bough with the tip of his tail, and there continued swinging to and fro, and making mouths at me. — At last I passed on, they still keeping me company, with the like menacing postures, till I came to our huts. The tails of these monkeys are as good to them as one of their hands; and they will hold fast by them. If two or more of us were together they would hasten from us. The females with their young ones are much troubled to leap after the males; for they have commonly two: one she carried under one of her arms; the other sits on her back, and clasps her two fore-paws about her neck. These monkeys are the most sullen I ever met with; for all the art we could use, would never tame them. It is a hard matter to shoot one of them, so as to take it; for if it gets hold with its claws or tail, it will not fall as long as one breath of life remains. After I have shot at one and broke a leg or an arm, I have pitied the poor creature to see it look and handle the wounded limb, and turn it about from side to side.

What is striking is William's sympathetic attitude. By contrast, here is a similar description from the pen of a French adventurer, Raveneau de Lussan, who took part with Dampier (though they are unlikely to have met) in a huge Anglo-French buccaneering expedition on the Pacific coast a few years later:

Monkeys [on Golden Island] almost as large as sheep also inhabit the forests but they rarely descend from the trees where they find their food. These creatures are so tough that even when shot through the head or shoulder with a pistol, they do not fall to the ground for frequently, notwithstanding their wounds, they are quick enough to hang by their tail, which is very long, and to wind it around the limb of a tree, where they remain hanging, knowing they cannot be captured there, since they usually select the highest trees for their retreat.

I cannot recall without laughing the conduct to which I was eyewitness of one of these creatures, who had been hit by several pistol shots that had carried away part of his stomach. I saw him hold on by one of his paws or hands, if so they may be called, to the limb of a tree, while with the other he pushed his intestines back into what was left of his stomach. Another one, on whom I fired with my pistol loaded with soft lead, was hit in the mouth. This creature, realising he was being strangled by the streams of blood, was wise enough to wash himself with some leaves from the tree where he sat.

De Lussan is capable of good observation; but his attitude is very different from Dampier's.

Dampier continues his gallery of animal sketches with descriptions of ant eaters, the sloth and the armadillo. Only the porcupine does he pass over in silence, as being 'well known'. He pauses with the alligator to differentiate between it and the crocodile, and to mention its strong smell of musk, which he would have cause to remember. He gives several varieties of snake, and tells us of:

a sort of spiders of a prodigious size, some near as big as a man's fist, with long small legs like the spiders in England: they have two teeth, or rather horns, an inch and a half, or two inches, long, and of a proportionable bigness, which are black as jet, smooth as glass, and their small end sharp as a thorn; they are not straight, but bending. These teeth we often preserve. Some wear them in their tobacco-pouches to pick their pipes. Others preserve them for toothpickers, especially such as were troubled with the toothache; for by report they will expel that pain, though I cannot justify it of my own knowledge. The backs of these spiders are covered with a soft yellowish down, as soft as velvet. Some say these spiders are venomous, others not; whether [which] is true I cannot determine.

The spider in question may be *Epeira curvicauda*, whose abdominal arched and elongated spines may be the horns Dampier describes. His description of ant armies is just as impressive:

sometimes a band of ants would happen to march through our huts, over our beds, or into our pavilions, nay, sometimes into our chests, and there ransack every part; and wherever the foremost went, the rest all came after: we never disturbed them, but gave them free liberty to search where they pleased; and they would all march off before night. These companies were so great, that they would be two or three hours in passing by, though they went very fast.

He gives equally profuse descriptions to a whole variety of fish and birds, and the keenness of his eye is no better illustrated than by his observation of the humming-bird, with which we must be satisfied before moving on:

The humming-bird is a pretty little feathered creature, no bigger than a great overgrown wasp, with a black bill no bigger than a small needle, and his legs and feet in proportion to his body. This creature does not wave his wings like other birds when it flies, but keeps them in a continued quick motion like bees or other insects, and like them makes a continual humming noise as it flies. It is very quick in motion, and haunts about flowers and fruit, like a bee gathering honey, making many near addresses to its delightful objects, by visiting them on all sides, and yet still keeps in motion, sometimes on one side, sometimes on the other; as often rebounding a foot or two back on a sudden, and as quickly returns again, keeping thus about one flower five or six minutes or more.

As I have said, Dampier was writing these fine descriptions for publication, twenty years later, having acquired in that time more experience and observation; but there can be no doubt that they were firmly based on the notes made by the 25-year-old who first saw the creatures he tells of.

Among the logwood-cutters, some had the job of felling the trees, using gunpowder to blow them from their roots if they proved too stubborn for the axe, while the more experienced men cut away the soft sappy outer layers to get down to the dye-yielding core. Some of the cutters at least exchanged their wood for more than just consumable commodities, for Dampier, now engaged in the business himself, tells us that the best wood went to captains prepared to purchase with 'bills payable at Jamaica'. Cutters were strong men, able to carry very heavy loads – Dampier says three or four hundredweight – of wood from the stacks to the ships.

Their recreation, which was also their chief means of getting food, was hunting, and their prey were the wild cattle and pigs that inhabited the hinterland. Hunting took place in Dampier's camp every Saturday, to stock the larder for the coming week. With his usual meticulousness, Dampier points out that 'the cattle in this country are large and fat in February, March and April; at other times of year they are fleshy, but not fat, yet sweet enough'. The manner of bringing the meat home shows how tough a logwood-cutter had to be. 'When they have killed a beef, they cut it into four quarters, and taking out all the bones, each man makes a hole in the middle of his quarter, just big enough for his head to go through, then puts it on like a frock, and trudgeth home, and if he chances to tire, he cuts off some of it, and flings it away.' What state their clothes were in after this treatment, and what their standards of personal cleanliness were, Dampier leaves to our imagination; but for the sake of their health, they cannot have neglected at least rudimentary hygiene.

It was sometimes easier to hunt down cattle when they were found swimming through the swamp from grazing ground to grazing ground. The animals in the water made simple targets from a canoe; but there was a danger attached to this approach: that of attack by alligators. Yet the alligators here weren't in any way as aggressive as those of the Isle of Pines.

> I have drank out of a pond in the dry time that hath been full of them, and the water not deep enough to cover their backs, and the compass of the pond so small, that I could get no water but by coming within two yards of the alligator's nose; they lying with their heads towards mine as I was drinking, and looking on me all the while.

It's likely that the alligators were so sedate because they had a plentiful supply of cattle and their bellies were full; but Dampier was right not to be over-confident: 'probably should a man happen in their way, they would seize upon him'.

When Dampier arrived, the group he was to join had just begun the task of carrying the cut logs down to the creek, a convenient place for loading them on board ship. Carrying the wood was the hardest, though least skilled work of all, and help was welcome. Dampier was engaged at a payment rate of one ton of wood per month. Once the carriage-work was over, Dampier's probation with them would also be over and he would become a fully fledged member of their team. These teams were loose associations that broke up and reformed in different combinations from time to time; but the three men with whom Dampier stuck were Scots: the oldest, who had been at the trade some time and was prosperous enough to own a pretty large periagua (a dugout canoe), was called Price Morrice. In this swampland a canoe was essential to get about.

The other two were younger men, former merchants, perhaps fallen on hard times, called Duncan Campbell and 'Mr George'. Neither of these men liked the work, and they were keen to leave on the first available ship. William himself probably saw his involvement in the work as short-term, a means to getting money quickly to further his career, though he may not have had any firm plan in his head at the outset. In any case, it's likely that a protracted time without travel would have made him bored and restless.

As a newcomer, Dampier's duty on his first hunt was merely to drive the cattle towards the guns, but he hadn't been there a week before he wanted to prove his mettle as a hunter in his own right. Was this arrogance, or another indication of an adventurous spirit, or a mixture of the two?

On the next Saturday's hunt, they travelled four miles by canoe, and then walked three miles more, through woods and savannah, before encountering any game. 'Here,' says Dampier insouciantly, 'I gave my companions the slip, and wandered so far into the woods that I lost myself.'

He was soon out of earshot of their guns. Had they kept an eye out for him? It's unlikely. But they weren't completely careless of him either, as events proved.

He recognized himself lost towards midday, and decided to rest until the sun had sunk a little lower, giving him his compass-bearing. It is an indication of the climate (this all happened in May) that within an hour or two he was so parched that he had to suck wild-pines; he had no water-bottle with him.

In the mid afternoon he set off again, heading north into open savannah. He recognized his surroundings and headed for home, but was still far from it when night fell. He lay down as far as possible from the woods in order to avoid the attentions of the mosquitoes, but they tormented him all night nevertheless, making sleep impossible. After what must have been a hellish four or five hours he rose, and at dawn made his way back to the creek where he and his companions had landed the day before. On his way he saw no cattle – frequent hunting had already made them shy – but he did encounter a flock of guans, and tried to shoot one, without success, because his aim was affected by exhaustion. At last he came to the path which led to the creek, and saw ('to my great joy') a hat upon a pole, and another when he reached the creek itself. He realized that these were signs that they would come back and look for him, and so he sat down to wait. The journey back to the encampment was easy by water, but almost impossible by land, because of the virtually impenetrable thickets along the banks.

Within half an hour his companions arrived, and one can imagine his relief at being reunited with them – 'for I have known several men lost in like manner, and never heard of afterwards'. The cool writing gives nothing away. Tough and pig-headed, driven by a need to prove himself, and always restless, Dampier was nevertheless probably called a bloody fool by his more experienced companions for wandering off.

He worked out his month as a carrier of logwood, and, in the meantime, noted the way cattle-hides were prepared for sale to the ships that put in on the coast. He, however, stuck to cutting logwood, in the company of Mr George and Price Morrice; Campbell sailed with a Captain Hall for New England to sell a cargo of logwood and bring back flour and other supplies. But Morrice had been too long at the job to work hard at it any more, preferring to carouse away any profit that he made, which 'retarded our business', as Dampier says, irritably.

Dampier himself persevered until he was brought to a stop by a pain in his right leg:

a hard, red and angry swelling like a boil . . . so painful that I was scarce able to stand on [my leg]: but I was directed to roast and apply the roots of white lilies (of which here is great plenty growing by the creek-sides) to draw it to a head. This I did three or four days, without any benefit. At last I perceived two white specks in the middle of the boil; and squeezing it, two small white worms spurted out: I took them both up in my hand, and perceived each of them to be invested with three rows of black, short, stiff hair, running clear round them; one row near each end; the other in the middle; each row distinct from other; and all very regular and uniform. The worms were about the bigness of a hen's quill, and about three-fourths of an inch long.

No sooner had he recovered from this infestation than, in June 1676, a much worse disaster struck: Campeachy Bay was struck by a hurricane. Dampier's description is the first accurate account of such a storm in the English language:

I was then cutting logwood in the western creek of the west lagoon. Two days before this storm began, the wind whiffled about to the south, and back again to the east, and blew very faintly. The weather also was very fair, and the men-of-war birds came hovering over the land in great numbers; which is very unusual for them to do.

Dampier pours scorn on the belief of his companions that this was a token of the arrival of a large number of ships:

> But that which I did most admire was to see the water keep ebbing for two days together without any flood, till the creek, where we lived, was almost dry . . . About four o'clock the second day after this unusual ebb, the sky looked very black, and the wind sprung up fresh SE and increasing. In less than two hours' time it blew down all our huts, but one . . . In it we huddled together till the storm ceased. It rained very hard the greatest part of the storm, and about two hours after the wind first sprang up, the waters flowed very fast in . . . This storm made very strange work in the woods by tearing up the trees by the roots . . . the poor fish also suffered extremely by this storm, for we saw multitudes of them either cast on the shore, or floating dead on the lagoons.

The hurricane left the entire settlement shattered. Dampier and his companions had one canoe left which was large enough to carry them all, and in it they set off for One Bush Key. There had been four ships at anchor here when the storm began. When they arrived, they found only one, and even though they offered money for food and drink, they could get none, because the ship was overburdened with other refugees already. They got news of the other ships however – one had been driven out to sea, one towards Man-of-War lagoon, and the third towards Beef Island (Carmen Island).

They decided to make for the ship, commanded by a New England captain called Skinner, that had been blown towards Beef Island. When they were a league away, they saw a flag made fast to a pole which in turn was attached to a high tree in the middle of the woods. Following a line of smashed trees, they found Skinner's ship, skewered by tree stumps beyond redemption and thrown two hundred yards inland. Here they were entertained, though Skinner was temporarily absent, having gone to liaise with one of the other distressed commanders, whose ship had stuck on a reef. The fourth ship had equally run aground. Four more ships riding off Trist met a similar fate; one of these was lost without trace.

There was no point in remaining where they were, as the storm had wiped out their livelihood; but before they left one more adventure befell Dampier. He and his companions decided to go ashore to shoot themselves a 'beef' for supper:

> Passing through a small savannah, about two or three feet deep, we smelt a strong scent of an alligator; and presently after I stumbled over one, and fell down immediately. I cried out for help, but my consorts, instead of assisting me, ran away towards the woods. I had no sooner got up to follow them, but I stumbled on him a second time; and a third time also; expecting still [always] when I fell down to be devoured. Yet at last I got out safe; but so frighted that I never cared for going through the water again as long as I was in the Bay.

I don't think William's companions failed to save him because he had made himself unpopular; it is more likely that they were simply too scared to try. Despite their codes of conduct, the behaviour of men in logwooding and buccaneer societies was often selfish and undisciplined.

The logwooders now transferred their home to Beef Island. The island had been a pirate refuge since the 1550s. It was owned by one Juan d'Acosta, a Spaniard from Campeachy Town, and inhabited by Indian refugees fleeing from the Spanish. The Spanish colonists had since their arrival established a reputation for cruelty amongst the local population, and it is worth pointing out, having already mentioned how the logwooders occasionally raided Indian settlements to carry off women and enslave them, that notwithstanding this, Beef Island became a place of retreat for the Indians, once it had fallen into the hands of the English. For centuries, because of their reasonable behaviour with the locals, the English would enjoy a huge advantage over the Spanish. Indian women, returning to their villages after living with the English, 'made known the kind entertainment they had met with . . . and persuaded their friends to leave their dwellings near the Spaniards, and settle on this island'.

D'Acosta had come to an accommodation with the local English and Scottish logwooders for the sake of his cattle, providing them with beef on condition that they didn't hunt themselves. By this means he was able to manage his herds sensibly, and the relationship he had with the logwooders was both cordial and mutually profitable. It was too good to last: jealous Spanish neighbours reported his collaboration with the 'enemy' to the local governor, and as a result d'Acosta was thrown into prison, where he languished for several years. The island was then left open to the English, who, together with French buccaneers who put in for meat, slaughtered the stock indiscriminately, breeding animals along with older cattle, thereby depriving themselves of a regular supply and equally turning the cattle wild. The same irresponsibility had led to an almost total reduction of cattle on Jamaica at the hands of the soldiers who took the island in 1655, with the result that the men subsequently starved.

Dampier had only been a logwooder for a few months before the hurricane struck, so he had no stocks to carry him over the lean period which followed while the logwood re-established itself. He was ruined. His money-making scheme had been shattered. He didn't complain, at least on paper. One thing was certain: he wasn't going to go back to Colonel Helyar's plantation. But he had to do something to make a living. Perhaps he was hankering after the sea again. He doesn't come clean about that immediately.

After describing the adventure with the alligator, he launches into a scholarly account of the east coast of Central America. He talks of everything, from the nature of the coast, to what can best be traded, to the likely relationship between the hippopotamus of Africa and the tapir, for which he invokes the supporting authority of a fellow mariner who had had first-hand experience of hippos in Africa. He distinguishes between fresh- and salt-water manatees – perhaps making an actual distinction between dugongs and manatees, both of which animals had been categorized indiscriminately as mermaids by earlier travellers. He describes everything from a stingless bee to the social status of the local Indians and the local Negro population. He describes the geography of the coast, and, ironically, anticipates his own later experience by mocking the privateers who had ambitions on the Pacific coast, believing it to be a land overflowing with gold and silver.

Privateers. Very soon Dampier admits that when the means of earning a living by logwooding gave out, he joined their company:

When the violent storm beforementioned took us, I was but just settling to work, and not having a stock of wood to purchase such provision as was sent from Jamaica, as the old standards [established cutters] had; I, with many more in my circumstances, was forced to range about to seek a subsistence in company of some privateers then in the Bay. In which rambles we visited all the rivers from Trist to Alvarado . . .

Privateers is what he always calls them, which is discreet, but not accurate. Only in his last two voyages could Dampier be described as a privateer. Not now. Almost in passing he mentions two buccaneer captains, Rives and Hewet, with whom he may have sailed. Hewet has perhaps been identified. If it is the same man, he was tried for piracy at Charleston in 1718 and hanged at White Point on 18th November of that year. He would have been an old man when he met his end.

Throughout his long association with buccaneers and pirates, of whom I'll say more in the next chapter, Dampier is at pains to distance himself from them, and he was more interested in what he was finding out about the world than the means by which he satisfied his curiosity. He was a great navigator, and in his later life he was hugely admired and sought after for this talent. He is fully aware of it, and he can be scathing about commanders under whom he serves who are less able than he is; yet in his early days he never wants command himself: it is as if the responsibility it brings with it would rob him of the independence and the freedom of mind he enjoys without it. But he had little talent for command, and, as will become apparent as his story unfolds, when he was tempted by it, he came unstuck.

But buccaneer and pirate he was, however he chooses to gloss over the fact in his work. Fortunately other mariners with whom he sailed were not so fastidious. What they record – events at which Dampier was present and in which he must have taken part – indicate a much more engaged personality than he would have us believe. It is good to bear this in mind as we continue his journey with him.

Writing of his experience on pirate and buccaneer ships two decades later, Dampier, eager to make an impression on the London society which had adopted him, says little or nothing of the activities in which the ships he travelled on took part. Working on pirate ships gave him greater freedom than sailing the world by more conventional means would have done. He might have argued that this was the only way in which he could fulfil his ambition. But he sidesteps any question either of the ethics or the morality of his choice. If he had qualms, he overcame them quickly. He was already familiar with the mores and manners of the buccaneering fraternity through his association with logwood cutters, and after the hurricane had spoilt his chances of getting rich through that work, he followed the example of his fellows by setting sail against the Spanish to compensate for his losses. His taste for travel and adventure was already established. He had no real idea of what he wanted to do with his life, other than follow where his curiosity led him. He was content to do that by whatever means were available to him. But he also *participated* in all the attacks and battles he and his fellow-chroniclers describe. He was not, as he sometimes wants us to believe, merely a fellow-traveller whom the freebooters allowed aboard with them out of the kindness of their hearts, so that he could pursue his work of scientific exploration. Dampier's blood was much redder than he would have us think.

They made an attack on Alvarado, taking the fort after a bloody fight lasting four or five hours, during which time the Spaniards had had time to hustle their most valuable goods to safety in the hinterland – a favourite device of theirs, and indeed often their only means of defending themselves. Spain had long ceased to be a great world power, or even a great seafaring nation, and her colonies were stretched too far and too thin for there to be any adequate defence of them against the attacks of England and France. The Dutch concentrated on undermining Spanish trade monopolies by dealing 'under the counter' with the Spanish co-lonials, who welcomed the chance to buy goods more cheaply than they otherwise could.

But after a year of this, the logwood trade in the Bay of Campeachy had revived, and Dampier returned to it. He still cherished the idea of making his fortune, or at least enough capital to make a go of things, and of returning home with it. He remained at the work for about a year longer, and when he had made enough, decided to return to England. He had been away now about four and a half years, and was twenty-seven years old. We have no record of how much money he had; but it must have been a substantial sum.

He sailed from Trist with Captain Chambers in April 1678, and arrived in Jamaica a month later. He didn't stay long, only to sort out his affairs with Mr Fleming, a merchant at Port Royal with whom he'd left a power of attorney when he first set out as a logwooder. Then he left for London with Captain Loader, travelling as a passenger, and arrived in England in August.

He makes no mention in his published work of what he did in the six months or so he was at home, but he must have visited his brother in Dorset, and perhaps he really thought he would settle down, for he married. It was not much of a marriage, and one cannot help feeling that it was a mistake.

He only mentions his wife once, as a passing reference. Long afterwards, he was in the East Indies, when the ship he was sailing with arrived at the Bashee (Batan) Islands, north of the Philippines: 'The northermost of them, where we first anchored, I called the Duke of Grafton's Isle, as soon as we landed on it; having married my wife out of his duchess's family, and leaving her at Arlington House, at my going abroad.'

Apart from one or two other references in legal documents, that is all we hear of his wife. William brought with him out of the Bay of Campeachy enough money to set up an establishment for himself, on the basis of which he found someone to marry. Perhaps he felt it was time to settle down; perhaps others put pressure on him. Perhaps it *was* a love match.

Perhaps he tells us no more of her directly because he felt that his private life was of no account to his readers, or because he felt that it was none of our business. She was a member of the Duchess of Grafton's household. We know that her Christian name was Judith, and that, although she was still alive in 1703, she died before her husband. He took good care of her welfare during their lives, and never abandoned his responsibility for her, but he can barely have seen her, and it is scarcely possible that they had children.

What she did, whether she lived in London or in the West Country, we do not know. It is sad to reflect on her life, as the wife of a man who was already (though he may not yet fully have known it) hopelessly lost to another passion. After the spring of 1679, except for brief periods, Dampier was at home – and even this we can only surmise – only for the years between 1691 and 1699, and from 1711 to 1715. The whole of the rest of his life was spent voyaging, and when he was in England he must have been so preoccupied with his business affairs as to have no time for domestic matters.

But when he left England for Jamaica again in 1679, he had no conscious intention of staying away for long. His plan was to trade with the logwood-cutters, and when he took passage with Captain Joseph Knapman on board the *Loyal Merchant*, he had brought goods with him from England, which he meant to sell at Port Royal 'and stock myself with rum and sugar, saws, axes, hats, stockings, shoes and such other commodities as I knew I would sell among the Campeachy logwood cutters'.

However, once he had sold his English goods, he changed his mind about going back to Campeachy, and spent the remainder of the year at Jamaica, 'in expectation of some other business'. While on the island he purchased from a fellow countryman, sight unseen, an estate in Dorset, presumably not far from that of his brother George. All the papers were properly drawn up and at Christmas he was just about to re-embark for England to take possession. His vacillation is clear: he wanted to go home and establish himself, and settle down with his new wife, whom he had scarcely got to know. And yet he was also drawn to the restless life he had begun to know too well.

At that point he met a Mr Hobby, who invited him to become his partner in a short trading venture to the land of the Moskito Indians. These people, for centuries loyal allies of the English, lived on what is now the east coast of Nicaragua – the Costa de Mosquitos.

It is worth a short digression to say something about the fate of this people. It is described by James Burney in his massive *Chronological History of the Voyages and Discoveries in the South Sea or Pacific Ocean*, of which volume four (from which I quote) was published in 1816:

> How would Dampier have been grieved if he could have foreseen
> that this simple and honest people, whilst their attachment to the

English had suffered no diminution, would be delivered by the British government into the hands of the Spaniards; which, from all experience of what had happened, was delivering them to certain destruction . . . The Mosquito [Burney's spelling] country and the native inhabitants, the best affected and the most constant of all the friends the British ever had, were abandoned in the summer of 1787 to the Spaniards, the known exterminators of millions of the native Americans, and who were, moreover, incensed against the Mosquito men for the part they had always taken with the British, by whom they were thus forsaken.

Objections had been raised against the handover in Jamaica and in the House of Lords, but it was considered politically expedient at the time. Burney speaks of 'some mercantile arrangement' or 'a desire to show civility to the prime minister of Spain'. He ends his account with a passionate plea to reconsider the issue or at least to save what remained of the Moskito nation. Admiral Burney, an elder brother of Fanny Burney, who had sailed with Cook in 1772 and 1776, was a man whose opinion would carry weight. But nothing was done.

Mr Hobby's proposal was pleasing to Dampier, who 'was willing to get up some money before my return, having laid out what I had at Jamaica'. He sent the contract for his new estate home – George would have dealt with the business there – 'with the same friends I should have accompanied to England, and went aboard [to] Mr Hobby'.

They set out from Port Royal on the first leg of their venture, but put in at Negril Bay, where they found a buccaneer fleet preparing to set sail, and still recruiting men. The captains of the fleet were all experienced, some of whom had served with the famous marauder, Henry Morgan: among them were John Coxon, Richard Sawkins and Bartholomew Sharp. The crew of Mr Hobby's ship, no doubt attracted by the promise of more excitement and greater gain, promptly defected to a man, 'leaving not one with him, beside myself . . .'

The temptation was too great. 'Being thus left alone,' Dampier continues, 'after three or four days stay with Mr Hobby, I was the more easily persuaded to go with them too.'

It was a fateful step. 'It proved,' as Dampier wrote elsewhere, 'to be a voyage round the world.'

A voyage which would last twelve years.

PART TWO

Roving

CHAPTER SIX

The Enemies of All Mankind

The Golden Age of piracy roughly spanned the twenty years following the Treaty of Utrecht. During that time such notorious men as Blackbeard Teach and Bartholomew Roberts operated, and it has been estimated that 5,500 men were engaged in piracy in the Caribbean between 1714 and 1724. But freebooters were active in the Caribbean and along the Pacific coast of South America long before that. As William Dampier's association with them was very close, it is worth looking at the way in which they went about their business.

Spain had no serious rivals in the New World until about the middle of the sixteenth century. The Portuguese had their ambitions in the East Indies, and the two nations had divided the world between them by the Treaty of Tordesillas in 1494, whereby all lands to the west of an imaginary line drawn down the centre of the Atlantic were to belong to Spain, and those to the east, to Portugal. The Portuguese proposed that the line be moved 700 miles west, which gained them the then undiscovered country of Brazil.

Spain laid formal claim to the New World in its entirety, and all the treasures that it contained. It bound up its colonies in exclusive trade agreements to ensure a mercantile monopoly. Ironically, the currency Spain introduced survived long after that monopoly had gone, and was recognized as legal tender all over the world. *Ocho reales* – the piece of eight – was a squarish, roughly cut, roughly stamped coin. No one is the same as the next. Each was chiselled out of a bar of silver and hammered into pieces of eight, four and two, according to weight. They were minted at Lima, Mexico City or Potosí. On one side, below the

Holy Cross, were the arms of Leon and Castile. On the other, there was an image of the Pillars of Hercules, wavy lines indicating the sea, and the legend *Plus ultra*. Formerly, the legend had been *Ne plus ultra*, but the Spanish, having reached America, wanted to stress that they could indeed go further.

However, over the years Spain lost its ascendancy as a nation, and the series of European wars emptied its treasury as fast as the coffers there were filled with the bounty of the western colonies. Meanwhile, other European countries, principally England, France and Holland, had no intention of respecting Spain's exclusive claim to so much wealth. Whatever the political situation on the chessboard of Europe, and however monarchs and diplomats paid lip-service to treaties and alliances, the dictum of 'no peace beyond the line' (the line being the longitude which divides the Azores) was taken seriously. Here, unofficial activity was welcome.

As we have seen, Dampier never referred to himself as a pirate, though he certainly was one at times during his career. He was also a privateer, and consorted with buccaneers. The difference between these three types of marauder isn't always precise. Broadly speaking a pirate is someone who preys on any other ship; an 'enemy of all mankind'. The pirate crew sails 'on the account', following the principle of 'no purchase, no pay' – in other words, no regular wage is given, but plunder is shared. Pirates owed no nation loyalty. When hailed, a pirate ship would say that it came 'from the seas', and the frightened crew of the other vessel would know immediately with whom it was dealing.

A privateer is one who attacks only the ships of an enemy nation, and does so under licence. The principle of 'no purchase, no pay' usually applied, but a few crews were paid a wage – a device which reduced the risk of discontent and mutiny. Essentially privateers sailed on privately equipped warships, funded on a commercial basis, with a remit to go after merchant shipping, while the regular navies engaged in formal strategic battles with one another. Privateers also operated in times of peace, not always officially, as agents of reprisal for damaging enemy actions. They flew the flag of their own country, or that of the nation from which they held their commission. Before attacking, they might run up a different national flag to delude a potential victim.

Their licences were known as Letters of Marque and Letters of Reprisal, issued and controlled by admiralties. Letters of Marque were impressive documents, festooned with seals and dressed in impenetrable legalese. The Prize Act of 1692 was introduced to regulate their terms. Booty from privateering expeditions was supposed to be strictly recorded and it was divided between the crew, the ship's owners, and, until early in the eighteenth century, the Crown. The system was open to corruption, however, and often a pirate venture would masquerade as privateering. Licences could be bought from local governors, not necessarily of the same nation as the captain making the purchase, or bought and sold between captains themselves. A legitimate privateer might also take an unlawful prize on the high seas when there was no one to police him, and simply not enter it on his books. Dampier himself notes that some governors were happy to sell blank commissions for captains to fill in as they pleased, though possession of such documents did not always save them from prosecution if caught.

Buccaneers have a long history. The word comes from the French *boucaner*, meaning to smoke or cure meat, which is the way these outcasts first earned their living. Learning the technique from the surviving Carib Indians in north-western Hispaniola, they cut thin strips of meat and dried them over a slow fire, into which they threw bits of hide and bone to add to the flavour. The cured meat was the colour and almost the texture of mahogany, but it would soften in water and it would keep for the length of a transatlantic voyage. These they would sell to Dutch merchants – interlopers defying Spain's bans on all foreign trade to her colonies – for six pieces of eight per bundle of 100. They would also sell hides and tallow – the latter being used in sealing the hulls of ships rotten with worm. Instead of money, they would also trade for gunpowder, lead shot and muskets, preferably the high quality, long-barrelled weapons from the gunsmiths of Nantes and Bordeaux.

Buccaneer society was almost exclusively male, and was made up of runaway slaves, deserters and young men who had escaped the bondage of indentured service. They found a refuge in the savannah land of north-west Hispaniola. The Spanish had abandoned their own settlements there, but the pigs and cattle they had originally taken with them had run wild and multiplied. These animals provided the buccaneers with a living. The long-barrelled muskets were very accurate, and the men became the best shots in the world. They had a saying that 'four muskets were better than one cannon', and when they later turned to the sea and ship-taking, they would strap twelve guns together and fire them all at once.

The fundamental social unit was made up of two men who depended upon each other completely. Much later, when women drifted into their company, it was not unusual for two such men to share a wife. For clothing, they wore leather straps bound around their legs, or trousers and boots of untreated hide, topped with a tunic and shirt. On their heads they had a peaked cap to keep the sun from their eyes as they aimed their guns. They never changed their clothes, and as they did all their own skinning and butchering, sucking the marrow (their 'brandy') from the bones as they did so, they stank and were caked with blood. They made something of a fetish of their ferocity, drinking gunpowder mixed with brandy, and no half-hearted Spanish punitive expedition was able to drive them away. How they withstood flies and biting insects is a mystery to me; and their lives must have been brutal and short.

In the course of time, the buccaneers began to launch attacks on Spanish shipping from long dug-out canoes called periaguas. Keeping the bow towards their prey, they would strafe their victim with musket fire, get under the rudder and jam it, and then board. Spanish attempts to starve them out by wholesale slaughter of the wild cattle merely intensified their attacks on ships, and in time they established what amounted to a colony on Tortuga, just off the north-west coast, and as far away as possible from the centre of Spanish power in the capital, Santo Domingo.

In time the word buccaneer lost its precise meaning, and was applied to any adventurer in the Caribbean, or one who made his living by attacking Spanish vessels.

In the regular merchant service there was little work during the winter months; what work there was at the best of times was given on a 'per voyage' basis. Conditions and pay were poor. Though he shared Dampier's enthusiasm for travel, the mariner Edward Barlow tempers it with morose reflections on the fate of sailors of the day:

Yea, I always knew that the worst of prentices did live a far better life than I did, for they had high days and other holy days to rest upon and take their pleasure; but all days were alike to us, and many times it fell out that we had more work on a Sabbath day than we had on other days; and the hardships I endured made me think many times that I had better to have taken any other employment upon me than have come to sea; but I had always a mind to see strange countries and fashions, which made me bear these extremities with more patience.

People were so well aware of the dreadful conditions in the seventeenth-century Royal Navy that press-gangs were necessary to recruit crews. Those who could afford to, bribed the press-masters to let them go ('the pressmaster carryeth the able man in his pocket'), with the result that the lowest of the low were all there was available to the Navy, though conditions were better than in the merchant marine, with more men to share the work and more control over the behaviour of officers. Barlow's comment, however, is:

There are no men under the sun that fare harder and get their living more hard and that are so abused on all sides as we poor seamen, without whom the land would soon be brought under subjection, for once the naval forces are broken, England's walls are down. And so I could wish no young man to betake himself to this calling unless he had good friends to put him in place or supply his wants, for he shall find a great deal more to his sorrow than I have writ.

Conditions did not improve with time. Samuel Johnson remarked with a certain amount of exaggeration, given the state of prisons at the time, that 'no man will be a sailor who has contrivance enough to get himself into gaol, for being in a ship is being in a gaol with the chance of being drowned . . . A man in gaol has more room, better food, and commonly better company.'

The average sailor of Dampier's day found life on board ship cheerless and severe. Below decks, it was dim, damp and cramped. In dark corners and in the belly of the ship where food refuse accumulated, rats and cockroaches bred in droves. Privacy was unknown: on a pirate ship with a large crew 200 men and more might be packed into a space less than 120 feet by 40. Everywhere there would be the smell of the bilges, of unwashed humanity, and of rotting provisions. In storms, everything would be soaked, and would stay that way for days on end afterwards. Not that such conditions freed the men from the fear of fire. In theory at least, no smoking or open flames were allowed below decks. Light for the powder room came from a lamp in the tin-lined lamp-room, shining through thick glass.

There were few remedies for sickness: some enlightened captains knew that fresh citrus fruit was the best remedy for scurvy, but usually the only attempt at hygiene was to wash down the decks with sea water or vinegar occasionally, and to fumigate the holds with burning sulphur. Apart from the cramps and coughs the eternal dampness caused, typhus and typhoid were common. In the tropics, you could also expect dysentery, yellow fever and malaria. This last disease was not yet identified: the name *mala aria* wasn't current until the 1740s, and the connection with mosquitoes wasn't discovered until long after that. Edward Barlow describes the flux encountered at Java:

> it being a disease that many die of in and about this island, especially cold country constitutions as English and Dutch . . . coming out of a cold country into such a hot climate, and . . . changing all our victuals and drink upon a sudden, it changeth our flesh into another nature; and if a man be not very moderate and careful, it is one thousand to one if he catch not some disease or other presently . . . which is seldom helped and killeth a lusty strong man in ten days.

Then there were the sharks:

> they are hungry and ravenous, and will seize upon any man if he should be swimming in the water, so that in some places men, as they have been swimming for recreation, have had their legs bitten off and also have been carried quite away and never seen more, so that great heed must be taken to them when anyone is swimming where those fish are.

Voyages could last from three months to three years and more. No wonder that rum was the most important commodity of all to the common tar.

Although there may have been the occasional variation in diet – in the case of pirates in the form of some delicacies from the table of rich passengers on a captured ship, or a cargo which included chocolate or marmalade – food was monotonous and vile. The staple was ship's biscuit, stored in barrels and keeping indefinitely – though it would taste increasingly stale after a year or so. It was made of a thick dough of flour, salt and water rolled out and baked hard, and stored in barrels, where colonies of the maggots of the weevil would soon establish themselves. Salted meat and fish was also stored aboard, but rotted and stank before it was all consumed, and as there was no alternative to it thereafter, it would not be thrown away. Sea cooks were often veteran sailors who had been wounded out of active service, which is why they are often portrayed – as is Long John Silver – minus a limb, peg-legged or hook-handed. They were made cooks in lieu of being pensioned off, but had no skill at their new work. At least in the regular navies the provision of food of some kind was usually assured, though Barlow comments with his usual pessimism:

> Merchants and owners of ships are grown to such a pass nowadays that it is better sailing with any other nation; for when they send a ship out for a voyage they will put no more victuals or drink in the ship than will just serve so many days, and if they have to be a little longer in this passage and meet with cross winds, then the poor men's bellies must be pinched for it, and be put to shorten their allowance.

All such privations Dampier endured, though he never complains, and scarcely mentions them. He doesn't appear to notice them. This suggests that he may have had an ascetic side to his nature. He didn't miss creature comforts, and perhaps he had never cared for any. He seems to have had little interest in sex, though he would never have mentioned personal sexual activity in his books. Many freebooters turned to homosexuality at sea. Dampier may have been homosexual, despite his marriage;

but there is no evidence for this. The fact that he was always drawn to exclusively male society has more to do with his taste for travel than his sexual orientation.

Mutiny – when it was at all feasible – was frequent, and the men often rose against their captain, seized the ship, turned pirate, and sailed off 'on the account'.

Food was always a problem. On pirate cruises the men would often be saved from starvation only by the sighting and taking of a merchantman. Islands where edible wildlife abounded were also favoured, and the Galapagos was for a time a popular haunt because the great tortoises there could be turned on their backs and kept on deck as living fresh meat until required. Similarly, shores where turtle could be found were popular ports of call. The fecund Juan Fernandez group, well off the coast of Chile and far enough south along the Pacific coast of South America to be away from the thin policing of Spanish frigates (Spain's empire was too widespread for the mother country, its exchequer eaten into by the cost of European wars, to afford to protect it adequately), became a regular rest and recuperation point for all manner of buccaneers, pirates and privateers between rounding the Horn and sailing north in search of prey.

In times of scarcity they would eat crackerhash – broken-up ship's biscuit shaken in a bag with the week's leftovers. A porridge might be made by adding a little water, but the drinking water itself, stored in rum barrels, became in the course of a voyage 'thick as treacle, blue as indigo, and with a smell you couldn't stand up against'. It was all there was to drink, apart from the occasional luxury of beer or rum. When pirates had access to alcohol, they drank until there was nothing left to drink.

In times of greater plenty, they had a dish known as salmagundi: it included any meats available, in any combination: pork, beef, fish, turtle, chicken and goat, for example. These were roasted and marinaded in spiced wine before being stewed with 'cabbage, anchovies, pickled herring, mangoes, hard-boiled eggs, palm hearts, onions, olives, grapes and any other pickled vegetables that were available'. The whole lot would then 'be highly seasoned with garlic, salt, pepper and mustard seed and doused with oil and vinegar – and served with draughts of beer and rum'.

The advantage of piracy was that it offered freedom and the chance to live an adventurous seafaring life without the drawbacks of wretched pay, poor clothing and harsh discipline. Floggings in the military and merchant marine were common. Keelhauling was still practised as late as Nelson's day. There were other punishments: men were forced to swallow cockroaches; or had their teeth knocked out. They could be made to choke on their own blood by being force-fed iron bolts. In 1704, Captain Staines of the *Rochester* had a man given 600 lashes with a tarred rope. In another case, a seaman called Richard Desbrough had one of his eyes cut out by his captain.

This was an age when cruel punishment was still common and public. At a time when a boy could be hanged for stealing a shilling, when everyday punishments included the use of the thumbscrew, branding on the forehead, pressing with weights, being nailed to a pillory by the ears and stoned, it was no wonder that anyone driven by poverty or unemployment (or for any other reason) to crime would not baulk at aiming high. The intellectual and material elite of the time, most visible in London society, has a very high profile for us; after all, these were the people who wrote and were written about; but they represented a small proportion of the population, the majority of whom were poor and unenlightened. William Dampier, not born to privilege, sought by what means he could to better himself, and it is not surprising that those whose form of rebellion at social unfairness took them outside the law were possessed of a healthy cynicism. As the pirate Charles Bellamy said in a well-known riposte to a captured captain who wouldn't join his crew:

> Damn ye, you are a sneaking puppy and so are all those who will submit to be governed by laws which rich men have made for their own security, for the cowardly whelps have not the courage otherwise to defend what they got by their knavery. But damn ye altogether. Damn them for a pack of crafty rascals, and you, who serve them, for a parcel of hen-hearted numbskulls. They vilify us, the scoundrels do, then there is only this difference, they rob the poor under the cover of law, forsooth, and we plunder the rich

under the protection of our own courage; had ye not better make
one of us, than sneak after the arses of those villains for employment?

Bartholomew Roberts, the most successful pirate of the early eighteenth century, put things more succinctly:

In honest service there is thin rations, low wages and hard labour;
in this [service], plenty and satiety, pleasure and ease, liberty and
power; and who would not balance creditor on this side, when all
the hazard that is run for it, at worst, is only a sour look or two at
choking. No, a merry life and a short one shall be my motto.

Of course, these are criminals justifying themselves, but the life did
have more to offer than unemployment and poverty at home, and pirate
crews counted among them a complete cross-section of careers and
nations: escaped slaves, runaway servants; but also physicians, naturalists,
scholars and gentlemen of broken fortune. Lancelot Blackburne, born in
1659, may have worked as a chaplain-gunner on board a privateer. Despite
a later chequered ecclesiastical career, he ended up in 1724 as Archbishop
of York.

Many wrote accounts of their adventures, which proved when pub-
lished to be extremely popular, though few come close to the calibre of
Dampier's. Two which do were written by fellow mariners of his, Basil
Ringrose and Lionel Wafer, filling in important gaps in his own narrative.

The average seaman was young, in his mid twenties, and his officers were
not much older. His gait, his sunburn and his gnarled hands soon marked
him so that press-gangs did not have to go far to seek experienced men,
even though such men would probably return to the sea voluntarily, for
despite its hardships, the nautical life would have opened up horizons
beyond the imagination of the bulk of the population, for whom it would
be exceptional ever to leave their home town or village. His dress is best
described by the naval historian, Marcus Rediker:

wide, baggy breeches, cut a few inches above the ankle and often
made of a heavy, rough red nap. The breeches were tarred as a
protection against the cold, numbing wetness. He frequently wore
a checked shirt of blue and white linen, a blue or grey 'fearnought'

jacket, grey stockings and a Monmouth cap. Some of his apparel he might have made for himself, so deft was he with needle and thread after years of mending sails at sea. Always making clever use of commonplaces, the seaman used bits of hardened cheese or 'ye joints of ye backbone' of a shark as buttons on a jacket.

Though very few pirates actually saved the money they earned through plunder, the income they achieved was vastly greater than that they would have got in regular maritime employment. Early in the seventeenth century, the share of one ordinary crewman from one prize might be £10. That was what most regular sailors earned in a year. In the course of a whole voyage, which might last a year or two, a seaman-pirate could earn up to £4,000, which would put him on a par with the richest members of society. London merchants might hope to make half that amount. The income of a pirate cruise could be almost unimaginably boosted by the taking of one great prize: when John Taylor and Oliver la Buze took the Portuguese East Indiaman *Nossa Senhora do Cabo* in 1721, they made £875,000 – an unimaginably fabulous sum – from the plunder.

Piracy in the Indian Ocean created a home market for exotic goods so great that legitimate businesses were founded on the back of it. One merchant, Frederick Philipse, made so much money that he became the richest man in colonial New York, with a 90,000-acre estate on the Hudson River. North American pirates specialized in the 'round' voyage to the Indian Ocean and back. The English colonies were already showing discontent with the motherland, and piracy was one way of developing an independent economy. The east coast of North America from Boston to Charleston offered a vast number of estuaries, bays and inlets to hole up in. The other presence in the Indian Ocean was British, with a settlement on Madagascar that amounted to a pirate kingdom.

As for the risks involved, mortality was something with which everyone in that age, and especially in the seafaring profession, was familiar. Captured pirates were rarely imprisoned: they were either hanged or pardoned. Often they were given the chance to buy their pardon and some didn't fail to pay up to £40,000 for it – a useful amount for the Exchequer. In practice, anyway, there was a general reluctance to hang pirates, because experienced seamen were regarded as a useful resource in time of war. Usually only particularly notorious captains were executed, often to appease Spain, the chief victim of their depredations. Both James I and James II declared general amnesties for pirates. Some pirates earned their pardons by reporting new discoveries – of islands or coastlines – knowledge of which would be useful to the nation. Stolen foreign logbooks, charts and atlases were even more valuable, for countries were not eager to share what they had found with the rest of the world.

Typically, a pirate crew would start off with a small boat of some kind – a yawl or a shallop, for example – and use it to capture a larger one, to which they would promote themselves. As they graduated to ships capable of sailing the high seas, they used to their advantage the practice vessels had of hailing each other to discover each other's nationalities, and to exchange news. They had their own pirate flags. There were many variations on the skull-and-crossbones theme, and there was also the terrifying red flag, which indicated that they would neither give nor accept quarter. Like the privateers, they were not above hoisting the flag of any nation which would conveniently aid them in taking a ship by surprise. To avoid a long chase, they might lie in ambush in a cove (a lookout could see for twenty miles from the top of a mainmast); or they might pretend to be in distress.

Pirates didn't often attack treasure ships, since these were usually accompanied by an armed escort: this became more frequently the case as the eighteenth century progressed and the international cooperation against sea robbery which went with the fading of longstanding enmities between the nations of Europe increased. Although the greatest prize of all was the Manila ship, with its rich cargo of Chinese silks and Indian spices, it was beyond even the dreams of most. Pirates chiefly preyed on merchant ships carrying commodities – silk often fetched a better price than gold, and indigo, spices, timber and tobacco were also favoured. Africans transported on slavers were similarly regarded as a commodity. When a ship carrying an important passenger was taken, he or she could be held to ransom. Pirate ships had very large crews – four or five times those of merchantmen – and the most frequent form of attack was to come alongside the victim in the small hours and board her, overwhelming the much smaller merchant crews by sheer weight of numbers. If attacking by day, they raised a terrifying racket to strike fear into their victims –

the ship's 'orchestra' was used to augment this – and they deliberately cultivated a reputation for brutality. It was rare for pirates to encounter much resistance: the goods the merchantmen's crews protected were not their own, and they were insured.

Once they had made their prey captive, the merchantman was rummaged, and relieved of the goods the pirates wanted. Because of the prevalence of syphilis among crews, the medicine chest was often one of the most valued prizes. The rummaging could take days – the open seas were empty enough for pirates to do their stealing at leisure. Plunder was not only taken for resale. Pirates needed to refit their own ships in order to stay at sea for months until their holds were full. If they took a ship for their own use, they would adapt it for its new purpose.

Ship design progressed fast in the seventeenth century, the 'round' Elizabethan form giving way to sleeker lines. Pirates favoured three-masted square riggers, which may not have been the fastest or most manoeuvrable ships available, but were big enough to take care of themselves: they weighed 350 tons and were 100 feet long. They could also carry crews of 200, together with twenty cannon and several smaller swivel-guns. Their holds were big enough for large cargoes, and the ships could remain at sea for longer than smaller vessels. In addition, the superstructures of captured merchantmen of this type could be stripped down to make the vessels into better fighting ships. The smaller brigantine, usually of about 150 tons with a length of 80 feet, could mount ten cannon and accommodate a crew of 100, and 100-ton sloops could mount four or five cannon more than that. The fast Dutch fluyt or flyboat was also greatly valued. It was of shallow draught (and could therefore be used inshore) – a single-decked square-rigged three-master, fast and adaptable. Thirty guns or so could be mounted on its deck and there was room for a sizeable crew. Two-masted schooners, usually with a fore-and-aft rig, of about 100 tons, were popular as well. They too were shallow-draught vessels and so could gain access to remote coves which provided safety from pursuers. Pirates were at their most vulnerable when careening – scraping and repairing their ships' hulls. Copper-sheathing was not introduced until the end of the eighteenth century, and after several months at sea a ship's bottom would be eaten away by the tropical-water mollusc known as the teredo worm. The Caribbean became popular with pirates not only for the rich pickings to be had there but also because of the many uninhabited islands and islets which provided hiding places.

Although there are many examples, excessive cruelty and violence for their own sake didn't occur as often as the pirate myth has made apparent – though they certainly existed. Equally, it was not always in the pirates' interest to destroy the ship they had seized, though if they did not want to take it over themselves, they would disable it by cutting down the masts or removing the rudder, so that the abandoned crew could not quickly sail to seek help or raise the alarm against their attackers. There is little evidence for anyone having been made to walk the plank, though a similar practice may have existed in antiquity. Something similar, however, equally reported in antiquity, was used by the pirates of our period: the practice of tying men back-to-back and throwing them into the sea. Throwing wounded captives into the sea was common. In most cases, unless they were important enough to be ransomable, women captives could expect little mercy: one crew took turns in raping a female prisoner before breaking her back over the ship's rail and throwing her into the sea.

Violence occurred if any of the crew of the merchant ship were suspected of lying about the size or value of the cargo, or concealing anything. Whippings and beatings were common, but harsher measures were reserved for victims too stubborn, brave or ignorant to give in to the pirates' demands. Slow matches were lit and inserted under the fingernails. A knotted cord tightened round the head would, if the torture continued, cause the victim's eyes to burst from his skull.

Captain Charles Johnson, whose contemporary *General History of the Robberies and Murders of the Most Notorious Pirates* is the greatest account of their activities in the late seventeenth and early eighteenth centuries, relates how Captain Edward Low, on learning that the captain of a Portuguese ship he had taken had bilked him of a bag of 11,000 moidores by letting it drop into the sea, 'raved like a fury, swore a thousand oaths and ordered the captain's lips to be cut off, which he broiled before his face, and afterwards murdered him and all the crew, being thirty-two persons'. Low was a sadist by any standards, however. He captured a French ship, removed her guns from her, and set her on fire. 'They took all the crew out of her but the cook, who, they said, being a greasy fellow would fry well in the fire; so the poor man was bound to the mainmast and burned in the ship, to the no small diversion of Low and his myrmidons.'

Montbars of Languedoc, known as 'The Exterminator', joined the buccaneers with the sole intention (or excuse) of 'punishing the Spanish for their cruelty to the American natives, about which he had read . . . One of his favourite methods of torture was to cut his victim's belly open and extract one end of his guts, which he nailed to a post. Burning wood pressed to the man's bare buttocks forced him into a ghastly dance of death to the limits of his insides, or his endurance.'

François L'Ollonais, who had suffered greatly himself in colonial forced labour, inflicted great cruelty as a buccaneer, as Alexander Exquemelin luridly describes. L'Ollonais was unable to get satisfactory information from some Spanish prisoners about the best way to a town he was intent on sacking.

> Having asked them all, and finding they could show him no other way, L'Ollonais grew outrageously passionate; insomuch that he drew his cutlass, and with it cut open the breast of one of those poor Spaniards, and, pulling out his heart with his sacrilegious hands, began to bite and gnaw it with his teeth like a ravenous wolf, saying to the rest: *I will serve you all alike if you show me not another way.*

Most pirates were experienced seamen and had come to their trade from the harsh backgrounds of the military and merchant naval services. The result was that rule aboard was surprisingly democratic. All the officers were elected, including the captain, and could be deposed at any time. There were exceptions to this rule, since a leader like Blackbeard terrified even his hardened crew; but as we will see from Dampier's experience, the captain's authority only lasted as long as his crew thought him worthy of it.

Life aboard was complicated by intrigues born of boredom over long inactive weeks and months at sea, but on the whole the system of ship's government, where it was introduced, seems to have worked. It needed to. There was little in the form of entertainment. Gambling could become invidious, and dangerous for the general security of the ship, splitting the men into losers and winners. Drunkenness was frequent but inevitable, especially after a spectacular prize had been taken – though it could lead to indiscipline and insubordination. It is hard to find enough reliable evidence about sex. Women, certainly, were sought after hungrily in the ports where the pirates spent their money, but women were not allowed on board for the obvious reason that they would provide the focus for rows – and the same went for young boys. On board ship, homosexuality was common, though in the regular services it could be punishable by death. The ship's musicians, usually men impressed from captured ships for their skill, were in great demand, to provide entertainment with jigs and ballads. In fact, so great was the demand that the musicians became exhausted. On a humane ship, they were allowed to lay down their pipes, concertinas and drums on a Sunday.

Another means of alleviating boredom was to hold mock-trials, crude dramas in which the practice and manner of the courts at home were satirized. The satire went home: these men knew what kind of summary justice the poor generally received at the hands of magistrates. Captain Johnson reports one such, which was played by the crew of Captain Anstis:

> *Judge*: Hearkee me, Sirrah, you lousy, pitiful, ill-looked dog; what have you to say why you should not be tucked up immediately and set a-sun drying, like a scarecrow? Are you guilty or not guilty?
> *Pris*: Not Guilty, an't please your Worship.
> *Judge*: Not Guilty! Say so again, Sirrah, and I'll have you hanged without any trial.

In most cases the pirate captain had no advantages over his men, beyond a larger share of the booty. He had no absolute right to the great cabin, and he did not even enjoy special or better food. His orders were only unquestioned in battle, and indeed he owed his rank chiefly to his prowess and bravery in the attack. Under him, the quartermaster was responsible both for meting out punishment to those who broke the rules of conduct, and for sharing out booty. The lieutenant was second-in-command, the boatswain was in charge of the day-to-day running of the ship, and the gunner was in charge of the gun crews, where the ship had cannon (many pirate ships had none, and their crews relied on small-arms, pikes, swords and boarding-axes). Finally, the carpenter often doubled as ship's surgeon.

Apart from scurvy and venereal disease, the most likely call for medical attention was to have one's wounds dressed after battle, or, if the wound was too great for that, to have the limb which sustained it amputated. For this purpose the carpenter's tools doubled as the surgeon's. Like the musicians, expert seamen were forced into service from captured ships. They were frequently given papers proving that they had joined the pirates under duress, for use in their defence if captured. Some of them, attracted by the money to be made and the freedom of the life, came willingly. In practice, when captured, whatever the circumstances, skilled men were acquitted, and unskilled seamen were condemned.

There were anarchic crews, and crews given over to unbridled cruelty, but to enjoy any sort of success there had to be at least a semblance of discipline and order. The kind of order most men who came to piracy were used to was inflicted by the regular naval services, however, and they would not stand for such usage again. We have seen that a kind of democracy was the norm on well-run pirate ships, and several of them had strict rules of conduct to which every crew member had to swear obedience. Such articles were drawn up by Captains George Lowther and John Phillips. Captain Misson, with his scholarly lieutenant, Caraccioli, was not only merciful and courteous to his victims, but ran his ship on lines which looked forward to communist principles. But apart from Misson, who was as much a philosopher and a political theorist as a pirate, the fullest and probably best-known articles are those of Bartholomew Roberts. As will be seen, they reflect common sense as much as anything, and though Captain Johnson, who reports them with the occasional gloss, says darkly that there were probably others 'too horrid to be disclosed to any except such as were willing to be sharers in the iniquity of them', they were sworn on the Bible, and, brutal as some of the punishments for infraction may seem to us, probably contributed greatly to the success of Roberts' two-year career:

> I. Every man has a vote in affairs of moment; has equal title to the fresh provisions or strong liquors at any time seized, and

use them at pleasure unless a scarcity (no uncommon thing among them) make it necessary for the good of all to vote a retrenchment.

II. Every man to be called fairly in turn, by list, on board of prizes, because over and above their proper share they were on these occasions allowed a shift of clothes. But if they defrauded the Company to the value of a dollar, in plate, jewels or money, marooning was the punishment. (This was a barbarous custom of putting the offender on shore on some desolate or uninhabited cape or island, with a gun, a few shot, a bottle of water and a bottle of powder, to subsist with or starve.) If the robbery was only between one another they contented themselves with slitting the ears and nose of him that was guilty, and set him on shore, not in an uninhabited place but somewhere where he was sure to encounter hardships.

III. No person to game at cards or dice for money.

IV. The lights and candles to be put out at eight o'clock at night. If any of the crew after that hour still remained inclined to drinking, they were to do it on the open deck (which Roberts believed would give a check to their debauches, for he was a sober man himself; but he found at length that all his endeavours to put an end to this debauch proved ineffectual).

V. To keep their piece, pistols and cutlass clean and fit for service. (In this they were extravagantly nice, endeavouring to outdo one another in the beauty and richness of their arms, giving sometimes at an auction at the mast, £30 or £40 a pair for pistols. These were slung in time of service with different coloured ribbons over their shoulders in a way peculiar to these fellows, in which they took great delight.)

VI. No boy or woman to be allowed amongst them. If any man were found seducing any of the latter sex, and carried her to sea disguised, he was to suffer death. (So that when any fell into their hands, as it chanced on the *Onslow*, they put a sentinel immediately over her to prevent ill consequences from so dangerous an instrument of division and quarrel. But then here lies the roguery; they contend who shall be sentinel, which happens generally to be one of the greatest bullies who, to secure the lady's virtue, will let none lie with her but himself.)

VII. To desert their ship or their quarters in battle was punished with death or marooning.

VIII. No striking one another on board, but every man's quarrels to be ended on shore, at sword and pistol. (Thus, the Quartermaster of the ship, when the parties will not come to any reconciliation, accompanies them on shore with what assistance he thinks proper, and turns the disputants back to back at so many paces distant. At the word of command they turn and fire immediately or else the piece is knocked out of their hands. If both miss they come to their cutlasses and then he is declared victor who draws first blood.)

IX. No man to talk of breaking up their way of living till each had a share of £1,000. If, in order to do this, any man should lose a limb or become a cripple in their service, he was to have 800 dollars out of the public stock, and for lesser hurts proportionately.

X. The Captain and Quartermaster to receive two shares of a prize; the master, boatswain and gunner, one share and a half, and other officers one and a quarter.

XI. The musicians to have rest on the sabbath day, but the other six days and nights none, without special favour.

In addition to these 'laws', complex compensation schemes were devised on pirate cruises, the payments to be drawn from a common fund, for the loss of a limb, an eye or a finger in battle.

William Dampier belonged to this world. The only means he had to his end 'of seeing the world' was by working on roving ships and – as was the custom – changing from ship to ship as the fancy took him. As we have seen, he also wanted to make money. He wasn't always unsuccessful at it, but none of his schemes ever came to anything. Either they were doomed to failure, or he could not make his comrades see the value of them, or there was not time to establish them, or the people he was with did not have the staying power to establish them. The riches of the Spanish colonial empire always remained just outside his grasp.

★

The Dutch arrived in the West Indies in 1600, when they landed on the barren island of St Eustatius. The English followed with landings on St Kitts in 1623 and Barbados in 1625. But Jamaica was the crowning glory of English expansion in the Caribbean. By Dampier's time, Jamaica, with a strong economy based on sugar, had come a long way since Penn and Venables took it for the Commonwealth in 1655. Spain continued to try to keep a firm grip on its trade monopoly with its colonies, forbidding them to engage in direct commerce with other nations; but at the best of times its merchant fleet was too small to supply demand. Humiliatingly, in 1669 the Spanish had to hire Dutch ships to make up their lack of vessels. In both 1656 and 1657 the Spanish fleet bringing treasure from the New World to the Old was destroyed, and thereafter no Spanish fleet visited the New World for seven years. Even after that, the fleets were smaller than formerly, and sailed every few years instead of annually. Spain was losing the race for trade in the New World and wasn't strong enough to support its claims by force. Port Royal, on the south side of Jamaica, became a centre for the 'illegal' trade with the Spanish colonies as a result of its superb harbour, which, being seven miles long and four wide, could accommodate 500 large ships. It was so deep that 'a ship of one thousand tons may lay her sides to the shore of the Point, and load and unload with planks afloat'. The Palisadoes, a spit of sand stretched across the bay like a long finger, was a natural breakwater creating the harbour out of what would otherwise have been a bay. Kingston was later to grow on the mainland side of this bay. Port Royal, named in honour of the Restoration, was crowded on to the tip of the sand-spit.

The port grew very fast. Jamaica as a whole welcomed 3,500 settlers in 1661, but 18,000 in 1668. Immigrants' numbers were increased by those who came either unwillingly or under the constraint of tightly binding contracts. As early as 1649, Bristol merchants had successfully petitioned Cromwell for 500 Scots, defeated in battle, to send as labourers to British colonies in North America and to the West Indies. After the Battle of Worcester two years later, thousands more Scottish prisoners-of-war were transported. In 1652, Irish Roman Catholics were sent over, to all intents and purposes as slaves. Following the failure of the Monmouth rebellion, Judge Jeffreys had 850 men transported to the West Indies.

Landless labourers at home were presented with a picture of the

Caribbean as a paradise on earth. From England, France and Holland they flocked there on long, binding contracts to be cheated, enslaved and exploited. Some lived to clear themselves of their indentures and prosper; but the vast majority remained as miserable as they had been at home; and the more spirited among them ran away. Those who could enlisted with the buccaneers. Legislation against them, designed to keep them in servitude, was harsh and detailed:

> in case one servant gets another with child the man shall after the expiration of his term serve the master or mistress double the time he had to serve at the time of the offence committed. And a manservant marrying without master's consent shall serve two years for such offence.

In the long term, however, the rate of immigration slowed, and by the turn of the eighteenth century Jamaica was beginning not only to be isolated from the motherland but to notice that the black population, still enslaved, was encroaching on the white. A memorandum of about 1720 notes that 'but one ship sailed from London for Jamaica from 25 of March last to the 18 November, which is near eight months, nor have we had any advice from that island since 17 of September to this time, which is almost 6 months'.

Packet boats plied between Britain and the Caribbean regularly between 1702 and 1710, taking 100 days each way for the voyage, but communication was pricey. A letter cost 1s 6d, and a packet 5s per ounce, even though the cost of the service was subsidized by the Crown.

Such was the ultimate diminution in the number of immigrants that proposals were introduced for increasing the number of white inhabitants and for promoting the further settlement of Jamaica. These included plans to send out 400 boys aged 12–15, and 200 girls aged 11–12 every year. The idea was that they would be young enough to adapt to life there, and that they would intermarry and found families. Inter-racial marriages and other liaisons were, however, naturally common, and a complicated systematization of the offspring of mixed races developed. The sacatra had the highest level of African blood; the scale then ran through the griffe and the marabou to the mulatto, who was half white and half black; and so on to the quarteroon or quadroon, one-quarter

African; through the métif and the mameluke to the octoroon, one-eighth black; to the mixed-blood.

At the height of its prosperity Port Royal had 'more plenty of running cash' in proportion to its size – it had a population of about 8,000 – than London. It also developed a reputation for drunkenness, godlessness and profligacy unmatched in the West Indies. Local whores had colourful names like Unconscionable Nan, Salt-Beef Peg and Buttock-de-Clink Jenny. In July 1661 alone the city council issued forty new licences for taverns, grog shops and punch houses. When the town was destroyed in an earthquake in 1692, there were those who saw the disaster as a Judgement of God: 'There is now resident in this place ten men to every house that selleth strong liquors . . . besides sugar and rum-works that sell without licence. All the tavern doors stand open as they do in London on Sundays in the afternoon.' And the seaman-satirist Ned Ward wrote of it in 1698, at a time when the battered phoenix had begun to struggle from the ashes: 'The dunghill of the universe, the refuse of the whole creation, the clippings of the element, a shapeless pile of rubbish confusedly piled into an emblem of chaos, neglected by Omnipotence when He formed the world into its admirable order.'

Visitors to the town were struck by how crowded it was. There were 2,000 buildings pressed tightly together, even reaching out into the harbour where dwellings had been constructed on piles driven into the sand. The rich merchants' houses were of an impressive size, and grander still were the governor's house and the king's warehouse. There were two prisons, the Bridewell for women and the Marshalsea for men, and three forts – Charles, James and Carlisle. Dominating all was the great church of St Paul. The best buildings were constructed of specially imported English brick. 'Almost every house', wrote a contemporary observer, Francis Hanson, 'hath a rich cupboard of plate, which they carelessly expose, scarce shutting their doors at night, being in no apprehension of thieves, for want of receivers . . .'

The prosperity was immense, and much of the product turned over here – silk, linen, plate, gold and silver – was bought by the resident merchants at knockdown prices from the buccaneers who used Port Royal as their base. It was also a centre for the slave trade. Twelve thousand captive Africans passed through it in the 1670s, and one letter at least, of 27th August 1678, exists among the accounts of the Earl of Carlisle, who was governor between 1677 and 1681, from the Committee of the Gambia Stock, urging him to get Sir Thomas Modyford to forward money which had been made on selling slaves and which was now owing to the Committee. Modyford was himself a former governor, who had been recalled as a result of Spanish diplomatic complaints – he had too close and obvious an association with the buccaneers, of which we will hear more – but who had subsequently been forgiven and was now Lord Chief Justice of the island.

The West Indies formed one corner of a great trade route upon which pirates, privateers and buccaneers regularly preyed. Eric Williams describes it in his history of the Caribbean, *From Colombus to Castro*:

> The combination of the Negro slave trade, Negro slavery and Caribbean sugar production is known as the triangular trade. A ship left the metropolitan country with a cargo of metropolitan goods, which it exchanged on the coast of West Africa for slaves. This constituted the first side of the triangle. The second consisted of the Middle Passage, the voyage from West Africa to the West Indies with the slaves. The triangle was completed by the voyage from the West Indies to the metropolitan country with sugar and other Caribbean products received in exchange for the slaves. As the slave ships were not always adequate for the transportation of the West Indian produce, the triangular trade was supplemented by a direct trade between the metropolitan country and the West Indian islands.

The buccaneers were great spenders, and in the early days when they were allowed to have their head completely, it wasn't unusual in Port Royal for a man to spend 3,000 pieces of eight in a night, or to give a girl 500 *reales* just to see her naked. These were fabulous sums. Few people today would be able to part with £100,000 and more on one fling, and either not feel it or not care about it!

The buccaneers were encouraged by local businessmen because their presence, in heavily armed ships, deterred Spanish or French interference. Equally, it was in the buccaneers' interests to protect their business partners. Nevertheless, there came a time when increasing respectability made their presence less welcome, as legitimate trade between nations became easier and more desirable. A letter exists dated 14th June 1680 from Captain Banister to the Earl of Carlisle, in which he writes: 'I am very sorry it was not your Excellency's good fortune to take that rogue Coxon as well as the two small vessels, for then the neck of privateering had been broken, for a great while at least; and forever if the Spaniards have the good luck to destroy these rogues in the South Seas.' Shortly before this, John Coxon had been one of the leaders of the expedition which Dampier had joined.

In 1681 an Act was proposed:

for restraining and punishing privateers and pirates by which it is made felony for any of the inhabitants of the island [Jamaica] to serve in an hostile manner under any foreign prince against any other foreign prince in amity with Great Britain without licence [*sic*] from the Governor, and every offender against this Act being duly convicted in the Supreme Court of Judicature within the island . . . shall suffer pain of death without benefit of clergy.

A little more than ten years earlier, matters had been very different. Sir Thomas Modyford, then governor, who had been in the habit of purveying commissions to privateers to operate against the Spanish, was privy to a plan laid by the nephew of his deputy governor to take the Spanish mainland town of Portobello. Henry Morgan had started his career as a soldier and had made his way to the Caribbean with Penn and Venables, but once there had quickly adapted to seaborne warfare. He was an accomplished and merciless strategist. By attacking Portobello, which he did in 1668, from the landward side, where the town's defences were weakest, he took it easily and his expedition netted 250,000 pieces of eight. He returned to a hero's welcome in Port Royal and soon set about further plans for attacking Spanish mainland towns. A projected attack on Cartagena foundered when Morgan's flagship was accidentally blown up in port; but he then turned his attention to Panama. This was highly significant because Panama was on the Pacific coast of the Isthmus of Darien, as it was then called. Panama was the main treasure port for the gold and silver brought from the mines in Peru and at Potosí (now in

Bolivia). It would have expected an attack from the sea, but even there no marauders had been seen since the days of the Tudor venturers.

Just before Christmas 1670 a huge buccaneer fleet under Henry Morgan sailed south from its mooring at Isla Vaca off the south-western coast of Hispaniola and made for San Lorenzo, where a fortress defended the mouth of the River Chagres. The Spaniards there defended themselves bravely but at last the fortress fell, and Morgan's ships sailed up the river as far as they could. Then the buccaneers transferred to smaller craft, and finally completed the journey to Panama on foot.

The city had good warning of their approach, and set up landward defences, as well as transferring as much as possible of the treasure on to ships and otherwise out of the city. When forced to retreat after a fierce battle, the Spaniards set fire to the city, leaving the buccaneers with relatively little, at least materially, to show for their victory. Alexander Exquemelin, who was one of their number, describes Morgan as a man of unexampled cruelty. What offended Morgan most in Exquemelin's account was that he had been described as one who had arrived in Jamaica as an indentured servant. Morgan claimed at least bourgeois origins, and successfully sued Exquemelin's English publishers. Exquemelin was himself a buccaneer, and may have vilified Morgan in revenge for the poor pickings Morgan's 'army' had to show for its efforts.

Despite a very muddy definition of what constituted peace between England and Spain in the Caribbean at the time, Morgan and Modyford were recalled to England. Later they both returned to Jamaica, Morgan in 1676 as lieutenant governor, having gained a knighthood. Although a maverick before, Morgan had never operated absolutely outside the Establishment, and now he took his official duties seriously. In May 1680 he issued a warrant calling for the apprehension of Sharp, Coxon and others concerned in taking Portobello – in which action Dampier also played a role as an ordinary seaman. Soon after that came another warrant warning residents of Jamaica against having dealings with 'the said villainous pirates lurking in and about this island and conceded by some wicked-minded men of their wicked complices'. Morgan complains bitterly of the difficulties he encountered in attempting to eradicate buccaneering. It was not for want of trying: Morgan strung up as many pirates as he could catch.

Morgan served under two governors, Carlisle and Sir Philip Howard, and had much to do with his old ally Thomas Modyford, and with that other old Jamaica hand, Hender Molesworth. Morgan acquired great estates, but when Hans Sloane came out to Jamaica in 1687 as physician to another governor, the Duke of Albemarle, he found Morgan, acting as Albemarle's deputy, wrecked by drink and weakened by dropsy. Morgan did not live much longer, refusing or being unable to shake off alcoholism despite Sloane's care and treatment.

Albemarle himself did not long survive his deputy. Described by Sloane as 'of a sanguine complexion, his face reddish, his eyes yellow, as also his skin, and accustomed by being at court to sitting up late and often being merry', he was not an ideal candidate for the post. Elsewhere described as 'this miserable son of the great George Monck', the most damning comment on him must be: 'How Albemarle was allowed to take up so important a post is a complete mystery, for he seems to have been well known for a fool.' He died early in the autumn of 1688.

Sloane stayed fifteen months on the island. He made a collection of 800 plants and collected as many manuscript memoirs of buccaneers and other seafarers as he could. Noting how local slave women fed their children on milk mixed with cocoa, he invented milk chocolate, which he was later to market successfully at home, along with quinine, which he also brought from Jamaica. These established a fortune with which he was able to purchase a great deal of land in Chelsea, London. He experimented with salting the flesh of manatees, finding that it responded to the treatment much like beef, and he discovered the calming properties of smoking tobacco mixed with poppy seeds. He and William Dampier would meet much later in London, and it is certain that they found plenty to talk about.

CHAPTER SEVEN

Crossing the Isthmus

Morgan's expeditions against Portobello and Panama inspired the expedition that Dampier joined after leaving Mr Hobby in the lurch early in 1680.

Dampier himself gives a very scant account of the adventures of the first year or so of the venture into which he had entered: the story is told in detail in another book by Basil Ringrose, Dampier's fellow buccaneer and friend – if one may judge him to have been so by the one sympathetic reference made to him by our mariner. Although it is a pity that Dampier gives us no account of this part of the expedition, he explains in his own published work that he hasn't done so because Ringrose's version needs no addition. It is true that Ringrose's book could hardly have been bettered by Dampier – though one does miss the keen eye for detail, especially for wildlife. Perhaps in the future Dampier's original journals will turn up: but it is likely that they are lost for ever. It may be that, as he chose to leave the narrative of these events to Ringrose, he found little to engage his attention on the crossing which his fellow explorer had not covered.

Dampier takes up his own story much later, from the time when he and Ringrose parted company. So we must join with Ringrose as we take the first steps of the journey. But not only Ringrose. Several other members of the expedition kept journals, and I will refer to them where they elaborate Ringrose's account.

Dampier joined the buccaneers early in 1680 as a man of some standing – he was a merchant-trader. And yet he enlisted on a par with the other men who had defected from *The Loyal Merchant*, the ship commissioned by Mr Hobby. He cannot have insisted on a higher rank than foremast man, but it was not unusual in those days to accept demotion: no dishonour or loss of esteem attended such a thing.

Dampier does not warrant any mention by name in Ringrose's account. On this first expedition together, he and Ringrose probably had only a slight acquaintance with one another. They were both members of Captain Bartholomew Sharp's crew, at least latterly; and we know from his own account that Dampier had little time for Sharp. But Dampier himself cannot have made a great impression on Ringrose. Perhaps he kept his head down; perhaps he simply kept himself apart.

Ringrose was born in Kent. He was literate and reasonably well educated. He had learnt Latin. It is possible that he was a runaway apprentice. He was bitten by the urge for adventure in the same way as Dampier, and his account of the crossing of the Isthmus of Panama – or Darien, as they called it – is lively and detailed. He did not have much stomach for buccaneering, but he stuck it out with Sharp and eventually returned to England with him. Then, turning into an entrepreneur, he left home again before his journal was published. It appeared as the second volume of Exquemelin's *Buccaneers of America* in 1685, having been edited with a strong bias towards Sharp by Sharp's friend, the cartographer William Hack. Sharp's own journal is more modest than Hack's elaboration of Ringrose's account, and it is fortunate that as a corrective, both Sharp's and Ringrose's manuscripts have survived.

Ringrose left England with Captain Swan of the *Cygnet* in 1684, and in the course of that voyage he was to run into Dampier once more; but he never saw his native land again. But I am getting ahead of myself. We must return to the spring of 1680.

The fleet Dampier joined first engaged in taking Portobello, which it did without much difficulty, though the booty was poor: £40 per man. After some reorganization the fleet then gathered at a convenient harbour called Boca del Toro. Ringrose gives its composition as follows:

	Tons	Guns	Men
Captain John Coxon, in a ship of	80	8	97
Captain Peter Harris	150	25	107
Captain Bournano	90	6	86
Captain Richard Sawkins	16	1	35
Captain Bartholomew Sharp	25	2	40
Captain Edmund Cook	35	0	43
Captain Robert Alleston	18	0	24
Captain Row	20	0	25
Captain Thomas Mackett	14	0	20

Bournano and Row were Frenchmen. Bournano had already established friendly relations with the local Indians. The original plan was to make their way inland to Tocamora, guided by the Indians, who had told Bournano that there was much gold to be had there.

Once the fleet had assembled, it made its way down the coast to the Islands of Samballas (the San Blas archipelago) to rendezvous with the Indians. Ringrose gives a vivid description of the buccaneers' first encounter with them:

Being here at anchor, many of the Indians, both men and women, came to see us. Some brought plantains, others fruits and venison, to exchange with us for beads, needles, knives, or any trifling bauble whereof they stand in need. But what they most chiefly covet are axes and hatchets to fell timber withal. The men here go almost naked, as having only a sharp and hollow tip, made either of gold, silver, or bark, into which they thrust their privy members, which tip they fasten with a string about their middle. They wear as an ornament in their noses a golden or silver plate, in shape like a half-moon, which, when they drink, they hold up while they lift the cup with the other. They paint themselves sometimes with streaks of black; as the women do in like manner with red. These have in their noses a pretty thick ring of gold or silver; and for clothing they cover themselves with a blanket. They are generally well-featured women: among them I saw several fairer than the fairest of Europe, with hair like the finest flax. Of these it is reported that they can see far better in the dark than in the light.

Pale Indians are mentioned in other journals, and were probably albinos.

These Indians had been in a state of perpetual war with the Spanish, and though a truce now existed between them, they still resented the European occupation of their lands.

Now the Indians were against the idea of an expedition to Tocamora, saying that the journey lay through bleak and barren mountains with small chance of obtaining provisions on the way. It is also possible that spring was the wrong season of the year for such travel – in any case the buccaneers were soon to be plagued by torrential rain. Instead, the Indians proposed to guide the buccaneers across the Isthmus of Darien to Panama. The English mariners liked this idea, but the two French captains, Bournano and Row, were against a long route march, and so parted company with the rest.

The seven remaining ships proceeded to Golden Island in the company of an Indian chief called Andreas, who could speak some Spanish. There the buccaneers learnt of another Spanish settlement, Santa Maria, east-ward along the coast from Panama and situated at the mouth of the river of the same name. Santa Maria was a collecting-point for gold mined in the mountains to be shipped to Panama. There was a garrison of 400 soldiers to guard it, but the rewards for taking it promised well, and if it did not yield sufficient riches to satisfy the buccaneers, then they could always proceed with their original plan and attack Panama as well.

Of the captains, Robert Alleston, Thomas Mackett and Bartholomew Sharp had all fallen ill. Sharp was sufficiently recovered by the time the expedition was ready to set off to lead his men, but Alleston and Mackett were too unwell to travel, and so they remained behind with a skeleton crew of thirty-five men to guard the fleet while the rest of the force, 331 men, William Dampier among them, undertook the venture. They did not expect it to take a very long time. A swift attack and retreat was the usual method of operation, before the Spanish had time to rally their forces.

They set off on 5th April 1680, each man equipped with three or four doughboys to eat, 'and for drink the rivers afforded enough'. They were a rough crowd, but there was some semblance of military order about them. Ringrose tells us:

Our several companies that marched were distinguished as follows. First, Captain Bartholomew Sharp with his company had a red flag, with a bunch of white and green ribbons. The second division, led by Captain Richard Sawkins with his men, had a red flag striped with yellow. The third and fourth, led by Captain Peter Harris, had two green flags, his company being divided into two several [separate] divisions. The fifth and sixth, led by Captain John Coxon, who had some of Alleston's and Mackett's men joined to his, made two divisions or companies. The seventh was led by Captain Edmund Cook, with red colours striped with yellow, with a hand and sword for his device. All or most of them were armed with a fuzee [light musket], pistol, and hangar [short cutlass].

The first part of the march went well. The going was good, the weather dry, and the path well-defined. They made a camp by an all-but-dried-out river bed. John Cox (not to be confused with John Coxon), a fellow member of the expedition who later became a commander, wrote in his own journal: 'We marched till 2 in the afternoon, then coming to an Indian house we took our quarters for this night, having the cold ground for our bedding and the spangled firmament for our covering.' Dampier, sharing these experiences, would have expressed himself less poetically. Cox's imagery is hardly original, however; and Bartholomew Sharp, in his journal, describes camping out in almost identical terms.

There another Indian 'captain', whose name was Antonio, came to meet them. Antonio encouraged them in their design on Santa Maria, and said that he would lead them there. He could not join them immediately as a child of his lay very sick indeed. 'However,' says Ringrose rather coldly, 'he was assured it would die by the next day, and then he would most certainly follow and overtake us.' Antonio warned them against sleeping in the long grass for fear of 'monstrous adders'.

The mariners discovered gold ore in rocks that lay in the river bed, which had been carried down from the mountains when the river was in flood, but this good omen was not encouraging enough for four of the men, who, finding themselves too tired to continue, returned to the ships. Dampier would have quickly latched on to the idea of gold, and in any case he only ever abandoned an expedition when a greater one beckoned. As we follow his life, it becomes increasingly apparent that he was addicted to travel, in the fullest sense of the word 'addiction'.

The following day they climbed a steep hill, and found on the other side of it a river, which Chief Andreas told them was the one at whose mouth Santa Maria stood. But it was not to be a simple matter of following its course from then on. They had to ascend and descend a huge mountain, and then cross and recross the meandering river, 'almost at every half-mile, sometimes up to the knees and at other times up to the middle in a very swift current'. By now it had begun to rain. They struggled on in sodden clothes, with no means of alleviating their discomfort and misery. Yet no one turned back. If Dampier had a stoical nature, it was far from unique. We can only guess at the toughness of the people of that period.

At about midday on 7th April they reached an Indian village and here they were visited by the local king of the Darien Indians, whose palace was half a mile distant. Basil Ringrose tells us:

His crown was made of small white reeds, which were curiously woven, having no other top than its lining, which was of red silk. Round about the middle of it was a thin plate of gold, more than two inches broad, laced behind, whence did stick two or three ostrich [*sic*] feathers. About this plate went also a row of golden beads, which were bigger than ordinary peas; underneath which the red lining of the crown was seen. In his nose he wore a large plate of gold in the form of a half-moon, and in each ear a great golden ring, nearly four inches in diameter, having a small hole in the centre by which it hung to the ring. He was covered with a thin, white cotton robe, reaching to the small of his legs, and round its bottom a fringe of the same, three-inches deep. So that by the length of this robe our sight was impeded, that we could see no higher than his naked ankles. In his hand he had a long bright lance, as sharp as any knife.

The king had come accompanied by three sons similarly attired and armed, his wife, clad in red blankets, and a small retinue of eight or nine. They were obviously accustomed to Europeans, and some trading took place, wherein 'we found them to be very cunning'. Another member of the expedition, who has left behind an anonymous manuscript record of the trip, noted that 'the king's daughters fancied much to be in our company, insomuch that some of our people by signs would ask them if they should live with them, and be their wives'.

It seems unlikely that William would have been swayed by such temptation; but none of the expedition members succumbed to matrimony. Bartholomew Sharp writes more directly in his journal: 'They are very beautiful, they are also very loving and free to dispose of themselves to Englishmen, answering them in all respects according to their desires.' The king arranged for each of the buccaneers to be given three plantains and some sugar cane, but that was the extent of his generosity. All other food had to be paid for.

Having rested for a day, they continued their journey on 9th April, following the river, and passing an Indian house or settlement from time to time, where they would be given plantain or cassava root. Ringrose noticed that the Indians counted the buccaneers by dropping one grain of rice per man that passed; but they could count no higher than twenty.

The following day started badly. Sharp notes in his journal:

> Saturday in the morning we got up as soon as it was day to provide to march whereat the same time one of our commanders, Captain John Coxon, had some words with another which was Captain Peter Harris, and upon the same Captain Coxon fired his gun and did conclude to return, but I persuaded him to the contrary.

The fraternity was always loose-knit and discipline was never more than shaky. In addition, Coxon was a troublemaker with a surly nature.

Later that day, a party of about seventy men, including Ringrose, and possibly Dampier as well, under Cook, Coxon and Sharp, embarked in native canoes and sailed downriver, led by Chief Andreas. Sharp says that there were not enough canoes for the whole troop. The going was no easier by river: 'For at the distance of every stone's cast we were constrained to quit and get out of our boats, and haul them over either sands or rocks . . .' At the end of every exhausting day they had to build huts to shelter in, though they were hardy men and did not complain.

Sharp gives us an optimistic account of the camp they made on the Sunday night:

An hour before night we came to a green bank which was situated by the river side and here we took up our lodging for the night, we having for supper a very good sort of wild beast called warr [the white-lipped peccary, *Dicotyles labiatus*] which is much like to our English hog and altogether as good, for here is great store of them in this part of the world. The navels [actually a gland] of these creatures grow upon their backs.

But there was a more serious problem than the rigour of the journey: the Englishmen had begun to suspect the Indians of splitting their party deliberately, to betray them to the Spaniards.

Their fears were groundless. They were reunited with the main party, which had travelled by land, a few days later, and they were relieved to see each other again. They had reached a rendezvous point used by the Indians when they set out to attack the Spanish. On Wednesday 14th April 1680 they all embarked in a flotilla of something over sixty canoes, provided by the Indians, fifty of whom now accompanied them as guides

King Golden Cap

and brothers-in-arms. Among them was a son of the king who was called Golden Cap by the buccaneers, on account of his distinctive headgear. There are various descriptions of it. It may have been a golden coronet, or possibly a captured and adapted Spanish helmet.

They set off early in the morning, and by midnight landed about half a mile from Santa Maria: 'The place where we landed was deeply muddy, insomuch that we were constrained to lay our paddles on the mud to wade upon, and withal lift ourselves up by the boughs of trees to support our bodies from sinking.' They hid deep in the woods, to avoid discovery by Spanish lookouts. They must have been exhausted, stinking and wretched. But they were within stabbing distance of their goal.

The next morning, roused by the noise of the reveille drum beating in the town, the force readied itself for the attack. Their caution, however, had been in vain, for the Spanish knew of their arrival, and were ready for them.

The fort consisted of a palisade of twelve-foot-high wooden stakes, from behind which the Spanish set up a brisk fire. But the vanguard of the buccaneers, led by Sawkins, quickly breached the wall and soon after that the battle was over. Sawkins was wounded in the hand by an arrow, but not seriously. The ease with which the town was won is fairly typical of such confrontations; the Spanish forces were composed of half-trained young soldiers, volunteers and amateurs, no match for tough fighting men. Ringrose says:

> In this action not fifty of our men had come up before the fort was taken, and on our side only two were wounded, and not one killed. Notwithstanding, within the place were found two hundred and three-score men, besides which number two hundred others were said to be absent, having gone up into the country to the mines to fetch down gold, or rather to convey away what was already in the town.

The Spanish, if they knew that they were going to be attacked, took anything of value out of a town into the jungle and hid it there. Buccaneers and pirates resorted to torture to discover the whereabouts of treasure thus concealed, but often did not dare stay long enough to find it, for fear of a counter-attack by Spanish reinforcements. In fact, though the battle of Santa Maria was so easily won – the Spanish lost twenty-six men and sixteen were wounded – the pickings were small. The town itself was disappointing: it wasn't really a town at all; more a collection of huts. Worse still, the buccaneers had missed by three days a consignment of three hundredweight of gold, which had just been taken up the coast to Panama. The gold transports took place only three times a year, so there was no point in waiting for the next. Captain Sawkins and a small troop set off down-river in a canoe in pursuit of the town's governor, priest and other chief men who had escaped before the attack, but any

hope of major booty at Santa Maria was gone. Dampier was as disappointed
as any of them, and the riches of Santa Maria were to stay in his mind
for the rest of his life.

In one respect the raid had been a success. Indeed, the buccaneers may
have guessed the real reason why the Indians had built up Santa Maria
so much to them. One of the Indian king's daughters had been forcibly
carried off by a member of the garrison at Santa Maria. She was now
restored to her people, but she was pregnant. The Indians were so furious
that they took large numbers of the captive Spaniards into the woods
and speared them to death, before the buccaneers stopped them, rounding
up the surviving prisoners in the fort and placing them under close guard.

The next thing to be decided was how to proceed with the expedition.
The discussion was short, although John Coxon would not give his
support unless he was elected to overall command, which he got. Coxon
was a short tempered and difficult man, but his force was the second
largest and could not be dispensed with. Sawkins and Sharp led the
vanguard of the attack on Santa Maria, but Sharp did not distinguish
himself in it.

I wish one of the chroniclers of this expedition had been more candid.
Why wasn't Harris, who commanded the largest force, elected leader?
Did Coxon have more experience, or a more cohesive gang? And how did
they endure the climate, and the privations of the crossing, in heavy
clothes which would dry slowly, or not at all, in such wet conditions?
How did they cope with leeches and mosquitoes? What diseases did they
suffer? There appear to have been no deaths due to sickness.

The next goal was Panama, 'that city being the receptacle for all the
plate, jewels and gold that is dug out of the mines of all Potosí and Peru'.
Many of the Indians returned home at this point, though Andreas,
Antonio and Golden Cap remained with the buccaneers. Some of the
Spanish prisoners had been sent back across the isthmus under a guard
of twelve men with the little booty taken at Santa Maria. The rest begged
the buccaneers to take them with them and not leave them to the mercy
of the Indians.

The expedition embarked in thirty-five canoes and a larger periagua
on 17th April. They rowed out into the Gulf of San Miguel, but before
they had reached the coast, the canoe in which Ringrose found himself

was in difficulties. Being heavy and consequently slow, it soon lagged behind the rest of the fleet. Abandoned by their comrades, they felt their way through shoal water and driving rain to try to catch up. When they did so, they were promptly abandoned again at a place where everyone had stopped to take on fresh water. The devil take the hindmost seems to have been the philosophy of the expedition, and despite a loose order, it is by incidents like this that we can most easily distinguish between a buccaneering venture and one run with formal discipline. Alone, lost, rainsodden and battered, Ringrose and his companions spent another miserable night before blundering on the next day.

On one of the many islets in the gulf they came upon a group of shipwrecked Spaniards from Santa Maria, who had followed the buccaneer fleet in an old, rotten canoe rather than stay behind and face the Indians. Their canoe had split on the rocks and left them stranded here. Brothers in misfortune, the English and the Spanish ate together. They were in great need of water, but soon they encountered some Indians from their expedition. However, on discovering that some of the Europeans were Spaniards – 'We told them they were *Wankers*, which is the name they commonly give to the Spaniards in their own language' – the Indians wanted to put them to death. Only Ringrose's intervention saved them, and the Spaniards were able to make their getaway in the surviving canoe; only one of their number was kept back by the Indians as a slave.

The Englishmen now joined the Indians in their own large canoe and the party set off in pursuit of the main force once more. Indeed, they thought they had caught up with them at one point, only to discover that they had run into a very large group of Spaniards, prisoners from Santa Maria who had been released on shore by the buccaneers. The Englishmen and the Indians now faced almost certain death; but the Spaniard who had accompanied them as a slave of the Indians told how merciful Ringrose had been to him and his companions. As a result, though not without some reluctance where the Indians were concerned, the Spaniards let Ringrose and his companions go on their way, and the next morning they finally caught up with the main expedition.

At long last the fleet of canoes assembled at the island of Chepillo, and on 23rd April, before sunrise, they came within view of Panama itself. A new city had been built a little way from the old after Morgan had sacked it, and was not yet finished, being constructed of brick and stone rather than wood. In the old city, the cathedral still rose, making, as Ringrose comments, 'a fair show at a distance, like that of St Paul's in London'. At Chepillo, Ringrose tells us, the commanders cruelly decided to hand over their Spanish prisoners to the Indians for slaughter. But the unarmed Spaniards, given a desperate courage by their terror, fought their way past the Indian lances into the safety of the woods with the loss of only one man.

The force was reduced by the temporary departure of Sharp and others on a cruise of his own in a captured Spanish vessel. To make matters worse, the Spanish were ready for them, word having arrived from Santa Maria. There is no record that Sawkins caught up with the 'chief men' of that town who had made their escape the day before the buccaneers attacked it. Riding at anchor off the island of Perico, close to Panama, were five great ships. Sailing towards them were three more: small men-of-war sent out to get them.

The buccaneers were tired from several days' hard rowing. There were sixty-eight of them in all. In the leading Spanish vessel alone there were eighty-six 'Biscayners, who have the repute of being the best mariners and also the best soldiers amongst the Spaniards'. The ship was commanded by High Admiral Don Jacinto de Barahona. His consorts were commanded by Don Francisco de Peralta, 'an old and stout Spaniard', with seventy-seven Africans, and Don Diego de Carabaxal, with sixty-five mulattos.

The battle was ferocious and bloody, and the buccaneers knew that if they did not win they would die. The canoes were more manoeuvrable than the ships. The English mariners managed to jam the rudder of Barahona's ship, and the admiral and his pilot were killed soon afterwards. Two-thirds of the crew were slaughtered before the survivors asked for quarter. Coxon boarded the ship, taking with him Captain Harris, who had been shot through both legs. Meanwhile, Sawkins had engaged Peralta, and after being rebuffed three times, took the ship when two powder magazines aboard exploded, killing many of the crew. The survivors were badly wounded or burned.

At the end of the engagement, the buccaneers had lost eighteen men, with twenty-two wounded. Peralta was their prisoner. They wasted no time, but made for the five large ships riding at anchor. The biggest of them, a 400-tonner, had been holed and set on fire, but they boarded her in time to rescue her. She was called *La Santissima Trinidad*. They renamed her the *Trinity*, and took her over. Of the other four ships, two they burned and two they commandeered. They were rejoined on 25th April by Captain Sharp and the rest of the buccaneers. Crewmen frequently changed ship on such expeditions. We simply do not know if Dampier had been away with Sharp during the battle, or if he had taken part in it.

Now things faltered. Captain Harris died of his wounds. The anonymous crewman who has left us a manuscript account of the voyage reports: 'the doctors cutting off one leg, it festered, so that it pleased God he died, so we lost that brave and valiant soldier'. Captain Coxon, who had not been valiant in the battle, was furious to find himself criticized for cowardice, and withdrew from the expedition, taking with him seventy men, together with Golden Cap, Antonio and Andreas.

Sharp writes of Coxon's departure in his journal:

> I think [his departure] will not redound to his honour, for he left
> about twenty of his men here wounded which was the greatest
> cause of our staying here, to get these men well again, for had we
> all been of his mind we had left thirty-four men to have perished
> there . . . This night came Captain Coxon on board my vessel to
> see if he could work upon me to go with him back but I would by
> no means condescend to an action so dirty and inhuman to leave
> poor English souls to the mercy of a bloodthirsty people, so he
> departed this night and carried away with him the best of our
> doctors [and] medicines . . .

Beneath the oratorical self-righteousness of Sharp's tone, there is genuine indignation. Thus Coxon departed, to pursue his own piratical career. He was to die among the Moskito Indians with whom he subsequently chose to live, many years later, in 1698.

Captain Sawkins, a genuinely brave and popular leader, was elected commander-in-chief. In the days that followed, the expedition took some small prizes, but made no attempt to launch an attack on Panama itself. An incentive to stay in those waters was, however, provided by the news that a treasure ship was on its way from Lima with a cargo of 100,000 pieces of eight. In the meantime, the governor of Panama sent a message to Sawkins, via some merchants who were quite happy to trade with the buccaneers, to ask what he intended to do. Sawkins replied with the demand for a ransom in exchange for sparing the city, and he also exchanged presents with the Bishop of Santa Martha, who was in Panama and who had been his prisoner when he had taken Santa Martha four or five years previously. The governor was not intimidated and asked Sawkins from whom he held his commission, so that the governor would know where to make his complaints for the damage already done to the Spanish fleet. Sawkins, who of course had no commission, sent a bombastic reply:

> That as yet all his company were not come together; but that when they were come up we would come and visit him at Panama, and bring our commissions on the muzzles of our guns, at which time he should read them as plain as the flame of gunpowder should make them.

But even this did not shake the governor. The buccaneer fleet stood off to the nearby island of Taboga, to recover after the battle and refit their new ships. John Cox notes in his journal for 25th May that 'Captain Sharp made himself a forestaff and I made myself a quadrant with which we made shift at present to navigate our ships.' I will return to the question of navigation, but for the present it is simply worth noticing that the buccaneers had found no navigational instruments on the prizes they had taken, which seems odd, even given the Spaniards' reputation for poor seamanship.

These activities took them through to just before the middle of May. But the men under Sawkins' command were growing restive. They had a reasonable fleet, but they were running short of provisions, and they did not have the patience to wait for the treasure ship. One French crew-member deserted to the Spanish, and this was to prove damaging to the buccaneers, for he was privy to their immediate plans.

Sawkins knew that he would not retain command if he did not pander to his men, and so towards the end of the month he arranged a raid on the nearby coastal town of Puebla Nueva. Here, on 25th May, at the forefront of the battle as usual, Sawkins was killed. His troop was routed. Our anonymous crewman was one of the party, and leaves us this account:

> Our valiant Captain Sawkins landed himself first and went into the savannah and saw abundance of people there, one mulatto met him, whom Captain Sawkins shot down. He returns back a little way, asked if the party were all landed and ready. Answer was made, yes. Then he said, follow me and do not lie behind for if I do amiss you will all fare the worse for it. He went up courageously with some brisk men with him, but there was provided mulattos . . . with their lances which came to oppose him. He fired his pistol and shot down one mestizo, the rest firing and loading as fast as they could, but the Spaniards coming in upon them so fast that killed Captain Sawkins and three men more; they took one alive, we heard him make a dreadful noise but could not rescue him, but was forced to retreat to our canoes, and go off as fast as we could.

On Sawkins' death, Captain Sharp once again took command of the fleet, and, coming on board the *Trinity*:

> asked our men in full council who of them were willing to go or stay, and prosecute the design Captain Sawkins had undertaken, which was to remain in the South Sea [the Pacific] and there to make a complete voyage; after which, he intended to go home round about America, through the Straits of Magellan. He added withal that he did not as yet fear, or doubt in the least, but to make each man who would stay with him worth one thousand pounds by the fruits he hoped to reap of that voyage. All those who had remained after the departure of Captain Coxon, for love of Captain Sawkins and only to be in his company and under his conduct, thinking thereby to make their fortunes, would stay no longer, but pressed to depart.

Ringrose continues, tellingly:

> Among this number I acknowledge myself to have been one, being totally desirous in my mind to quit those hazardous adventures, and return homewards with those who were now going to leave us.

Yet, being much afraid and averse to trust myself among wild Indians any farther, I chose rather to stay, though unwilling, and venture on that long and dangerous voyage. Besides which danger of the Indians, I considered that the rains were now already up, and it would be hard passing so many gullies, which of necessity would then be full of water and consequently create more than one single peril to the undertakers of that journey.

Dampier, who shared these hazards, would not have been so discouraged; but I can sympathize with Ringrose, who was exhausted and longed for nothing more than to be home. The buccaneers were the first to have spent any time on that coast since Drake's day. Home was a year away at least, and the tedium of life at sea had begun to tell. Ringrose did not have Dampier's voracious curiosity, and the fact that he can give vent to such a personal confession is one mark of the difference between the two men. In the event, Dampier also remained with Sharp at this point.

On the last day of May, following Sharp's speech, a further sixty-three men left the expedition, taking the remaining Indians with them. The parting of the ways took place on the island of Cayboa, where there was a plentiful supply of fresh food in the form of tortoises and red deer.

On the same island, Ringrose had an unusual experience. While he was washing himself under a mançanilla tree, there was a shower of rain, and the water dropped from the leaves on to his skin. Shortly thereafter his skin broke out into red blotches, which he attributes to a poisonous quality in the tree. The blotches *may* have been caused by his having recently fed on the large oysters found on the island, 'the biggest that ever I ate in my life, insomuch that I was forced to cut them into four pieces, each quarter of them being a good mouthful'. However, if the tree he'd been standing under *was* the poisonous euphorbiaceous *Hippomane mancinella*, which grows in tropical America and has both apple-shaped fruit and a blistering milky juice, Ringrose's own deduction is the correct one!

From Cayboa, Sharp's expedition set sail to find a safe haven to careen their ships and prepare themselves for a cruise along the Pacific coast, in search of whatever pickings they could find. It was to be a difficult year.

CHAPTER EIGHT

Ranging the Pacific Coast

Taking their Spanish prisoners with them, Sharp and his men, William Dampier and Basil Ringrose among them, set sail from Cayboa at about five in the evening on Sunday, 6th June 1680. Their original intention was to make for the Galapagos Islands, where the then plentiful giant tortoises would have provided them with ample food; furthermore, the Galapagos group was sufficiently remote for the fleet to careen in preparation for the projected long cruise without fear of being surprised by any Spanish force. Freebooters were always at their most vulnerable when their ships were out of the water.

This plan misfired, and poor navigation rather than contrary winds seems to have been to blame. By mid June, they found themselves a long way south of Panama. One of their principal captives, Captain Peralta, advised them to make instead for the island of Gorgona. A certain cordiality existed between the buccaneers and their captives. Sharp, admittedly in Hack's sanitized version of his story, tells us that he had a cultivated conversation with Peralta about the comets that had appeared in the sky above Quito in 1679.

The Spaniard, who would have been in hopes of being ransomed in due course, did not baulk at volunteering practical information. He even praises the buccaneers' seamanship. He is not an exception. It is so common for Spanish prisoners to accommodate their captors that I wonder, when reading the English accounts, how much of a euphemism the word 'questioned' is. It is unlikely that eminent prisoners were tortured; but we have ample evidence of lesser mortals being dealt with brutally if they did not cooperate.

Dampier never tells us of such things. He chose to concentrate his narrative on what really interested him; but he is not above self-editing. Ringrose is franker, though he was shocked at the cruelties he reports. Shortly after leaving Gorgona, the buccaneers took a Spanish ship with 3,276 pieces of eight aboard; they shot the vessel's chaplain and threw him overboard before he was dead. It is possible that the chaplain had given some particular cause for offence, for the buccaneers were not always so cruel. Later, when they themselves were short of water, they did not take the supply of a small Spanish prize.

Peralta told Sharp that the local Spanish population avoided Gorgona because it always rained there. Dampier recollects in his book *A Discourse of Winds*, which he wrote much later, how on another visit to Gorgona:

we boiled a kettle of chocolate . . . and having every man his calabash full, we began to sup it off, standing all the time in the rain; but I am confident not a man among us all did clear his dish, for it rained so fast and such great drops into our calabashes that after we had supped off as much chocolate and rainwater together as sufficed us, our calabashes were still above half full; and I heard some of the men swear that they could not sup it up so fast as it rained in. At last I grew tired with what I had left and threw it away, and most of the rest did likewise.

Sharp optimistically thought that if they laid up there for a while, the Spanish would think they had gone away, and that in consequence they would have the advantage of the element of surprise when they set out on their voyage of plundering. Ringrose was far less sanguine:

At this time it was that I seriously repented my staying in the South Seas and that I did not return homewards in company of them that went before us. For I knew, and could easily perceive, that by these delays the Spaniards would gain time and be able to send advice of our coming to every port all along the coast, so that we should be prevented in all or most of our designs wheresoever we came. But those of our company who had got money by the former prizes of this voyage overswayed the others who had lost all their booty at gambling.

It's unlikely that Dampier was of the same opinion as Ringrose; he wasn't ready to go home for a long time yet.

They careened and refitted at Gorgona during a rare spell of dry weather, stripping all the high superstructure off the *Trinity*. A mainmast cracked, and the carpenters had to repair it. The Spaniard who had carried off the Indian king's daughter to Santa Maria, one José Gabriel, died here of an unidentified 'malignant fever'.

The party was in a quandary about where to sail for next, but one of their number suggested a raid on Arica, the town used as a collection-point for the silver from Potosí, Chiquisaca, and other neighbouring mines. The expedition set off on 25th July. By this stage John Cox had command of one of the consort ships, and on their way down the coast, ill-served as they were by their Spanish pilots, who seem to have been genuinely inefficient and not so by design, they lost contact with him, but were reunited when they arrived at the Isla de Plata, or Drake's Island, so called because it was here that Sir Francis Drake was said to have distributed the plate he took from the Spanish in the 1570s. Ringrose gives a detailed account of the coastline and islands passed on their route. Like Dampier, he collected such information avidly, to pass on to fellow mariners and to their governments. Those pirates and buccaneers with sufficient education and expertise to gather and expound new geographical discoveries contributed greatly to man's knowledge of the world, and if discoveries already made by enemy or rival nations and kept secret could be revealed, so much the better. The special value of Dampier's geographical observations lies in his masterly grasp of pinpointing locations, though this was several decades before John Harrison's chronometer enabled seamen to measure longitude accurately.

At Drake's Island they adapted the *Trinity* further. While working on her, many of the men suffered badly from sunburn. They had with them a handful of Moskito Indians, expert at spearing fish and turtle, and here they caught, killed and salted several tortoises and goats, turning more tortoises on their backs until they chose to kill them for fresh meat. Continuing on their way, they took one or two small prizes, but they sailed south as far as Guayaquil without meeting any resistance from the Spanish. Off Guayaquil, however, they fought and took a substantial Spanish vessel, whose commander was the brother of Admiral de Barahona, whom they had killed in the action off Panama. They took him prisoner, along with several other distinguished Spaniards whom they found aboard, and from him they learnt that the coast was alerted against them, and that the viceroy of Peru had powerful ships in readiness to engage them. They made an abortive attempt on the city, but the news they had received did not deter them from pursuing the long voyage south towards Arica.

When they finally reached Arica it was the end of October and the men were exhausted and dispirited. Supplies were so low that water was changing hands for thirty Spanish dollars a pint. To make matters worse, Arica was prepared for them and they were easily seen off. Instead, they made an attack on the nearby port of Hilo, where they took the sugar-works. This they did in full view of a large Spanish force which merely looked on – though it later transpired that it was largely made up of unarmed boys under the command of a local English merchant. They found no fresh meat but quantities of chocolate, which was an excellent remedy for scurvy.

They negotiated Hilo's ransom with the Spaniards there for eighty head of cattle. The Spanish prevaricated, and negotiations dragged on for three days before the frustrated buccaneers smashed up the sugar-works and carried off what plunder they could. Even so, they almost fell foul of a force of 300 Spanish horsemen sent to rescue the town. Dampier almost certainly took part in this attack, alongside Ringrose. We can only imagine the role he played, though by the yardstick of later exploits it was probably not a small one.

With little to show for their work, the buccaneers set sail for Coquimbo, a port well to the south. Nerves were beginning to fray. On 28th November Don Peralta 'was taken very frantic, his distemper being occasioned, as we thought, by too much hardship and melancholy'. But he recovered the next day.

They sailed into Coquimbo a few days later, and made plans to take the town whose port it was, La Serena, without delay. The Spaniards had been forewarned of their arrival, and, not having adequate forces to defend the town, had evacuated it, taking with them most of the provisions the buccaneers had hoped to benefit from. La Serena was a substantial and beautiful town, and Sharp's party, having taken possession, set about negotiating a ransom to the total value of 95,000 pieces of eight. But once again the Spanish prevaricated, and, having gained time, opened irrigation sluices and flooded the town in the hope of driving the buccaneers from it. In response, the English set La Serena on fire and marched back to their ships, fighting off an attempted ambush by 250 horsemen on the way. But the Spanish had not finished with them yet. Ringrose writes:

> They blew up a horse's hide like a bladder, and upon this float a man ventured to swim from shore and come under the stern of our ship. Being arrived there, he crammed oakum and brimstone, and other combustible matter, between the rudder and the stern-post. Having done this, he fired it with a match, so that in small time our rudder was on fire and all the ship in a smoke. Our men, both alarmed and amazed with this smoke, ran up and down the ship, suspecting the prisoners to have fired the vessel, thereby to get their liberty and seek our destruction.

The fire was discovered in time, and it did little damage. The buccaneers thought their most prudent course now was to withdraw, which they did, after having set ashore Don Peralta and the rest of their worthy prisoners. They were becoming a liability, and a drain on provisions.

The dispirited Englishmen then sailed on until they reached the two islands of Juan Fernandez, off the coast of modern Chile, on Christmas Day, in honour of which they fired three volleys. They anchored off t he island closer to the mainland – though still a comfortable 100 miles from it.

Juan Fernandez had once been briefly colonized by the Spanish, who had abandoned it because life was easier on the mainland; but they had left behind their goats, which had multiplied and run wild. The island on which the buccaneers found themselves was naturally fecund, and it was a much-used stopping place for rest and refitting after rounding Cape Horn, both for Dampier on this and later voyages, and for all those mariners who came after him.

This was not a peaceful Christmas. The weather was stormy, and now, with a little leisure, the restiveness of the men came to a head. They had worked hard all year, but had very little to show for it. Sharp, who may have been a perfectly capable commander, had not brought them luck, and had none of the charisma of Captain Sawkins. He was turfed out of command on Twelfth Night, 1681, and replaced by one John Watling, 'he having been an old privateer and gained the esteem of being a stout seaman'. How one longs for Dampier's comments on all this. But the politics of ship life don't interest him at all. Yet he must have been involved: it would hardly be possible to be otherwise, in such an isolated, claustrophobic and tiny community.

Watling had a busy time during his first few days of command. Captain Edmund Cook's servant, William Cook, was discovered to have a paper about him with every man's name on it. He was suspected of having planned to give it to the Spanish if captured and so was clapped in irons on 7th January. Or was he? There is some confusion about who was actually put in irons, for there was more drama concerning the two Cooks the same day. Ringrose notes in his unpublished, and more candid, journal:

> This day William Cook servant to Captain Edmund Cook confessed that his master had often buggered him in England, leaving his wife and coming to bed to the said William, once in Jamaica and also in these seas before Panama, also searching his writings found a paper with all our names which was suspected he had designed to have given to the Spanish prisoners, so this evening our captain thought fit to put him in irons.

From this it may safely be inferred that it was Edmund, not William, who was shackled, and this is borne out by Sharp who writes baldly: 'William Cook servant to Edmund Cook in the morning impeached the said Edmund Cook for buggering him several times and by order of the new commander he was put in irons.'

In Hack's version of Sharp, the story is much the same: 'the first thing he (Watling) had to exert his unjustly-gotten power upon, was in the putting of Edmund Cook into irons, upon the accusation of a servant of his, of the same name, that the former had several times acted the sodomite with him'.

Edmund Cook had been in trouble before. They had taken a Spanish vessel on 1st May and renamed her the *Mayflower*. Captain Cook was put in command of her, 'but upon some disgust or other (he) left his *Mayflower* and went on board the great ship [the *Trinity*] as a private soldier; Captain Bart. Sharp being commander-in-chief, puts [as] commander of the *Mayflower* one John Cox.' This report by the anonymous crewman whose account has come down to us indicates the degree of intrigue which had developed by Christmas. The *Mayflower* was later sunk off the coast of Guayaquil, having been damaged in a collision with the *Trinity*.

On Sunday 9th January, Watling revived a rule which had been enforced under Sawkins: that of observing the Sabbath. Sawkins had seen the wisdom of forbidding gambling, at least on Sundays, and had once angrily thrown the dice overboard when he had caught men gaming.

Sawkins and Watling were by no means as strict as some of their colleagues in observing the Sabbath. In 1694 Père Labat was made to say Mass for a group of buccaneers at Martinique. One of the men misbehaved during the service and was insolent when rebuked; upon which Captain Daniel, his commander, shot him dead.

On 12th January the buccaneers were forced to make a hasty departure from Juan Fernandez, as three men-of-war had been sighted bearing down on the island. In their haste to be gone, they left one of the Moskito Indians, called William, behind. He had gone inland and could not be found in time. He was to be Juan Fernandez' first famous castaway, and we will meet him again, on a return voyage with Dampier. Watling fled from the Spanish warships, but he was right to show caution, since they kept in a tight group and were big ships: the two principal vessels weighed 800 and 600 tons.

Watling did not reward the confidence the men had placed in him. Wishing to attack Arica again, he sailed north and first captured Iquique. There they noticed that the Indians 'ate much and often of certain leaves which were in taste much like to the bay leaves in England, by the continual use of which their teeth were dyed to a green colour'. Were they coca leaves? Or a kind of betel leaf? Dampier, who evidently tasted them, gives no report of their effect.

Among the prisoners Watling took there were two old men, whom he interrogated regarding the defences of Arica. Believing one of them to be lying, he had him shot out of hand. In the version of Ringrose's account doctored by William Hack, a dramatic incident is inserted at this point to the greater glory of Captain Sharp:

> Our old commander . . . was much troubled in his mind and dissatisfied at this cruel and rash proceeding, whereupon he opposed it as much as he could. But, seeing he could not prevail, he took water and washed his hands, saying: *Gentlemen, I am clear of the blood of this old man; and I will warrant you a hot day for this piece of cruelty, whenever we come to fight at Arica.*

Of course, writing well after the event, it wasn't hard to credit Sharp with prophetic powers; and one shouldn't forget that Sharp had been in command when they shot the Spanish chaplain.

The attack on Arica was a disaster. It took place on 30th January, the anniversary of the execution of King Charles I and therefore, as Ringrose implies, a day of ill-omen. But the attack failed principally because of Watling's poor strategy. Failing to take the fort, he turned his attention on the town, and only when he thought he had subdued it did he return to the attack on the fort. But then the town rallied. Arica had had intelligence from Iquique of the projected assault, and was well prepared. In the fray, a great many of the buccaneers met their end, including Watling himself, two quartermasters and a boatswain. They also lost three of their surgeons, who, having got drunk, were captured by the Spaniards, and, being valuable trained men, were neither offered for ransom nor returned.

Following this débâcle, Sharp, who rallied the men enough to organize an orderly retreat, once again took command. The anonymous account gives a very forthright version of how he did so, and John Cox comments: 'Our former new Captain, Jno. Wattkyns [*sic*] being killed at this place Captain Sharp would have thrust himself Captain again . . .' We know that Dampier had no love for Sharp, and though Watling sounds worse, it was probably this return to power of the old commander that decided him to leave Sharp's company.

Fortune still failed to smile on the adventure, as the little fleet rambled on up and down the coast. There were skirmishes, and small prizes were taken, but there was nothing like the splendid booty Sharp had promised.

It was not long before another group of men had decided to leave him. The split occurred at Drake's Island, where they had returned after attacking Hilo again, on Sunday 17th April 1681.

Amongst these defectors – accounts vary, but Dampier and Ringrose give their number as forty-seven, composed of forty-four buccaneers, two Moskito Indians, and one Spanish Indian – were Dampier himself, and a friend of his, whom I must now introduce: a young surgeon called Lionel Wafer, of whom we'll hear much more. Also with them was Captain Edmund Cook. They were given the *Trinity*'s longboat for their voyage, together with supplies and two canoes. They also had with them 'five slaves taken in the South Seas who fell to our share'. Their intention was to sail back to the Isthmus of Darien, and recross it to the Caribbean coast.

Basil Ringrose remained with Sharp. It was a long way back to the isthmus, and then there would be the demanding crossing, the unrelenting rain, and possibly hostile Indians to face. Ringrose had been frightened by the Indians' treatment of Spanish prisoners. It is likely too that he thought his quickest way home lay with Sharp. In this he was probably correct.

Before taking up the narrative of Dampier's voyage after he had left Sharp, I think it is worth following Ringrose and Sharp home.

Soon after the departure of Dampier and his companions, Ringrose was able to prove himself useful in a very important way, as another account of Sharp's voyage printed in Exquemelin's book relates:

> From Chero we went to the island of El Cavallo, where we lost our interpreter, who had done us good service all along, and at this place ran away from us, as we judged, unto the Spaniards, leaving behind him all that he had purchased [gained] in the voyage, which was worth nigh 500 pound in money and goods. What should be his intent in this action we could not know, except to betray us unto that nation.

He must have thought it worth his while. Five hundred pounds was a small fortune then. The account continues:

He was a Dutchman by birth, and his name James Marquis, and was very intelligent in the Spanish *lingua*, and besides that in many others. After his departure we had no great need for an interpreter, neither now did we much want one; yet, in what occasions we had, we made use of one Mr Ringrose, who was with us in all this voyage, and being a good scholar and full of ingeniosity had also good skill in languages. This gentleman kept an exact and very curious *Journal* of all our voyage from our first setting out to the very last day; took also all the observations we made, and likewise an accurate description of all the ports, towns, and lands we came to.

Now down to just over sixty men, Sharp continued his cruise for several months, taking one or two important prizes, before heading for Paita. On their way, at the end of July, they encountered and took *El Santo Rosario*. 'In this vessel,' writes Ringrose, 'I saw the most beautiful woman that I ever saw in the South Sea'; but we learn no more of her. In the ship was some money, 620 jars of wine and brandy, and much more important cargo besides, though the buccaneers failed to recognize that 700 pigs of what they took to be tin were in fact silver. They took one pig to make bullets of, and left the rest where it was. When they got to Antigua at the end of their voyage they sold the remaining third of that pig to a merchant, who recognized it for what it was and later sold it in Bristol for £75. Each pig had therefore been worth £225. 'Thus we parted with the richest booty we had gotten in the whole voyage, through our own ignorance and laziness,' Sharp records ruefully, adding that 'the plate was not yet thoroughly refined and fitted for coin; and this was the occasion that deceived us all'.

He did, however, take a prize of equal worth from the ship – a large Spanish 'waggoner', or collection of charts, of the whole coast of South America. The Spaniards wept when it was taken, for it was of enormous strategic value, and Sharp, who had it translated, and redrawn (most beautifully) by his friend Hack, was able by presenting it to King Charles II in 1684 to purchase his pardon. For reasons of security, only a very small number of copies were made. One ended up in the possession of a certain William Hill of Lincoln's Inn who sold it to the South Sea Company in 1711, having purchased it from Hack eighteen years earlier for £70. Hill had to sell it to get out of debt. It was offered for sale in London by Bernard Quaritch in 1914 at £650. Charles II's copy, together with the Spanish original, are in the British Library.

Having rummaged the *Rosario*, they turned her loose and continued towards Paita, which they reached at the end of August. They had hoped to take the city, but found it well prepared against them, and so decided to start the long voyage southwards along the coast towards the Horn. They encountered ferocious seas, especially where the south-west coast of Chile breaks up into a mass of islands, and were often hard put to find safe havens from them; but the *Trinity* was a well-found ship, as she seems to have withstood the buffetings she received without complaint.

On 27th October, they encountered a small group of Indians in a boat: a man, a woman and a youth of eighteen or so. The buccaneers sent a canoe after them, and the Indians tried to escape by leaping into the water. The man was shot dead, the woman escaped, and the youth was taken. 'He was covered only with a seal's skin, having no other clothing about him. His eyes squinted, and his hair was cut pretty short.' He gave them to understand by signs that there were other Indians in the vicinity, but they made no contact with them. The youth, whom the buccaneers christened Orson, was extremely strong. When a foraging party returned to the ship bearing large limpets, and mussels 'which were six-inches-and-a-half long', Orson was able to open them with his bare hands, 'which our men could not so readily do with their knives'. Orson remained their prisoner, but Ringrose does not tell us what became of him.

By early November they were looking for the Straits of Magellan, but, failing to find the entrance, sailed on far to the south, leaving the coast behind them. On 17th November they saw icebergs, and Ringrose noted their latitude as 58° 23' South, but on 20th in the evening they caught a small white 'land-fowl', which gave them hope that they might not be too far away from 'some coast or other'.

The long voyage continued, and it is a measure of the discontent mounting on board that on 7th December Sharp gained intelligence of a plan to shoot him on Christmas Day. He defused the situation by issuing a generous extra ration of wine.

They did not see land again until 28th January 1682, which to their great joy and relief they discovered to be Barbados. Two days later they anchored off Antigua. It was agreed that the *Trinity* should be given to 'them of our company (seven or eight in number) who had no money left of all their purchase in this voyage, having lost it all in play'. The remainder of the company split into two groups and travelled back to England as passengers.

Ringrose left Antigua with Sharp on the *Lisbon Merchant*, under Captain Robert Porteen, on 11th February, and arrived home on 26th March 1682, almost two years since the beginning of the original expedition. And there, for the moment, we will leave him.

After a short period of respectability, during which he held the rank of captain in the Royal Navy, Bartholomew Sharp seems to have run out of money; but he soon managed to scrape £20 together, with which he bought a hulk. This he equipped with 'a dozen or two pieces of beef', a little cheese and butter, and a crew of sixteen. He sailed it to the mouth of the Thames and with it took a French vessel in the Downs. This he commandeered; then, pausing only to rustle cattle on Romney Marsh with which to provision his trip, set off once again on a pirating expedition. We last hear of him in 1688 on the island of Anguilla, an infamous pirate rendezvous, where he was acting governor.

CHAPTER NINE

Return across the Isthmus

It is at the point of departure from Sharp that Dampier takes up his own narrative. He was now an experienced mariner of twenty-nine, and probably one of the older members of the crew that left the *Trinity* in April 1681.

Dampier and his companions faced a voyage of about 600 miles back to the Gulf of San Miguel, where they hoped to make contact with the Cuna nation of Darien Indians who had assisted them before, and make their way back following the river of Santa Maria. They took their supplies from the *Trinity*, and for three days before parting company they sifted flour and 'rubbed up 20 or 30 pound of chocolate with sugar to sweeten it,' as Dampier tells us. From the outset they established a rule which would apply once they were on dry land again: that if any man became a straggler, he would be shot. This was intended for the security of the whole group: if a wounded or sick man fell into the hands of the Spaniards, they would torture out of him information about his companions. In the event, the rule was not enforced.

The weather was good to begin with, but when a stiff sea-breeze stirred up the water they had to cut up an old animal hide and erect it round the sides of the launch to keep their provisions and ammunition dry, for they were in danger of being swamped. Their greatest fear was of Spanish patrols, but they reached Cape Passao (Passado) without incident, and there had the luck to come upon a small trader at anchor, which they swiftly took, and transferred to it. They kept the crew with them as prisoners. Dampier says, 'in taking her we were safe from being described: we did not design to have meddled with any when we parted with our consorts, nor to have seen any if we could have helped it'. They would not have set their prisoners ashore because they would have raised the alarm.

The buccaneers now continued their journey north in greater security and comfort, and at a better speed, than if they had kept to their open boats. Reaching Gorgona on 24th April, they hung back, fearing an ambush, for the Spanish would by now have learnt that the main fleet had careened there. When night fell and they did pluck up enough courage to go ashore, they found that the Spanish had erected a large 'house', big enough for 100 men, together with a huge crucifix. The captive crew told them that a large, fourteen-oar periagua was anchored in the mouth of 'a river on the Main' – perhaps at Punta Reyes – which came over to Gorgona on patrol every three days or so. If the periagua sighted the buccaneers, she was to make haste to Panama and alert a newly formed fleet of three warships.

The buccaneers only spent a day here, scraping the barnacles from the hull of their prize to make her sail more smoothly, 'that if ever we were chased we might the better escape'. They replenished their fresh water and set sail again as soon as possible, through rainy weather, but providentially with the wind at the south-west. Nearing the Gulf of San Miguel, they had a close shave; sighting two large ships only four or five miles to the west of them, they hurriedly furled their sails and stood close in to the shore. Luckily they were not spotted. The following day they landed, cleaned their guns and dried their ammunition. They expected to reach the Gulf the next day, and also expected their enemies to be waiting for them. Passing Point Garrachina that evening, they arrived at their destination at eight in the morning. They anchored and sent a canoe to scout. Just as Dampier had feared, it discovered a vessel lying in wait for them.

The buccaneers' own ship was lying just off a large island, and now the men landed on it in another canoe. Once ashore, they spread out and awaited events. After high water, a canoe came over cautiously from the enemy ship, and the three men in it landed on the island, falling into the ambush the buccaneers had set. They were one Spaniard and two Indians, who when questioned described what the buccaneers were up against. It turned out to be a huge Spanish force, which the buccaneers would have no hope of escaping from unless they moved quickly and made contact with the Indians. A degree of their fear is apparent in Dampier's tone as he writes: 'for we did not question but we should get a good commerce with the Indians, by such toys as we had purposely brought with us, or else force our way through their country, in spite of all their opposition'. In his unpublished and always slightly more candid manuscript he notes, with more confidence but less 'political correctness', 'for we very well know the hearts of the Indians'.

Dampier had gained a position of authority (though not command) among his shipmates, owing to his skill as a navigator. He tried to persuade them that the best course of action was to make their way by stealth in their ship up the Congo River, a wide waterway which lay a short distance from the island where they were anchored, but of which no one else in the party had any knowledge. That in itself is a testimony to Dampier's powers of observation and strength of memory. 'But all the arguments I could use were not of force sufficient to convince them that there was a large river so near us, but they would land somewhere, they neither knew how, where, or when.'

Dampier's impatience with their recalcitrance is obvious. They managed to make their way up the Gulf in their ship, rowing and towing against the wind all night, and brought her into a little creek four miles west of Cabo San Lorenzo, where they landed, unloaded their gear, and sank the ship. It was 1st May 1681. What they did with their prisoners, Dampier does not relate. It seems unlikely that they simply let them go. Perhaps they left them on some remote island. Perhaps they simply killed them.

As they prepared to march up country, their Moskito Indians caught enough fish to make a meal. They started their march at three in the afternoon, after the heat of the day had passed. Within two days they had made contact with the local Indians, who received them in a friendly manner. The buccaneers paid for their food, 'which we ate all together, having all sorts of our provisions in common, because none should live better than others, or pay dearer for anything than it was worth'. A sensible arrangement. Internal dissent was the last thing they needed, on top of all their other difficulties.

After a hearty supper on the evening of the second day, Dampier and

his companions negotiated with the Indians for a guide who would take
them a day's march further north – as far, in fact, as the dwelling of an
Indian who could speak Spanish. They set out for his house on the
following morning, having agreed to pay the guide with a hatchet for his
pains.

The Spanish-speaking Indian lived on the banks of the River Congo,
eight miles away. As they marched, one of their number, 'being tired,
gave us the slip'. Dampier does not say who he was. Perhaps he dreaded
being shot as a straggler. In any event I wonder how he imagined he
would survive alone.

The Indian who they hoped would guide them turned out to be surly
and unhelpful, but as he was their only hope they dared not threaten
him. On the other hand, he was unmoved by their offers of machetes,
beads, money and knives. Luckily, they did find a way to win him over.
Dampier tells us:

'One of our men took a sky-coloured petticoat out of his bag and
put it on his wife; who was so much pleased with the present, that
she immediately began to chatter to her husband, and soon brought
him into a better humour.'

The real cause of the man's brusqueness, it turned out, was a wounded
foot, which meant that he could not guide them; but a deputy was found.
The buccaneers were eager to be gone, for this Indian was in contact
with the Spaniards aboard the ship they had avoided in the Gulf. By
using the River Congo, he could reach it, he said, in a 'tide's time'.
Dampier felt justifiably aggrieved that his companions hadn't taken his
earlier advice. They had been travelling for three whole days and were
still well within the clutches of their enemies.

On the fourth day they marched twelve miles through driving rain,
'though the difference whether it rained or shined was much at one with
us,' Dampier notes mournfully in his manuscript, 'for I do believe we
crossed the river 30 times this day, for the Indians have no paths to
travel from one part of the country to another, therefore do guide
themselves by the rivers . . .' Fear of the Spanish was replaced by anxiety
about how to get guides and food. Dampier and some companions managed
to shoot two 'fat monkeys'. In his manuscript he points out that 'although

what we bought was in common yet what we killed was not'. Nevertheless, some of the monkey meat was given to those of their companions who were already sick and weakened by the march. Eggs and other extra delicacies were also obtained for them.

Lionel Wafer was their only surgeon. The following day he was the victim of an accident which increased their worry. Dampier's version of what happened differs slightly from Wafer's, so I will give Wafer's as being more likely to be accurate:

> I was sitting on the ground near one of our men, who was drying of gunpowder in a silver plate; but not managing it as he should, it blew up and scorched my knee to that degree, that the bone was left bare, the flesh being torn away, and my thigh burnt a great way above it.

They did not shoot him: apart from anything else, he was far too valuable a crew member. But he could not carry his load. One of the five African slaves was deputed to carry his gear and medicine chest. Dampier, nursing his grievance, notes that they could have come this far up-river in their canoe, with far less stress and in a far shorter time, 'if I could have persuaded them to it'. Why hadn't they listened to him? Had his bluntness let him down? Or had they simply not trusted his judgement?

Wafer was able to walk, though Dampier tells us that he 'marched in great pain'. By the sixth day two other men, Robert Spratlin and William Bowman, had become unable to stand the pace. But there was no question of anyone shooting them. The going was becoming very rugged indeed. Dampier says: 'The last time we forded the river, it was so deep, that our tallest men stood in the deepest place, and handed the sick, weak, and short men.' At this crossing Spratlin and Bowman decided they could go no further, and were left behind to fend for themselves, or recover and then do their best to catch up.

Dampier's thoughts had long since turned to how he could preserve his journal, otherwise by now it would have been ruined:

> Foreseeing a necessity of wading through rivers frequently in our land-march, I took care before I left the ship to provide myself a large joint of bamboo, which I stopped at both ends, closing it with

wax, so as to keep out any water. In this I preserved my journal and other writings from being wet, though I was often forced to swim.

It's sad that after he took such trouble, none of them has survived for us. However, his care is an indication of how important his record was for him, and it's certain that he knew of its worth to others.

That night was a miserable one. The rain pounded down and the river rose alarmingly, so fast that it forced them to abandon the huts they had built for the night. They found what shelter they could under trees, scattered about, not setting a watch, as a tremendous thunderstorm raged about them. Sodden and wretched, none of them slept, but nevertheless four of the five slaves took this opportunity to slip away into the night. One of their number was the man who carried most of Wafer's equipment, and he took it with him, together with Wafer's gun and all his money. Wafer was left 'deprived of wherewithal to dress my sore'; the others were left with nothing but the surgeon's medical knowledge to help them.

After the storm, the river's level sank, but that was cold comfort, for it was still too deep to ford. But as there was no other way forward, they were forced to try to swim. Swimming was not a skill learnt by all buccaneers, and so a means had to be found of hauling them across, together with all the gear. That meant getting a line over first, and the man chosen to swim over with it was one George Gayny. His manner of doing the job was foolish and dangerous, since he fastened the line around his neck, and tragedy was almost bound to strike, particularly as the river was in flood and Gayny was not unencumbered.

One man stood by the line [ashore] to clear it away to him. But when Gayny was in the midst of the water, the line in drawing after him chanced to kink or grow entangled; and he that stood by to clear it away, stopped the line, which turned Gayny on his back; and he that had the line in his hand threw it all into the river after him, thinking he might recover himself; but the stream running very swift, and the man having three hundred dollars [probably Spanish silver dollars] at his back, was carried down and never seen more by us.

There is an element of the moral tale here: if he hadn't been carrying his 'purchase', which he would entrust to no one else, Gayny might have survived. His body was found later downstream by Spratlin and Bowman, still with the money on his back. They did not have the strength to climb down to where he had been washed ashore, but left him, 'being only in care how to work their way through a wild, unknown country'. Bowman was to learn nothing from Gayny's example, though he turned out to be luckier.

At last the party crossed the river by felling a bank-side tree tall enough to bridge it, and having passed that hazard they came upon a plantain 'walk', or plantation, which they hungrily ransacked. At this point their guide, wishing to return to his own home, handed them over to another, an old man, who agreed to take them further on their way. Here, too, they parted company with their Spanish Indian. He had made arrangements at a settlement they had passed earlier to work for the owner and marry his sister; but as it was close to the Spanish ship, the buccaneers had not let him go immediately for fear of betrayal, despite the fact that the man had previously sailed for a long time with Sawkins.

They next came to a large Indian settlement, where they were made welcome, though the provisions the Indians had to give them were few; and here Lionel Wafer remained, together with two other men, John Hingson and Richard Gopson. Wafer describes the latter as 'an ingenious man, and a good scholar; and had with him a Greek Testament which he frequently read, and would translate extempore into English to such of the company as was disposed to hear him'. Gopson had served an apprenticeship to a pharmacist in London. What course led him to buccaneering we are never told; probably he had his own reasons for keeping it to himself.

The others pressed on after a short stay, forcing two Indians from the settlement to act as guides for their further journey. The Indians were unwilling to go, as it was the height of the rainy season, and the trek lasted another fortnight. Ploughing through the rainforest and crossing and recrossing the river, they made their weary way, until at last, to their 'great comfort', they came within sight of the sea. At La Sound's Key, they found a French privateer (I use Dampier's word) at anchor, under the command of a Captain Tristian, who took them aboard. From his crew they bought knives, scissors and looking glasses to give to their guides as a reward before bidding them farewell, together with a present of half a dollar each from each of the buccaneers.

The French ship was ready to sail, and William Dampier and his companions went with her to rendezvous with a fleet that stood off Springer's Key, about fifteen miles away. Here they met with Captain Coxon again, in company with another Englishman, Captain Peter Wright, a Dutchman called Yankey, and some other French commanders, among whom was Captain Row. The commanders of the fleet now held a lengthy discussion, which lasted a week, about where to sail for. Eventually they settled for a raid on the town of Coretaga (perhaps Cortago), which lay some way up Carpenter's River in what is now Costa Rica. Dampier and his friends were attached to the ship of one of the French captains, Monsieur Archembo, because his was the only vessel that was undermanned.

Dampier took a dim view of the Frenchmen he was obliged to mess with. He found them 'the saddest creatures that ever I was among; for though we had bad weather that required many hands aloft, yet the biggest part of them never stirred out of their hammocks, but to eat or ease themselves'. Soon afterwards, the English buccaneers left Archembo to his own devices and took over a Spanish tartan (a fast coaster) which had been taken by Captain Wright, putting themselves under his command.

This was just as well, for the fleet could not hold together and the original design was aborted, especially as Captain Tristian had had a narrow escape from a flotilla of Spanish warships which had come out to find them. They split up, Dampier remaining with Wright. 'We past by Scuda, where 'tis said Sir Francis Drake's bowels are buried', on their way to cruise along the coast of Cartagena, but chiefly they foraged for food, and no great enterprise distinguished the voyage. Dampier, as usual, kept his eyes open and recorded everything of interest that he saw. His experience with mançanilla apples bears out Ringrose's:

> We found plenty of soldiers [soldier-crabs] . . . One time our men
> found a great many large ones, and being sharp-set had them dressed

[cooked], but most of them were very sick afterwards, being poisoned by them: for on this island were many manchineel trees, whose fruit is like a small crab [apple], and smells very well, but they are not wholesome; and we commonly take care of meddling with any animals that eat them. And this we take for a general rule, when we find any fruits that have not been seen before, if we see them pecked by birds, we may freely eat, but if we see no such sign, we let them alone . . .

Dampier was by no means the only mariner to follow this sound advice. Dampier's tartan now returned to La Sound's Key. Here there was to be a reunion:

It was in the evening when we came to an anchor, and the next morning we fired two guns for the Indians that lived on the Main to come aboard, for by this time we concluded we should hear from our five men, that we left in the heart of the country among the Indians, this being about the latter end of August, and it was the beginning of May when we parted from them. According to our expectation the Indians came aboard, and brought our friends with them: Mr Wafer wore a clout about him, and was painted like an Indian; and he was some time aboard before I knew him. One of them, named Richard Cobson [*sic*] died within three or four days after, and was buried on La Sound's Key.

Wafer notes in his account that Gopson's death was in accordance with a prophecy made by an Indian oracle he had consulted when he reached the coast.

It is now time to introduce Lionel Wafer more fully. He was born around 1660, and made his first voyage under Captain Zachary Browne of the East India Company on the *Great Anne* in 1677, where he served as an assistant surgeon or loblolly boy – loblolly being a kind of gruel served to the sick. He spent the next three years sailing in the same capacity in the East and West Indies. His name suggests possible Huguenot descent and he is elsewhere called Weaver, Weber and DelaWafer. Apart from what we learn of him through Dampier's books and his own writings, we know little of him. He was active among the buccaneers until about 1688, and served two years in prison at Jamestown, Virginia, on charges of piracy. He returned to England in 1690 and his book, *A New Description of the Isthmus of America*, was published after Dampier's, in 1699. They shared the same publisher, James Knapton, and Dampier's manuscript contains a transcription of part of Wafer's journal. Both books, appearing at such a turbulent time in European history, would have been read not only as stories of adventure and travel, but as practical guides for future political, mercantile and military development.

In the late 1670s, Wafer was working as a free man with his brother on the Angels Estate in Jamaica, owned by Sir Thomas Modyford and next door to Sixteen Mile Walk, where Dampier had worked. It was while he was in Jamaica that he met Edmund Cook, and with him joined the expedition across the isthmus which I have described. It is possible that he and Dampier crossed each other's paths in Jamaica, though neither makes any allusion to a meeting there.

The Darien Indians, among whom he and his two companions, Gopson and Hingson, found themselves, were of the Cuna nation. Their chief, who according to some sources was the successor to Antonio, was called Lacenta. Unlike Wafer, Gopson and Hingson were uninjured, but were worn out by the struggle through the jungle. At the settlement where they found themselves, they were presently joined by the two other stragglers, Robert Spratlin and William Bowman. Bowman had narrowly escaped death, having been swept away when crossing the river by means of a wet and slippery log bridge. He had managed to get to the shore, despite being 'a weakly man, a tailor by trade' and having 400 pieces of eight in a bag on his back.

All five of them remained for about three months with the Indians. The Indians cured Wafer's burns with local herbal remedies, the chewed herbs applied as a poultice; but they treated the Englishmen in a distant and surly manner which the Europeans found difficult to understand. 'Some of them looked on us very scurvily, throwing green plantains to us, as we sat cringing and shivering, as you would bones to a dog.' Only one young Indian, who had been in service with the liberal Bishop of Panama and spoke quite good Spanish, treated them well, though he had to do so secretly. This kind Indian was later to be one of their guides to the sea; but not before a plot had been foiled by Lacenta to burn the Englishmen alive, so strongly did feeling run against them.

The Indians' attitude changed when the two guides taken by Dampier and his companions returned, laden with their rewards. The Indians' experience of the Spanish had taught them always to be wary of Europeans, and now they were pleasantly surprised to find the English behaving decently. In fact these guides had returned *after* Wafer and his companions had set out for the coast; but, being abandoned by their own guides, the Englishmen had been forced to return to the settlement. Now they were greeted with smiles and friendship. In his manuscript journal as transcribed by Dampier, Wafer notes here: 'It will not be amiss to take notice what an alteration the hope of gain causeth in the heathens as well as Christians, for this made those that were our enemies before to be now our friends.' This succinct comment did not make it to the published version.

The positive change of mood was further bolstered by Wafer's ability to cure, by skilful bleeding, Lacenta's principal wife. Letting blood was considered in those days to be a legitimate form of medical treatment, and it was frequently effective.

Lacenta was a paramount chief wielding absolute power, and his friendship was invaluable. Wafer describes Lacenta's house as being surrounded by a grove of stately cotton trees – 'four Indians and myself took hand in hand round a tree, and could not fathom it by three foot'. A man of his time, Wafer comments that the grove 'would make a pleasant artificial wilderness, if industry and art were bestowed on it'.

Lacenta's wife had already been bled by the painful hit-and-miss method used by the Indians. They fired tiny arrows from a miniature bow into her arms, 'and if by chance they hit a vein which is full of wind, and the blood spurts out a little, they will leap and skip about, showing many antick gestures, by way of rejoicing and triumph'. Wafer continues:

I was by while this was performing on Lacenta's lady, and perceiving their ignorance, told Lacenta, that if he pleased, I would show him a better way, without putting the patient to so much torment. Let me see, says he; and at his command I bound up her arm with a piece of bark, and with my lancet breached a vein. But this rash attempt had like to have cost me my life. For Lacenta seeing the blood issue out in a stream, which used to come only drop by drop, got hold of his lance, and swore by his tooth, that if she did otherwise than well, he would have my heart's blood. I was not moved, but desired him to be patient, and I drew off about 12 ounces, and bound up her arm, and desired she might rest till the next day, by which means the fever abated, and she had not another fit. This gained me so much reputation, that Lacenta came to me, and before all his attendants bowed and kissed my hand . . . after which I was taken up in a hammock, and carried on men's shoulders . . . Thus I was carried from plantation to plantation, and lived in great splendour and repute, administering both physick and phlebotomy to those that wanted. For though I lost my salves and plasters, when the Negro ran away with my knapsack, yet I preserved a box of instruments and a few medicaments wrapped up in an oil-cloth, by having them in my pocket . . .

Wafer became a favourite, adopted native costume, and learned their language. His book is one of the first great anthropological studies.

These actions secured the gratitude of the locals, and Wafer tells us that Lacenta was anxious for him to remain permanently, promising his daughter to the young surgeon in marriage. Wafer, who did not want to remain, had to make some excuse to return to the coast. Seeing Lacenta furious one day at his lack of success in chasing peccary, Wafer promised to return with a gift of some English hunting dogs. In fact, Lacenta was probably happy to see Wafer go, as the Cuna Indians were jealous of their own racial purity. Lacenta felt honour-bound to offer Wafer such a high reward for his services. According to Wafer, Lacenta showed him a forest of bloodwood as an inducement to him to return, which dyewood an ill-fated Scottish colonizing expedition looked for in vain in 1698.

At last, Wafer and the rest were accompanied to the coast by more or less the same route that Dampier had followed, though it took them half the time, and then the reunion occurred which has already been described by Dampier. But Dampier doesn't mention the practical joke Wafer decided to play on his old shipmates:

We went aboard the English sloop [*sic*], and our Indian friends with us, and were received with a very hearty welcome. The four Englishmen with me were presently known and caressed by the ship's crew; but I sat a while cringing upon my hams among the Indians, after their fashion, painted as they were, and all naked but only about the waist, and with my nose-piece . . . hanging over my mouth. I was willing to try if they would know me in this disguise; and 'twas the better part of an hour before one of the crew, looking more narrowly upon me, cried out, Here's our doctor; and immediately they all congratulated my arrival among them.

Wafer and his friends joined Dampier in Captain Wright's company, and Wright now joined forces once again with Captain Yankey. They cruised together for some time, despite a squabble between the two commanders over a prize which each claimed he had the right to. In this dispute the men sided with Yankey, but Wright did not yet part company with him. Weeks passed in sometimes abortive trading with local Spaniards, and the taking of petty prizes as the occasion arose. They touched at Curaçao and at Aves Island, where a powerful French force under the Count d'Estrées had been wrecked a few years earlier. Dampier relates a gothic incident from that mighty shipwreck, which underlines his own dislike of drunkenness:

> There were about forty Frenchmen on board in one of the ships where there was good store of liquor, till the after part of her broke away and floated over the reef, and was carried away to sea, with all the men drinking and singing, who being in drink, did not mind the danger, but were never heard of afterwards.

It was the effect of drunkenness, rather than the thing itself, which Dampier hated, and he disapproved strongly of indiscipline too, which he regarded as leading to inefficiency and time-wasting. These are thoughts worth bearing in mind when we consider his later career. As a commander he was a poor disciplinarian; and it is probable that he took to drink as well.

★

As usual, Dampier kept a careful note of the coastlines and islands they encountered and the wildlife found on them, but one senses a certain weariness growing within him and a restlessness to be doing something more worthwhile. At the beginning of February 1682, at Los Roques, they met with a French man-of-war to which they sold ten tons of sugar they had taken, and here we get a hint of how much Dampier's standing had risen. He was now thirty:

> I was aboard twice or thrice, and very kindly welcomed both by the captain and his lieutenant, who was a Cavalier of Malta; and they both offered me great encouragement in France, if I would go with them; but I ever designed to continue with those of my own nation.

Perhaps the memory of Captain Archembo's crew was still green, but despite his resolution one has the feeling that he was aware of his worth and was flattered by the approach.

At length the little fleet made its way to Tortuga, or Petit-Guaves, the old French-controlled buccaneer haunt off the north-western coast of Hispaniola. Dampier notes:

> I have seen above twenty sail at a time in this Road [anchorage] come to lade salt, and these ships, coming from some of the Caribbe Islands, are always well stored with rum, sugar and lime-juice to make punch, to hearten their men when they are at work, getting and bringing aboard the salt; and they commonly provide the more, in hopes to meet with privateers, who resort hither . . . purposely to *keep a Christmas*, as they call it; being sure enough to meet with liquor enough to be merry with, and are very liberal to those that treat them.

From here they sailed to Trinidad and to Isla Blanca, where Dampier describes the iguanas, notes that their flesh is good eating, and differentiates between the marine and land species.

Back at Tortuga, Yankey and Wright decided to part company, and Dampier also parted from some of his friends. He elected to stay with Wright, but Wafer and John Hingson opted to sail with Captain Yankey. Sailing with Yankey as his quartermaster was another survivor of the original expedition, who had parted company with Sharp alongside Dampier and Wafer. His name was John Cook, a man of whom Dampier always speaks warmly, and who may have commanded the return voyage from Drake's Island to the Gulf of San Miguel. We will meet him again in the course of the next major voyage Dampier was to undertake. (I must apologize to the reader for having to introduce a name so similar to some already encountered. John Cook is not to be confused with John Cox or Edmund Cook. The similarity of so many names has often been a trial to me during the researching of this book!)

Peter Wright took his crew as far afield as Caracas in Venezuela, but the pickings remained as slim as ever, and finally, possibly because his ship was becoming unseaworthy, possibly because his men were restive, he set sail for Virginia, where they arrived in July 1682.

There were already rumblings of rebellion in the North American colonies against the autocratic power of the distant motherland. An item in the State Papers for 24th April 1678 notes 'considerations upon the present troubles in Virginia, with the means by which they may be settled, to the great benefit of the Crown and the good of that colony'. The colonists were protesting against heavy English taxation, and in 1676 and 1677 there had been a full-scale rebellion named after its ringleader, Nathaniel Bacon. In the 1680s there are reports of near anarchy and rebellion in Massachusetts, New Hampshire, New York, Pennsylvania and even Bermuda. Colonial governors had collaborated and would collaborate with pirates, and although that did not guarantee that sea-rovers would be treated to a sympathetic reception, they had a better chance of it here than elsewhere.

William Dampier, and some of his fellows, parted company with Wright at Chesapeake Bay. He stayed there nine or ten months, but we don't know what he did while he was there, nor why he stayed ashore for a long time. He must pretty soon have tired of the 'green flats and tobacco plantations'.

He deals with the period with his usual reticence, though he does allude to 'troubles' that befell him, and as 'troubles' is often a euphemism for imprisonment, it is possible that he was gaoled as a pirate. However, he cannot have been in prison for the whole time, for he also tantalizingly refers to lodging with 'a gentlewoman'.

It is impossible to guess at a romantic attachment. Dampier's nature was not inclined to love, and though we know that he took care of his wife materially, nothing leads us to suppose that his relationship with Judith was an ardent one, even on the rare occasions that he was with her. Dampier was still young and adventurous; and he had married in haste. Of sexual relationships of any kind, if they existed at all, he breathes not a word. Even his friendships were few. His only real relationship was with travel and exploration.

It is possible that he worked on a plantation in Virginia, and he may have engaged in a short buccaneering voyage to Carolina; but whatever he did, he leaves us virtually no record. Almost all we get is one sentence: 'That country is so well known to our nation, that I shall say nothing of it.' As always, he considers his personal affairs of no account to us.

What he *does* tell us is that after six months or so in Virginia he suffered once again from a noxious worm (probably the guinea-worm, *Filaria medinensis*) which bred under his skin on the ankle. He describes the experience with his usual combination of graphic detail and scientific detachment:

> These worms are no bigger than a large brown thread, but (as I have heard) five or six yards long, and if it breaks in drawing out, that part which remains in the flesh will putrefy, and be very painful, and endanger the patient's life; or at least the use of that limb . . . I was in great torment before it came out: my leg and ankle swelled and looked very red and angry; and I kept a plaster to it to bring it to a head. At last drawing off my plaster out came about three inches of the worm, and my pain abated presently . . . I knew well enough what it was, and presently rolled it up on a small stick. After that I opened it every morning and evening, and strained it out gently, about two inches at a time, not without some pain, till at length I got out about two foot.

Apparently, however, this method was not good enough, for Dampier soon afterwards paid an African slave a fee of one white cockerel in exchange for a cure which consisted of the application of some powder, 'and mumbling some words to himself, he blew upon the part three times, and waving his hands as often over it, said, it would be well speedily'. The man had used exactly the same method to cure the galled back of a horse which belonged to an acquaintance of Dampier, and in both cases he was entirely successful:

> He bade me not open it in three days; but I did not stay so long; for the next morning, the cloth being rubbed off, I unbound it, and found the worm broken off, and the hole quite healed up. I was afraid the remaining part would have given some trouble, but have not felt any pain there from that day to this.

While Dampier remained at Chesapeake Bay, Captain Yankey's crew had not been idle. For some time Dampier's former companions had continued to sail with Yankey, but he was a disputatious man. When they took a Spanish prize which John Cook, as quartermaster, or second-in-command, had every right to lay claim to command under privateering law, he would have none of it. Cook had already taken charge of the Spanish vessel, and into it with him had come some of Yankey's men and all those remaining buccaneers who had recrossed the isthmus, so that for the moment Yankey had to accept the situation. This all took place at Isla Vaca, a favourite meeting-point for rovers off the south-west coast of Hispaniola.

Yankey saw his chance when reinforced by the French commander, Tristian, who was still cruising in those seas. He persuaded Tristian that Cook had no right to the vessel, on the slender grounds that he carried no 'commission', or Letter of Marque. Together with some other French captains, they took the prize ship back from Cook, and confiscating all arms and goods from him and his crew, turned them ashore and sailed for Tortuga. However, Captain Tristian took pity on the despoiled Englishmen, and brought about ten of them aboard his own vessel, among them John Cook, John Hingson, Lionel Wafer, and Cook's own second-in-command, Edward Davis. Then he sailed after the rest of the fleet to Tortuga.

Cook and his men bided their time. Once anchored in the road between Tortuga and the mainland, Tristian and many of his crew trustingly or naïvely went ashore. Seizing the opportunity, Cook turfed out the remaining members of Tristian's crew, and with his companions promptly sailed off, taking Tristian's ship, which they aptly renamed the *Revenge*, back to Isla Vaca, where they picked up the rest of their number. They then promptly took a rich French merchantman, and one other French vessel 'of good force'.

They decided on a cruise in the Pacific, because the Caribbean was becoming too hot for buccaneers. In response to bitter complaints from Spain, English men-of-war, in touch with the governors of Jamaica and other West Indian islands in English hands, were on the lookout for any ships or men involved in the attacks on Portobello and Panama, and the crossing of the isthmus. Port Royal was no longer a safe haven. In addition, their impudent attacks on French ships had turned the third major European power in the Caribbean against them, as well as the French privateers.

But first they needed to recruit more good men, and they knew where to find them: in Virginia. Not too many questions were going to be asked there, either, and they needed somewhere to refit for their enterprise.

Dampier, then staying at Point Comfort, must have felt his heart quicken when he saw the sails:

> They went for Virginia with their prizes; where they arrived the April after my coming thither. The best of their prizes carried eighteen guns; this they fitted up there with sails, and everything necessary for so long a voyage; selling the wines they had taken for such provisions as they wanted. Myself, and those of our fellow-travellers over the Isthmus of America, who came with me to Virginia the year before this (most of which had since made a short voyage to Carolina, and were again returned to Virginia), resolved to join ourselves to these new adventurers: and as many more engaged in the same design as made our whole crew consist of about seventy men. So having furnished ourselves with necessary materials, and agreed upon some particular rules, especially of temperance and sobriety, by reason of the length of our intended voyage, we all went aboard our ship.

They set sail in one vessel from Accomac on 23rd August 1683, with John Cook as their commander. The Caribbean days were over.

CHAPTER TEN

From America to Africa, Then Back round the Horn

John Cook was perhaps a Creole, a native of St Kitts, 'a brisk bold man'. For his master, or navigator, on the voyage, he had chosen one William Ambrosia Cowley. Dampier may have acted as his mate. Why Dampier himself did not get Cowley's job is a mystery, because Cook had travelled with him long enough to have some idea of the man's capability. It could be that Cowley thrust himself forward: he comes across as a self-centred and vainglorious man, and he may have deceived Cook into thinking him a better 'sea-artist' than in fact he was. He claims to have been an MA of Cambridge University, but he is so boastful in other departments that one may doubt even that, though he must have been a competent seaman. At the beginning of his *Journal*, Cowley states his innocence of connivance in piracy, and says that Cook hired him to take the ship to Tortuga for a fee of 500 pieces of eight. Only when they were at sea did he learn their true design. This was a common way of getting a pilot to sail on a freebooting venture; but Cowley, in the later course of his narrative, protests far too much to be considered innocent.

Cowley's own account of the venture that was about to begin is useful in that it fills in the gaps Dampier chooses to ignore. In his book, Dampier tells us blandly, 'I shall not trouble the reader with an account of every day's run, but hasten to the less known parts of the world, to give a description of 'em; only relating such memorable accidents as happened to us, and such places as we touched at by the way.' He does, however, recount one event on the voyage out from Virginia which serves to place Cowley (the master) in his proper light. Dampier's indignation is evident in his demonstrative language:

we scudded before the wind and sea some time, with only our bare poles; and the ship, by the mistake of him that conned, broached to, and lay in the trough of the sea; which then went so high that every wave threatened to overwhelm us. And indeed if any one of them had broke in upon our deck, it might have foundered us. The master, whose fault this was, raved like a madman, and called for an axe to cut the mizzen shrouds, and turn the mizzen mast overboard, which indeed might have been an expedient to bring her to her course again. Captain Davis was then quartermaster, and a more experienced seaman than the master. He bid him hold his hand a little, in hopes to bring her some other way to her course. The captain also was of his mind. Now our main yard and fore-yard were lowered down a port last, as we call it, that is, down pretty nigh the deck, and the wind blew so fierce that we did not dare to loose any head-sail, for they must have blown away if we had, neither could all the men in the ship have furled them again; therefore we had no hopes of doing it that way. I was at this time on the deck with some others of our men; and among the rest one Mr John Smallbone, who was the main instrument at that time of saving us all. Come! said he to me, let us go a little way up the fore-shrouds, it may be that may make the ship wear; for I have been doing it before now. He never tarried for an answer, but run forward presently, and I followed him. We went up the shrouds half-mast up, and there we spread abroad the flaps of our coats, and presently the ship wore. I think we did not stay there above three minutes before we gained our point and came down again, but in this time the wind was got into our mainsail, and had blown it loose . . .

After this adventure, their first port of call was the Cape Verde Islands, which they reached following a terrible storm which lasted more than a week. Their reason for coming here, which Dampier does not mention, was to seek and take a better ship for their long cruise. Arriving at the island group, they anchored off Sal, which as its name implies was rich in naturally occurring salt-pans. Otherwise it was a barren place, save for a few flamingos, of which Dampier gives us a beautiful description, a fine example both of his keen eye and his ability to paint an accurate and glowing pen-portrait:

> a sort of large fowl, much like a heron in shape, but bigger, and of a reddish colour. They delight to keep together in great companies, and feed in mud or ponds, or in such places where there is not much water: they are very shy, therefore it is hard to shoot them. Yet I have lain obscured in the evening near a place where they resort, and with two more in my company have killed fourteen of them at once; the first shot being made while they were standing on the ground, the other two as they rose. They build their nests in shallow ponds, where there is much mud, which they scrape together, making little hillocks, like small islands, appearing out of the water, a foot and a half high from the bottom. They make the foundation of these hillocks broad, bringing them up tapering to the top, where they leave a small hollow pit to lay their eggs in; and when they either lay their eggs, or hatch them, they stand all the while, not on the hillock, but close by it with their legs on the ground and in the water, resting themselves against the hillock, and covering the hollow nest upon it with their rumps, for their legs are very long; and building thus, as they do, upon the ground, they could neither draw their legs conveniently into their nests, nor sit down upon them otherwise than by resting their whole bodies there, to the prejudice of their eggs or their young, were it not for this admirable contrivance, which they have by natural instinct. They never lay more than two eggs, and seldom fewer. The young ones cannot fly till they are almost full grown; but will run prodigiously fast; yet we have taken many of them. The flesh of both young and old is lean and black, yet very good meat, tasting neither fishy, nor any way unsavoury. Their tongues are large, having a large knob of fat at the root, which is an excellent bit: a dish of flamingos' tongues being fit for a prince's table.

When many of them are standing together by a pond's side, being half a mile distant from a man, they appear to him like a brick wall; their feathers being of the colour of new red brick: and they commonly stand upright, and single, one by one, exactly in a row (except when feeding) and close by each other. The young ones at first are of a light grey; and as their wing-feathers spring out, they grow darker; and never come to their right colour, or any beautiful shape, under ten or eleven months old. I have seen flamingos at Rio la Hacha, and at an island lying near the Main of America, right against Curaçao, called by the privateers Flamingo Key, from the multitude of these fowls that breed there: and I never saw of their nests and young but here.

Dampier's descriptions of all the fauna and flora he encountered on his present voyage, as well as of the towns, bays, islands and coastlines he sailed to, are as vivid as this. Flamingos are familiar creatures to us; but it is worth remembering that the vast majority of his contemporary readers were learning about them, and everything he described, for the first time.

The population of the island of Sal, according to one account, consisted of a 'governor, a lieutenant, two officers and a boy'. 'They were all black,' the egregious Cowley tells us, 'but scorn to be counted anything but Portuguese; for if any man call them Negro, they will be very angry, saying, that they are white Portuguese.' The governor presented the freebooters with a few lean goats, which were the best on the island. In return, Cook, 'minding more the poverty of the giver than the value of the present', gave him a good coat, since he was dressed in rags, and for headgear had 'an old hat not worth three farthings; which yet I believe he wore but seldom, for fear he should want before he might get another'. Theirs was the first ship to anchor at Sal in three years. They took on salt and gave the islanders some powder and shot. There was little other trading. A second surgeon, Herman Coppinger, who was to accompany Dampier through subsequent adventures, bought a lump of ambergris, whose authenticity Dampier, having seen the real thing before, doubted. His doubts were borne out by another shipmate, John Read of Bristol, who was to have his own effect on Dampier's life as the long voyage unfolded.

They touched at the slightly more prosperous St Nicholas, and then at Mayo, where the people would not allow them to land because an English ship had recently been there and held the governor to ransom after a double-cross in order to obtain cattle. The captain responsible was George Bond, who later defected to the Spanish, and whom we will meet again. The result of this for John Cook's crew was that they could get no meat here. And Dampier tells us little more. He tells us nothing of the friendly Dutch ship – 'a Holland ship bound for Virginia with Negroes,' as Wafer tells us (an interloper, or illegal trader, in fact) – from which they took 'six casks of Canary . . . with some victuals and lemon, telling him they might as well rob him as he the King, he being bound to rob the King of his duties'.

This was an act of piracy which Dampier passes over in silence. Equally he tells us nothing of another encounter with a Dutch ship off St Iago, which they attacked, but which proved to be a big East Indiaman of fifty guns and 400 men, who 'strook her ports alow, and presently running out her lower tier of guns was ready to receive us,' as Cowley tells us, and sent the freebooters off with their tails between their legs. This was the reason why they did not anchor at St Iago, the richest of the Cape Verdes, with good trading. Dampier simply states the fact; he does not tell us why.

They left the Cape Verdes in the hope of picking up a favourable wind to take them down to the Straits of Magellan; but contrary winds forced them to change course and make instead for the Guinea coast of Africa, where they anchored in the mouth of the River 'Sherborough', some way from an English factory, or trading station, of the same name. Today this is by Sherbro Island in the southern province of Sierra Leone. Dampier, as usual with an eye to where money could be made, notes that a local logwood was traded here.

They careened their ship and cleaned her, close to a large town whose occupants were familiar with Europeans and gave the freebooters a friendly reception. Dampier becomes disingenuously bland again. He says they filled their water-casks; 'and buying up two puncheons of rice for our voyage, we departed from hence about the middle of November, 1683, prosecuting our intended course towards the Straits of Magellan'.

Ambrosia Cowley is more honest than Dampier, for he tells us graphically in his manuscript journal what else happened in November 1683. I am not aware that what follows has been published before, so it is worth quoting at length, the more so as Cowley fills in crucial gaps purposely left by Dampier, who as we know didn't want to draw attention to the fact that he was involved in acts of piracy:

> We made the land in Sorolone in Guinea where we spied a sail to the eastward of us; he standing to us and we to him, but we could not make what he was before dark. About eight o'clock at night we came up with one another. We hailed him in English, but he answered us with his guns which roared at us as long as they could see, placing some shot in us, we stood a little way from him, keeping a good eye on him till day; and, getting the weather-gage of him, when it was day we were clear to fight him, and seeing him a goodly ship, he being too high-minded to show his colours, but when he saw us bear down to him resolving to board him, he heaved up his Majesty's colours which made us bear up round under his stern, giving him a gun to leeward to satisfy him that we were his friends, but would not speak with him by reason he would not speak with us the night before. So that we stood with the land and never knew what ship it was.

Then there was the much more significant taking of a Danish slaver with sixty black girls loaded. The Danes were neutral in any war affecting the English at that time, so once again Cook's crew performed an act of outright piracy. The slaver was well stocked with fresh water, food and brandy. She was ideal – a 'lovely ship'.

If Dampier were to be believed – and it has to be said that he omits unwholesome facts rather than lies directly – the ship in which they sailed for the Pacific was the same as the one they set out in from Virginia; but this was *not* the case. They probably took *two* ships across the Atlantic. Again it is to Cowley that we must look for the truth, though he puffs himself up shamelessly in what follows:

> We being gotten under the land, we came to an anchor at the mouth of the Sirilono River. As soon as the day broke we saw a lovely ship pass by us to the west, and our anchor being almost up, they got it up in great haste, making sail after him; but he outsailed us. That made them angry and some of the rashest would have fired upon him, which if we had, he had sunk us in the sea, for he had

36 good guns mounted and about 70 men as they say, the number of his men I know not so exactly, but did the number of his guns. The wind taking him short, he tacked and stood into Sirilono River, he coming to windward of us, some of our men would have fired a broadside into him, which I hindered, our broadside consisting but of four guns, and I knowing myself in as much danger if taken as any of them, I being but a jackdaw amongst rooks. I promised them I would take him with more safety and less danger if that they would be content. Those men left the management of the fight to me. The tide of ebb being done, the Dane got into an anchor and we could not get in that side while he was at anchor. The English agent [presumably of the local factory] came aboard of him, and the captain of the Brandenburg ship that lay by him with the Brandenburg agent. [Brandenburg was another nation friendly to England at that time.] The English agent seeing a ship without sent his boat to us to know whether we were a Company ship [i.e., belonging to the Royal African Company] or an interloper; the messenger telling us that if we were a Company ship we should fire and he would come aboard. We being willing to get him out of that ship, we fired a gun; but the tide of flood being come we were under sail and he did not come out of his ship as we would have had him. We kept the other two men of the agent's [who had managed to board before the flood tide] aboard and sailed into the river. I roused about thirty men to go down below having their arms by them, and when I stamped on the deck to come up and enter him, keeping with me about eighteen men, ordering the quartermaster [Cowley's superior, Edward Davis!] whom I called to put the helm a-port and so put the helm hard a-starboard [this was a preconceived stratagem to delude the Danes; the helmsman deliberately turned the ship in the opposite direction to command], and the boatmen to let go the anchor and four men ready to lash them together with a guard for their security, the rest all hands to enter; he having some jealousy [suspicion] of us was cleared [for action], but I laid him aboard on his bow, and his foretopmast yard being squared and his braces fast, took the [?bolt-rope] of our foretopmast, that our ship swung along his side, our anchor not holding, but we presently lashed, and our

men entering the first time; but were driven back again, but then the captain and I entered, they all following, we having her in in half a glass, they killing and wounding but five men, for our ship was so low that we lay under her guns. When they were made masters of that ship they went and secured the ship of the Duke of Brandenburg, a ship of four guns, for fear of their doing us damage. Sending all the prisoners ashore, except the officers, giving them victuals with them until we had made the other ship fit for sailing from thence . . .

Hearing of another, much larger ship belonging to the Duke of Brandenburg in the vicinity, of forty guns and 250 crew, they made haste to depart. They sank their original vessel 'by reason she should tell no tales' and, putting their remaining prisoners ashore, made off for the mouth of the Sherbro. Here, Cowley had another adventure:

I went on land with the doctor [he does not say which one, but it cannot have been Coppinger or Wafer] and one mulatto that could speak the language, and treated with the king for watering the ship, presenting him with a cask of brandy and four bars of iron, and some Indian clothes which pleased him very well. He sent his people down to fill our water for us, and treating us very kindly, with the king presenting each of us one of his black women to sleep by us as long as we stayed there. The doctor stayed with his mistress but I went aboard by reason I did not like her hide.

The poor doctor caught a fever on shore and died at sea in late November, 'much lamented', says Dampier, who also states that there was then left to them only one doctor – Lionel Wafer. At the time Coppinger was only an assistant surgeon.

We do not know what happened to the sixty African slave girls on board the Dane, but either they were turned loose with the Danish crew, or, which is more likely, sold to another trader before the freebooters set sail for the Horn.

The ultimate fate of the Brandenburg ship is not known, but the Danish slaver, well victualled and crewed, and rechristened *The Batchelor's Delight*, set sail for the South Seas. They crossed the Atlantic without incident, though weathering storms. Off Brazil they 'observed the sea to be as red as blood,' writes Cowley, 'occasioned by a prodigious shoal of shrimps which lay upon the water for many leagues together'. This was no doubt plankton, for in the vicinity they also saw a great many whales. 'One hundred,' says Cowley, 'to every one seen in the northern hemisphere.'

They reached the Sebald de Wart Islands on 28th January 1684. These islands had been discovered and rediscovered, named and renamed, and even today they are known either as the Falklands or the Malvinas, depending on one's point of view. Here Cowley claims to have discovered an island which he 'named' after Samuel Pepys, and he describes it in detail. In his manuscript Cowley gives a latitude of 47°40' (for Pepys Island) and half-guesses that it might be one of the 'Sibble d'Wards'. James Burney, in his *Chronological History*, comments sternly:

> The editor of Cowley's journal, William Hack [whom we now meet again, embroidering another fellow mariner's work], might possibly believe from the latitude mentioned by Cowley that the land seen by him was a new discovery. To give it a less doubtful appearance, he dropped the 40' of latitude, and also Cowley's conjecture that the land was the Sebald de Weerts, and with this falsification of the journal he took occasion to compliment the Honourable Mr Pepys, who was then Secretary of the Admiralty, by putting his name to the land, giving as Cowley's words: 'In the latitude of 47° we saw land, the same being an island not before known. I gave it the name of Pepys Island.'

Hack embellished his account with a drawing of Pepys Island, in which he introduces an Admiralty Bay and a Secretary's Point.

Dampier's own account would have cleared the whole matter up except for the fact that for a long time no one realized that he and Cowley were aboard the same vessel at the same time. In his manuscript, Dampier writes: 'we made the Sebald de Weerts . . . The two northermost lie in 51°S., the other in 51°20'S. We could not come near the two northern islands, but we came close by the southern.' Burney comments: 'In consequence of the inattention or oversight in not perceiving that Dampier and Cowley were speaking of the same land, Hack's ingenious adulation of the Secretary of the Admiralty flourished a full century undetected, a Pepys Island being all the time admitted in the charts.'

They made no stop at the Falklands, but continued for the Strait of Le Maire, but the sea and wind were against them and so they altered course to round the Horn to the east and south of Staten Island. Cowley says:

> we came abreast of Cape Horn the 14th day of February, where we were choosing of Valentines, and discoursing of the intrigues of women. There arose a prodigious storm, which did continue till the last day of the month, driving us into the lat. of 60° 30' S., which is further than any ship hath sailed before south, so that we concluded the discoursing of women was very unlucky, and occasioned the storm.

Cowley is prone to exaggeration, but his estimate of their southerliness is borne out by Dampier, who does not, however, mention the Valentines. During the storm, they managed to fill twenty-three barrels with rain-water, and they kept themselves warm by drinking vast quantities of brandy: 'They found that they could bear to drink three quarts of burnt brandy a man in twenty-four hours, without getting intoxicated.'

Continuing on their way, they were alone in the sea until 19th March 1684, when they spied a sail. Thinking her to be a Spanish vessel, they prepared an ambush, but when the ship drew closer, they found she was a friend, the *Nicholas*, whose captain was John Eaton. Eaton had originally set out as a trader, but had switched to freebooting. He had seen some action off the coast of Brazil, and had sailed through the Straits of Magellan with another trader, Captain Charles Swan of the *Cygnet*, in whose ship our old acquaintance Basil Ringrose was travelling in the capacity of supercargo (commercial agent). The *Cygnet* and the *Nicholas* had separated soon afterwards, in a storm which *The Batchelor's Delight* had also weathered, but they would meet again soon.

Eaton and John Cook kept company together. Cook gave Eaton bread and beef, and received fresh water in return. They sailed on for three days and on 22nd March anchored at Juan Fernandez. Ominously, however, Dampier noted in his journal: 'We consorted at Juan Fernandez but did not well agree all the voyage for Eaton's men were but young beginners to the trade and (our) men old privateers and allowed themselves on that score and would not agree on equal terms.'

It was here that Dampier and those of his companions who had been at Juan Fernandez before with Sharp and Watling over three years earlier were reunited with William, the Moskito Indian who had been abandoned on the island when the English were forced to make a run for it in 1681. The story of finding William, as Dampier tells it, will seem familiar to anyone who has read *Robinson Crusoe*:

This Indian lived here alone above three years, and although he was several times sought after by the Spaniards, who knew he was left on the island, yet they could never find him. He was in the woods, hunting for goats, when Captain Watling drew off his men, and the ship was under sail before he came back to shore. He had with him his gun and a knife, with a small horn of powder, and a few shot; which being spent, he contrived a way of notching his knife, to saw the barrel of his gun into small pieces, wherewith he made harpoons, lances, hooks and a long knife; heating the pieces first in the fire, which he struck with his gun-flint, and a piece of the barrel of his gun, which he hardened; having learnt to do that among the English. The hot pieces of iron he would hammer out and bend as he pleased with stones, and saw them with his jagged knife, or grind them to an edge by long labour, and harden them to a good temper as there was occasion. All this may seem strange to those that are not acquainted with the sagacity of the Indians; but it is no more than these Moskito men are accustomed to in their own country, where they make their own fishing and striking instruments, without either forge or anvil; though they spend a great deal of time about them . . .

With such instruments as he made in that manner, he got such provision as the island afforded; either goats or fish. He told us that at first he was forced to eat seal, which is very ordinary meat, before he had made hooks; but afterwards he never killed any seals but to make lines, cutting their skins into thongs. He had a little house or hut half a mile from the sea, which was lined with goatskin; his couch or barbecue of sticks lying along about two foot distant from the ground, was spread with the same, and was all his bedding. He had no clothes left, having worn out those he brought from Watling's ship, but only a skin about his waist. He saw our ship the day before we came to an anchor, and did believe we were English, and therefore killed three goats in the morning . . . and dressed them with cabbage, to treat us when we came ashore. He came then to the sea to congratulate our safe arrival, and when we landed, a Moskito Indian, named Robin, first leapt ashore, and running to his brother Moskito man, threw himself flat on his face at his feet, who helping him up, and embracing him, fell flat with his face on the ground at Robin's feet, and was by him taken up also. We stood with pleasure to behold the surprise, and tenderness, and solemnity of this interview, which was exceedingly affectionate on both sides; and when their ceremonies of civility were over, we also that stood gazing at them drew near, each of us embracing him we had found here, who was overjoyed to see so many of his old friends come hither, as he thought purposely to fetch him.

Dampier is loud in his praise of the island, which provided not only an amplitude and variety of fresh food, but good grass for grazing, and timber for building. He maintains that Juan Fernandez could support up to 500 families, and that as it has only two bays with decent anchorages, it would be very easy to defend. During their stay there, the freebooters sowed carrot seed, turnip seed, and 'garden seeds for salading'. Dampier may have considered colonizing the island. He did not regard England as a home to which he would one day return. By now, it must have seemed as remote as a dream.

Subsequently, in 1687, five mariners who elected to leave the service of Edward Davis and remain on the island, managed to repel two Spanish attacks, though on the second occasion one of their number went over to the enemy. Despite the fact that the Spanish had already attempted to destroy the goat population in order to make the island less hospitable, the men lived there pretty well for three years until taken off by Captain John Strong in 1690.

Dampier and his shipmates remained at Juan Fernandez for over a fortnight, putting those of their men with scurvy on a diet of fresh meat and vegetables, together with herbal cures. They were fortunate in having fallen in with Eaton, who had no fewer than four doctors on board. But when they set sail again on 8th April, John Cook was himself beginning to sicken.

They made their way north, keeping well out to sea to avoid Spanish patrols. On this voyage, Dampier took note of the vast mountain range along the Chilean coast. In their journey, they only took one small prize, a timber-ship, on 3rd May, before arriving at the Lobos Islands six days later with their capture. They cleaned their ships, interrogated their prisoners, and took three more vessels, all laden with flour. In the biggest of the three they found a letter from the viceroy of Lima to the president of Panama, explaining that he was sending these supplies as enemies had been sighted on the coast, 'and desired him to be frugal of it, for he knew not when he should send more'. They also found a large cargo of quince marmalade, and a 'stately mule', sent as a gift to the president. Cook and Eaton were concerned at the fact that the alarm had been sounded despite their precautions, but it was not they who had alerted the Spanish. Behind them, Captain Swan had come round the Horn, and attempted to trade at Valdivia.

In view of Spanish preparedness for them, they decided to stand off for the Galapagos Islands, of which Dampier gives a detailed account. He describes the wildlife in particular detail – then, as now, extraordinarily tame; then more plentiful, but unprotected from the direct depredations of man:

> The Spaniards, when they first discovered these islands, found multitudes of guanoes [iguanas], and land-turtle or tortoise . . . I do believe there is no place in the world that is so plentifully stored with those animals. The guanoes here are as fat and large as any that I ever saw; they are so tame, that a man may knock down twenty in an hour's time with a club. The land-turtle are so numerous that 5 or 600 men might subsist on them alone for several months, without any other provision. They are extraordinarily large and fat, and so sweet that no pullet eats more pleasantly.

It is interesting to note in passing that when Raveneau de Lussan, the French buccaneer, found himself on San Juan de Cueblos Island in 1685, he discovered that the English had destroyed so many of the native tortoises there in order to salt them that 'as a result, we remained an entire month on the island with only two tortoises to feed 330 men every forty-eight hours'. Dampier continues relentlessly: 'There are great plenty of turtle-doves so tame, that a man may kill 5 or 6 dozen in a forenoon with a stick.'

At the Galapagos, Ambrosia Cowley launched himself into a spree of bestowing patriotic names on all the islands, despite the fact that they already were named, and archly informs us that he took the liberty of naming one islet after himself. He also describes sitting on a giant tortoise. Later, to curry favour with Eaton, he attempted to attribute the discovery of the group to him.

They spent twelve days on the Galapagos, recuperating and deciding what to do next, as well as stashing a large quantity of flour as a reserve which they knew they could come back to in case of need. Interrogating one of their Indian prisoners, they learnt that the town of Realeja on the coast of what is now El Salvador was a place of sufficient wealth to merit an attack. They set sail on 12th June, pausing only at Cocos Island to stash more flour. Their fleet was augmented by the largest of the prizes they had taken. The others had either been released or sunk.

Meanwhile, Captain Cook, who had remained ill, suddenly died when they were within sight of Cape Blanco. Interestingly Dampier notes that 'it is usual with sick men coming from the sea, where they have nothing but sea air, to die off as soon as ever they come within the view of the land'. They came to anchor and Cook's body was taken ashore for burial. In his manuscript, Dampier tells us that 'we had always someone who spoke good Spanish that actually went ashore on such occasions, whereby we often trepanned [duped] both Indians and Spaniards'.

As they were digging the grave, three Indians appeared and questioned them very keenly. As they became suspicious, the freebooters seized them, though one managed to get away. The two others were taken aboard the *Nicholas*, and interrogated by Eaton, who learnt that they were gathering information for the president of Panama. They also volunteered the information that there was a big cattle ranch three miles away, 'where we might kill what we pleased'.

A raiding party was organized, Dampier among them, and they set off. They arrived at the place but then disagreed about what to do: whether to kill three or four cattle then to carry back immediately, or wait until morning and drive a larger number of animals down to the shore. Dampier didn't like the idea of staying overnight, and managed to persuade half the company to return to the ships with him; but the other twelve remained. When by four the following afternoon they had not reappeared, a search party set out in a canoe, and found them stranded on a small rock, in water up to their waists, about half a mile from the shore. They had been ambushed by a large party of Spaniards, and had fought their way back to the beach, only to find their own canoe set on fire. The tide was partly out and they saw the rock in the bay as the only place of refuge, so they set out for it, sending the tallest men ahead to see if the water that had already risen between the rock and them was fordable. It is likely that none of them could swim. They made the best of their way to the rock, while from the shore the Spaniards mocked them and fired the occasional round at them, having only a handful of firearms, and probably not much ammunition. For seven hours they perched on the rock as the tide came in and the Spaniards watched in hopes of seeing them drown, as they would certainly have done if the rescuing canoe had arrived an hour later than it did.

Thus reunited, the company gathered to elect a new commander, and according to privateering practice, Edward Davis was chosen to succeed John Cook. This would have pleased Dampier, for Davis was one of the few men we know for sure he was close to.

Raveneau de Lussan tells us that Davis was born in Holland, and there are possible mentions of him in other sources before we meet him, though whether these refer to the same man is in doubt. He and Dampier were to meet and compare notes in London at the end of the century. He was a good sailor and a temperate man.

They learnt that Realeja had been warned of their presence, and so abandoned their design on that town for the time being, making instead for the neighbouring islands of Mangera and Amapalla. Dampier observed what he had noted elsewhere, that in the churches of native towns under Spanish control, the images of the Virgin and the saints were depicted like Indians, in something approximating Indian dress. They took the local Spanish friar prisoner, the only European on the islands, and made contact with the Indian Magistrate and the Indian Secretary, the latter a man of some standing, the only Indian who could both speak and write Spanish, who kept the records and accounts of the islands.

Captain Davis and his men met these two at Amapalla. It appeared that the Secretary had no love for the Spaniards, who held the Indians in subjection, and so he was disposed to be friendly to Davis, who told him that he and his men were 'Biscayers' come to seek assistance in careening their ships. Biscay mariners were highly skilled and intrepid, and were frequently commissioned by the Spanish authorities to chase pirates. Notwithstanding this, the Biscayers were known to turn pirate themselves if a Spanish prize ever presented itself. From Dampier's manuscript it seems that the Secretary was not necessarily well disposed to the English, but did admire 'Biscayers', at least by reputation, since he'd never met any before. Davis spoke no Spanish, but had men with him who did.

The Indians welcomed them, and the whole company made their way to the church. Dampier leaves us a moving description of it:

> that is the place of all public meetings, and all plays and pastimes are acted there also; therefore in the churches belonging to Indian towns they have all sorts of vizards, and strange antick dresses both for men and women, and abundance of musical hautboys and strumstrums.

He also leaves us a sad record of their entertainments:

> Their mirth consists in singing, dancing, and sporting in those antick habits, and using as many antick gestures. If the moon shine they use but few torches, if not, the church is full of light. They meet at these times all sorts of both sexes. All the Indians that I have been acquainted with who are under the Spaniards, seem to be more melancholy than other Indians that are free; and at these public meetings, when they are in the greatest of their jollity, their mirth seems to be rather forced than real. Their songs are very melancholy and doleful; so is their music; but whether it be natural to the Indians to be thus melancholy, or the effect of their slavery, I am not certain. But I have always been prone to believe that they

are then only condoling their misfortunes, the loss of their country
and liberties, which although these that are now living do not know,
nor remember what it was to be free, yet there seems to be a deep
impression in their thoughts of the slavery which the Spaniards
have brought them under, increased probably by some traditions
of their ancient freedom.

Such sensitive observation is rare in the annals of the time.

Unfortunately, the Indians were not to enjoy better treatment from
their new guests. Davis intended to shut them into the church, reveal
his true identity, and then bargain with them in a friendly way for
their help. He had specifically ordered his men not to open fire in any
circumstances. But in ushering the Indians into the church, one of the
freebooters gave one of the Indians a less than gentle shove, which
immediately, in this delicate situation, gave rise to general panic. The
Indians 'sprang out of the church like deer', leaving Davis and his men
alone with the friar and the Secretary, at which point, for reasons that
are unclear, possibly suspecting betrayal, one of the Englishmen shot the
Secretary dead.

This might have been disastrous for the freebooters; but astonishingly,
perhaps through the intercession of the friar, perhaps because the Indians
were already so fatalistic and broken in spirit, the locals still helped their
murderous guests, feeding them beef, which must have been a relief to
them after a long diet of fish, and giving them the opportunity of a
leisurely refit during August. Here, however, began the first of the serious
altercations between the crews of Eaton's and Davis's ships over division
of spoils, which led to Eaton's parting company with *The Batchelor's
Delight*. The dispute arose, as Dampier had foreseen, because Davis's ship
was the larger and better equipped, and had the more experienced crew.
They therefore laid claim to the lion's share of any booty. Eaton sailed
first from Amapalla. When Davis left the next day, 3rd September, he
released the friar and, in atonement and thanks, left behind the prize
ship with half a cargo of flour.

Later, on 21st September, they met up with Eaton again at Isla de
Plata; and 'he was very willing to have made up those differences which
first parted us, and I did what I could to persuade our men to it, but

could not,' writes Dampier. 'Captain Eaton seeing the unreasonableness of our men he went away the next day and we never saw him afterwards.' If Eaton had ignored the wishes of his own crew, he might have been turfed out of office; and the same would have gone for Davis, with whom Dampier stayed.

Ambrosia Cowley elected to go on board with Captain Eaton when the two ships separated. Before continuing Dampier's travels, I think it is worth a brief digression to follow Cowley and Eaton home, especially as Dampier and Swan were later to follow in their path, and some of Cowley's observations are in marked contrast to Dampier's.

Cowley represents himself as usual as being at the centre of the stage, and depicts Eaton and his men as far superior to Davis's crew. When he finally left Davis, and after a short further cruise along the South American coast, Eaton set out across the Pacific. The voyage was a harsh one: scurvy was rife and rations ran low. Arriving at length at Guam, they were able to recuperate. There, Eaton passed himself off to the Spanish governor as an explorer financed by France. The governor duly sent him provisions, and Eaton sent him a diamond ring worth £20. The next day, the hard-pressed governor asked for some gunpowder, for which Eaton refused payment. The governor thereupon sent him a diamond ring worth £50. In such a gentlemanly way was business transacted.

Less gentlemanly was the way in which the rebellious local Indians, who resented the Spanish yoke, were treated. The governor, José de Quiroga, too weak to do more than trade even with enemies at his remote island outpost, nevertheless managed to 'conquer and unpeople' all the northern islands of the Ladrones group. Cowley describes the local Indian race as huge, being seven and a half feet tall. And, as a measure of his true character, he describes the following event, apparently without blushing. (The islanders had attacked the *Nicholas* on her arrival, but that hardly excuses what happened afterwards.)

We took four of these infidels prisoners, and brought them on board, binding their hands behind them, but they had not been long there, before three of them leaped overboard into the sea, swimming away from the ship with their hands tied behind them. However, we sent the boat after them, and found a strong man, at the first blow, could not penetrate their skins with a cutlass. One of them had received, in my judgment, forty shots in the body before he died; and the last of the three that was killed had swum a good English mile first, not only with his hands behind him as before, but also with his arms pinioned.

Allowing for Cowley's propensity for exaggeration, such cruelty cannot be condoned even by the standards of the time.

At the beginning of April 1685, Eaton set sail again, this time for Canton, and there refitted his ship. Here, his crew had the opportunity to make themselves rich for life, for thirteen Tartar vessels arrived, laden with silks and satins. But the men of the *Nicholas* showed themselves to be inexperienced freebooters indeed, by declaring that they would not degrade themselves by dealing in pedlar's goods. They were only interested in gold and silver. As we've seen, the textile cargoes they ignored were worth far more, but Eaton could not persuade them to take them.

They remained in the East Indies until the end of the year, by which time, at Timor, the disaffected and homesick crew broke into open mutiny. Cowley and about twenty of his shipmates quit the *Nicholas* and, buying a large local boat, set sail for Cheribon in Java, a Dutch outpost. They took ship from here to Batavia (Jakarta), and thence Cowley and two others travelled home, arriving in London on 12th October 1686. His book was not published until thirteen years later.

Eaton ended up as a captain in the Royal Navy, and died commanding the *Suadadoes* prize in the West Indies in 1698, providing Sir Walter Scott with the inspiration for his novel *The Pirate*.

CHAPTER ELEVEN

Dampier's Second Cruise
along the Pacific Coast

While Davis and Dampier had been cruising the coast with Eaton, Captain Charles Swan in the *Cygnet* was sailing round the Horn in their wake.

Swan's story so far had been an unfortunate one. Fitted out by a syndicate of London merchants to trade with the Spanish along the Pacific coast of South America, he had met with nothing but ill luck. He had been given a hostile reception by the Spaniards with whom he tried to trade on the East Coast of South America. Undaunted, once round the Horn, Swan persevered in his intention of trading, but he was double-crossed and ambushed by the Spanish at Valdivia. Total disaster was averted by the presence of mind of Basil Ringrose, and the caution of one of Swan's officers, Josiah Teat.

Ringrose, who had proposed the voyage in the first place and, as we have seen, was travelling as supercargo on board the *Cygnet*, hereafter earned Swan's mistrust. When he later considered Ringrose's motives for suggesting such a trading voyage to Swan, Dampier is forced to admit:

> I am a little at a stand when I consider Mr Ringrose, his method.
> I confess he was an ingenious gentleman, but was extremely beside
> his mark in proposing two such places as Valdivia and the Gulf of
> Nicoya to trade in, the one being only a garrison, the other a port
> of poor mulattos.

I wonder how fair this is. Ringrose knew the coast as well as Dampier, so he could not plead ignorance as an excuse. Perhaps he was desperate to sell a trading plan, and this was the best he could come up with.

Perhaps he was simply over-optimistic, and hoped the Spanish would be tempted by the low prices the English could offer. On the other hand, Valdivia was far from the main power centres of colonial Spain, and set in rich countryside. A few years later, in 1697, Lionel Wafer would recommend it to the Lords of Trade and Plantations in London as being ideal for English colonization.

After Valdivia, Swan refitted at Juan Fernandez and then made his way up the coast to the Gulf of Nicoya near where Captain John Cook had been buried. Early in August 1684 he fell in with a group of buccaneers under a Captain Peter Harris, a nephew of the Peter Harris who had been fatally wounded off Perico a few years earlier. Harris had taken Santa Maria with some profit after making his way across the isthmus and was now sailing in a ship taken from the Spanish. Swan's remaining men, seeing how much money Harris's crew had made, went over to him and Swan was forced to join forces, opening a trade with him in clothing and ammunition. He jettisoned that part of his cargo which would now be of no use, to make room for extra men from Harris's company. The two captains then cruised together for the rest of the summer. Swan was able to vent some of his resentment of the Spanish when they arrived at Manta on 28th September. Finding nothing in the town, which had in fact been sacked by Davis two days earlier, he burnt it to the ground, including the church, which was 'a very fine one, adorned with a great deal of carved work'.

Four days later, on 2nd October, Swan and Harris arrived at Isla de Plata and there encountered *The Batchelor's Delight*. Davis, Dampier and the rest of his crew were debating what course to take next, and were happy to join forces with Swan and Harris. Now they regretted parting with Eaton, and sent a ship to look for him to strengthen their force, but he had set off across the Pacific long since. Swan traded with Davis, then threw overboard the remainder of his unusable goods, such as anchors, knives, beads and looking-glasses, but retained luxury items like silk, muslin and stockings, together with a quantity of iron, both wrought and in ingots, which was saved for ballast. Swan had seniority over Harris, but he was a reluctant freebooter at first, and for some time religiously put aside ten shares of his booty for his London owners. He wrote sadly to his wife:

Assure my employers that I do all I can to preserve their interests, and that what I do now I could in no wise prevent. So desire them to do all they can with the King for me, for as soon as I can I shall deliver myself to the King's justice, and I had rather die than live skulking like a vagabond for fear of death.

Notwithstanding this, he turned out to be a shrewd and efficient brigand, influenced by the treachery with which the Spanish had served him. He was a good leader and a tough disciplinarian, though able to rally and cheer his men when the need arose. He seems to have had a sense of humour, and to have been more sophisticated than most men of his calling. Only towards the end of his career does a kind of madness creep in.

The fleet began its cruise by attacking Paita, but finding nothing there, Swan set the place on fire. This was the second town he had destroyed. Not bad going for a man who continually protested that he had been forced into buccaneering.

There followed an attack on the major port and shipyard of Guayaquil, though they were only able to take a bark laden with Quito woollen cloth, and three slave-ships, containing 1,000 young Africans of both sexes.

The attack on the town itself failed for several reasons: at first, owing to a failure of communication between the ships, one of them opened fire and so betrayed their presence; then an attempt by Davis and forty men to find a way to the town through the thick red mangrove swamps failed. Next, coming within sight of the town on another attempt at night, they saw it lit up and wide awake – though this may have been on account of a religious festival. Matters were made worse by the cowardice of one of Swan's men, who cut the rope securing one of their two Indian guides and gave him a chance to get well away before he raised the alarm.

After this they withdrew without a shot being fired on either side. But at least they had their four prizes laden with cloth and slaves. To Dampier's frustration, his companions elected to leave the slaves behind with their ships, taking only the cloth bark and forty of the strongest male slaves, together with about thirty more selected by Swan and Davis between them.

Seeing such a good investment slip, Dampier's irritation is great. What follows is another indication of how little his thoughts were on ever returning home to Judith and his estate in Dorset:

There was never a greater opportunity put into the hands of men to enrich themselves than we had, to have gone with these Negroes, and settled ourselves at Santa Maria, on the Isthmus of Darien, and employed them in getting gold out of the mines there. Which might have been done with ease: for about six months before this, Captain Harris (who was now with us) coming over land from the North Seas [the Caribbean, in this context] with his body of privateers, had routed the Spaniards away from the town and gold-mines of Santa Maria, so that they had never attempted to settle there again since. Add to this, that the Indian neighbourhood, who were mortal enemies to the Spaniards, and had been flushed by their successes against them, through the assistance of the privateers for several years, were our fast friends, and ready to receive and assist us. We had, as I said, 1,000 Negroes to work for us, we had 200 tons of flour that lay at the Galapagos, there was the river of Santa Maria, where we could careen and fit our ships; and might fortify the mouth so, that if all the strength the Spaniards have in Peru had come against us, we could have kept them out. If they lay with their guard-ships of strength to keep us in, yet we had a great country to live in, and a great nation of Indians that were our friends. Beside, which was the principal thing, we had the North Seas to befriend us; from whence we could export ourselves, or effects, or import goods or men to our assistance; for in a short time we should have had assistance from all parts of the West-Indies; many thousands of privateers from Jamaica and the French Islands especially would have flocked over to us; and long before this time we might have been masters not only of those mines (the richest gold mines ever yet found in America), but of all the coast as high as Quito. And much more than I say might then probably have been done.

But these may seem to the reader to be but golden dreams. To leave them therefore . . .

And he resumes his narrative. But he never forgot the missed opportunity, and in a later voyage touched on the possibility again, with equal lack of success. His companions were not the sort of people with the staying power for that kind of project, and who knows, perhaps Dampier wasn't the type for it either.

They sailed on for Lobos and for Isla de Plata, where they divided the cloth. But as usual among freebooters, dissent wasn't far from the surface. Davis's crew counted Moskito Indian hunters among them, who could harpoon turtle for them. Swan had no such skilled men, nor did he have any flour; but had to depend on Davis for provisions. There were those in Davis's crew who were not keen to see Swan fed, since they argued he had not been as bold in the project against Guayaquil as Davis. But at last the differences were resolved, and they continued their cruise together.

All the time, Dampier indefatigably kept up his observations, and his dedication is all the more impressive when one considers the discomfort, the lack of light, space and privacy, in which he wrote. No detail escapes him. Looking at the shore-life at Gorgona, for example, he remarks: 'Here are a great many periwinkles and mussels to be had at low water. Then the monkeys come down by the seaside and catch them, digging them out of their shells with their claws.'

And yet sometimes it seems as if he were a solitary voyager. He tells us so little of the circumstances in which he was sailing. Usually he tells us only about the discoveries the sailing led him to. Even allowing for the conventions of his time, and Dampier's naturally private nature, I find myself frequently frustrated by the relative lack of what you might call local colour, anecdote, and the sharing of personal hopes and fears. Even Dampier's manuscript, which is already in a late stage of preparation for publication, carries little such material. Might the lost original journals have given us more? It is tempting to think so, but I doubt it. Dampier would have had to husband his paper and ink, and I believe he was temperamentally inclined simply to omit most matters which did not make a direct contribution to new knowledge. It is, as always, for his extraordinary eye for detail and his sympathetic disposition towards newly met local peoples, together with his ability to learn from them as well as about them, that we must value his work. To learn as much as he did, and to learn empirically, Dampier must also have possessed the quality of modesty, which does come through in his published work, especially when one compares it with such writers as Cowley and de Lussan. If this quality seems to sit oddly with the arrogance which surfaces in his letters and in some of his relationships, it is because he was better at dealing with ideas and experiences than with his peers.

Intercepting a packet-boat and seizing its mail, they learnt that the Spanish Atlantic fleet had arrived at Portobello, and that the silver fleet from Lima to Panama was being urged to make haste, so that the bullion could be carried across the isthmus and transferred to galleons which would take it back to Old Spain. This would be a rare chance, since the Atlantic fleet only came over once every three years, and so the freebooters prepared to sail to Panama, where they intended to intercept the Lima fleet. On 16th February, they anchored off Pacheca Island in the Bay of Panama. The Lima fleet had not yet arrived. They opened a correspondence with the president of Panama, dealing with an exchange of prisoners. The English had taken prisoners from the prizes they had seized in their cruise since leaving Isla de Plata, and had lost at least one man captured by the Spanish while hunting onshore a few days earlier. Their first letter had been taken ashore by one of their prisoners, but he, being mistaken for a buccaneer, was killed by the Spanish. The English did not know this, and as the deadline for his return with an answer was now up, they sent a second, more strongly worded missive to the president:

> If you refuse this last demand and think that the imprisonment of three or four Englishmen is more advantageous to you than the lives of so many of your countrymen as are already and what else shall fall into our hands, then you may keep them and we will send you the heads of these for a beginning; and then do our countrymen the least hurt in their lives or bodies and by the help of God we will colour your land, rivers and sea with Spanish blood of men, women and children the whole time that we remain in these seas, turning our former mercy into cruelty, showing no mercy nor giving quarter to any.
> We will bring our ships near your walls that you may have the

pleasure of seeing them [i.e., the Spanish prisoners] hanged at our yardarms.

We will make you know that we are the commanders of the whole South Seas, so consider what to choose for we wait your sentence of life or death with impatience, if death you shall certainly have the heads by Monday morning, & c.

From the Commanders of the whole South Seas.

Feb. 22, 1685.

This letter, Dampier tells us, 'wrought so powerfully among the common people that the city was in an uproar'. Which is hardly surprising. An exchange of prisoners took place shortly afterwards. Whether Davis, who had a reputation for leniency, or Swan, the self-styled reluctant buccaneer, would have carried out their threat, I do not know; but there's no doubt that there would have been bloodshed.

Davis and Swan moved their anchorage to Taboga Island and here a Spanish merchant offered to enter into a little black-market trade with them. They agreed, but when the merchant returned in the night, it was not with a bark laden with goods, but a fireship, which blew up near them, forcing them to cut their cables and 'scamper away as well as we could'.

Swan had been warned by his astrologer, in whom he placed much faith, to beware of fire, and the astrologer had reiterated the warning that same evening. Luckily they had again moved anchor, this time to Perico, where they had more sea-room to make their escape than they would otherwise have done. They later learnt that the fireship had been devised by the traitorous Captain George Bond – the same man who had double-crossed the natives of Mayo in the Cape Verdes shortly before Dampier attempted to land there with Cook in 1683.

Dampier takes this opportunity to scoff at the decay in Spanish seamanship:

The Spaniards of Panama could not have fitted out their fireship without this Captain Bond's assistance; for it is strange to say how grossly ignorant the Spaniards in the West Indies, but especially in the South Seas, are of sea affairs. They indeed build good ships, but this is a small matter: for any ship of good bottom will serve for these seas on the south [Pacific] coast. They rig their ships but untowardly, have no guns, but in three or four of the King's ships, and are meanly furnished with warlike provisions, and as much at a loss for the making any fireships or other less usual machines. Nay, they have not the sense to have their guns run within the sides upon their discharge, but have platforms without for the men to stand on to charge them; so that when we come near we can fetch them down with small shot of our own boats. A main reason of this is that the native Spaniards are too proud to be seamen, but use the Indians for all those offices. One Spaniard, it may be, going in the ship to command it, and himself of little more knowledge than those poor ignorant creatures: nor can they gain much experience, seldom going far off to sea, but coasting along the shores.

This is a grim picture: amateurish Spaniards without adequate defences pursued by pirates at whose mercy they would find themselves totally, were it not for the inability of the pirates to agree with one another or maintain discipline for any length of time.

This theme continues: the next day in the morning, Dampier reports, 'we came again to anchor close by our buoys, and strove to get our anchors again; but our buoy ropes, being rotten, broke'. This hardly demonstrates great efficiency in *English* seamanship, and this is not the only example. On one occasion a tide was missed because the entire crew of Swan's tender overslept.

While they were 'puzzling' about their anchors, they saw a large fleet of canoes, twenty-eight in all, pass by Taboga. When they came within call, Dampier and his companions learnt that they were fellow freebooters, a mixed force of French and English which had come over the isthmus by what was becoming a well-used road. The newcomers were commanded by François Grogniet and Captain l'Escuyer. They brought news of another group of 180 English seamen, led by Captain Francis Townley.

The forces now all combined together, to the dread of the people of Panama. The Englishmen went aboard the English ships, and Grogniet, the senior French commander, was given a Spanish flour prize as his ship. In gratitude, he offered Davis and Swan fresh commissions, blank ones issued by the governor of Tortuga for the convenience of 'privateers' to fill out for themselves. Davis's own commission was old, having been inherited from John Cook, so he was glad to accept one; but Swan already had an Order from the Duke of York, which commanded him 'neither to give offence to the Spaniards, nor to receive any affront from them'. After the incident of Spanish treachery at Valdivia, where he had had men killed, Swan felt that he had received affront and therefore had an official imprimatur to proceed as he did. As for the French commissions, they were of notional value only, and existed to give the appearance of official sanction to what were piratical activities.

On 2nd March 1685, the fleet sailed south to the Gulf of San Miguel to meet Townley. Swan also wanted to send letters home over the isthmus and via Jamaica. They were met on their way by Townley himself, who had resourcefully already taken two Spanish merchantmen, one laden with flour, the other with Pisco wine, brandy, sugar and oil. He distributed the alcohol freely, since he needed the empty jars for water. They also met up with two more freebooters, Captains William Knight and Henry More. Swan turned More out of the prize ship he commanded and gave it to Peter Harris, on the grounds that Harris deserved it and More looked like a leader of a gang of mutineers rather than a captain. More accepted this ruling and joined Swan's crew as one of his men.

At the end of March they were back in Panama Bay, a fleet of nine ships in all. Here an attempt was made to depose Davis from command because he was too mild, but Davis shook off the threat. In a manuscript note, Dampier writes: 'I opposed them and by the assistance of one John Fitzgerald, an Irishman, made them quiet.' This is another small indication of the position of seniority, or at least respect, that Dampier held among the men; and we can take it as true, because Dampier was never boastful. He fails to tell us what his actual position was. He was thirty-three years old, and his age and experience would have qualified him for officership. But as always he seems shy of any real authority he might have held amongst the freebooters, preferring to distance himself from them.

In the meantime, they learnt that the long-awaited Lima fleet was at sea. During April and May, they hung around in the bay, sailing from one island to another. So large was their number that they had to send a raiding party to seize extra coppers from a sugar-mill for cooking food and making chocolate, for they didn't have enough for so many men. In April another French force arrived, under Laurent de Graff, Row, Le Picard and Desmarais. Raveneau de Lussan was in their company.

Dampier was especially taken with Chepillo Island, where he found and described a whole variety of fruit trees, and the avocado pear. Late in May they took prisoner three Spanish seamen, who had come out from Panama in search of food. From them they learnt that the freebooters' presence among the islands had cut the city off from its supply of plantains, and the poor were near to starvation. They also told the English that news had reached Panama of the death of Charles II (he died on 6th February) and the coronation of the Duke of York as James II. The other news was that the Lima fleet was expected daily. This must have come as a blessing to the freebooters, for they had been cruising the bay too long. The fact that they could do so with impunity is a measure of how weak the Spanish forces were. News of their presence had reached Jamaica by now, and Colonel Hender Molesworth wrote of it in enraged tones to the Earl of Sunderland. One cloud on the freebooters' horizon was news of the death of Golden Cap, who had been their staunch ally among the Indians on the expedition of 1680; but with it came the further news that another Indian leader, Josepho, had allied himself to the buccaneers.

On 28th May, once the morning rain had cleared up, they saw the Lima fleet. After such a long period of indolence they must have been at some shifts to clear their decks and get ready for action. Davis, Swan and Townley made a battle plan. The French and the English now had ten sail, but the fleet ranged against them had fourteen, as well as periaguas and canoes; and six of the ships were large ones. The flagship mounted forty-eight guns, with a crew of 450, and the others did not come much behind. *The Batchelor's Delight* was the largest of the Anglo-French force, with thirty-six guns and 156 men. The Spaniards looked set to engage, which, according to letters the freebooters had intercepted, was against their instructions. What they did not know was that the fleet had, for security, unloaded its treasure down the coast at Lavelia before coming on to deal with these intruders.

The first setback after the fight had begun was that Captain Grogniet hung back, unwilling to engage. In his manuscript Dampier tells us:

The Spanish admiral and the rest of his squadron began to play at us, and we at them, as fast as we could. They might have laid us aboard if they would; but they came not within small-arms shot, intending to maul us in pieces with their great guns.

The freebooters had the advantage:

for being to windward of the enemy, we had it at our choice, whether we would fight or not. It was 3 o'clock in the afternoon when we weighed, and being all under sail, we bore down right afore the wind on our enemies, who kept close on a wind to come to us; but night came on without anything except the exchanging of a few shot on each side.

During the night the freebooters thought they could see a light in the Spanish flagship's top, and kept to windward of it. Later the light was put out, but then reappeared. Still believing the light to mark the position of the Spanish fleet, they continued sailing to windward of it, but when dawn broke they saw that they had been deceived: one Spanish bark had carried the light, but the rest of the fleet had come round and got the weather-gauge of the Anglo-French ships, and was now bearing down on them with full sail.

Dampier tells us what happened next:

So we ran for it, and after a running fight all day, and having taken a turn almost round the Bay of Panama, we came to an anchor again at the Isle of Pacheca, in the very same place from whence we set out in the morning.

The plans of the last several months having now come unstuck, the English ships parted company frostily with the cowardly Captain Grogniet. The Anglo-French alliance was over. De Lussan defends Grogniet against any charge of cowardice, and accuses the English of gross impiety and the desecration of Catholic churches. In any case, there could be no agreement on an absolute commander for so large and disparate a force.

The remaining English commanders considered what to do next. They were reunited at Cayboa, just outside Panama Bay, and planned an attack on the rich inland city of Leon. Dampier describes it as 'the most pleasant place in all America'. To do this they needed canoes to make a landing in, and so set about cutting down trees to make as many as they would need. Meanwhile, they sent an expeditionary force of 150 men off to sack Puebla Nueva, which they found bare of provisions. On 20th July they were ready to make for Realeja, which is the port for Leon.

They were a strong force of 640 men in eight ships. On 9th August they anchored and 520 men in thirty-one canoes made for Realeja. As they rowed, a storm blew up, threatening to swamp them. Dampier does not lose an opportunity to draw conclusions about the nature of the 'tornado', which had come at them from the shore:

> The fierceness of the wind continued about half an hour, and abated by degrees; and as the wind died away, so the fury of the sea abated: for in all hot countries as I have observed, the sea is soon raised by the wind, and as soon down again when the wind is gone, and therefore it is a proverb among the seamen: Up wind, up sea; Down wind, down sea.

They managed to land, having negotiated the mangrove swamps and the Spanish defensive breastwork, but not without alerting local Spanish Indians, who ran ahead to Leon to raise the alarm. Dampier was left with fifty-nine men to guard the canoes. Clearly by now he was officially some way up the chain of command. The rest made their way the twenty miles across country to Leon. When they got there, the Spanish put up some resistance but soon fled. The attacking force had straggled on the road to Leon, however, and Spanish patrols were able to pick off those who were isolated, including one hardy old seaman by the name of John Swan, who refused to surrender and went down fighting, though he was, Dampier tells us, eighty-four years of age – a very great age indeed for a man in his profession to have reached.

Unable to negotiate a huge ransom for the town – 300,000 Spanish dollars, and food for 1,000 men for four months – with the Spanish, who prevaricated, as usual, the English set the place on fire and, marching back to the coast, turned their attention to Realeja. Built close to swamps, the port was never free from a noxious stench, and was an unhealthy place. Several of the men caught typhus here. The locals cultivated guavas, and Dampier notes their medicinal qualities: 'When this fruit is eaten green, it is binding; when ripe, it is loosening.'

At Realeja it was the same story as at Leon: token resistance by the Spanish, followed by some petty pillaging by the English, who then, this time it appears without provocation, set fire to the town. Apart from 150 head of cattle and 500 packs of flour, they got nothing out of the venture. They did manage to redeem one of their men who had been taken prisoner by giving up a high-born Spanish woman they had captured.

On 25th August, Davis and Swan decided to part company. After all the bickering that had gone before, it was an amicable parting, and they complimented each other with salutes of cannon; but the fact was that there had been fundamental disagreement since Guayaquil. Davis wanted to continue to cruise the South American coast; Swan wanted to set off to the west. Other old acquaintances separated now as well. Lionel Wafer and John Hingson stayed with Davis; Basil Ringrose remained with Swan. Townley decided to keep Swan company, while Harris and Knight consorted with Davis.

Dampier's own choice will come as no surprise, given his temperament:

I had till this time been with Captain Davis, but now left him, and went aboard of Captain Swan. It was not from any dislike to my old captain, but to get some knowledge of the northern parts of this continent of Mexico. And I knew that Captain Swan determined to coast it as far north as he thought convenient, and then pass over for the East Indies, which was a way very agreeable to my inclination.

Rather disingenuously he adds a note in his manuscript to the effect that 'I came into these seas this second time more to indulge my curiosity than to get wealth, though I must confess at that time I did think the trade lawful.' Some of the Moskito Indians evidently also joined Swan.

To finish Davis's story: he sailed for the Galapagos Islands and retrieved the cache of flour there, somewhat eaten away by doves. He also filled some eight-gallon jars with tortoise oil, which was as good as butter. At Cocos Island some of his crew became incapacitated by drinking too much coconut milk, an incident reported by Wafer:

And one day among the rest, being minded to make themselves very merry, they went ashore and cut down a great many cocoa trees, from which they gathered the fruit, and drew about twenty gallons of the milk. Then they all sat down and drank healths to the king, queen & co. They drank an excessive quantity; yet it did not end in drunkenness. But however that sort of liquor had so chilled and benumbed their nerves that they could neither go nor stand, nor could they return on board ship without the help of those who had not been partakers in the frolic; nor did they recover it under four or five days' time.

Davis made his way south, cruising and taking what pickings he could. He spent Christmas 1686 at Juan Fernandez. It is possible that he made the first sighting of Easter Island on his travels, though it was not officially discovered until 1722.

Another year of cruising followed, during which one incident occurred, related by Wafer, which would have earned Wafer Dampier's sympathy. On the beach at Vermejo (Huarmey), Peru, the crew came across a large number of corpses which 'seemed as if they had been not a week dead; but if you handled them, they proved as light and dry as a sponge or piece of cork . . .' It appeared that a community of Indians had buried themselves alive here a good generation earlier rather than give themselves up to the Spanish, and there are still the remains of an ancient Chimu cemetery here to this day, the bodies dessicated by the sand.

Of these dead bodies I brought on board a boy of about 9 or 10 years of age, with an intent to bring him home for England, but was frustrated of my purpose by the sailors, who having a foolish conceit that the compass would not traverse aright so long as any dead body was on board, threw him overboard, to my great vexation.

Wafer also notes the shock of an earthquake at Callao felt at sea on the ship 150 leagues from the shore: 'so sudden and violent that we took it for granted she had struck upon a rock'.

At last, at the end of 1687, *The Batchelor's Delight* rounded the Horn and headed for home. If indeed she had survived that long, and had not been replaced by another prize ship. She reached the Caribbean, and after various adventures Davis, Wafer and Hingson arrived in Virginia, via Philadelphia and Pennsylvania. In Virginia the three spent most of their time in prison in Jamestown. Times had changed, and freebooters were looked on with far less tolerance than before. James II had issued a proclamation against pirates in May 1687, promising amnesty under certain conditions and within a time limit to those who gave themselves up. This Davis and his friends may not even have been aware of. They were finally allowed to return to England in 1690, and most of their goods were restored to them two years later. They were, however, fined £300, which went towards the building of William and Mary College at Williamsburg.

After separating from Davis and Wafer, Dampier, with Swan and Townley, sailed towards Guatemala. The typhus that had taken hold at Realeja had now laid half the crew low, and several had died. Townley set off in nine canoes to forage for refreshment for the sick men, but he returned on 2nd October with a story of a bad landing, in which those of the men who had not waxed and sealed their cartridge boxes had wet their gunpowder, followed by a Spanish ambush. At length the buccaneers reached the island of Tangola, where they took on water, and then sailed on to Guatulco. After a few days here, they pursued their way along the unfamiliar coast, meeting few people and unable to take any prisoners from whom to learn more about where they were. At least the men began to recover their health, as towards the end of the month they came close to Puerto Angel. Here a canoe sent into a lagoon to fish was trapped by the Spanish, who cut off the narrow strait separating it from the sea. They were prisoners for three days, until Townley sent reinforcements to rescue them.

Finally they managed to take a prisoner who told them of a Lima ship at present anchored at Acapulco. In his manuscript, Dampier makes an interesting comment:

Though prisoners may sometimes conceal the whole truth in things pertaining to themselves, yet in matters relating to the country whether of its riches or many factories they would commonly relate without any scruple for most men never look beyond the present time not supposing any future damage; beside, we had men aboard that had not such admiration for the Spaniards.

Townley, who wanted a better vessel for himself, was for going to take it, and most of his men and Swan's supported him in this design, though Swan counselled getting provisions instead, and preparing to cruise for the big Manila ship which came over from the Philippines to Acapulco laden with oriental riches every year. Dampier supported Swan, with whom we now sense he had a closer friendship. They were outvoted, much to Dampier's frustration. In the event Townley's attempt on the ship in canoes was foiled by a violent storm, which nearly drowned him and all his men. They returned to the mother ships 'tired, hungry and sorry for their disappointment'.

A short time afterwards they took a mulatto woman and her three children, and made her their guide, which enabled them to fall upon a Spanish mule caravan she'd told them about, robbing it of flour, chocolate and cheese. They also killed some cattle. When the time came to let the woman go, however, there was a curious incident:

> we gave the woman some clothes for her, and her children, and put her and two of them ashore; but one of them, a very pretty boy, about 7 or 8 years old, Captain Swan kept. The woman cried, and begged hard to have him, but Captain Swan would not, but promised to make much of him, and was as good as his word. He proved afterwards a very fine boy for wit, courage, and dexterity . . .

Perhaps Swan thought he could create a better life for the boy as a ship's hand or as his page than the boy would have enjoyed if he'd let him stay at home.

There is no suggestion that Swan's action was sexually motivated, but it was a cruel thing to do, and other actions followed. Late in November, when they were near the shore, two Spanish horsemen rode up. One took out a bottle and raised it to the seamen's health, upon which a mariner levelled his musket and shot the man's horse. His companion rode off, and the English came ashore and tried to seize the first Spaniard, but he fought them off with his machete. Their likely motive was that they wanted to take him prisoner and interrogate him, for the whole coast was strange to them. About this time too, sleeping on the damp sand, Dampier began to feel unwell. The illness turned out to be dropsy (a morbid accumulation of watery fluid in parts of the body), and it came close to ending his life.

They continued to cruise, Swan principally in hopes of finding rich towns or mines, Townley still eager to take the Lima ship. These different interests gradually diverged to the point where the two captains decided to part company, especially when it became apparent that despite their vigilance they had missed the Manila ship early in 1686, when they had dropped their guard to go ashore and kill and salt cattle. Townley returned to Peru, and Swan continued up the coast.

At length the *Cygnet* came to the wealthy silver-mining town of Santa Pecaque, which Swan and his crew resolved to take. As the town lay some way up-river, a force of 140 men set off in eight canoes to do the job. From the start it was an ominous venture. Swan's astrologer, who seems to have been very accurate, told him of the great danger they were in, and the men, who once they had landed took refuge in a church for the night, were disturbed by 'grievous groanings which hindered them from sleeping'.

Swan's aim here was to load provisions and nothing more. At first, things went well, for the men managed to capture some horses, and on 17th and 18th February 1686 they loaded maize on to them and took it down to the canoes. Swan did not want his men to get separated from each other, lest a weak force might encourage the Spanish to attack, and on 19th he wanted everyone to return to the canoes with laden horses; but his men said they would not leave until all the provisions available were put into the canoes. The raiding party divided into two, and even more unwisely the men strung themselves out along the road. As Swan had feared, the Spanish launched an entirely successful ambush and killed over fifty of the English, whose mangled corpses Swan found the next day, though the fact that the Spanish did not press home the attack indicated that the English gave a good account of themselves. Among those killed was 'my ingenious friend Mr Ringrose,' as Dampier tells us. 'He had no mind to this voyage, but was necessitated to engage in it or starve.' Dampier, who was still sick, took no part in this adventure.

Having come this far along the coast, Dampier begins to speculate about how it would be if the voyage were continued, in the hope of establishing the north-west passage, suggesting a better way of finding it than had hitherto been attempted might be by approaching it from the Pacific, not the Atlantic side. This original proposition was not to result in a voyage, however, and with his dislike of cold climates, he was content to theorize.

After the tragedy at Santa Pecaque, the *Cygnet* made for the uninhabited Tres Marias Islands, where they careened her. Dampier attempted a cure for his dropsy:

> I was laid and was covered all but my head in the hot sand: I endured it near half an hour, and was then taken out and laid to sweat in a tent. I did sweat exceedingly while I was in the sand, and I do believe it did me much good, for I grew well soon after.

Captain Swan now proposed to the crew an idea which he had already discussed fully with Dampier in private: to sail across the Pacific to the East Indies. Dampier was almost certainly navigator. 'I had still a mind to make further discoveries and my advice and counsel was ever accepted by the company as much as any one man's, and indeed it was ever a design between Captain Swan and myself to promote it.'

After such an unrewarding time on the coast of America, the crew were generally in favour, though they still took some persuading. In revenge for Santa Pecaque, the Spanish prisoners were left on the barren Tres Marias Islands. The *Cygnet* took in fresh water and prepared for the voyage. There were undercurrents: it was a long way and no one knew how long it would take. Swan himself had no intention of continuing a career of piracy once they arrived, though he knew that the promise of rich pickings in the Philippines and the East Indies was what persuaded his crew. Swan's ultimate hope was that he would be able to make his way back to England. The *Cygnet* was a fine ship and could well have made it, even after so long a time at sea.

But it was not to be.

CHAPTER TWELVE

Westwards across the Pacific

Dampier and Swan set out from Cape Corrientes on 31st March 1686. Ahead of them was a daunting voyage, for though they planned to make landfall at Guam (the remote island in mid-Pacific then held by Spain), there was no guarantee that they could re-provision there, and they had at best supplies for sixty days, at a rate of half a pint of maize per man per day. This was to be their staple diet, for apart from the maize they had only a little salted jew-fish. To make matters worse, there was a large number of rats aboard, and it was impossible to prevent them from taking their share of the maize.

The distance to Guam was reckoned by the Spanish to be about 2,300 leagues, and by the English to be 300 or 400 leagues less. Though the Spanish estimate was the more accurate, Swan tried, without spectacular success, to persuade his men that 'the English books did give the best account of the distance'. 'But some thought,' says Dampier, 'that he would carry them out of the world, for about two thirds of our men did not think there was any such way to be found.' Dampier dismisses these as 'unthinking rabble'. When his temper shows, it shows!

The crew of 150 men was divided between two ships: the *Cygnet* and a small prize bark commanded by Josiah Teat. For the first twenty days the sailing weather was so fair, and they made such good daily runs, that the men became more optimistic and clamoured for an increase in the daily food ration. This is the more understandable when we read in Dampier's manuscript journal that:

There was not any occasion to call men to victuals for the kettle was boiled but once a day, which being made ready at noon, all hands were aloft to see the quartermaster share it, wherein he had need to be exact, having so many eyes to observe him. We had two dogs and two cats aboard, they likewise lived on what was given them, and waited with as much eagerness to see it shared as we did.

Swan was with great reluctance persuaded to increase the daily allowance from eight spoonfuls of maize to ten. As for Dampier, still an austere man at this stage in his career:

I do believe that this short allowance did me a great deal of good, though others were weakened by it, for I found that my strength increased, and my dropsy wore off. Yet I drank three times every twenty-four hours; but many of our men did not drink in nine or ten days' time, and some not in twelve days; one of our men did not drink in seventeen days' time, and said he was not adry when he did drink; yet he made water every day, more or less.

Dampier doesn't have any reason to lie, yet going seventeen days without water seems such an exceptional feat that one wonders if for once he is accurate. Another crewman was caught stealing food, and every man on the ship gave him three blows with a two-and-a-half-inch thick rope across the bare back. 'Captain Swan began first, and struck with a good will; whose example was followed by all of us.'

They saw no fish ('not even a flying fish') or birds for nearly 5,000 miles, and then came upon a flock of boobies, which they supposed came from an isolated group of small islands, possibly the Dawsons, which however they did not sight.

The voyage was tedious in the extreme, and the crew began to grow restive, resenting the fact that they had allowed themselves to have been persuaded to come at all, but Swan and Dampier did their best to allay their fears, and the following wind continued to aid them. At last, on 20th May, at 4 o'clock in the afternoon, they came in view of Guam. Dampier remarks drily:

It was well for Captain Swan that we got sight of it before our provision was spent, of which we had enough for three days more, for, as I was afterwards informed, the men had contrived to kill first Captain Swan and eat him when the victuals was gone, and after him all of us who were accessory in promoting the undertaking this voyage. This made Captain Swan say to me after our arrival at Guam, *Ah! Dampier, you would have made them but a poor meal*; for I was as lean as the captain was lusty and fleshy.

Guam was maintained by the Spanish as a staging post for the Manila ship on its return journey from Acapulco to the Philippines, but owing to its isolation and weak defences, and to the rebelliousness of its native population, the governor was not able to do other than keep on friendly terms with any ships that put in here, and most of these were more in need of assistance and reprovisioning than in a position to do battle. Dampier is at particular pains to describe the versatile qualities of all parts of the coconut, which can provide not only food and drink, but oil, crockery, and coir for the making of cable. He is also loud in his praise of the breadfruit, which he had not encountered anywhere else, and it's possible that his account of its usefulness would inspire later expeditions in the Pacific, the most famous of which was that of Captain Bligh to Tahiti in 1787. His description of it is the first in English, as are his descriptions of the plantain and the banana, fruits then unknown at home.

By the time Dampier reached Guam the local Indians had been terribly reduced or driven away, though some still clung to the outer islands of the group. He tells us that they were 'affable and courteous', though afflicted with leprosy. He is vastly impressed, as many other travellers to the island were, by their outrigger canoe, or proa, of which he gives a lengthy technical description in which he takes great delight, concluding:

I do believe they sail the best of any boats in the world. I did here for my own satisfaction try the swiftness of one of them. Sailing by our log, we had 12 knots on our reel, and she run it all out before the half-minute glass was half out, which, if it had been no more, is after the rate of 12 mile an hour; but I do believe she would have run 24 mile an hour. It was very pleasant to see the little boat [outrigger] running along so swift by the other's side.

The locals tried to persuade Swan to join them in an attempt to overthrow the governor, 'but Captain Swan was not for molesting the Spaniards here'.

Provisions were scarce on the island, though the crew laid in a great store of coconuts, and the governor did what he could for Swan, after there had been an exchange of civilities and Swan had sent ashore four yards of scarlet cloth, a piece of broad silver and gold lace as presents. Hogs and citrus fruit augmented the diet of coconuts and breadfruit, and Swan paid for them with ammunition. There were, however, complications: 'We had a delicate large English dog; which the governor did desire, and had it given him very freely by the captain, though much against the grain of many of his men, who had a great value for that dog.'

The dog must have been one of the pets that had crossed the Pacific with them. Swan had an ulterior motive for the gift: he wanted the governor to give him a letter of recommendation to merchants at Manila, for his private intention was to sail to the English colony at Fort St George [Madras], and trade between there and the Philippines. We do not hear if Swan got the letter, but his plan was never to be realized. In the meantime, the English sailors once again missed the chance of capturing the Manila ship, now on its return journey, and thus called by Dampier the 'Acapulco ship':

> While we lay here, the Acapulco ship arrived in sight of the island, but did not come in sight of us; for the governor sent an Indian proa with the advice of our being here. Therefore she stood off to the southward of the island, and coming foul of the same shoal that our bark had run over before (on the approach to Guam), was in great danger of being lost there, for she struck off her rudder, and with much ado got clear, but not until after three days' labour. For though the shoal be so near the island, and the Indians go off and fish there every day, yet the Master of the Acapulco ship who should (one would think) know these parts, was utterly ignorant of it. This their striking on the shoal we heard afterward, when we were on the coast of Manila; but these Indians of Guam did speak of her being in sight of the island while we lay there, which put our men in a great heat to go out after her, but Captain Swan

persuaded them out of that humour, for he was now wholly averse to any hostile action.

The governor was clearly keen to get the English on their way as soon as possible, however, and, sending them a present of a number of pickled delicacies and other good things to eat, told them that as the west monsoon would soon be upon them, 'therefore it behoved us to be jogging from hence, unless we were resolved to return back to America again'. Swan thanked him for his advice and sent the friar who had acted as go-between ashore with gifts of a large brass clock, an astrolabe and a telescope. So delighted was the friar that he returned presents of six hogs and a roasting pig, several bushels of potatoes and fifty pounds of Manila tobacco. Acting on the friar's advice, who told them that it was a good place for provisioning, they sailed on 2nd June for Mindanao in the Philippines, where they dropped anchor twenty days later after an uneventful voyage.

Most of the Philippines at the time were under Spanish dominion, but Mindanao was not, the local inhabitants keeping the Muslim faith. Dampier was quickly aware of the potential spice trade that could be developed, especially in nutmegs and cloves, and indeed one of the local headmen, Raja Laut, obliquely proposed an English settlement there to promote the clove trade. The locals themselves, however, did nothing to cultivate their naturally growing spices, for fear that the Dutch would come and put them under subjection, since the Dutch were very jealous of their monopoly in the spice trade.

One can see Dampier's mind working in the same way as when he saw the possibility of running the mines at Santa Maria:

Yet although the Dutch take such care to destroy them, there are many uninhabited islands that have great plenty of spice-trees, as I have been informed . . . near the Island Banda there is an island where the cloves falling from the trees do lie and rot on the ground, and they are at the time the fruit falls three or four inches thick under the trees . . .

The prospect of creating a trading station here was very attractive to him, and he speculates on the best sea-routes to and from it, avoiding the Dutch colonies. Among the crew there were enough craftsmen, such as 'sawyers, carpenters, joiners, brickmakers, bricklayers, shoemakers, tailors & c.', to build and maintain a settlement, and they were well provided both with raw materials and arms and ammunition. They had capital, and the *Cygnet* might have been sent home to bring the news to her owners, together with their share of the profits of the voyage so far. They were even accustomed to the climate. Once more we see how little intention Dampier had of returning to England. He had been away from home for about six years, and even then he had only been there briefly. He had no need of his homeland.

Despite the presence of a thriving black market, the trading post was just another golden dream. On a later occasion, when convinced there was gold on a certain island not far away, he sighs: 'but I fell among rooks and could not accomplish what I designed'. Poor Dampier. He was never able to make any money.

He is on firmer ground when describing the practice of chewing betel 'nuts', as he says, and noticing fruit bats as big as kites. He discusses the various nations and languages of Mindanao, but warns of their natural laziness and their tendency to poison people who they believe have offended them. He describes the mores and nature of the coastal people with whom he and his companions had most to do. One custom he particularly noticed, never having come across it before, which he ascribed to the lack of general trade they had with the outside world:

When strangers arrive here, the Mindanao men will come aboard, and invite them to their houses, and inquire who has a comrade . . . or a *pagally*, and who has not. A comrade is a familiar male friend; a pagally is an innocent platonic friend of the other sex. All strangers are in a manner obliged to accept of this acquaintance and familiarity, which must first be purchased with a small present, and afterwards confirmed with some gift or other to continue the acquaintance; and as often as the stranger goes ashore, he is welcome to his comrade's or pagally's house, where he may be entertained for his money to eat, drink or sleep . . . The richest men's wives are allowed the freedom to converse with her pagally in public, and may give or receive presents from him. Even the sultan's and the general's wives, who are always cooped up, will yet look out of their cages when a stranger passeth by, and demand of him if he wants a pagally; and to invite him to their friendship, will send a present of tobacco and betel-nut to him by their servants.

Dampier describes the people as small, and does not mention that they were especially attractive. He says that their teeth were black, but sound, which may mean that they dyed their teeth. They were also prone to what Dampier calls leprosy, but which was more likely to be a form of herpes, and to smallpox and cholera; but they had plenty of herbal remedies to hand. They were fond of music and dance.

The more or less enforced fraternization did not lead to good relations. The Mindanaoans, who were a poor race, but acquisitive, may also have had ulterior motives from the moment the *Cygnet* and her little consort sailed into their harbour. At any rate, tobacco and betel-nut were all the mariners got from them for nothing.

The sultan himself was a man in late middle-age. Much of the real power, however, lay in the hands of his brother, Raja Laut, who filled the offices of prime minister and commander-in-chief. Raja Laut could both speak and write Spanish.

Using Henry More, the freebooter who had joined him in the Gulf of San Miguel, as a go-between, Captain Swan exchanged presents with the sultan and his brother. Swan knew that the season of the year would oblige them to stay until the weather became favourable for sailing again, and he was lavish in his gifts. He sent 'three yards of scarlet cloth, three yards of broad gold lace, a Turkish scimitar and a pair of pistols' to the sultan, and rich textiles to Raja Laut. No doubt he was pleased not to have jettisoned this part of his original cargo along with the rest when he joined the freebooters. When, the following day, Swan was invited ashore, he went in very great pomp, 'with a flag flying in the boat's head, and two trumpets sounding all the way'. Perhaps this was a political move to impress the sultan, for Swan was a clever man; but there was already an element of the vainglory to which Swan was gradually to give way.

Swan was entertained with tobacco and betel-nut, and given two English letters to read. One, written on gold-lined paper in a fine hand, was from the English East India Company, and made inquiries about the possibility of establishing a fort. The other had been left by a certain Captain Goodlud, for the benefit of any Englishmen who came after him. It described trading-rates with the Mindanaoans in detail, and ended with a caveat: 'Trust none of them, for they are all thieves; but *tace* is the Latin for a candle.' It later emerged that Goodlud had been robbed by one of Raja Laut's men. The man was brought before Swan with the request that he impose whatever punishment he pleased. Swan sensibly refused to have anything to do with it. Raja Laut thereupon passed sentence himself, and the punishment was harsh enough. Dampier describes it thus:

> He was stripped stark naked in the morning at sunrising, and bound to a post, so that he could not stir hand nor foot, but as he was moved, and was placed with his face eastward against the sun. In the afternoon they turned his face towards the west, that the sun might still be in his face, and thus he stood all day, parched in the sun (which shines here excessively hot) and tormented with the mosquitoes or gnats. After this the general would have killed him, if Captain Swan had consented to it. I never did see any put to death, but I believe they are barbarous enough in it. The general told us himself that he put two men to death in a town where some of us were with him; but I heard not the manner of it. Their common way of punishing is to strip them in this manner, and place them in the sun; but sometimes they lay them flat on their backs on the sand, which is very hot; where they remain a whole day in the scorching sun, with the mosquitoes biting them all the time.

Swan, notwithstanding his own mercy to the Mindanaoan thief, offered Raja Laut the right to punish any of his crew who offended Mindanaoans. This Raja Laut refused to accept, but Swan hereafter punished his men when he thought he had cause with great severity, in sight of the Mindanaoans, and not always with justice. Dampier, who is almost always fair-minded, remarks on his behaviour with a disapproval which is the greater for his having been Swan's friend and supporter. With regret, Dampier remarks:

At that time Captain Swan had his men as much under command as if he had been in a King's ship; and had he known how to use his authority, he might have led them to any settlement, and have brought them to assist in any design he had pleased.

After reading the letters and witnessing the punishment, Swan started to consort frequently with the chief men of Mindanao, especially Raja Laut, with whom when he dined he had his trumpeters sound throughout the meal – which seems a little excessive, though once again we must take Dampier's word for it. The ships were careened, and Swan sold the sultan some of the iron and lead he had aboard, in exchange for rice. Meanwhile the men fraternized with the locals, and from this arose another incident which shows that all was not well with the state of Swan's mind.

The crew were frequently entertained by displays of local dancing, in which the Mindanaoans took enormous pleasure. One of the crewmen, John Thacker, was himself an excellent dancer – he had learnt to dance 'in the music houses about Wapping' – and he was relatively well-off, having husbanded his share of the booty. He also dressed better than his comrades. He danced for the locals, to their great delight. For a joke, some of his fellow crewmen encouraged Raja Laut's belief that Thacker was of noble extraction, and told him that many of the others were equally so, having come aboard only out of curiosity to see the world. But when Swan came to know of it, he had Thacker, who was innocent of the whole business, soundly flogged.

Mindanao was a terrible place for the teredo worm, the mollusc that bores into a ship's planking below the waterline, and although the *Cygnet* was protectively sheathed with tar and horsehair between inner and outer boards, it was still necessary to replace much of the honeycombed main planking. Ominously, when he saw that the ship was double-sheathed, Raja Laut seemed concerned, as if he'd hoped she would be totally unseaworthy by now.

By the end of the year they were ready for setting off again, and many of the men, especially those who had run through their money, were eager to do so. Swan, however, showed no such inclination, and remained ashore, telling Dampier that he would not lend himself to any further freebooting ventures, and that 'no prince on earth' was 'able to wipe off the stain of such actions'.

From his attitude it is clear that Swan took a high, if not histrionic, moral line *vis-à-vis* his association with men whom he regarded as no better than pirates. He wasn't far wrong in his assessment of his companions, but how he squared this with his own actions is a small triumph of human nature over human reason.

If Swan had any other plans in mind, he did not confide them in Dampier, and was 'commonly very cross'. He did, however, give orders to continue to make the *Cygnet* ready for the sea. He still had command, though his hold on it weakened when the ship was moved from her river anchorage to the sea-road. Significantly, it was at about this time that he punished Josiah Teat. Dampier notes that Swan punished Josiah Teat 'out of jealousy'; and this action marked the beginning of the schism which was soon to divide the crew completely.

Meanwhile, those of the crew who still had money were spending it freely ashore, both on their pagallies and on women servants whom they had bought or hired from the locals to be their concubines. Equally, they bought or rented houses – 'for houses are very cheap' – and showed every sign of settling down, though they were being thoroughly fleeced by the Mindanaoans.

Dampier was becoming increasingly aware that Raja Laut was duplicitous. He lied about the availability of cattle to be hunted, and seemed to be putting obstacles in the way of their departure. Dampier complained to Swan, who was furious at the news in Dampier's presence, but with the Raja he was 'very mute, being a man of small courage'. Dampier despaired of his captain. He saw the whole enterprise falling apart, half the crew disaffected, the other half going native. His hopes of establishing a permanent and profitable settlement were evaporating, and he had no power to do anything to prevent it.

Further complications followed, the Raja continuing to prevaricate about helping the English to obtain beef to salt for the voyage. Another of the Raja's servants was brutally punished, and the Raja refused to honour a debt of twenty ounces of gold owed to Swan and lent by him out of his owners' share. Meanwhile Christmas and New Year had passed, and the easterly monsoon was well up, 'the only wind to carry us farther into the Indies'. Some of the men, including Dampier, bought a periagua secretly and absconded with it, intending to sail to Borneo, but Swan learnt of the design and put a stop to it. Otherwise, Swan did nothing, and the division between the two halves of the crew increased.

By mid January 1687, matters had come to a head. One of the merchants aboard, Mr Harthop, who had been involved with Ringrose and Teat at the action at Valdivia, strongly urged Swan to come to a decision. In response, Swan ordered all his men aboard on 13th January. But two days before that date an unfortunate discovery was made on board by Dampier's fellow seaman John Read, of whom Dampier speaks highly, though he was later to change his opinion of him.

Read was an educated man, and kept a journal. With the captain on shore, he took it into his head to look at Swan's own account of the voyage. This contained a long diatribe directed against the crew, naming names. When Teat saw the book, he seized on the opportunity to incite those aboard to mutiny.

Dampier himself and the surgeon's mate, Herman Coppinger, were ashore when all this was going on. When they came aboard, innocently, as Dampier says, on 13th January, they were detained by the mutineers. Whether they remained willingly, Dampier does not confirm or deny.

Once the plot was discovered on shore, Swan made some half-hearted attempts to mollify his rebellious crew, but a curious lassitude seems to have overtaken him. Dampier speaks of him with neither approval nor warmth. The *Cygnet* sailed the next day, leaving Swan and thirty-six crew members at Mindanao. Several others remained too, but these men, as Dampier informs us darkly, had died, the victims of poisonings by the Mindanaoans. On the *Cygnet*, John Read was now captain, Teat master, and Henry More quartermaster. Perhaps Dampier was master's mate again; perhaps he was given no chief office, not having been among the leaders of the mutiny. Still, it is hard to imagine that he was reluctant to leave Swan. Most of the men were bored and sickened with the life at Mindanao, and it isn't hard to imagine how restless Dampier became. In his manuscript, he writes: 'Of the two evils I thought to choose the least, and therefore came away with the ship, with a resolution to leave her the first place we came to near an English factory.' He also notes: 'I thought I should in time persuade them to return and fetch Captain Swan . . . but I missed of my aim.'

One of Dampier's shipmates at the time was a certain Kerrill Roffey, of whom a little must be said: Roffey later became a captain in the Royal Navy, and had as his lieutenant for a time one George Fisher. Fisher was the man who caused Dampier's downfall after the *Roebuck* expedition, which is described in Part Three of this book. After Swan's crew split up at Mindanao, Roffey was left behind. Later rescued by the Dutch, he worked for them until he could get a passage home, and one of his jobs was to destroy spice trees in order to preserve the monopoly and maintain high prices.

As the *Cygnet* sails away, Dampier settles down to close observations of the winds, with the calculation of latitudes, and daring speculation about the date-line. In the coming weeks, there was much to attract his eye. Until the end of February, they cruised the Philippines, taking a modest prize, until on 26th they departed for the Pulo Condore group of islets in the mouths of the Mekong River, luckily passing the dreaded Paracel Reefs on their way without so much as seeing them. Here they careened, and took in water, laboriously cutting bamboo pipes to siphon it from the water-holes.

At Pulo Condore the locals made their women available for very little money, and many of the crew took advantage of this. Dampier was more interested in their customs and religion, though he does record the deaths of two sailors from poison administered at Mindanao. Their livers were discovered to be 'black, light and dry, like pieces of cork' – so that they may not have died so much of deliberate poisoning, suggests John Masefield, as of cirrhosis, from drinking too much arrack after a long period of privation.

From here they ranged the Gulf of Thailand, before returning towards Pulo Condore. They exchanged news with a junk laden with pepper, from which a 'Portuguese' seaman came aboard them. Soon afterwards they had an affray with a Malay vessel, whose crew attacked the men in the *Cygnet*'s canoe with krises, 'stabbing five or six of our men before they knew what the matter was'. One of the survivors, Daniel Wallis, 'leapt into the sea, who could never swim before nor since; yet now he swam very well a good while before he was taken up'. Dampier would meet Wallis again much later on, at the Cape of Good Hope, and travel home with him. They stayed in touch, for in his manuscript he reports Wallis as 'a young man, now living at Weymouth'. Henry More was stabbed to death in the attack.

Meanwhile, matters were not going well aboard the *Cygnet*. Herman Coppinger tried to run away at Pulo Condore, but was brought back forcibly. Dampier had sympathy for the surgeon:

> I had the same thoughts, and would have gone ashore too, but waited for a more convenient place . . . and being sufficiently weary of this mad crew, we were willing to give them the slip at any place from whence we might hope to get passage to an English factory.

It was now the end of May 1687. Aged thirty-five, Dampier began to feel the first intimations that life was not endless.

Forced by the winds, they sailed up into the South China Sea. Dampier gives us a description of the Chinese he encounters, built up both from personal experience and tales he hears, not forgetting to report the state of the seas and winds. They are caught in a tremendous typhoon, the worst Dampier has yet experienced, and as it abates, St Elmo's Fire appears in the rigging and shrouds. In the first identifiable description in English of this phenomenon, Dampier reflects on its nature, and as always inclines to a scientific rather than a supernatural explanation. The *Cygnet* touches at the Piscadores Islands, at Macao; passes Hong Kong, sails on for Formosa. At last, on 5th August, she arrives at the Bashee Islands (Batan), and the English crew give the islands names. Dampier names one after the Duke of Grafton, telling us in passing, as I mentioned earlier, that he does so because he married his own wife 'out of his duchess's family'. I wonder, though, how often Judith was in his thoughts, and whether he ever felt guilty about his treatment of her.

Here they found a pale metal like gold, but none of them was certain that it *was* gold. Dampier would have liked to buy some, and clearly thought that it would have been a good investment, but had no share in the iron in the *Cygnet*'s hold for which it was bartered. He brings away a wealth of impressions instead: the houses, streets, clothes, boats, geography, cultivation, are all described in enthusiastic detail.

The Bashee Islands gained their collective name from a native drink, made:

> with the juice of the sugar-cane, which they boil, and put some small black sort of berries among it. When it is well boiled, they put it into great jars, and let it stand three or four days and work. Then it settles, becomes clear, and is presently fit to drink. This is an excellent liquor, and very much like English beer, both in colour and taste.

Food was not so appealing. Goats' stomachs were stewed and eaten with their contents, together with raw fish, and roasted locust.

As for religion and customs, Dampier could find scant evidence of idolatry or of hierarchy. He witnessed an execution, the pathetic description of which is worth repeating:

> While we lay here we saw a young man buried alive in the earth; and 'twas for theft, as far as we could understand from them. There was a great deep hole dug, and abundance of people came to the place to take their last farewell of him: among the rest, there was one woman who made great lamentation, and took off the condemned person's earrings. We supposed her to be his mother. After he had taken his leave of her and some others, he was put into the pit, and covered over with earth. He did not struggle, but yielded very quietly to his punishment; and they crammed the earth close upon him, and stifled him.

They remained here for some time, not sailing away until the beginning of October. Most of the men were homesick and tired, and Dampier still longed to escape, though he confesses himself 'well enough satisfied, knowing that the farther we went, the more knowledge and experience I should get, which was the main thing I regarded'. Adventure was like a drug to him. Perhaps he had become afraid of anything else.

Their route now took them back to the Philippines. On 16th October they put in at the south-eastern end of the island of Mindanao to make repairs, and there met a friendly prince who was a neighbour of their old sultan. By now, Dampier tells us, he and some of his shipmates had learnt Malayan, so the prince was able to tell them in his own language that Captain Swan was still alive, and had been fighting in local wars alongside the sultan; but now hoped to sail to Madras at last, and was negotiating the purchase of a ship. Hearing this, Dampier, who thought that Swan, with all his faults, was a better commander than Read or Teat, tried to persuade the crew to put themselves back under Swan's authority, and with some success; but word of this reached Read and Teat, and before the crew could be swung round, they were brought into line. Presumably Read and Teat did not learn that Dampier was behind this revolt, or they would have left him at Mindanao. As it was, they 'made all possible haste to be gone'.

Much later, Dampier learnt that Swan and his surgeon were murdered in the water by Raja Laut's men as they tried to get aboard a Dutch ship and so make their escape. It is possible that Raja Laut killed Swan on account of the gold he still had. Many of his other men did get away in Dutch sloops, though others, including Mr Harthop, died at Mindanao.

The aimless cruise continued. They touched at Timor and at Sulawesi. At Buton Island, Dampier noticed the cockatoos, and the sultan presented Captain Read with a boy remarkable for having two rows of teeth in each jaw. Then, on 5th January 1688, the *Cygnet* touched on the north-western shores of Australia, at 16° 50' latitude. Her crew were the first Englishmen to set foot there.

Dampier is as observant as ever, but he is not impressed. The land was desert or scrub, and they saw few birds and no animals, though Dampier mentions the track of what was probably a dingo. What is most striking is his view of the local natives. In his manuscript account he gives a simple description, quite in keeping with his usual scientific objectivity:

> They are people of good stature, but thin and lean, I judge from want of food. They are black, yet I believe their hair would be long if it was combed out; but for want of combs it is matted up like a Negro's hair. They have, all that I saw, two front teeth of their upper jaw wanting, both men, women and children.

The last remark refers to ritual tooth extraction practised by some tribes. In the published account of his *New Voyage*, however, Dampier is ferocious in his description of them. This is very unusual, for he is normally sympathetic, or at least open-minded, in his response to anything new. He describes their 'swords' as being made of wood 'and shaped somewhat like a cutlass'; what he actually saw was probably boomerangs.

As far as their physical appearance is concerned, he is remorseless. Comparing them unfavourably with the *Hottentots*, whom he would meet later in South Africa, he says, 'setting aside their human shape, they differ but little from brutes'.

As he goes on, I suspect that a general irritation with the place has transferred itself to the natives themselves:

> They have great heads, round foreheads, and great brows. Their eyelids are always half-closed, to keep the flies out of their eyes; they being so troublesome here, that no fanning will keep them from coming to one's face; and without the assistance of both hands to keep them off, they will creep into one's nostrils, and mouth too, if the lips are not shut very close . . . They have great bottle-noses, pretty full lips, and wide mouths . . . They are long-visaged, and of a very unpleasing aspect, having no one graceful feature in their faces.

It is remarkable that for the first time Dampier's curiosity loses its sympathetic quality.

Dampier is equally scathing about their primitive way of life, deprecating their want of clothing, habitation, and general lack of development. They spoke a guttural language he could not understand, and ran away at any attempt to make contact. Dampier describes finding a native settlement whose menfolk attempted to defend it against the frightening newcomers. The English fired a gun over their heads to scare them, which succeeded. The great early-nineteenth-century chronicler of the buccaneers, Admiral James Burney, writes:

> It deserves to be remarked to the credit of human nature, that these poor people, in description the most wretched of mankind in all respects, stood their ground for the defence of their women and children, against the shock and first surprise at hearing the report of firearms.

At length, some of the men became familiar with the English, and allowed themselves to be dressed in some old European clothes. The English hoped that in return for this dubious favour they would carry fresh water from some wells they had found, down to the ship's canoes: 'But all the signs we could make were to no purpose, for they stood like statues, without motion, but grinned like so many monkeys, staring upon one another.' Dampier adds: 'I did not perceive that they had any great liking to them [the clothes] at first, neither did they seem to admire anything that we had.' Another time the crew took some of the natives on board ship and gave them a good meal of rice with boiled turtle and manatee. 'They did greedily devour what we gave them, but took no notice of the ship, or anything in it, and when they were set on land again, they ran away as fast as they could.'

Although we will return to encounters with Australian natives later, it is worth noting here a very similar experience of James Cook when he made his first landfall in Australia just under a century later, as told by Alan Moorehead in *The Fatal Impact*:

Some odd things were happening on shore as the *Endeavour* approached. One group of natives, about a dozen in all, went up on a rise to watch, and when the vessel's boat came near they beckoned the sailors to come ashore. On the other hand, no notice at all seemed to be taken of the *Endeavour* herself. There she was, 106 feet long, with her high masts and her great sails, and when she passed within a quarter of a mile of some fishermen in four canoes, they did not even bother to look up. Then when she had anchored close to the shore a naked woman carrying wood appeared with three children. 'She often looked at the ship,' [Joseph] Banks tells us, 'but expressed neither surprise nor concern. Soon after this she lighted a fire and the four canoes came in from the fishing: the people landed, hauled up their boats and began to dress their dinner, to all appearance totally unmoved by us . . .' There are some interesting aspects in all this. The sight of the *Endeavour* had apparently meant nothing to these primitives because it was too strange, too monstrous, to be comprehended. It had appeared out of nowhere like some menacing phenomenon of nature . . . and by ignoring it or pretending to ignore it no doubt they hoped that it would go away.

They sailed from New Holland, as Australia was called, on 12th March 1688. Dampier's descriptions here are scanter than anywhere else. For the moment his mind was firmly occupied with the question of getting away from the *Cygnet*, as while they were still at New Holland:

> I did endeavour to persuade our men to go to some English factory; but was threatened to be turned ashore, and left here for it. This made me desist, and patiently wait for some more convenient place and opportunity to leave them, than here; which I did hope I should accomplish in a short time, because they did intend, when they went from hence, to bear down towards Cape Comorin.

Instead, the *Cygnet* continued her meandering course among the East Indies, avoiding busy routes for fear of Dutch patrols. To make matters worse Captain Read captured a local proa out of Achin, on the point of north-west Sumatra, took some of her poor cargo of coconuts, sank her and took her four crewmen prisoner. Dampier comments angrily:

> It was not for the lucre of the cargo that Captain Read took this boat, but to hinder me and some others from going ashore . . . and he thought that by robbing and abusing the natives, we should be afraid to trust ourselves among them.

Early in May, having encountered contrary winds, they arrived at the Nicobar Islands, and here Dampier at last succeeded in persuading Read to let him go ashore. Read agreed because he thought Dampier would not easily be able to get on to another ship from here, and so (as Read feared) raise a hue and cry against him. Once he'd got the captain's assent, Dampier made all possible haste to get ashore in case Read should change his mind again, but he was not out of the woods yet. The locals were neither friendly nor unfriendly, but it was clear they didn't particularly want him left with them.

Soon afterwards a boat was sent back to the shore to fetch him and his sea-chest back again. What had happened since his departure was that several other disaffected members of the crew, taking courage from his example, were also clamouring to leave. They were Robert Hall, Herman Coppinger, and another man whose name Dampier simply gives as 'Ambrose'. After much altercation, they were allowed to go, with the exception of Coppinger, who was the ship's surgeon and whom, therefore, they could not afford to release, though he was desperate enough to threaten them with a gun, which the quartermaster wrested from him. With them went the four sailors from the Achin proa, and the 'Portuguese' (though the manuscript describes him as Chinese) who had joined them from the junk they'd encountered in the Gulf of Thailand.

The *Cygnet* sailed away. She made for Sri Lanka, but could not bear in to it, and so anchored off the coast of Coromandel. By then dissent was rife, and Read was deserted by half the crew. Most of those who left him joined the army of the great moghul, but soon deserted, and we lose their traces in petty villainy, disease and death. Read headed across the Indian Ocean, setting a course for the great pirate haven of Madagascar, where he left the *Cygnet*. We last hear of him in a vessel headed for New York. Josiah Teat took over command of Swan's old ship, which must have been one of the best built of her time, given the length of her voyage to date. He joined forces with Captain William Knight, who however abandoned him when, on a cruise together, the *Cygnet* at last began to founder. Teat brought her back to St Augustine Bay in Madagascar, where she sank. What became of Teat and the rest of the crew thereafter, history does not relate.

Dampier must have watched the *Cygnet* sail away with mixed feelings, since Great Nicobar was well away from any trade route. Yet his predominant sense must have been one of relief. He had companions, and he did not fear the locals:

> I am of opinion that there are no people in the world so barbarous as to kill a single person that falls accidentally into their hands, or comes to live among them, except they have before been injured by some outrage or violence committed against them. Yet even then, or afterwards, if a man could but preserve his life from their first rage, and come to treat with them (which is the hardest thing,

because their way is usually to abscond, and rushing suddenly upon their enemy to kill him at unawares) one might, by some sleight, insinuate oneself into their favours again, especially by showing some toy or knack that they did never see before, which any European, that has seen the world, might soon contrive to amuse them withal; as might be done generally even with a little fire struck with a flint and steel.

This is just a shade optimistic, and in our day the tricks he advises would not work, but the philosophy behind his idea is encouraging.

They had no intention of staying long on the island and quickly purchased a canoe from the locals in return for an axe, which one of their former fellow crewmen had smuggled to them. They loaded it up with their gear, with the intention of rowing themselves across to Sumatra.

This was not to be as easy as it seemed. No sooner had they launched and got underway than the canoe capsized, dumping them and their belongings into the sea. They got ashore with difficulty and preserved all their goods, but Dampier's and Hall's journals and draft maps were wet and the next three days were spent carefully drying them, and everything else, at great fires on the beach. In the meantime the Achinese converted the canoe into an outrigger, and equipped her with a mast and a matting sail. They then made an experimental coastal tour of the island to trade for supplies, but early on, fearing attack, Hall fired his gun over the heads of some natives. After that it was impossible to treat with anyone, let alone to land, for they were seen off by large numbers of locals everywhere they went. At last, on the north coast, Dampier hit upon a stratagem that worked:

I took my gun, and presented at them; at which they all fell down flat on the ground. But I turned myself about, and to show that we did not intend to harm them, I fired my gun off to sea, so that they might see the shot graze on the water. As soon as my gun was loaded again, we rowed gently in, at which some of them withdrew. The rest standing up, did still cut and hew the air, making signs of their hatred, till I once more frighted them with my gun, and discharged it as before. Then more of them sneaked away, leaving only four or five men on the bay. Then we rowed in again, and Mr

Hall taking his sword in his hand, leapt ashore; and I stood ready with my gun to fire at the Indians if they had injured him. But they did not stir till he came to them and saluted them.

Thus peace was made, and it was to the great relief of both sides. Dampier and his companions were at last able to trade with the modest means at their disposal for equally modest provisions, for the islanders were not rich. They turned down an offer of hogs in order not to offend their Achinese friends, who were Muslims. Their staple was mellory, a kind of breadfruit.

They were ready for the crossing now, and awaited the arrival of the western monsoon, which was imminently expected, with impatience.

CHAPTER THIRTEEN

The Worst Voyage of His Life

The eight of them set out in their canoe at four in the afternoon on 15th May 1688. Three Englishmen, four Achinese, and 'the mongrel Portuguese' as Dampier now calls him – so that we may assume that this member of the crew was a half-caste. The crossing from the Nicobars to Sumatra was the toughest Dampier ever made.

He and Hall were the only competent open sea mariners, and took turns to steer the boat while the others rowed. They set off with a will, for they were in hopes of reaching Sumatra before the western monsoon really started to blow. Dampier had a pocket compass and a pocket book in which he had noted 'an account of the bearing and distance of all the Malacca coast, and that of Sumatra, Pegu, and Siam'. Their vessel was very light, and they soon had cause to be grateful to the Achinese for lashing the outriggers, and making one for each side of the boat, for otherwise she would have overset before they had run a mile. She sailed very crank – lightly – too, and sat low in the water, being designed for rowing, so that they could not rest for a moment in the management of her.

They thought they had made good progress in the first two days and began to look out for Sumatra, but the first land they saw, to their horror, was Great Nicobar again, and only about twenty-five miles away. A strong current against them, which 'made a great noise that might be heard near half a mile', had retarded their progress. On the following day the wind freshened, but the sky clouded over so that they could not take an observation on the sun, especially at noon. Worse was to come:

We had then a very ill presage, by a great circle about the sun (five or six times the diameter of it) which seldom appears, but storms of wind, or much rain ensue . . . I must confess that I was a little anxious at the sight of this circle, and wished heartily that we were near some land. Yet I showed no sign of it to my consorts, but made a virtue of necessity, and put a good countenance on the matter.

He did not have to dissimulate for very long. The wind got up with frightening speed, and was soon bearing down against the side of the boat violently. The poles supporting the twin outriggers bent so much that it looked as if they would break. If they had, the canoe would have capsized and the men would all have drowned. They had been caught in a violent south-westerly gale which increased all afternoon, and it was lucky that they got the canoe's back to the wind and sea, for otherwise she would have been swamped. It was still bad enough, but luckily the vessel was light and narrow enough to bend with the force of the storm:

the sea still swelled higher, and often broke, but did us no damage, for the ends of the vessel being very narrow, he that steered received and broke the sea on his back, and so kept it from coming in so much as to endanger the vessel, though much water would come in, which we were forced to keep heaving out continually.

Dampier was a strong man, physically and spiritually, but it was a long time since he had been able to relax, and he had only recently shaken off the effects of the dropsy which had dogged him for many months. Now, with the storm at its height and all the men exhausted, darkness began to fall. It was the night of 18th May. Dampier is not given to broad reflections on life and mortality, but thinking back on that time, he writes:

The sea was already roaring in a white foam about us; a dark night coming on, and no land in sight to shelter us, and our little ark in danger to be swallowed by every wave; and, what was worst of all, none of us thought ourselves prepared for another world. The reader may better guess than I can express, the confusion we were all in. I had been in many eminent dangers before now, some of which I have already related, but the worst of them all was but a play-game in comparison with this. I must confess that I was in great conflicts of mind at this time. Other dangers came not upon me with such a leisurely and dreadful solemnity. A sudden skirmish or engagement, or so, was nothing when one's blood was up, and pushed forwards with eager expectations. But here I had a lingering view of approaching death, and little or no hopes of escaping it; and I must confess that my courage, which I had hitherto kept up, failed me here; and I made very sad reflections on my former life, and looked back with horror and detestation on actions which before I had disliked, but now I trembled at the remembrance of. I had long before this repented of that roving course of life, but never with such concern as now. I did also call to mind the many miraculous acts of God's providence towards me in the whole course of my life, of which kind I believe few men have met with the like. For all these I returned thanks in a peculiar manner, and this once more desired God's assistance, and composed my mind, as well as I could, in the hopes of it . . .

At the time there can have been little leisure for such thoughts. Hall and Dampier took turns to steer. At 10 o'clock a thunderstorm began, and they were grateful for the rain, because their water-bumkins were empty. Even so the hard rain chilled them, for fresh water is always colder than sea water. 'In this wet starveling plight we spent the tedious night.'

But despite the storm they had held their course east throughout the night, and though the foul weather continued, daylight brought some relief. At 8 o'clock one of the Achinese sighted land, believing it to be Weh Island off the north-west coast of Sumatra. Encouraged, the exhausted men hoisted a small sail and set a course for it through the violent waters. All day they sailed, until they could see that the land was not Weh Island at all, but a great mountain on Sumatra itself, perhaps Silowaih Agam. When the wind dropped at 10 o'clock that night, they took to the oars, for though they were almost worn out, they found the strength to get them to land. On the morning of the 20th, the wind freshened again and at last, at five o'clock in the afternoon, they put ashore in the estuary of the River Passanjan.

I. William Dampier, aged about forty-six, from the portrait by Thomas Murray.

2. An East Indiaman of Dampier's day.

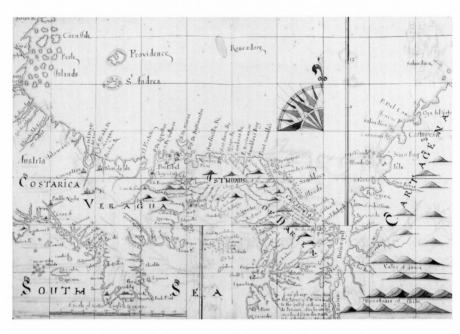

3. William Hack's map of the Isthmus of Darien (Panama).

4. Sir Henry Morgan, 1635–88.
One of the most adventurous and successful buccaneers, his notorious exploits
against the Spanish inspired the
expedition against Panama which
Dampier joined.

5. Sir Edward Spragge,
Admiral of the Blue Squadron and
Dampier's commander in the
Third Dutch War.

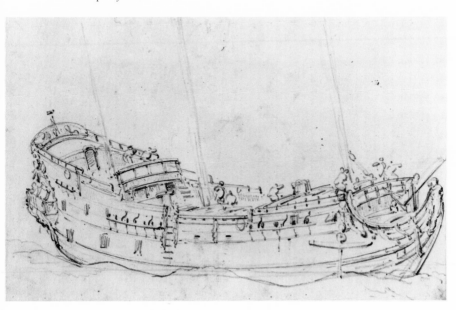

6. A fifth-rater of similar type to the *Roebuck*.

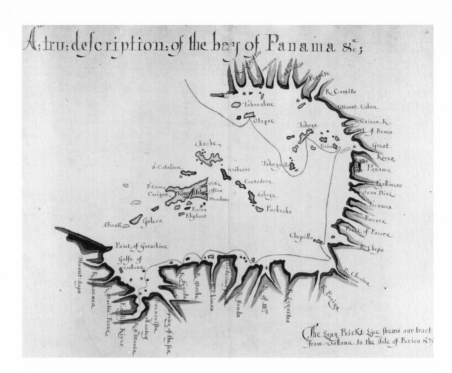

7. Hack's map of the Bay of Panama.

8. The rescue of William, the Moskito Indian abandoned on the island of Juan Fernandez.

9. A Dutch fluyte, called by the English flyboats or flutes.

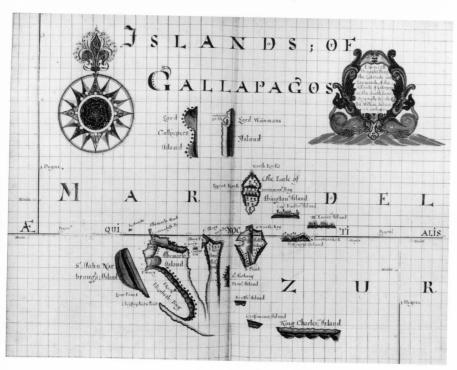

10. Hack's map of the Galapagos Islands.

11. The Darien Indians' manner of bloodletting, as described by Lionel Wafer.

12. Jeoly, the 'painted prince' whom Dampier brought home with him at the end of his first circumnavigation.

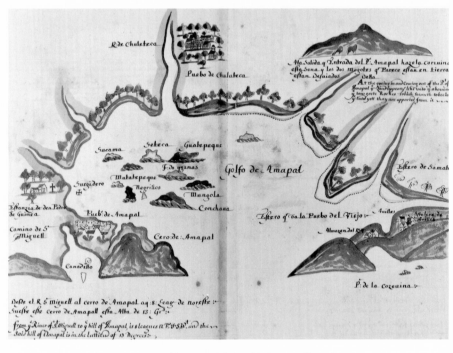

13. Hack's map of the Gulf of Amapalla.

14. Admiral Sir George Rooke, 1650–1709, by Michael Dahl. Rooke presided over Dampier's court martial at the end of the troubled voyage of the *Roebuck*.

15. Naval Secretary Samuel Pepys, 1633–1708, by Sir Godfrey Kneller. John Evelyn and Dampier were guests at a dinner party given by Pepys in August 1693.

16. Admiral Sir Cloudesley Shovell, 1650–1707. One of the greatest naval commanders of his day, Shovell lost his life in the massive shipwreck of his fleet off the Isles of Scilly five years after Dampier's court martial, at which he sat in judgement.

17. Edward Russell, 1653–1727, Earl of Orford and Admiral of the Fleet, by Sir Godfrey Kneller. Orford met Dampier through the president of the Royal Society, and sponsored his proposals for the voyage to Australia.

18. Alexander Selkirk is taken off the island of Juan Fernandez after his four-year sojourn there.

19. Woodes Rogers, commander of Dampier's last expedition, portrayed with members of his family in later life by William Hogarth.

The Achinese took them to a nearby fishing village. They were only thirty-four leagues – about 102 land miles – from Achin, which lies, it will be remembered, on the north-western tip of Sumatra. Dampier and his companions were exhausted, and all had caught fever and were probably suffering from exposure. The Achinese told their friends in the village the whole story of their adventure, and how Dampier, Hall, Ambrose and the Sino-Portuguese were in some ways fellow sufferers. Thus the Europeans were treated with great kindness. The local nobles arranged a spacious house for all of them to live in, and showered the Europeans with so many gifts that, as they could not refuse them for fear of giving offence, they were forced to let go the young buffalo, goats, and so on under the cover of night. The other presents of food – eggs, fish, chickens, rice, plantains, and so on – they gratefully accepted. Their Achinese companions shared the house, but now that necessity did not drive them all together, kept to their own part of it, and observed the niceties of their religion. All eight men were ill, and had to take turns to look after each other, each group – ludicrously, after all they had been through together – in its own separate religious camp. Dampier was so unwell that he could hardly stand, and whetted his penknife in an attempt to let his own blood; he failed because he could not get the knife sharp enough.

They spent twelve days here and, as they showed no improvement, they begged to be taken to Achin. Three of the Achinese had already left them, though still ill themselves, but the remaining five men were taken by proa to the town at the beginning of June. There was an English East India Company factory here, and after examination by a local bureaucrat, they were provided with lodgings by an Irishman called Driscoll who worked for the Company. Sadly, Ambrose and the anonymous Sino-Portuguese died soon afterwards. Dampier and Hall scarcely survived themselves. Dampier, who does not relate what happened to the remaining Achinese, was the least sick of the three survivors; if that is true, it is a miracle that Hall, at least, also recovered. Dampier writes:

Mr Driscal and some other Englishmen persuaded me to take some physick of a Malayan doctor. I took their advice, being willing to get ease; but after three doses, each a large calabash of nasty stuff, finding no amendment, I thought to desist from more physick; but was persuaded to take one dose more, which I did, and it wrought so violently that I thought it would have ended my days. I struggled till I had been about twenty or thirty times at stool, but it working so quick with me, with little intermission, and my strength being almost spent, I even threw myself down once and for all, and had above sixty stools in all before it left off working. I thought my Malayan doctor, whom they so much commended, would have killed me outright. I continued extraordinary weak for some days after his drenching me thus; but my fever left me for above a week; after which, it returned upon me again for a twelvemonth, and a flux with it.

Not that this terrible bout of dysentery stopped him from exploring. As soon as he felt well enough, he was up and about, first visiting a Captain Bowry, who had a house at Achin, and who, apart from being enormously kind to Dampier and his friends, very much wanted William to enlist with him as his boatswain on a voyage to Persia. All looked set fair, but Bowry panicked when a small but powerful Siamese man-of-war sailed into port with an ambassador to the queen of Achin on board. Relations between the English and the Siamese had been more than cordial until a year earlier – indeed, an Englishman, one Captain Williams, had been admiral of the Siamese fleet – but then a certain arrogant naval lieutenant called Weldon managed to insult the Siamese nation and kill a number of its nationals, which, according to Alexander Hamilton, a Scottish merchant who flourished in the East Indies at the end of the seventeenth century and wrote a brilliant account of his life there, 'fatally reversed this happy position'.

Bowry made a run for it when the Siamese ship arrived, taking Dampier and Hall with him and treating them well; but adverse winds drove them back to Achin, by which time more English ships had arrived, whose presence allayed Bowry's fears.

Dampier was too ill to travel to Persia with Bowry, but a Captain Weldon (it seems unlikely that he was the same man as the one just mentioned) soon arrived in the *Curtana* from Madras. Weldon had slaves aboard to sell at Achin, and was then bound for Tonkin to trade. Dampier shipped with him in July 1688; not least because he had a surgeon aboard, and Dampier was still very weak. With him travelled Robert Hall, whose enthusiasm for new adventures more than matched Dampier's own, for he was in poorer health than William, and hadn't the additional encouragement of the command of a sloop, which Weldon had promised our mariner, as he proposed to purchase one at Tonkin.

What Dampier's rank was aboard he does not say. On their way they called in at Malacca (Melaka), where they took a pilot aboard, and at Johor, whose inhabitants are described by Alexander Hamilton as 'lazy, indolent, perfidious and cruel'.

At length they arrived at Tonkin, which corresponds approximately to the northern part of Vietnam. Here Dampier was to spend several months, at times as a tourist, at leisure, and his description of the country in all its aspects is correspondingly long. Most of what he describes is familiar to us, through reading and television, if not at first hand; but it is not hard to imagine, and it is worth re-emphasizing, the impact of hearing what Dampier had to tell for the first time. Though there were Dutch and English factories at the capital, Cachao, the Europeans there were principally occupied with trade. They seldom travelled far inland, nor were they on close terms with the local population.

Dampier complains of the ill-made streets of Cachao. He had been away from home so long that he had forgotten that the streets of London and the lanes of Somerset were scarcely better. He notes that the people are addicted to gambling, that they dye their teeth, that silk-producing countries generally have a huge poor underclass which chiefly subsists on rice, which must be made available to them cheaply. Dampier takes notice of their housing, social life, language and industries. He notes that the country is ruled by two kings, one of whom has all the executive power yet defers to the other, who is kept a prisoner in his palace. He sees that the chief officials are eunuchs who are not only castrated, but, as the old naval term has it, 'docked smack smooth'. He tells the story of one official, still intact, who, seeing that he will not rise in his career without the operation, performs it on himself.

He notices and lists the cannon available to their army, from falcon to demi-culverin. He pulls himself up on an error he committed in Mindanao, which was to ascribe to the natives the chewing of betel-nuts.

It is a slice of arek nut wrapped in a betel leaf that is chewed. 'Every man here has a box that will hold a great many of these pellets, in which they keep a store ready made up, for all persons, of what quality soever, from the prince to the beggar, chew abundance of it.' He becomes aware of the importance of etiquette, and observes the use of chopsticks, but manages to escape an unattractive meal:

> My friend, that he might better entertain me and his other guests, had been in the morning a-fishing in a pond not far from his house, and had caught a huge mess of frogs, and with great joy brought them home as soon as I came to his house. I wondered to see him turn out so many of these creatures into a basket, and asking him what they were for, he told me, to eat; but how he dressed them I know not; I did not like his dainties so well as to stay and dine with him.

Though still suffering from dysentery and seriously weakened by it, Dampier did not hesitate when a chance to travel inland, alone except for a guide, presented itself. The price of rice was high in the capital, and Weldon and some others had set off to collect cargoes of it from provincial ports. Perhaps Dampier was too unwell to make the journey with them. As usual, he had no money, except for two dollars (he does not tell us whether Dutch or Spanish) he had earned 'by teaching some of our young seamen plain sailing' – a simple form of calculation by which a ship's position can be determined. One of these he gave to his guide as his fee.

They set out towards the end of November 1688, making only short journeys every day, because of Dampier's weakness. He no longer had a fever, but he seems to have lived chiefly on small oranges and other fruit, which were the worst things for diarrhoea. Didn't he know that? Or was it that he needed vitamins? Or perhaps he couldn't afford anything else to eat. He was thirty-seven years old, a good age for the time he lived in and the career he followed. But, tough and hardened though he was, he didn't spare himself.

They found no inns on the way, but spent the nights in private houses, borrowing a pot to cook their rice. Indefatigable as ever, he tells us:

Usually after supper, if the day was not shut in, I took a ramble about the village, to see what was worth taking notice of, especially the pagoda of the place. These had the image of either an horse, an elephant, or both, standing with the head looking out of the doors. The pagodas themselves were but small and low. I still made it dark night before I returned to my lodging, and then I laid me down to sleep. My guide carried my sea-gown, which was my covering in the night, and my pillow was a log of wood. But I slept very well, though the weakness of my body did now require a better accommodation.

It was as a result of a similar ramble that he almost came to grief: he came across a small tower near which was a number of stalls stacked with meat. Around them was a great crowd of people, mainly men and boys.

This made me conclude that it was some great market, and that the flesh I saw was for sale. Therefore I went in among the crowd, as well to see the tower as to buy some of the meat for my supper, it being now between 4 and 5 o'clock in the afternoon. My guide could not speak English, neither could I speak the Tonkinese language, so I asked him no questions about it, and he too went readily with me, it may be not knowing my intent was to buy.

First of all he looked at the tower, a flimsily built but large structure, about twenty-six feet high. Then he turned his attention to the stalls, where he saw there was fruit as well as meat. The pork was cut up into quarters and sides, but not into any smaller pieces.

I, as was customary in the markets, took hold of a quarter and made signs to the master of it, as I thought, to cut me a piece of two or three pound. I was ignorant of any ceremony they were about, but the superstitious people soon made me sensible of my error, for they assaulted me on all sides, buffeting me and rending my clothes, and one of them snatched away my hat. My guide did all he could to appease them, and dragged me out of the crowd; yet some surly fellows followed us, and seemed by their countenance and gestures to threaten me; but my guide at last pacified them and fetched my hat, and we marched away as fast as we could.

Later, Dampier learned that he had interrupted a funeral. The tower was the tomb, which was to be burned. In the meantime:

> I was both weary and hungry, and I think my appetite was raised by seeing so much food, for indeed at first sight of it I concluded to have had a good supper; but now I was likely to sup only on rice, or a yam roasted, and two eggs as I used to do. For though there were fowls to be bought at every house where I lay, yet my pocket would not reach them . . .

He made his way to the town of Hean, but as his flux had increased, and strength decreased, he threw himself on the mercy of the French missionaries there. Their common language was Spanish; Dampier tells us that he understands the language better than he speaks it. When it failed him, he fell back on the Latin he remembered from school. They discussed the progress of Christianity in Tonkin, and as the missionary was a Roman Catholic, we can imagine Dampier being politely noncommittal in his conversation, though in his book he argues strongly that the French priests were merely replacing the idols of the native religion with images of the saints, without doing anything more fundamental to convert the beliefs of the people, and that their gifts of rice to the poor were a greater inducement to conversion, especially in lean times, than any religious arguments. Despite his contempt for their missionary efforts, he was very happy to teach them how to make gunpowder, which he had learnt from a technical work, first published in 1669, covering all aspects of navigation and nautical lore, called the *Mariner's Magazine*, by Captain Samuel Sturmy. Dampier's efforts were successful, and as this was the first time he had actually made gunpowder himself, he was all the more pleased.

Soon afterwards he returned to Cachao, but found himself again so weakened by his illness that he could not wander about. He stayed in a house there that belonged to a Captain Bowyer. When Captain Weldon was ready to return to Achin, Dampier travelled with him. He had never got the promised schooner, but then he would have been too ill to command her, and it was probably for this reason that the scheme was abandoned. On the way back to Achin, Dampier takes note of the country of Cambodia and sermonizes at length on the virtues of trade. There was no ill-will between Weldon and him, and on arrival back at Achin, Weldon offered to take him on to Madras. Dampier declined, as he had friends at Achin, and did not wish to travel on in his weak condition to a place where he knew no one. At Achin, therefore, he took leave of Captain Weldon, and of his friend Robert Hall, who had made a perfect recovery – he probably took better care of himself than Dampier did – and who was now to accompany Weldon to Madras. Dampier probably met Hall again in London, for he tells us that his friend later took ship for home in the *Williamson* from Madras.

It was now the spring of 1689. Early in that year, Dampier, wishing to send letters home, especially relating to the fate of the *Cygnet*, gave them to our old acquaintance Edward Barlow, then mate of the *Rainbow*, commanded by Captain Poole. From a hint Dampier drops in his surviving works, we learn that the piratical crew of the *Cygnet* may have changed her name after abandoning Swan, in the traditional way (Swan never saw himself as a freebooter, and therefore would not have done so). Dampier never heard that his report had been delivered to the *Cygnet*'s owners, but that is hardly surprising in view of the fact that on her arrival home, the *Rainbow* fouled a man-of-war in bad weather and lost her longboat, which contained 500 Spanish dollars' worth of 'musk-in-wood', which was Barlow's private stake in the voyage, and, probably, Dampier's packet of letters with it. It is possible that some of Dampier's other papers were lost in the same accident.

Dampier now spent some time concentrating on his recovery, but that did not prevent him from investigating every aspect of life at Achin and in the surrounding countryside. He must have noted with special interest the binding qualities of the dried rind of the mangosteen, and he also gives us an early description of marijuana:

> They have here a sort of plant called ganga, or bang. I never saw any but once, and that was at some distance from me. It appeared to me like hemp . . . It is reported of this plant, that if it is infused in any liquor, it will stupefy the brains of any person that drinks thereof; but it operates diversely, according to the constitution of the person. Some it keeps sleepy, some merry, putting them into a laughing fit, and others it makes mad; but after two or three hours

> they come to themselves again . . . What other use this plant may
> serve for I know not; but I know it is much esteemed here, and in
> other places too whither it is transported.

Did he try it? He does not say, but from his description it seems unlikely.
Perhaps he didn't feel well enough to take the risk, for it's unlike him
not to be experimental.

The principal exports of the place were gold and pepper, and the East
Indies merchant Alexander Hamilton confirms that gold-dust was the
main export of the area. Local money was made of copper or block-tin
in the form of coin, and the lowest-denomination coins were called 'cash'.

Both Dampier and Hamilton remark on the extreme severity with
which crimes were punished. Both mention amputation of hands or feet;
Hamilton adds impaling. It's tempting to imagine Hamilton and Dampier
meeting. They were both at Achin at the same time, for each writes of
an English ship, the *Dorothy*, under Captain Thwaite, arriving in the
harbour to trade. The queen of Achin sent Thwaite two dancing girls to
entertain him, and Dampier's description of their traditional dance shows
that the style then was as it is now: 'rather writhing their hands and
bodies with several antick gestures than moving much out of the place
they were in'. As the East India Company was at war with the great
moghul, Thwaite abused the queen's hospitality by capturing one of the
moghul's ships, then also in the harbour. There was a great uproar, and
Dampier and others ashore had to take refuge on another English ship
in order to avoid the risk of imprisonment. As a result of the upheaval
Dampier's flux returned with a vengeance, even preventing him from
keeping his journal. But the affray soon blew over, and he was able to
get ashore again.

By May 1689, Dampier was well enough to travel again, and shipped as
mate aboard a trading sloop. Soon afterwards her captain fell ill and Dampier
was made commander. He took in a cargo and was preparing to sail for
Pegu, but at the last moment his orders were cancelled and he had to
trans-ship his cargo to another vessel. Another disappointment soon followed. An unemployed captain bought a quarter share of the sloop and
consequently took command. As a mere employee, Dampier had to eat
humble pie and, needing the work, accept again the position of mate.

This time they prepared to sail for Malacca, with a cargo of opium. Dampier had a row with the supercargo about the course, but the captain supported his mate, and though they nearly ran ashore shortly afterwards, Dampier was able to redirect the helmsman and save them from trouble. Anchoring to take in water at Pulo Verero, they met a Danish ship whose surgeon, Dampier discovered, was none other than his old comrade Herman Coppinger, but he tells us little of any conversation they had, beyond Coppinger's concern that his ship might not be able to take in pepper at Johor on account of an exclusive trade agreement they had discovered the Dutch had there.

When they arrived at Malacca with their opium, they learned that William and Mary had been crowned king and queen of England. This did not mean that the Dutch would not guard their trade monopolies any less fiercely, but English traders were at least exempt from duty. However, opium was 'prohibited goods', though 'a great commodity here at this time'.

They pretended they had not come in to trade at all, but to refit their vessel. Under cover of this pretence, Mr Coventry, the supercargo, found a Dutch buyer, but then the plot thickened. The Dutchman undertook to pay a price for the opium which equalled the value of all his considerable property. Then he discovered that the opium was of grossly inferior quality. Mr Coventry insisted that he be paid the agreed price, upon which the man absconded. Coventry then exerted pressure on the man's wife, who co-managed their business, through the local magistrate, who at first be-rated Coventry for not having done the business with him! Dampier adds:

> I saw this Dutchman on board his own vessel when he had bought the opium, and he was very pensive and sad. He had a pretty fine house without [outside] the gates [of the town], and a garden which maintained his family with pot-herbs, salading and fruits, besides some for the market. This was managed by his wife, and he himself had two sloops, and either employed them in trading among the Malayans [a name Dampier uses for all the local inhabitants of this area] for pepper, carrying them such commodities as they wanted, especially opium, or by hiring himself and the sloop to the Dutch East India Company . . .

When the magistrate obliged the wife to pay (no doubt taking a cut for his trouble), 'she complained they were utterly undone, for the opium, when it came to be examined, was really very bad, and worth little or nothing'. Although Dampier's tone is sympathetic to the Dutchman, he continued to work for Mr Coventry, and says nothing at all in criticism of the supercargo's actions.

The Dutch were much better disposed towards the English after the accession of William of Orange to the British throne, and Coventry was able to do some more reputable trading before returning to Achin at the end of the year. On their way, they stopped off at a little Dutch fort on Pulo Dinding. Here they found the Dutch colony in great fear of the Malayans, with whom they nevertheless traded, and this fear gave rise to an amusing incident – amusing at least to read about. The Dutch and the English exchanged courtesies, and the governor of the little colony invited the English to dine:

> the food was brought into the dining room and placed on the table. The dishes and plates were of silver, and there was a silver punch-bowl full of liquor. The governor, his guests, and some of his officers were seated, but just as they began to fall to, one of the soldiers cried out: Malayans, and spoiled the entertainment; for immediately the governor, without speaking one word, leapt out of one of the windows, to get as soon as he could to the fort. His officers followed, and all the servants that attended were soon in motion. Every one of them took the nearest way, some out of the windows, others out of the doors, leaving the three guests by themselves, who soon followed with all the haste they could make, without knowing the meaning of this sudden consternation of the governor and his people.

Fear of the Malayans was not peculiar to Pulo Dinding, though its isolation must have increased the nervousness of the colonists. Indeed, the uproar which ruined the dinner party had been caused by a Malay attack on a Dutch boat which was out catching fish for the governor's table. They returned to Achin without incident.

At Achin at Christmas-time 1689, our mariner ran into Edward Morgan, who, he tells us now for the first time, was one of the crew of the *Cygnet*.

Morgan's story is complex. It's enough to say here that he and Herman Coppinger remained with the *Cygnet* until she reached the coast of Coromandel, where they left her and enlisted in the Danish ship which we have already seen Dampier meet. Morgan's path was to cross significantly with Dampier's again, so it is worth introducing him briefly here.

Early in 1690 Dampier set off on another trading voyage, this time to Madras. Here he met a trader by the name of Moody, who arrived from Mindanao in April. With him were three of Dampier's former shipmates from the *Cygnet*, from whom he learnt the fate of Charles Swan. Also with him was the 'painted prince' Jeoly, and his mother.

Jeoly, to whom I will return, was a princeling in his late twenties, brought by Moody from the Philippines. He and his mother were extraordinary in that their bodies were covered with tattoos. Tattoos were little known in Europe – the tradition of tattooing among sailors dates from the time of Cook's voyages in the late eighteenth century – and so he was a great curiosity. Jeoly was to accompany Dampier home – the last, for this voyage, of our mariner's ill-fated money-making schemes.

Dampier and Moody hit it off well. Moody, who spoke fluent Malay, was ordered by the governor of Madras to go to Indrapore (Inderapura) on the west coast of Sumatra, and take over the management of an English factory there. Moody wanted Dampier to go with him, but Dampier had already been offered the post of mate on a ship bound for the Bay of Bengal, which he had a great desire to visit, out of pure curiosity. To woo him from that purpose, Moody offered to buy a small ship at Indrapore and make Dampier commander of it, sending him with Jeoly and his mother to their home island of Meangis (?Kepulauan Talaud), 'by which means I might gain a commerce with [Jeoly's] people for cloves'.

Dampier was never a man to ignore the possibilities of a business venture, and he immediately agreed to this proposition. They sailed together from Madras in July in the *Diamond*, commanded by Captain Howel. But contrary winds forced them from their route to Indrapore and they were forced to put in at Bencouli (Bengkulu), where there was an English settlement, Fort York.

James Sowdon, the governor, offered Dampier the post of gunner, telling him that he would do the East India Company more service here than elsewhere, and offering him twenty-four dollars a month salary. Dampier, who had picked up some knowledge of fortifications on his travels, was tempted. He consulted Mr Moody, who delayed his answer for a week:

> and then, being ready to be gone to Indrapore, he told me I might use my own liberty, either to stay here, or go with him to Indrapore. He added, that if I went with him, he was not certain, as yet, to perform his promise, in getting a vessel for me to go to Meangis with Jeoly and his mother; but he would be so fair to me, that because I left Maderas [*sic*] on his account, he would give me the half share of the two painted people, and leave them in my possession. I accepted of the offer, and writings were immediately drawn between us.

Dampier also accepted Sowdon's offer.

We learn little of what Jeoly's emotions were, but Dampier treated him well and was soon conversing with him and his mother in Malayan, of which Jeoly had some knowledge. Jeoly told our mariner all about Meangis, and Dampier learned that there were plenty of cloves, nutmegs, and a greater treasure to be had there. 'There is abundance of gold in Meangis,' Jeoly told him.

Jeoly also said that he had five wives, one of whom had tattooed him.

> He was painted all down the breast, between his shoulders behind; on his thighs (mostly) before; and in the form of several broad rings, or bracelets, round his arms and legs. I cannot liken the drawings to any figure of animals, or the like, but they were very curious, full of great variety of lines, flourishes, chequered work, &c., keeping a very graceful proportion, and appearing very artificial, even to wonder, especially that upon and between his shoulder-blades.

Jeoly had been captured by Mindanaoans with his father and mother, and sold into slavery at Mindanao, where he had languished for at least four years. Jeoly had asked Captain Read to take him from Mindanao back to his own country, though there is no suggestion that Dampier had known him before he met him at Madras. Moody had bought him for sixty dollars and, in a sense, rescued him.

At Bencouli, Dampier had no employment for Jeoly and his mother, so they found work for themselves – she mended their clothes after a fashion, for they were unused to wearing clothes at all, and he made a sea-chest out of a few boards and nails begged of Dampier. 'It was but an ill-shaped thing, but he was as proud of it as if it had been the rarest piece in the world.' They lived in a house outside the fort. Then, soon afterwards, they both became ill, and despite Dampier's care for them – not only was he fond of them but went to great lengths to get them the best attention – the mother died.

> I did what I could to comfort Jeoly, but he took on extremely, insomuch that I feared him also. Therefore I caused a grave to be made presently, to hide her out of his sight. I had her shrouded decently in a piece of new calico, but Jeoly was not so satisfied, for he wrapped all her clothes about her, and two new pieces of chintz that Mr Moody gave her . . .

Bencouli was an unhealthy place, and it is possible that Jeoly's mother had succumbed either to dysentery or typhus.

Meanwhile, Dampier did his best to fulfil his duties as the governor's gunner. He made gunpowder, and overhauled the defences of the fort as well as he could, given the incompetence of those with whom he had to work. It is hard to imagine why he was ever tempted to throw in his lot with the governor.

James Sowdon was a former book-keeper who had risen to the rank of governor when his predecessor and all his officers were carried off unexpectedly by disease. He was a weak and duplicitous man who drank heavily. Dampier calls him 'brutish and barbarous'. Alexander Hamilton describes how four local princes referred their disputes to Sowdon, who 'soon determined their differences in favour of the two that complained, and because the others seemed dissatisfied with his determination, ordered both their heads to be struck off, which ended their disputes effectually, and made them afterwards to make up differences among themselves . . .' Sowdon was eventually recalled to Madras, disciplined, and replaced by Charles Fleetwood. Dampier, on closer acquaintance with Sowdon, was appalled at the governor's behaviour, at the impression he made on the local people, and at the damage it did to trade and good relations.

Sowdon now tried to cheat Dampier of his pay. In retaliation, Dampier had the stakes which partly marked out a second bastion for the fort (he had completed the marking-out of a first) removed – 'and put them to seek a new method, for I knew none of them did understand how to do it'.

Dampier wanted to get away. He tells us, 'I began to long after my native country, after so tedious a ramble from it . . .' I doubt if he was homesick. The lines I've quoted were written for publication. He was expressing a conventional emotion, expected by his readers, and his publisher probably insisted that he put in some such thing. But he certainly needed to leave Bencouli, and he did want to get Jeoly back to England.

Jeoly was still very unwell. His survival was vital to Dampier, who intended not only to show him for money in England, but to persuade merchants there to equip a ship in which Dampier could return with Jeoly to Meangis and the other islands in its small group, and establish a trading post there. Dampier had himself touched at Meangis during the wanderings of the *Cygnet*, so he had a sketchy knowledge of the place.

There were still difficulties to be overcome; not least, getting away from Sowdon:

Upon these projects, I went to the governor and council, and desired that I might have my discharge to go for England with the next ship that came. The council thought it reasonable, and they consented to it; he [Sowdon] also gave me his word that I should go. Upon 2nd January 1691, there came to anchor in Bencouli Road the *Defence*, Captain Heath commander, bound for England, in the service of the Company. They had been in Indrapore, where Mr Moody then was, and he had made over his share in Prince Jeoly to Mr Goddard, chief mate of the ship. Upon his coming on shore, he showed me Mr Moody's writings, and looked upon Jeoly, who had been sick for three months, in all which time I tended him as carefully as if he had been my brother. I agreed matters with Mr Goddard, and sent Jeoly on board, intending to follow him as I could, and desiring Mr Goddard's assistance to fetch me off, and conceal me aboard the ship, if there should be occasion; which he promised to do, and the captain promised to entertain me. For it proved, as I had foreseen, that upon Captain Heath's arrival, the governor repented him of his promise, and would not suffer me to depart. I importuned him all I could; but in vain; so did Captain Heath also, but to no purpose. In short, after several essays, I slipped away at midnight (understanding the ship was to sail away the next morning, and that they had taken leave of the fort), and creeping through one of the port-holes of the fort, I got to the shore, where the ship's boat waited for me, and carried me aboard. I brought with me my journal and most of my written papers, but some papers and books of value I left in haste, and all my furniture; being glad I was myself at liberty, and had hopes of seeing England again.

Thus he made his escape. Materially, he had as little as when he set out. But in knowledge and experience of unknown countries, he had become one of the richest men in the world.

The *Defence* left for the Cape of Good Hope on 25th January 1691. To begin with, it was not a comfortable voyage. Many of the passengers and crew, Dampier included, had picked up sickness at Bencouli. The water was bad, black as ink, and stowed among the cargo of pepper in the hold, which made it very hot to drink. Also, the *Defence* had been at sea three years, and meat that has been salted that long was, as Dampier says with restraint, 'but ordinary food for sickly men to feed on'. He was continuously anxious for Jeoly. To alleviate the suffering of his passengers and crew, Captain Heath broke open a private store of tamarinds, and distributed them.

Eventually they reached the Cape of Good Hope. There is no room here to record all Dampier's impressions. He continued to be ill, but his eye misses nothing:

There is a very beautiful sort of wild ass in this country, whose body is curiously striped with equal lists of white and black; the stripes coming from the ridge of his back, and ending under the belly, which is white. These stripes are two or three fingers broad, running parallel with each other, and curiously intermixed, one white and one black, over from the shoulder to the rump.

There are few earlier accurate descriptions of the zebra.

His description of the Hottentots is not as extreme as that of Ambrosia Cowley, who had passed this way on his own way home some years earlier, and William shows less simple revulsion for their habits. He describes them instead with a modern disinterestedness which reveals the scientist in him. He paints a picture of a race already degraded by contact with Europeans, and reduced to drudges by the local Dutch colonists. They only come to life when dancing in the moonlight, which Dampier describes movingly. His feelings towards them are more of sympathy than revulsion:

> They all seem very busy, both men, women and children, dancing very oddly on the green grass by their houses. They traced to and fro promiscuously, often clapping their hands and singing aloud. Their faces were sometimes to the east and sometimes to the west; neither did I see any motion or gesture that they used when their faces were towards the moon, more than when their backs were toward it . . . In the grey light of morning I walked out again, and found many of the men and women still singing and dancing, who continued their mirth till the moon went down, and then they left off . . .

By contrast with the Hottentots, the Dutch appeared to live an idyllic existence. Dampier praises the fine white wine which they were already producing, and the wonderful climate of the Cape restored his health in no small way.

The *Defence* sailed from South Africa on 23rd May on the last stage of her voyage home, in a small convoy of English ships. They touched at St Helena, where 'many of the seamen got sweethearts'. One married, another got engaged and brought his betrothed back to England with him. Dampier says:

> several other of our men were over head and ears in love with the Santa Hellena maids, who though they were born here, yet very earnestly desired to be released from that prison, which they have no other way to compass, but by marrying seamen, or passengers that touch here.

Most of these girls were half-English.

Love was not for Dampier, who stayed ashore only two days, to get supplies for himself and the still-languishing Jeoly. Mr Goddard evidently left Jeoly's care entirely to Dampier. They left St Helena on 2nd July, and shortly before they crossed the Line, had a distant sight of Captain Thwaite's *Dorothy*, bound again for the East Indies.

At length the seas grew greyer and colder, and at last, on 16th September 1691, the *Defence* reached the anchorages of Deal Road. Dampier was home.

Immediately, economic matters pressed. Poor Jeoly was sold off a share at a time until finally Dampier had no more interest in him. 'I fell among rooks,' he laments again; but he needed money and had no choice. It must have been hard for him to see poor Jeoly taken away from him, as they had a genuine fondness for one another. Dampier also regretted the loss of his investment.

Jeoly was put on display as a rarity. A broadsheet advertising him still exists. Part of it reads:

> This admirable person is about the age of 30, graceful and well-proportioned in all his limbs, extremely modest and civil, neat and cleanly; but his language is not understood, neither can he speak English.
>
> He is exposed to public view every day (during his stay in Town) from the 16th day of this instant June, at his lodgings at the Blue Boar's Head in Fleet Street, near Water Lane, where he will continue for some time, if his health will permit.
>
> But if any persons of quality, gentlemen or ladies, do desire to see this noble person, at their own houses, or any other convenient place, in or about this City of London, they are desired to send timely notice, and he will be ready to wait upon them in a coach or chair, any time they please to appoint, if in the daytime.

We see from this that he was still alive nine months after his arrival in England. There is no evidence that he was treated badly, but he must have felt lonely and abandoned. Had Dampier discussed with him his plans to return to Meangis? If so, the shattering of that dream must have been frightful. Once Dampier had sold his share in him (and it is likely that Goddard did the same), he did not see him again. Now he was surrounded by people with whom he could not even communicate. Whether he ever fully recovered his health is unlikely, especially as he arrived on the bleak northern island of Britain at the onset of winter. We do not know how long he lasted. Dampier simply tells us that he died of smallpox at Oxford.

PART THREE

The *Roebuck* Voyage

CHAPTER FOURTEEN

An Interlude at Home

Between his arrival home in 1691 (soon after his fortieth birthday and twelve years since he had left England) and the publication of *A New Voyage round the World* in 1697, we know little of Dampier's life. He tells us nothing in his published writings. He must have visited his brother, George, in Dorset, and he must have been curious enough to have a look at the estate he had bought there so many years earlier. Was George looking after it? Or was he obliged to sell it to raise some cash? And where was Judith? Did she live down there, or in London? Had she remained in the household of the Duchess of Grafton, or left it? What would she and William have had to say to each other? It is scarcely conceivable that they could have taken up the reins of their marriage after so long – could their relationship be called a marriage? Women married to mariners were used to long periods of separation, but these two had had no life together before he went away, and even if he had not originally intended to be away long, there is nothing in Dampier's writings, even allowing for the fact that he was such a reserved man about his personal life, to suggest that he missed her. What if the Santa Maria gold mine scheme had worked? What if he had been able to settle at Mindanao or Meangis? It is hard to believe that he felt great ties to his country, or to anyone in it. Yet, once he was home, he involved himself in society with energy.

This was to take a while, however. One of the ways in which he must have passed the 'missing' years between 1691 and 1697 was by working up his journal for publication, though how he met his publisher, James Knapton, and when, is not certain. It is likely that Knapton approached him. London was a relatively small place then, and Dampier would have quickly come to the attention of a publisher who had seen the potential of the fashionable interest in travel. Following the publication and success of Dampier's first book, Knapton was to publish a whole string of books about nautical exploration, and inspire many imitators.

Let us deal with what we know. There are clues to pick up. In *A New Voyage*, Dampier makes a passing reference to being at anchor at the Groyne (Corunna) in July 1694. Dampier's biographer, Clennell Wilkinson, has argued against the likelihood of this, suggesting that 1694 might be a copyist's error for 1691 – when Dampier might have been at Corunna on his way home. However, evidence has recently come to light which suggests that he was indeed there in 1694.

In August 1694, Dampier was promoted to second mate on a galley which was one of a small fleet of four ships at Corunna, destined to trade with Spanish colonists in the West Indies and to salvage wrecked Spanish treasure-ships. However, the fleet never reached the Caribbean. Eighty-five of the 200-odd crewmen mutinied, took control of one of the ships, renamed her the *Fancy*, and went off 'on the account' under the command of Henry Every, who was to become one of the most successful pirates in history.

Dampier was not one of those who joined the pirates. From what we know of him, he may have been tempted; but other considerations – almost certainly not moral scruples, however – must have stopped him. He may not have felt like another long cruise. It is possible that his affairs in England were more pressing or interesting than another 'ramble'. In any event, he remained with the fleet, and returned to England on 8th February 1695. In London, Dampier and others went to law to recover unpaid wages – as usual, Dampier's finances pressed hard. In both 1695 and 1696 Dampier appeared in court, both in a civil law suit and in criminal proceedings against some of the crew of the *Fancy* who had been arrested on their return to England.

All this sheds interesting light, as we will see, on Dampier's demeanour and attitudes during the period of his captaincy of HMS *Roebuck*, and goes some way towards explaining why he got on so badly with his lieutenant, George Fisher, on that voyage. Fisher does not emerge as a particularly attractive or reliable character, but his persecution complex may not have been completely without foundation when one considers that two at least of the officers on board the *Roebuck* were fellow seamen of Dampier's on the Spanish expedition described above; and that Dampier always expressed himself well-disposed towards Every and his crew, and let three of them go when he encountered them at Bahia in Brazil. I will return to this; but I think it's worth mentioning now.

Before we leave this subject, and deal with what we know of how Dampier spent the rest of his time before the *Roebuck* voyage, I hope it is worth making a small digression about the remarkable Henry Every.

He was a close contemporary of Dampier, born in Plymouth about 1653, and served as an officer in the Royal Navy before turning pirate. In 1694, he was first or second mate of the *Charles*, or possibly the *Duke*, a privateering vessel bound for the Spanish Caribbean with the fleet described above. Pay to the crews of the fleet was delayed, and it lay for several months off Corunna. On 7th May 1694, when the captain of the *Charles* was incapacitated with drink in his cabin – a not uncommon occurrence with him – Every took command. 'I am bound to Madagascar,' he said, 'with the design of making my own fortune, and that of all the brave fellows joined with me.' Renaming the ship the *Fancy*, they sailed off around the west coast of Africa, attacking three English ships at the Cape Verdes, and two Danes near Principe Island off the mainland. Arriving at Madagascar, he refitted and then cruised for the pilgrim fleets bound from Surat to Mocha and Mecca. Merchants travelled with the fleets to trade spices and textiles for coffee and gold; and ships belonging to the great moghul sailed with them too.

Every's greatest *coup* was the taking of one of the moghul's treasure-ships, the massive *Ganj-i-Sawai*. This huge vessel carried forty guns and 400 muskets to defend her, but she was no match for the skilfully deployed little pirate fleet which Every now commanded. The taking of this prize became an inspiration for a number of plays and other works of fiction. In truth, Every's crew committed appalling atrocities upon the men and women on board the ship, and there were massive diplomatic repercussions in India when the great moghul took reprisals against the officers of the East India Company. An embarrassed England did all it could to bring the villains to book. Every himself was now master of a vast treasure, which has been estimated at £1,000 per share. He decided to retire, but after various adventures he succumbed to a fatal desire to return home, where he was bilked of his money by local businessmen, who probably knew full well where it had come from, and died in poverty at Bideford in Devon.

Another involvement of Dampier was with a Scottish plan for establishing a colony on the Isthmus of Darien. Scotland and England still had separate parliaments, and the scheme was derived from an Act of the Scottish parliament for 'Encouraging Foreign Trade'. It was the brainchild of William Paterson, a businessman who was also one of the founders of the Bank of England, and became a director, though he sold out after a quarrel at the end of the first year. A man 'of more imagination than judgement', in 1695 he was involved in the foundation of the Company of Scotland Trading to Africa and the Indies. Scotland wanted to assert itself as a trade rival to England, and although commerce in the East Indies was oversubscribed, there were still possibilities in the West, especially as Spain's grasp on power there had been consistently weakened by the depredations of the buccaneers. Even before publication of *A New Voyage*, Dampier's reputation had gone ahead of him, because Paterson sought his acquaintance, and from him received a copy of Lionel Wafer's detailed description of the isthmus. As we have seen, Dampier's manuscript, preserved in the British Library, contains a transcript by him of Wafer's work. I cannot say for sure why Dampier made such a transcript. The two men were friends; Dampier considered Wafer's work valuable, and may have wanted to incorporate part of it into his own.

Commercial espionage is nothing new, and it wasn't long before rumours of the Scottish plan reached the ears of the Lords of Trade and Plantations in London. They summoned Dampier in June 1697 and asked him what he knew of the Darien scheme. He told them that the man they really ought to be talking to was Lionel Wafer, so the two seafarers appeared again before the authorities on 2nd July. They gave Wafer a special grilling, and he responded with a monograph called *An Answer to Queries Proposed by the Honourable Council of Trade*. The English took the report seriously, and wanted to put a stop to Scottish ambitions in the area. They proposed to annex Golden Island in the San Blas Archipelago and its adjacent port for the Crown. Dampier and Wafer both deposed that a settlement of 500 people would be perfectly viable in Darien. They apparently neglected to mention the vile climate and the incidence of diseases, fatal to Europeans not inured to them. In fairness, Wafer does state in an undated manuscript report to Thomas, Duke of Leeds, that one proviso would be 'agreement . . . with the Court of Spain'. He further suggests, very sensibly, a number of other places ripe for colonization by the English, including the estuary of the Rio de la Plata, and the countryside surrounding Valdivia. He warns off the islands close to Cape Horn: they were full of 'wild Indians'; 'nor do I find the Spaniards have any settlement in these parts worth the taking notice of, and to be sure if there were honey the bees would be there'.

Meanwhile, Paterson's business partner, Fletcher of Saltoun, entertained Wafer at Pontack's Coffee House. Wafer was also talking privately with a consortium of English businessmen about an expedition to exploit the big dyewood grove which Lacenta, the Indian chief, had shown him as an incentive to return. These businessmen advanced some money to Wafer to delay publication of his book, so that they could keep the knowledge it contained to themselves. This deal did not prevent Wafer from negotiating a fee of £750 with the Scots to advise and even act for them. He put his affairs in London in order and travelled to Scotland using the cover-name of 'Mr Brown', ready to sail from there to Darien on behalf of the Scots if necessary. £50 had been paid down; but now the Scottish businessmen looked to see if they could get all the information they needed from Wafer, and then deny him the balance of his fee. Wafer, entirely naïve, told them all they needed to know, and they duly cheated him of the balance, making an excuse for the pretended abandonment of the project and paying him an *ex gratia* fee of twenty guineas for his trouble. A good deal of skullduggery, accusation and counter-accusation followed, both within the Scottish Company and in London, where Wafer returned to find that his two-timing had been revealed to the Lords of Trade and Plantations. In this connection Dampier was interrogated on 13th July 1698. Dampier told them with a certain *froideur* that he knew nothing of Wafer's dealings, and that in any case he did not think Wafer capable of doing the Scots any great service – which must have been a lie to save Wafer, for Wafer's knowledge of Darien was immense.

In the meantime the Scottish expedition was organized, and set off. The Scottish colonists reached Crab Island, near Anguilla, and there a pilot offered himself to them in the person of none other than Captain Robert Alleston, of the original Darien expedition of 1680, who rejoiced in the reputation of being 'one of the oldest privateers now alive', according to the journal of Hugh Rose. It is a pity that Rose does not tell us how old, exactly.

Alleston duly took them to Golden Island, where they met another two old acquaintances of ours, the Indian chief Andreas, who reminisced happily about Davis and Sharp, and Captain Tristian, who had been 'forced to live a great while among the Indians', whose language he now spoke.

The colonists made it to the mainland and also established a settlement, New Edinburgh, on Golden Island, but the rest of their story is a tragic one of mismanagement, bad luck – they never found Lacenta's dyewood grove, if indeed it ever really existed, or any gold – and disease. In the end, a local war with the Spanish put an end to the entire venture in 1700. A result of this disaster was the Act of Union between England and Scotland in 1707. King William had supported the development of Scotland, and this horrific product of ill-advised and by now anachronistic rivalry between the two nations led to their joining. King William died five years before the union he hoped for was achieved.

As for Wafer, as we have seen he published his book in 1699 with James Knapton. Dampier allowed him to reproduce one of his maps. Wafer's book sold well, and gave rise to several spin-offs, including a delightful and anonymous optimistic conflation of both Wafer's and Dampier's works from which one quotation (originally in Wafer) must be taken:

They [the Indian women] take great care of their husbands when they have made themselves drunk: for when they perceive him so, they get one or two more women to assist them to take him up, and put him into his hammock, where, as he lies snoring, they stand by, and sprinkle water to cool him, washing his hands, feet and face, stroking off that water with their hands as it grows warm.

Wafer remained in London until at least 1704, and was in touch with Paterson again before that year with new schemes for Darien. Nothing came of them, and it's assumed that he died in London sometime during or before 1705, though there is no proof of this. But interest in the South Seas remained alive, and, long after Dampier's and Wafer's deaths, exploded in the great financial madness and collapse of the South Sea Bubble in 1720.

It is disappointing that Dampier kept no journal of his activities during this period of his life, but the lack of one indicates that he undertook no major voyage. In preparing the record of his twelve-year journey he spared no pains, and it is accepted today that the work is wholly his own, though he tells us himself that he sought the help of friends in polishing his style. That is typical of him: he is not falsely modest in the things he knows about, but when he is uncertain of something, or feels that he is venturing into an area where he is underqualified, he will seek help from someone he believes more expert, and quote their authority with due credit. He was, however, not spared the slander of envious tongues, for he writes aggrievedly in his second book, *A Voyage to New Holland*:

> Others have taxed me with borrowing from other men's journals; and with insufficiency, as if I was not myself the author of what I write, but published things digested and drawn up by others. As to the first part of this objection, I assure the reader, I have taken nothing from any man without mentioning his name, except some very few relations and particular observations received from credible persons who desired not to be named; and these I have always expressly distinguished in my books, from what I relate as of my own observing.

The manuscript in the British Museum is in the handwriting of a copyist with marginal emendations by Dampier, and it is not as full as the final version. The finished book was published in 1697. *A New Voyage round the World* was an immediate success and ran to several editions over the next three decades, as well as being translated into Dutch, French and German. Its maps were beautifully engraved by Herman Moll. Dampier had the sense (or was advised) to dedicate it to Charles Montague, Earl of Halifax, and President of the Royal Society at the time. The dedication pleased Halifax, and the book must have done so too, for Halifax recommended Dampier to Edward Russell, Earl of Orford, among whose posts was treasurer to the Navy. As a result Dampier was provided with a sinecure which he would enjoy for the rest of his life: an income of eight pounds and fifteen shillings per quarter, which came with a post as a land-carriage man at the Customs House. It cannot have been much more than an honorary position as an excise officer, and there is no evidence that Dampier fulfilled any consistent function there, but the regular money was welcome. The success of *A New Voyage* also brought in some funds, though it is likely that Knapton simply paid Dampier a flat fee for his work.

Few books of this type had appeared since Samuel Purchas and Richard Hakluyt had published their travel anthologies, with only modest success, at the beginning of the century. Exquemelin's *History of the Buccaneers of America* appeared in an English translation in 1685.

Dampier's work established a new, serious, analytical kind of travel writing, made readable by the brilliance of Dampier's style, which was often emulated. The Royal Society was impressed and Dampier was able to use his influence with its members to have his brother George's cure for 'the bitings of mad creatures' published in *Philosophical Transactions*, with a gloss by Sir Hans Sloane.

Dampier published a supplement, *Voyages and Descriptions*, which contained a detailed account of his travels in the East Indies, as well as of his life as a logwood-cutter, together with his influential technical work, *A Discourse of Winds*.

A word must be said about this remarkable piece of work. Without any of the sophisticated navigational instruments that began to make their appearance towards the end of the eighteenth century, but by observation and deduction, Dampier was able to compile a reliable handbook of ocean passages and of the different qualities of various winds, especially the trades. Writing as recently as 1931, Captain A. Colquhoun Bell states that Dampier's 'directions for using the Atlantic Trade winds are still the best that can be given, and will be found, with little alteration, in the Admiralty handbook upon ocean passages'. The *Discourse* was used and commended by every variety of commander, from Cook to Nelson. Cook, of course, was Dampier's true heir, and knew all his works, taking them with him on his own voyages of exploration.

Captain Bell has this to add in respect of the *Discourse*:

> though written with none of these [modern] aids, [it] is nonetheless
> a practical handbook, which has been rearranged but never super-
> seded. The seaman who consults the paragraphs on winds and
> weather at the beginning of each volume of *Admiralty Sailing Directions*
> is probably unaware that he could get the same information from
> the *Discourse of Winds*.

Dampier was working on winds at about the same time as his contemporary, the astronomer and mathematician Edmond Halley. Joseph C.
Shipman, who has written about Dampier the scientist, finds that Dampier's maps surpass Halley's; and that where Halley's study of 1686 is
more complete, Dampier's is of greater practical application. Dampier
was also, incidentally, a good meteorologist. To this may be added that
the *Discourse* contains the most beautiful descriptions of weather – cloud
patterns, storms and winds.

As a man well versed in the practicalities of navigation, Dampier was
also able to correct to some extent previously erroneous measurements
of distance between one coast and another, or to pinpoint with greater
accuracy the location of islands, through re-examining the calculation of
longitude. This could not become an exact science until the invention
of the marine chronometer, but a rough estimate could be obtained by
'dead-reckoning'. This meant keeping a record both of the compass bearing
and the distance sailed every day. Latitude was found by measuring the
altitude of the sun with a backstaff or a quadrant – 'shooting the sun' –
and making a calculation based on the reading. Of course this wasn't
possible when the sky was overcast. The backstaff had been invented by
John Davis in 1595. Its advantage over the more primitive cross-staff was
that the navigator didn't have to squint into the sun to take a reading,
but stood with his back to it and measured its shadow. Some of these
instruments were fairly easy to construct if you knew how – Ringrose
describes making a quadrant, for example, which was a precursor of the
sextant and the octant. The compass and the astrolabe completed the
basic equipment of the late-seventeenth-century navigator, though
there were several more instruments. Samuel Sturmy lists a large number

in his compendious *Mariner's Magazine*, together with instructions on how to make some of them. His all-embracing book, with sections on navigation, surveying, gunnery, astronomy and fortification, also contains tables of longitude and latitude, together with other tables and means of calculation; the book must have been a godsend to all mariners. Even so, it is extraordinary that there are no more stories of shipwrecks and lost ships than there are. What is interesting about Dampier, especially in his early voyages, is that his lowly rank meant that he did not always have access to either the instruments aboard ship or to the charts. Even Captain Swan kept his instruments in his cabin, though he must have given Dampier free use of them. For Dampier, whose interest in navigation had also led him to explore the field of compass variation, it must have been very frustrating at times; but the scale of his achievement in these technical areas is all the more impressive as a result. At least in measuring the angle of deviation from the true north and south line of the compass needle, he would have had his own instrument. And even when he does not know why something should be, since he is the first to notice it, he records that it is so, for other minds to work on.

Voyages and Descriptions, the supplement to *A New Voyage round the World*, was dedicated to the Earl of Orford, whose other offices included membership of the Privy Council, and Principal Lord of the Admiralty. Dampier addresses him with suitable gratitude. Knapton advertised *Voyages and Descriptions* well in advance of its publication in February 1699, though it did not sell as well as the first volume. By then, its author was already at sea again.

Knapton sought out similar works, and soon had several collections of voyages in print, as well as Lionel Wafer's *A New Voyage and Description of the Isthmus of America*. Wafer is careful to mention his connection with Dampier. Basil Ringrose's journal was worked up for publication and appeared as a new fourth book in the third edition of Exquemelin. Its editor justifies its inclusion on the grounds that it was 'said by Mr Dampier to be very exact'. The cartographer William Hack, who will be remembered as the London associate of Captain Sharp after the latter's return from the South Seas, produced a collection of *Voyages* which contains Ambrosia Cowley's account, and again stresses the Dampier connection. A seaman who sailed with Dampier on the latter's ill-fated third major voyage (described in Part Four of this book), William Funnell, wrote an account of it aping Dampier's style – not very adequately, it is true; but for some time the work was passed off as Dampier's own. By that time, Dampier himself had stopped writing.

The taste for travellers' tales lasted, with a few dips, virtually throughout the eighteenth century. Though scorned by such people as Samuel Johnson, for whom London was world enough, it continued as a result of the voyages of George Anson, who sailed round the world in the early 1740s, and Philip Carteret, who travelled with Admiral John Byron in 1764–6. The voyages of James Cook between 1768 and 1779 represent the apogee of English maritime exploration. Like Cook, Anson and Carteret took Dampier's books with them as guides.

Alongside the travel writing was a fashion for fictional works featuring seagoing adventurers as the hero. Charles Johnson, who has nothing to do with the Captain Charles Johnson who wrote the *History of the Most Notorious Pirates*, was a prolific though mediocre playwright whose most successful piece was produced at Drury Lane in 1713. It was called *The Successful Pyrate*. The hero, Arviragus, is a pirate king who lives in Madagascar. He is loosely based on Henry Every, and the central event of the plot is the taking of the *Ganj-i-Sawai*. Johnson perpetuates the myth that Every carried off the moghul's granddaughter from the ship and the plot is a fairly humdrum romance. What is interesting is the figure of Arviragus himself. He is a hero who has modern counterparts. A former naval officer with a superb war record, he was unjustly cashiered. Now a rebel, loosed from society's ties and in a sense at war with it, he is nevertheless cast as a benevolent dictator with democratic pretensions. Unlike the lesser characters, Johnson has him speak in blank verse, and though it is not particularly inspiring stuff, it's worth looking at because it shows well the romantic view of the free-spirited rover held by the city-bound dreamer and armchair traveller of the early eighteenth century. Ruling his island of Madagascar, there is not a little of Prospero in Arviragus too. Speaking of his crew, he says:

Have they not ranged the globe to serve my cause,
With me they made a circle round this world,
Disclaimed relation, country, friendship, fame,
They toiled, they bled, they burnt, they froze, they starved,
Each element and all mankind their foe,
Familiar to their eyes saw horrid Death,
In every climate, and in every shape,
When, in this isle, our shattered barks found rest,
With universal voice they called me king.
And when th' oppressor laughs, when right and wrong
Entangled lie in law; while Wealth is judge,
When Merit begs despised; while Justice sleeps,
Or winks for bribes, unpunished, may I fall,
Like some o'erweening tyrant, who believes
Himself a law, and governs by his lust.

As early as 1676 Wycherley had introduced naval characters to the stage, but Manly and Freeman in *The Plain Dealer* have little to do with nautical matters, and the first writer to produce fiction from first-hand experience of the sea was Smollett, whose *Roderick Random* wasn't published until 1728. Smollett's descriptions are graphic, and have the *imprimatur* of authenticity.

Dampier's influence on fictional literature was considerable, both as a source of material and as a stylist. Coleridge refers to him in *Table Talk* as a man 'of exquisite mind', and advises travel writers to use his style as a model. Sir Walter Scott and Andrew Lang both pay him homage. Nearer his own time, Defoe owes much to him for background in several of his novels, notably *Captain Singleton*, *A New Voyage round the World by a Course Never Sailed Before*, and, most famously, *Robinson Crusoe*, though he never acknowledges the debt. In fact, when describing (in 1724) nautical travel writers, he is patronizing – not without justification in the case of some of them; but generally his rudeness is ungrateful:

It has for some ages been thought so wonderful a thing to sail the tour or circle of the globe, that when a man has done this mighty feat he presently thinks it deserves to be recorded, like Sir Francis Drake's. So, as soon as men have acted the sailor, they come ashore and write books of their voyage, not only to make a great noise of what they have done themselves, but, pretending to show the way to others to come after them, they set up for teachers and chart-makers to posterity. Though most of them have had this misfortune, that whatever success they have had in the voyage, they have had very little in the relation, except it be to tell us that a seaman, when he comes to the press, is pretty much out of his element, and a very good sailor may make but a very indifferent author.

And so on.

Jonathan Swift's Gulliver refers directly to 'my cousin Dampier' in the introductory letter to his *Travels*. Swift's maps are pastiches of Dampier's, and his lands are located vaguely close to the lands Dampier visited. Setting out on his voyage to the country of the Houyhnhnms, Gulliver meets with Captain Pocock, of Bristol, 'who was going to the Bay of Campeachy to cut logwood . . . He was an honest man, and a good sailor, but a little too positive in his own opinions, which was the cause of his destruction, as it hath been of several others.' It is unlikely but not impossible that Swift knew Dampier: the thumbnail sketch of Captain Pocock bears a resemblance to our mariner. *Gulliver's Travels* was published in 1726, eleven years after Dampier's death: Swift had certainly read Dampier's work, and must have known, perhaps through mutual acquaintances, something of his stubborn character, and of the downfall which followed Dampier's command of HMS *Roebuck*. Swift, an outsider like Dampier, would have been sympathetic to his plight.

Swift also leans heavily on Dampier, and Samuel Sturmy, from whom he lifts one complete passage, for descriptions of storms and for technical nautical terms. Swift's Yahoos are a conflation of Dampier's Australian Aborigines and the Hottentots of the Cape of Good Hope.

The success of Dampier's book led to lionization in London. He is alluded to by the journalists of the day, notably by the dominant partnership of Addison and Steele. He was in vogue, his company was sought. At about this time he had the portrait painted by Thomas Murray. The man-about-town Charles Hatton wrote to his relative, Christopher, First Viscount Hatton, in May 1697, that 'I have discoursed with Dampier. He is a blunt fellow, but of better understanding than would be expected from one of his education.' Less patronizing but similar in his assessment of the mariner was John Evelyn, whose diary entry for 6th August 1698 reads:

> I dined with Mr Pepys, where was Captain Dampier, who had been a famous buccaneer, had brought hither the painted prince Job [*sic*], and printed a relation of his very strange adventure, and his observations. He was now going abroad again by the King's encouragement, who furnished a ship of 290 tons. He seemed a more modest man than one would imagine by relation of the crew he had assorted with. He brought a map of his observations of the course of the winds in the South Seas, and assured us that the maps hitherto extant were all false as to the Pacific Sea, which he makes on the south of the Line, that on the north end running by the coast of Peru being extremely tempestuous.

This opinion of the Pacific – that it only deserves that name south of the equator – is borne out in Dampier's own writing.

The expedition Evelyn refers to is HMS *Roebuck*'s voyage to New Holland. Dampier, having been given a captaincy in the Royal Navy, was its commander. It is a mark of Dampier's importance that Pepys invited him to dinner; and it is a pity that Pepys's poor eyesight had long since obliged him to abandon his own diary, for we can imagine a livelier assessment of our mariner coming from him than the dry one we get from Evelyn. Still, Pepys and Evelyn were both active members of the Royal Society, and Evelyn was sufficiently enthusiastic about Dampier to suggest that a medal to commemorate him be struck. It should be added that Dampier was one of a number of people thus recommended in Evelyn's *Numismata: A Discourse of Medals*, which appeared in 1699. Others, less distinguished, included poor Jeoly and, rather sweepingly, 'the rest of the buccaneers'. Perhaps it was their trail-blazing qualities that Evelyn admired.

One wonders, however, how much the lionization of Dampier was a fashionable thing of the moment. Perhaps it wasn't. Among the professionally involved, Dampier's reputation was made, and the setbacks of the next few years could not shake it. He had brought a spirit of scientific exactitude to travel writing, and it was precisely in tune with the expectations of the educated late-seventeenth-century mind. Dampier was a practical man, not a theorist, modestly making the discoveries he had made available to others, and leaving them to draw their own conclusions. In his mid forties, with a wealth of experience behind him, he found both his opinion and his company sought by the greatest minds in the land.

A month after dining with Pepys, Dampier was consulted by the Council of Trade and Plantations regarding the best way of fitting out an expedition to root the pirates out of their stronghold in Madagascar. By then, he was busy with the preparations for his new voyage, this time with official backing and blessing.

The book resulting from this voyage was the slimmest and the least polished that Dampier wrote, but the nature of the expedition was very different from what he had been used to. In February 1703, Dampier produced the account of his *Voyage to New Holland*, dedicated to the Earl of Pembroke, who was President of the Privy Council. It was to be his last book. His eye for detail is undiminished, and he brought back with him not only specimens of the flora, but the first descriptions of the fauna of Australia. Though the artist who accompanied him was not good, Dampier's own descriptions enable us easily to identify species which still exist in the same locations.

Nevertheless, there is a certain heaviness in Dampier now. It was not the easiest of voyages, and it was to end in disaster.

CHAPTER FIFTEEN

Captain Dampier, RN

The explorations of Janzoon in 1606 and Tasman in 1642–3 and 1644 had established beyond a doubt the existence of a Southern Continent. From his letters it is clear that Dampier had deduced that New Holland was a distinct land mass, not attached to the supposed vast continent of Terra Australis Incognita. He saw, too, that here was a great opportunity for exploration, and he considered it likely that gold would be found there.

Lord Orford asked him to put up a proposal for the expedition. Orford would have read the passages in *A New Voyage* where Dampier described his fleeting acquaintance with the Southern Continent, and it is likely that his imagination would have been fired by it. The drawback was that, although the authorities were persuaded to back an expedition, they did not want to invest too much money in it. It was not until the North American colonies were lost seventy-seven years later that Australia would become important to Britain. But, in case there were riches to be had there, it seemed a good idea to send out a man with some experience of those seas to reconnoitre. And from his wanderings in the *Cygnet*, Dampier knew that if New Holland itself yielded nothing, yet there were islands and countries lying off its north coast which 'might probably be visited with good advantage'. But there is also truth in the remark by Admiral Burney that the *Roebuck* voyage was 'one of the few instances which the early navigations afford of a voyage being undertaken expressly for the acquisition of knowledge, without a prospect to other immediate advantage'. There was peace in Europe at the time. King William III was Dutch, and Dutch possessions lay closest to the great unknown southern land. It was natural that interest in it should be keen.

The attention paid to Dampier in London must have emboldened him. He was highly thought of, and he had cordial relations with many eminent and powerful members of the Royal Society. He was never invited to become a member, nor would he ever have been treated by any of them as an equal, for his background was rural working class, and he had no hope of ever belonging to the Establishment. Perhaps he was over-confident. He had never commanded a ship, still less an expedition, and so far his life of exploration had been one of opportunism, not of planned discovery. The Navy was far from being the organization it was to become. Under William III matters had begun, very slowly, to improve. Samuel Pepys had achieved great things, but there was still a long way to go. The bulk of the crews were pressed men, and the officers were not all professional sailors. Interestingly, however, the ordinary seamen's love for and loyalty to a good captain is described in many sources.

There was no established uniform. Army red was the colour of the officers' coats – dark blue was still far in the future. Discipline was harsh and arbitrary. Captains and their senior officers frequently fell out and even came to blows. The threat of mutiny was ever present. In these circumstances Dampier might have bitten off more than he could chew. It is to his credit that, despite all his disadvantages, he managed to complete the task set him, though he would receive no credit for it. He had a poor ship and an inexperienced crew, which led him to choose people he knew from the old days where possible. He was especially cursed in his first lieutenant, a career officer of inflexible manner whose personality clashed totally with that of his captain; though to be fair to George Fisher the reservations he had about Dampier were understandable from his point of view, if not justifiable. Dampier was a newcomer to the Navy, and knew neither its ways or the finer points of its etiquette. Fisher comes across as a peevish snob; but he did know the Navy, and he was loyal to its rules and traditions. He may also have had influential friends to help him when the final confrontation came.

Fisher knew that Dampier was a former buccaneer – Dampier's past career was not a secret – and he suspected from the first that his captain had it in mind to run away with the ship. These suspicions were deepened by the fact that Dampier had engaged at least two old associates for the voyage; though the real reason for this was that they were experienced seamen whom Dampier knew and trusted. Fisher was making trouble for his captain before the *Roebuck* even sailed. Indeed, the whole voyage had a subplot of intrigue and insubordination, which will be described in the next chapter.

Dampier's proposals to Orford are long and detailed:

> Your Lordship has been pleased to make me a proposal of some voyage wherein I might be serviceable to my nation. I know there are several places which might probably be visited with good advantage, but as there is no larger tract of land hitherto than the *Terra Australis* (if that vast space surrounding the South Pole, and extending so far into the warmer climate be a continued land, as a great deal of it is known to be) so 'tis reasonable to conceive that so great a part of the world is not without very valuable commodities to encourage the discovery . . .

His requirements are modest and sensible:

> If I be pitched for an expedition of this kind I would desire to have a commission as unlimited as might be, with respect either to time or place, for in so long a voyage, and an attempt so full of difficulties, 'tis impossible to foresee a thousand accidents which may require the going somewhat aside from the principal design; and may at the same time offer a yet more valuable opportunity of some collateral discovery. I would desire but two vessels well provided of all necessaries; and considering the temptations our seamen have had of late to break loose and turn pirate [a reference to Henry Every?] when they come into the nether parts of the world I should be glad that some good encouragement might be proposed to those who should go in this voyage upon their return.

This is sensible advice: if the men knew they would be well rewarded when they got home, they would be in better heart for the long and tough voyage; and Dampier must have known that he would not get a prime crew for a venture that, despite Orford's encouragement and the enthusiasm of others, would be viewed as a low priority by the Admiralty.

There is no evidence that Dampier's suggestion about remuneration promised to the men on their return was acted upon.

There was another problem. Despite his acceptance by London society, the Navy knew that Dampier was an ex-buccaneer, possibly a pirate. Well and good if their masters granted Dampier a captaincy, but old buccaneers accepted into the Service had turned bad before. Bartholomew Sharp was one example in recent memory. How aware Dampier was of this difficulty is not certain. He did his best to get the voyage organized, despite obstacles, disappointments and difficulties reflected in a flurry of letters during the summer of 1698.

He was not offered two ships, but one, the *Jolly Prize*. Dampier looked her over and wrote a hurried note to the Secretaries of the Lords of the Admiralty to say that she was in no way fit 'for the service intended'. She was too small for such a long voyage.

At about the same time he was arranging that his Customs House salary be paid to his wife Judith during his absence. This was agreed to without any problems. In August he had a ship, the *Roebuck*. She was not ideal, but she would do. By the end of the month he had gathered forty-six men to crew her. He objected to the master appointed to her, who was 'a very old man', and requested that John Knight replace him, asking that Knight be transferred to him from the *Dunwich*, where he was gunner. Knight had been on the aborted 1694 Spanish Caribbean expedition with Dampier.

Work on the *Roebuck* was progressing meanwhile. The new rigging was almost finished, the carpenters would soon have completed their tasks, and then she would be ready to take in her supplies.

The letters continue through the autumn and into winter. In October Dampier asks that an allowance of 'Dr Cockburn's Electuary against dysenteries' be sent to him. But there are delays over the provisioning of the ship, though he does get John Knight aboard as a mate, and manages to sail the *Roebuck* to the Downs in preparation for departure. Delays now were to play a crucial role, for it would soon be too late in the season to approach New Holland via the favoured route under Cape Horn, which would have brought him to the east coast of the Southern Continent. But official sailing orders were still wanting.

These he finally gets at the end of November. They give him a wide brief, but it is now too late for Cape Horn. He must sail via the Cape of Good Hope, and thus he will arrive on the north-west coast of New Holland. One can imagine Dampier tearing his hair at the bureaucracy, something new to him, and the appalling delays. He negotiates goods to use for trade with the local populations, such as axes and machetes, beads and looking-glasses, and finally, in January 1699, he is ready to leave. But there have been other problems: ominously, there is already dissent and discontent among the officers.

Though Dampier's account of the voyage hardly mentions the troubles that he had, they did not end with sailing. There is a certain weariness in his account from the outset. What is more, the book went to the press unfinished, since its completion was delayed by another voyage, and finally appeared in two parts. The tone is set on the first page of the Dedication:

> The world is apt to judge of everything by the success; and whoever has ill fortune will hardly be allowed a good name. This, my Lord, was my unhappiness in my late expedition in the *Roebuck*, which foundered through perfect age near the island of Ascension. I suffered extremely in my reputation by that misfortune, though I comfort myself with the thoughts, that my enemies could not charge neglect upon me.

And there is bitter self-defence at the beginning of the Preface:

> It has always been the fate of those who have made new discoveries, to be disesteemed and slightly spoken of, by such as have either no true relish and value for the things themselves that are discovered, or have had some prejudice against the persons by whom the discoveries were made.

He goes on to repudiate charges of plagiarism and dullness, and though he tries to be dignified, his underlying fury reminds me of the early letter to Colonel Helyar from Jamaica.

The *Roebuck* sailed on Saturday, 14th January 1699. She was a fifth-rater of His Majesty's Navy, an old ship of 292 tons, only ninety-six feet long, and twenty-five in the beam. Dampier had a final complement of fifty men, and his armaments were twelve guns. He had wanted seventy men and twenty guns. He was provisioned for twenty months. His principal officers were: George Fisher, lieutenant; Jacob Hughes, master; Philip Paine, gunner; James Brand (who may have been responsible for the less-than-skilful drawings done on the voyage), clerk; William Borthwick (or Brothwick), surgeon; Robert Chadwick and John Knight, mates.

The *Roebuck* made a good run to the Canary Islands, where she took on wine and brandy, and once the men were 'refreshed', she made sail again, this time for the Cape Verdes. Dampier notes how the *Roebuck* was greeted with relief by an English merchantman, the *Newport*, commanded by Captain Barfoot, who was loading salt and bound for Newfoundland. There had been various reports of pirates in the vicinity recently, and Barfoot was pleased to have one of the king's ships keep him company while he was engaged in the vulnerable business of loading.

Dampier decided that he would have to put in at one more major port before making the run down to New Holland. He knew that once he got there, all the place would afford him would be fresh water, and he was not even confident of that. His men were inexperienced in long voyages, and most of them had never been to the Southern Seas – only two of them had ever crossed the Line. It would be necessary to inure them to the hardships of the voyage by degrees. Dampier therefore decided to call at a friendly port on the coast of Brazil to rest and recover before making the long push south. If it seems odd that he crossed the Atlantic, rather than coasted down the western shores of Africa, it must be remembered that in the days of sail, ships had to take advantage of the most favourable winds and currents, and the route Dampier chose was the most effective for the outward voyage to New Holland, especially as he had no intention of calling at the Cape, but wished to pass it well to the south.

They crossed the equator on 10th March, and Dampier made all the haste he could away from it, to avoid foul weather frequently found there. He notes the inexperience of his men with some anxiety, and there is a hint of how ill-equipped they were. The equatorial storms, he writes:

would not only retard my course, but endanger sickness also among my men, especially those who were ill provided with clothes, or were too lazy to shift themselves when they were drenched with the rains. The heat of the weather made them careless of doing this, but taking a dram of brandy, which I gave them when wet, with a charge to shift themselves, they would however lie down in their hammocks with their wet clothes, so that when they turned out they caused an ill smell wherever they came, and their hammocks would stink sufficiently . . .

The undercurrent of ill-feeling aboard was becoming increasingly difficult to ignore. Dampier took solace in confirming the observations he had already taken on previous journeys in these waters and discussed in his *Discourse of Winds*. Technical matters of navigation must have comforted his mind greatly in view of the human problems with which he had to contend:

> And indeed I think I may say this of the main of the observations in that treatise [the *Discourse*], that the clear satisfaction I had about them, and how much I might rely upon them, was a great ease to my mind during this vexatious voyage; wherein the ignorance, and obstinacy withal, of some under me, occasioned me a great deal of trouble.

He originally intended to put in at Pernambuco (Recife), the most convenient port from the point of view of the plan of his whole voyage, but decided against it. His crew was already disaffected with the voyage, Lieutenant Fisher was proving a very great thorn in his side, and any attempt to persuade the men that they would soon pick up a favourable trade wind to drive them south fell on deaf ears. In short, Dampier feared a mutiny.

Pernambuco's anchorages were several miles out from the town, and if he stopped there he could not rely on the protection of its fort in the case of his men turning against him. He decided to move south along the coast, aiming for Bahia (Salvador).

On board, the situation was very tense; Dampier was 'forced to keep myself all the way upon my guard, and to lie with my officers, such as I could trust, and with small-arms upon the quarter-deck, it scarce being safe for me to lie in my cabin, by reason of the discontents among my men'.

The Portuguese were England's oldest allies, and the *Roebuck* had a warm welcome at Bahia – not least because the governor, Don Juan de Lancastrio, claimed descent from the House of Lancaster, and regarded the English as his countrymen. What is more, Dampier was able to anchor comfortingly close to the town guns. Here, his patience finally at an end, Dampier put the troublesome Lieutenant Fisher ashore in irons, a severe action which would lead to many problems for him on his return home.

Here also, he met with three former members of Henry Every's crew, but made no move to arrest them, which was his duty as an officer of the Royal Navy. Fisher accuses him of being in collusion with them; and it is likely that he knew them personally from the abortive Spanish Caribbean expedition of 1694. Fisher, probably with justification, accused Dampier of being sympathetic to pirates, and to Every's men in particular.

The pressure on the voyage was relieved during their stay at this prosperous and cosmopolitan mercantile town, and Dampier becomes his old self as he provides us with a wealth of detail about the place and the animals and birds to be found in the surrounding countryside, including one of the earliest descriptions of the anaconda. The men were in a better frame of mind, too – at least for the time being. Pepys has written, and Dampier would have known, that 'Englishmen, and more especially seamen, love their bellies above everything else, and therefore it must always be remembered, in the management of the victualling of the Navy, that to make any abatement from them . . . is to discourage and provoke them in the tenderest point . . .'

They were at Bahia from 25th March until 25th April. With Fisher off the ship, Dampier takes a more confident grasp of command. It has frequently been said that Dampier was not a good commander, but I do not find this. Once Fisher was off the ship, the trouble Dampier experienced was small, especially when one considers the demands that were put on his crew, who were not fired with his enthusiasm for exploration, and who had small hopes of any great reward from the cruise. Dampier wasn't used to command, and probably didn't care for it much – the responsibility was too much of a tie – but he would not shirk it. He had an old, leaky ship, a green crew and a tight budget. With the means at his disposal, he was to achieve an impressive amount.

Among the jobs that needed to be done aboard was the scraping, rinsing and burning of the now empty beer barrels to remove all trace of beer from them so that they could be used for water. Dampier also took in rum, sugar and oranges. As soon as he was ready, he made haste to depart, for the malign influence of Fisher was still able to exert some power:

> I had like to have been involved with the clergy here (of the Inquisition, as I suppose) and so my voyage might have been hindered. What was said to me of them, by some of my company that went ashore, I know not; but I was assured by a merchant there, that if they got me into their clutches (and it seems when I was last ashore they had narrowly watched me) the governor himself could not release me. Besides, I might either be murdered in the streets, as he sent me word, or poisoned, if I came ashore any more; and therefore he advised me to stay aboard.

And so the *Roebuck* set out once again, with fair weather. Dampier describes the seabirds they encountered, including this account of the storm-petrel:

> The petrel is a bird not much unlike a swallow, but smaller, and with a shorter tail. 'Tis all over black, except a white spot on the rump. They fly sweeping like swallows, and very near the water. They are not so often seen in fair weather, being foul-weather birds, as our seamen call them, and presaging a storm when they come about a ship, who for that reason don't love to see them. In a storm they will hover close under the ship's stern, in the wake of the ship (as 'tis called) or the smoothness which the ship's passing has made on the sea; and there as they fly (gently then) they pat the water alternately with their feet, as if they walked upon it, though still upon the wing. And from hence the seamen give them the name of petrels, in allusion to St Peter's walking upon the Lake of Gennesareth.

He also made detailed notes of the compass variations he observed, deferring to Halley's interpretative skill, but offering his own contribution modestly, for the use of others. In passing one can remark quickly a similar generosity of spirit in his brother George, who in his naïve but confident letter carrying the information about the cure for the 'bitings of mad creatures' is at pains to say that he requires no fee – only the satisfaction of having his knowledge made available to all. In fact, Dampier's tables were accurate enough to help the famous later navigator Matthew Flinders improve the construction of the ship's compass by the addition of 'Flinders' Bars'.

The voyage continued. In the open ocean they met the *Antelope* of London, commanded by Captain Hammond. This was a welcome encounter, because it gave an opportunity to exchange news and supplies. The *Antelope* was homeward bound from the Cape, where she had recently put in, and was able to give the *Roebuck* mutton, cabbages, pumpkins, butter, stockfish and parsnips. They parted company early in June, and the *Roebuck* made her lonely way south-east until at last her crew sighted land at the end of July.

They coasted along, seeking an anchorage, and found one at last on 7th August 1699 in a sound to which Dampier gave the name Sharks' Bay, from the number of those fish he saw there, and which is known as Shark Bay today. They had arrived in the middle of the west coast of Australia. The completion of the voyage was a miracle of navigation, when that science was still in its infancy and large tracts of the seas through which they had sailed were uncharted. Nevertheless, the difficulty of ascertaining longitude accurately meant that Dampier had arrived sooner than he had calculated. Among the many drawbacks of the *Roebuck*, she did not carry accurate hourglasses.

They landed and cut wood, though the trees were small and they found themselves in an arid scrubland. They saw few land-birds, but noticed a stumpy speckled lizard which looked as if it had a head at each end of its body. Dampier remarks:

> Though I have often eaten of snakes, crocodiles and alligators, and many creatures that look frightfully enough, and there are but few I should have been afraid to eat of, if pressed by hunger, yet I think my stomach would scarce have served to venture upon these New Holland guanoes [lizards], both the looks and the smell of them being so offensive.

It must have been really vile to turn a seaman's invincible stomach, 'which ostrich-like could well-near digest iron'. They also encountered a small mammal which Dampier describes as a sort of racoon, probably the kangaroo-rat. They searched for fresh water and dug for it, but could find none.

They caught turtles for food. Dampier made a collection of shells found on the beach, the bulk of which he subsequently lost in the wreck of the *Roebuck* at the end of the voyage, along with many of his books and papers. He was more fortunate in the collection of plants he made, probably on Enderby and East Lewis Islands, which on his return was deposited with Dr John Woodward, by order of the Royal Society, and is now at the Sherardian Herbarium in Oxford. The Latin names of two of the new species take note of their discoverer: *Clianthus dampieri* and *Beaufortia dampieri.*

They also caught sharks, which were large – one was eleven feet long – and were good eating. In the stomach of the largest they found 'the head and bones of a hippopotamus', which seems very unlikely, but it is not possible to determine what the creature actually was.

They careened their ship and continued their exploration of the coast, lowering a plumb-line tipped with wax to pick up particles of sand from the seabed, to determine its nature. They had a copy of one of the charts Tasman had made, and Dampier suspected the presence of a group of islands, but they found nothing of great interest in their exploration, nor any fresh water. They touched at Rosemary Island in what is now the Dampier Archipelago, just off the coast from the modern town of Dampier, and sailed on, following the shoreline north-east. On 30th August, near the area now known as Dampier Land, they saw 'many great smokes' near the shore. They dropped anchor and Dampier went ashore in the ship's boat the next day with about ten of his men, armed with cutlasses and muskets in case of trouble. They saw three native men on a hill near the shore, but the men ran away before they reached the beach. Climbing the same hill, they found themselves looking over an open plain dotted with 'things like haycocks', which may have been ant-hills. They searched for water with what was becoming depressing lack of success, and then returned to their landing place to dig for it.

While they were working, nine or ten aborigines cautiously approached to watch from a distance. The English tried to make contact with them, and when one of them advanced towards them a little, Dampier went out to meet him, 'making all the signs of peace and friendship' he could; but when he got within fifty yards of the man, the native retreated. That afternoon, Dampier took just two of his men from their group and deliberately wandered off with them. The aborigines followed at a distance, but more confidently now that they outnumbered the Europeans. Unfortunately things then began to go wrong:

We knew by what rencounter we had had with them in the morning that we could easily out-run them [which says something for the fitness of the sailors after so long at sea]. So a nimble young man that was with me, seeing some of them near, ran towards them; and they for some time ran away before him. But he soon overtaking them, they faced about and fought him. He had a cutlass, and they had wooden lances, with which, being many of them, they were too hard for him. When he first ran towards them I chased two more that were by the shore, but fearing how it might be with my young man, I turned back quickly, and went up to the top of a sandhill, whence I saw him near me, closely engaged with them. Upon their seeing me, one of them threw a lance at me, that narrowly missed me. I discharged my gun to scare them, but avoided shooting any of them; till finding the young man in great danger from them, and myself in some; and that though the gun had a little frighted them at first, yet they had soon learnt to despise it, tossing up their hands and crying, Pooh, Pooh, Pooh; and coming on afresh with a great noise, I thought it high time to charge again, and shoot one of them, which I did. The rest, seeing him fall, made a stand again, and my young man took the opportunity to disengage himself and come off to me. My other man also was with me, who had done nothing all this while, having come out unarmed, and I returned back with my men, designing to attempt the natives no further, being very sorry for what had happened already. They took up their wounded companion: and my young man, who had been struck through the cheek by one of their lances, was afraid it had been poisoned, but I did not think that was likely. His wound was very painful to him, being made with a blunt weapon, but he soon recovered of it.

The young man's name was Alexander Beale.

They had no more contact with the local people after this. Dampier writes of them with just as much disgust as he did when he was first in New Holland with the *Cygnet*, and guesses that as they were now on about the same part of the coast, they belonged to the same tribe. He makes what observations he can about their poor encampments and lowly manner of life, and in these he is not without sympathy; but no other race he ever encounters is treated with less. It is ironic that the very people which excited so much loathing in him were in fact close cousins, members of a Caucasian race which had migrated south when the Eurasian land mass was linked to the Australian. Later visitors were to disagree with Dampier about them. Charles Darwin found them 'good humoured and pleasant . . . far from being such utterly degraded beings as they have usually been represented'. Charles Pickering, the American naturalist, said, 'I would refer to an Australian as the finest model of the human proportions I have ever met; in muscular development combining perfect symmetry, activity and strength, while his head might have been compared with the antique bust of a philosopher.'

Dampier and his crew were beginning to find the whole New Holland enterprise frustrating. Dampier writes gloomily: 'If it were not for that sort of pleasure which results from the discovery even of the barrenest spot upon the globe, this coast of New Holland would not have charmed me much.'

When he returned to the water-hole it had been dug to a depth of nine feet, but without yielding a drop. Another well was more successful, but the little water they got from it was so brackish that they could not use it to drink. At least it was good enough to use in making burgoo, or porridge. There was no food to be had, and they did not trust the bean-like vegetable they saw growing on 'a creeping sort of shrub-like vine', since the locals did not appear to have harvested it. The only land animals they saw were more lizards, bandicoots, a speckled snake, and, once, three half-starved wolf-like creatures which must have been dingoes. The sea was more promising, but they had no turtle-net to catch green turtle. They were, however, able to catch fish, and shellfish were plentiful. Dampier says the sea was 'plentifully stocked' with whales, which makes sad reading for us.

There was no fresh water, there was nowhere to careen the ship, it was the middle of the dry season, and scurvy was breaking out among the men. New Holland did not seem to promise much. It was time to depart, and, with a certain reluctance, as if he knew he was throwing in the sponge, or, worse, letting a tremendous opportunity slip, Dampier does so.

In the second part of his *Voyage to New Holland*, Dampier is again enthusiastic about the possibilities he believes the country to have, and describes what he had proposed to do if only circumstances hadn't been against him. His chief complaint is that he was forced to sail via the Cape of Good Hope to the at least partially known western side of the continent. How different would his impressions have been if he had reached the fertile south-east of Australia?

He also justifies his decision not to sail south along the coast and by following it find a way to the eastern seaboard at last. The decision stems largely from his dislike of cold latitudes, which he believed he would encounter:

> I confess I was not for spending my time more than was necessary
> in the higher latitudes, as knowing that the land there could not
> be so well worth the discovering as the parts that lay nearer the
> Line, and more directly under the sun. Besides, at the time when I
> should come first on New Holland, which was early in the spring,
> I must, had I stood southward, have had for some time a great deal
> of winter weather, increasing in severity . . .

Dampier was wrong in thinking that the land further south would be of less value than that nearer the equator; but he was used to the rich commodities associated with the tropics, and could not see beyond them, despite his knowledge of the unhealthy climate. But even if he had wanted to, it is unlikely that his men would have stood for further exploration. They had never had much of a stomach for the voyage, and now, as they sailed away from the coast, their predominant feeling was one of relief. Dampier too, once he has justified himself, adds that 'I began to bethink myself that a great part of my time must have been spent in being about a shore I was already almost weary of, which I might employ with greater satisfaction to my mind, and better hopes of success in going forward to New Guinea.'

His brief from the Admiralty had been broad; he was not being negligent in his duty. He could not possibly have known that he was letting slip the greatest discovery in the world that still remained to be made, but he was too good a navigator not to realize that he was failing to investigate something significant. Circumstances were against him. He probably hoped that one day he would have the opportunity to return and finish the job. Ironically, in 1606, the explorer Torres had discovered the straits which bear his name and which separate New Guinea from Australia; but this important route from the west to the east of Australia remained a secret until Cook sailed through them in 1770. Dampier believed that Australia and New Guinea were joined.

On 8th September they shaped their course for Timor, where they knew they would find fresh water. Dampier was getting back to familiar territory as well. On 14th, to their 'great joy', they saw the tops of the mountains of the island rising above the clouds. It was a little before sunset. But they were not out of trouble yet. It took them several days to find a good anchorage. When they did so, they found themselves in the Dutch-controlled half of the island. The other half was governed by the Portuguese, who would have given Dampier a friendlier welcome, though neither nation welcomed strangers in this remote area. They were jealous of their trade and suspicious of commercial espionage. To make matters worse, the last ship to call here had been a French pirate which had attacked the settlement and burnt down a number of houses.

Dampier had to negotiate carefully with the governor simply to be allowed to take on drinking water, and this despite the fact that the *Roebuck* was a king's ship, and England and Holland were allies. It emerged, however, that a misunderstanding had arisen between Dampier and the governor owing to the behaviour of the officer Dampier sent ashore as negotiator. This man, whom Dampier for some reason had sent in place of his clerk, James Brand, who had opened the negotiations, deliberately tried to antagonize the governor in order, as Dampier later suspected, to prevent his captain's being able to continue his voyage of exploration and to force him to go to Java, and thence home. Dampier later caught the man stirring things up with the crew, telling them that in these waters they were at the mercy of the Dutch. Whether he took any action against the officer, we do not know; but he was able to smooth things over, rectified the false impression the governor had, maintained cordial relations with him, and got his water. Unfortunately, there were to be mutinous rumblings from other officers, who also wanted to go home. They may have been justified. The *Roebuck* was not built to withstand the kind of voyage she had already made, and Dampier himself knew that if while in these seas they encountered storms such as the one he had experienced in the *Cygnet*, she would not be able to withstand them. Nevertheless, he was able to contain the situation.

The ship needed careening again, and Dampier now cast about urgently to look for somewhere to do it. He had made contact with the local Portuguese, who had been friendly but unhelpful. He sailed to Babao (Babar) in the hope of hunting buffalo and catching fish. He also wanted to rest his men, of whom he was most careful. There were other considerations. His salt was running low, and he had a disastrously incompetent carpenter on board, who had already so wasted the ship's supply of pitch that they would have to make a compound of oil and lime to caulk the *Roebuck*. Despite many difficulties, they managed to clean her hull, and at least there was enough to eat. They stayed at Babao until 12th December. It is noticeable that in his descriptions and comments during this period Dampier becomes much more his old self again – if he was writing, as he must have been, from original notes, it is clear that he feels happier and more confident again. How he must have hated the restrictions of this voyage, after his twelve years of free roving alongside men of a similar spirit. At the same time he was aware of his duty, and was determined to stick it out, though with how much good will, no one can tell.

They continued to cruise among the neighbouring islands, passing the volcano on Gunong Api on St Stephen's Day. They were to see several volcanoes, active and erupting.

On New Year's Day 1700 they sighted New Guinea, and landed there on Twelfth Night. They explored, and a few days later might have been ambushed by a group of local tribesmen, but they were still in the ship's boat, and Dampier threw ashore some gifts, upon which the locals put down their weapons, 'and came into the water by the boat's side, making signs of friendship by pouring water on their heads with one hand, which they dipped into the sea'. They saw massive fruit bats which smelt like foxes, and a great variety of birds and fish. Dampier had by now recovered much of his vitality and enthusiasm. Sailing on, they ventured among the islands to the north-east of New Guinea, naming the headland on what is now New Ireland, Cape St George, and discovered a 'bay' which is in fact St George's Channel. The opposite cape they named after Lord Orford, and drank his health. Cape Orford lies on what is now New Britain. Needing to take in wood and water, and seeing locals on shore very numerous and apparently unfriendly, Dampier ordered shots to be fired above their heads to scare them away. His brusqueness was based on previous experience of local Indians, 'dull in everything but treachery and barbarity'. He was able to wood and water safely, but he cannot have been surprised when his attempts to trade with the locals failed. At another place he was not above shooting at the locals ('our design being rather to fright than to kill them') when they would not trade for some hogs. It may have been a pure accident that the locals were killed – but such behaviour is very different from what had been usual for William up to now.

The entries from the *Roebuck*'s log by her master, Jacob Hughes, are also revealing in this context. The entry for 10th March reads:

> as we were coming in and nigh the shore, the natives were very
> populous gazing on us, whereupon we fired two or three shots over
> them which made them run in a frightful manner; in doing this we
> civilised them, for as we brought to, they stood, five or six of them,
> on shore with coconuts in their hands, beckoning us on shore . . .
> the blacks fear us very much.

And an entry for 30th March is even less attractive: 'Our captain went ashore to seek a commerce and having given something to one of the natives he [the native] ran away, which caused our people to rassle [ransack] their houses.' Hughes describes other acts of bullying over the following few days.

Sailing around New Britain, a fine bay was named Port Montague, which lies near what is now Dampier Strait. Soon afterwards, Dampier was to discover that New Britain was an island distinct from New Guinea. He named it so – 'Nova-Britannia' – and a little flurry of namings followed, after the great and the good of England: Cape Anne, Cape

Gloucester and Rooke Island. By a quirk of fate, Admiral Rooke sat as the senior member of the court-martial which Dampier was to face on his return. Dampier named the island after him because Rooke had been a lieutenant under Admiral Sir Edward Spragge on *The Royal Prince*, on which it will be remembered Dampier had served before the mast.

But by now his pinnace needed repairing, and there was only one man competent to do the work (not the carpenter, one must assume from Dampier's comments about him). Worse, the easterly winds were setting in. The *Roebuck* was still bearing up, but only just; and Dampier was beginning to wonder whether in his unquenchable desire for new discoveries, he had not pushed her too far.

The time had come to make for home. After some delays and diversions owing to contrary winds, the *Roebuck* anchored in Batavia Road at the end of June 1700. The Road was crowded, mainly with Dutch ships, but there were some English vessels with which Dampier exchanged news. Here, the Dutch authorities allowed Dampier to provision his ship, but the *Roebuck* herself was in need of attention, and her condition was not helped by the carpenter: 'I supplied the carpenter with such stores as were necessary for refitting the ship, which proved more leaky after he had caulked her than she was before. So that I was obliged to careen her, for which purpose I hired vessels to take in our guns, ballast, provision and stores.' This meant an unwelcome delay. Batavia was notorious for sickness, and Dampier and all his men were exhausted. It was probably here that the useless carpenter died. One wonders why Dampier kept patience with him for so long.

They were not, however, to sail until 17th October, when they departed in company with three Dutch ships. They made the Cape of Good Hope with fair weather, but the *Roebuck* could scarcely go on. On 22nd February 1701, at Ascension Island, the end came. She sprang a leak which the pumps could not keep up with. 'At half an hour after eight in the night we sprung a leak in the larboard bow about four streaks from the keel which obliged us to keep our chain pump constantly going . . .'

Once at anchor, Dampier ordered the powder room cleared so that they could search for the leak there. He then consulted his officers and the carpenter's mate, John Penton, 'who was the only person in the ship that understood anything of carpenter's work'. The mate said that he thought he could stop the leak if he could cut through the inner lining planking. Dampier was doubtful, but the mate had stopped a smaller leak before perfectly well. However, once the cut had been made, they still couldn't get to the leak because it was up against one of the foot-hook timbers, which are the ribs that run between the floor and the top timbers. The planking around the leak was so rotten that it 'broke away like dirt'. The leak 'was very large, and the water gushed in with great violence', writes Dampier in his deposition to the Admiralty.

> I went down to view it, and the carpenter's mate and the boatswain told me it could not be stopped, unless the timber was cut. I made answer that I never was in any ship where timbers were cut to find leaks, but am no shipwright, therefore advise you that understand it to be very cautious not to weaken or endanger the ship more.

This seems quite diffident of him. Every precaution was taken in case the plan should go awry. 'But after they had cut the timber, notwithstanding all that could be done the leak so increased that with pumping and baling we could not stay in the place where the leak was.'

They worked valiantly throughout 23rd February, the carpenter's mate in particular determined not to give up; but by the following afternoon they were obliged to run her into as shallow water as possible, and hoist out the boat, to save themselves and as much as was of value as possible. They made a raft to take sea-chests ashore, and took some of the sails to make themselves tents. Luckily, there was a fresh-water spring on the side of a nearby mountain. It is still known as Dampier's Spring.

They were cast away here until early April, when they were picked up by His Majesty's ships *Anglesey*, *Hastings* and *Lizard*, together with the East-Indiaman *Canterbury*. Dampier went aboard the *Anglesey* first, but the warships having to steer a course for the Cape Verdes to take in water, the crew of the *Roebuck* all went aboard the *Canterbury*, which brought them home in August 1701. Dampier was absolved of all responsibility for the loss of his ship; but he found that Lt Fisher had arrived well ahead of him, and, with an obsessive sense of injustice, had spent the last two years preparing a case against him. Dampier had already written to the Admiralty on 22nd April 1699 describing his reasons for putting

Fisher ashore, but Fisher's case had to be heard, and as there had also been trouble with the disciplining of the boatswain later in the voyage, Dampier now faced a court martial.

CHAPTER SIXTEEN

Homecoming and Disgrace

A few months before Dampier arrived back in England, a long-drawn-out trial had ended with the execution of William Kidd.

Kidd was a Scotsman, born in about 1645. He went to sea early, and had a notable career as a privateer in the Caribbean, before retiring to New York in 1691, where he married a wealthy widow and settled down, starting a family and becoming a businessman. However, he became bored with the life, and in 1695 sailed for London in the hope of returning to his old trade. Here he found a New York business acquaintance called Robert Livingston, and together the two men set about looking for backers for a voyage. After much effort they attracted the attention of the Whig peer, Lord Bellomont, who persuaded four of his fellows – including Lord Orford – to back the venture. They were not the only ones involved – a City of London merchant and King William III had made up the consortium.

England was then at war with France, and the idea was to send Kidd to take French ships; but he had another commission as well: to hunt down pirates in the Indian Ocean. Kidd would take their booty and the profits would be divided among the interested parties.

The plan went wrong when Kidd turned pirate himself, attacking a pilgrim fleet in August 1697 which was under the protection of three British men-of-war, one of which, the *Sceptre*, was commanded by our old acquaintance Edward Barlow. Kidd was seen off, but he continued to cruise, and took several prizes, including a rich trading vessel commanded by an Englishman, owned by Armenians, and carrying cargo belonging to a senior official in the court of the Great Moghul. This had serious repercussions for him and he became a wanted man. He made his way back to New York and from there tried to negotiate a pardon from Lord Bellomont, who was now in Boston as governor of New York, Massachusetts Bay and New Hampshire. Bellomont's career would have been damaged if he had helped Kidd, and so he had him arrested and sent back to England. Kidd, by now a sick man, was examined by George Rooke and others at the Admiralty, and sent to Newgate, where he languished for a year, still protesting his innocence. He tried to get help from his backers, and wrote to Lord Orford for aid, but his powerfully placed former business partners washed their hands of him. He was sentenced to death, hanged, and his body then tarred and hung in chains at Tilbury Point, where it remained for eight years.

Kidd was a privateer who had become respectable but had then returned to his old ways. His trial was fresh in people's minds when Dampier came to face his court martial. Dampier was a former privateer, buccaneer, pirate – a general ne'er-do-well. But he had not run away with the king's ship entrusted to him, and he had discharged the duties assigned to him conscientiously and to the best of his ability in the circumstances. If it had not been for Kidd, the authorities might have been more lenient. Dampier stood accused of maltreating an officer, but such behaviour was not unusual in the Navy of the day. The main problem for the court was that Fisher knew his rights and insisted on them in a loud voice. He had been importuning anyone who would listen since his arrival back in England. However, similar charges regarding Dampier's later behaviour towards his boatswain on the same voyage were dropped. The sentence he received was harsh enough; but it might have been worse.

The papers placed before the court have been preserved and tell the melancholy story of Dampier's and Fisher's disagreements in a long series of accusations and counter-accusations. Fisher's journal of events is written in the third person. It is in a clerk's hand and the style is far more polished than that of Fisher's letters. Fisher was fastidious in the preparation of his case.

When the *Roebuck* lay in the Downs prior to sailing, she was in company with ten other men-of-war under the command of Admiral Sir Cloudesley

Shovell. Shovell's flagship was the *Swiftsure*, a third-rater of 326 crewmen. Fisher was on shore – with permission, as he carefully mentions, when the *Swiftsure* made a signal for lieutenants to come aboard. He made haste to obey. There he found Dampier on the quarter-deck, who drew him aside and told him that he had a secret to impart: Jacob Hughes, the master, had overheard two of the crewmen, drinking with the boatswain, saying that 'when they came to sea they would heave the master overboard and run away with the King's ship'. The boatswain is not named, but we know from Jacob Hughes's log that the boatswain for the voyage, John Norwood, did not come aboard until 24th November 1698, a good fortnight after Sir Cloudesley had sailed, so this boatswain was replaced. The two other crewmen were John Knight and James Gregson. Gregson certainly knew Dampier of old, and may also have been a member of the 1694 expedition. Fisher told Dampier that he should make the matter known to the Admiral, which Dampier promised to do; but in fact he took no action, though Fisher says he reminded him of this duty several times.

Two other incidents occurred before the *Roebuck* weighed anchor. On 5th November 1698, two of Sir Cloudesley's captains, Cleasbie and Jumper, and his secretary came aboard Dampier's ship, 'with an order to examine if our crew were seamen', as Fisher puts it – in other words, to make an inspection. Fisher ordered the boatswain to take the pinnace, moored alongside, out of the way astern, but the boatswain 'answered with an oath he would not obey his commands when the captain was on board, so that the captains and secretary were forced to come over the boat to come in'. Fisher complained of his treatment by the boatswain to Dampier in front of the Admiral's captains, who took it upon themselves to tell Dampier that he should protect his lieutenant and back up his orders, and then themselves reprimanded the boatswain. Dampier took all this meekly; he was very aware that he did not know the ropes as far as naval deportment was concerned and he was feeling his way. William Jumper was a senior captain, and commander of the *Swiftsure*. Dampier must however have been angered by his lieutenant's officiousness.

On 17th November, Fisher requested Dampier to have James Gregson punished – 'still finding him a refractory and dangerous fellow'. Dampier seemed unwilling to do this, until Fisher told him that the Lords of the

Admiralty 'ought to be acquainted with it'. Fisher must have had an inkling that Gregson was still plotting mutiny. Dampier ordered Gregson to be tied to the gangway for an hour, but then had him released without a flogging or any such thing. When Fisher insisted, Dampier had Gregson tied up again and had Fisher order the boatswain to give him six blows on his back with his clothes on – a very mild punishment. Dampier told Fisher that he would put Knight and Gregson ashore before the ship sailed, and Fisher undertook to find two replacements for them; but again nothing was actually done. By now, Fisher is accusing Dampier darkly of protecting the two men because they were his 'old acquaintance'; and Dampier's resentment of his junior's officiousness had probably increased.

Nothing else is mentioned before sailing, though Fisher reports a curious incident on 28th January: 'Last night as walking on the deck with the captain and the captain's clerk [James Brand], Fisher was taken ill and three drops of blood fell from his nose and fainting went to his cabin.' Can he have had a fit of some kind? His reaction seems extreme for a nosebleed.

Two days later, the *Roebuck* arrived at the Canaries, and a violent spat is recorded:

> They came to an anchor in Santa Cruz Road, where was the *Experiment* galley, Captain Trevars commander, who came on board and desired a hogshead of small beer, which the captain granted and ordered Fisher to see it done. Fisher thereupon ordered the cooper to break a butt, and as he was going to do it he met the purser on the deck who threatened to break his head if he obeyed Fisher's order therein. Fisher therefore before Captain Trevars complained to his commander . . . in which Captain Trevars seconded him saying, if you suffer your lieutenant to be thus used it may be of ill consequence in your voyage.

This is important because Trevars produced an affidavit for Fisher, testifying that Dampier would not back him up. It is hard to explain Dampier's behaviour: perhaps he resented Fisher's appealing to other captains to support him. But he should not have allowed Fisher's authority to be undermined. Had the two men simply taken against one another from the start? There is no doubt that Dampier, together with Borthwick the surgeon and Brand the clerk, as well perhaps as the purser, had ganged up on Fisher, which would have given him reason to suspect them. Fisher may have been a prig, but he was a professional officer with a distinguished career behind him – one of a new breed of sailor. Did Dampier represent the old, untutored ways to him? A day after the incident with the beer barrel, Dampier, Borthwick, Brand and Fisher were ashore with James Barnaby, the midshipman – not a boy officer in those days, but a kind of NCO – an experienced seaman with authority for the working of the vessel amidships. They had all dined together, at Dampier's invitation, and Dampier was 'morose'. The word gives us pause. In the course of this voyage, we have the first indications that Dampier had begun to drink, sometimes heavily. Up until 1691, at least, there is little trace of this and he even boasts about his abstemiousness, as we have seen. Accusations of drinking made against Dampier were always made by his enemies, however.

In any event, in his 'morose' mood, Dampier accused Fisher of having beaten Barnaby up. Fisher, and Barnaby himself, denied this, but Dampier threatened to have Fisher put in irons anyway. Fisher retorted that they were not so far away from home that he couldn't report this behaviour to the Admiralty. According to Fisher, Brand thereupon whispered to him that he should cane Barnaby. This is a very surprising suggestion, but Fisher interpreted it as designed to create a scuffle in which the others could 'run him through'. Of Brand, Fisher says: 'This was a base, impudent fellow and would frequently say the ship would not go home these seven years, and sometimes that she would never go home.'

Fisher's evidence is not consistent. In a letter to the Lords of the Admiralty of 22nd December 1699, dictated to a clerk soon after he got home, he varies his theme slightly and states that while still in the Downs Dampier had brought aboard one Andrew Gastior, a Spaniard whom he wished to enlist in the crew and whom he planned to make an officer. In fact Gastior, aka Andrés García Cassada or Andrew Gasher, had been on the 1694 expedition destined for the Spanish Caribbean, and was another old acquaintance of Dampier.

Fisher told Dampier that this was against the law, but Dampier kept him on board anyway. At Santa Cruz, Fisher writes: 'my captain sent the same Spaniard to inform the Spaniards on shore that I had beaten and abused him several times, upon which they promised to take away my life, which they had done, but one James Barnaby . . . informed them to the contrary'. He goes on to say that when Dampier finally sent him ashore in irons at Bahia the same Andrew Gastior came to him in prison, 'and told me he would go no further in the ship. I asked him his reason for it, to which he replied that the captain was a great rogue and would turn pirate . . .' Gastior also confessed that Dampier had tried to get him to kill Fisher, and Fisher gives further elaborations injurious to Dampier's reputation. He must have been bitterly disappointed that Dampier did not, in fact, turn pirate.

Fisher's accusations smack at the very least of exaggeration as they continue. Approaching the Cape Verdes he accuses Dampier, whose skill as a navigator can have been doubted by no one, of almost wrecking the ship. In his own third-person account of events, Fisher

> asked the captain what he designed to do. He answered (as if crying) he did not know what the master designed to do. Said Fisher, if you let him do what he pleases he will knock the King's ship at head, the master being then so drunk he could not stand on his legs. The captain walked off the quarterdeck and Fisher ordered the helm at lee, and if the ship had not stayed she had run ashore, she having all the small sails set at the same time.

This is suspect. It shows Dampier abandoning his post and casts Fisher in a heroic role. Jacob Hughes's entry in his logbook for 19th February 1699 states:

> this morning at 4 o'clock made the Island St Iago. We came within four miles of it so tacked and lay by until day, from five this morning until twelve at noon plied for the Road of St Iago, we having variable winds could not get in but continued plying. This Road is very rocky except one spot of sand.

All very routine, and the handwriting here is as firm and even as it is throughout the log, so Hughes probably didn't have a hangover. We shouldn't forget either that Hughes got the decrepit old *Roebuck* all the way to Australia and back to Ascension Island. The only element in Fisher's description that is worrying is Dampier's demeanour. It is highly unlikely that he was drunk at such a time; but it is possible. However unsympathetic Fisher appears, there must have been concrete reasons for the stand he took.

At this early stage in the voyage, Fisher and Dampier must still have been getting on, for a few days later, on 23rd February, sailing from St Iago, Dampier asked Fisher to 'club for a bowl of punch'. Fisher agreed, and was joined by the surgeon, the purser and the clerk. But it wasn't long before there was trouble. Dampier began by praising the privateering life, but then, in the course of their drinking, according to Fisher,

> the captain said, had he commanded one of the King's ships in the late war, all Frenchmen he took in privateers he would have tied back to back and thrown overboard, adding all the King's captains were fools they did not do it. Fisher replied it was a very cruel thought and that the French would have retaliated it, but he swore he would have done it. The doctor said it was barbarously intended. The captain answered it would have made a quick end of the war. Fisher said it would rather have prolonged it and created an irreconcilable hatred, and that if all nations would give no protection to pirates, but hang them as soon as taken, it would be of good service to all traders abroad. The captain demanded what he meant by pirates. Fisher answered: such as Every and his men were. He [Dampier] swore if he met with any of them he would not hurt them, nor a hair of their heads. Fisher answered that he being now one of the King's captains, and had the King's commission, ought as he conceived whenever he found such to secure them and bring them to justice . . .

The deliberate confrontation here is clear, and what happened shortly afterwards in Bahia shows that Dampier was as good as his word. Fisher was twenty years Dampier's junior and one can imagine that Dampier would have regarded any of his old crewmates as worth ten of this upstart. The reference to Every was certainly meant to needle him.

Nevertheless, two days later they were all drinking together again. This time it was Dampier who started the confrontation. He sent for James Gregson. By now Fisher must have been convinced that Gregson and Knight – Dampier had gone to great lengths to get Knight enlisted in his crew – were old pirate colleagues of the captain. When Gregson arrived, Dampier said to him: 'I beg your pardon for punishing you in the Downs, but it was to please one man.' Fisher, shocked at this and appalled that Dampier should apologize to 'so base a fellow':

> set the bowl down, pulled off his hat without saying one word, withdrew into his own cabin and reflected on other things had passed, particularly what the clerk had said, viz. that they would find Captain Dampier another sort of man when he came on the other side of the equinoctial line.

Fisher had complained to Dampier of James Brand's behaviour, of course, but Dampier had taken Brand's part. Fisher thought that Brand was acting as a kind of *agent provocateur* on Dampier's behalf.

Meanwhile, there were further confrontations. The purser abused Fisher over some spoiled biscuit, and Dampier supported the purser. On 10th March, according to a letter to the Lords of the Admiralty written by Fisher some months later:

> The cook came to me and told me that the beer was out and the men was all a-complaining they were a-dry. I call out for the cooper and ordered him to go and see if the beer was out; he came and told me it was. Then I ordered him to broach another [barrel], my captain never having ordered me to the contrary. I told the captain there was a butt of beer broached by my orders. He sent for his cane and then for the cooper, and broke his head for obeying my orders . . . Then he sent for me and asked me what made me to order a barrel of beer to be broached, but before I could make any reply he fell to caning me.

Fisher fled to the forecastle, but Dampier pursued him:

> I desired the men to take notice of it and told my captain that he must answer for striking of me before your Lordships, but he in a scornful manner told me he had got me out of your Lordships power, and did not give a farthing for what your Lordships could do to him . . . Then he presently ordered me to be confined to my cabin and after I was confined he came into my cabin and caned me there.

Fisher continued to suspect a mutiny, and a note was thrown into his cabin by one of the crew which said that the anonymous crewman had heard the clerk swear that if he were captain he would hang Fisher 'and two or three more'. On 16th March Dampier ordered all hands on deck and asked them bluntly if they were planning a mutiny, to which the unanimous answer was No.

Dampier, no doubt seizing on the excuse, thereupon accused Fisher of fomenting mutiny, and had the ship's corporal clap him in irons. Fisher was confined to his cabin:

> where he lay in great misery and all this while without any cause alleged, and under it the captain caned him violently and locked him up close, that with the heat, being under the sun, and forced to ease nature there, he was almost stifled to death, as no doubt was intended . . .

In the letter already referred to, Fisher adds: 'I did tell him [Dampier] what a great rogue I heard he was.'

Three days later, Dampier had three men — Alexander Beale, John Boate and (in Fisher's version) Owen Harris — chained to the gangway and interrogated about the mutiny. Fisher believed that the whole thing was a put-up job to implicate him in plotting mutiny, but 'because the three poor men would not swear falsely against him they were ordered into irons, and the boatswain [John Norwood] to his cabin because he was a good man and would not hearken to their wicked advice'. This is not the only time that Fisher begins to bleat and to protest too much. As for the three crewmen, Alexander Beale at least fought off the aborigines on the coast of Australia with Dampier and was rescued by him: there is nothing to indicate any ill-will between the two men. John Gregson, however, was perfectly willing to testify against Fisher.

Fisher's dates and those in Hughes's log do not always agree, and I have used Hughes's as probably being more reliable. According to him, Fisher was put ashore at Bahia on 28th March. Dampier arranged with the governor for him to be taken back to Europe as soon as a ship could conveniently be found. Fisher says he was 'put into a castle amongst Negroes, mulattos, and condemned persons, and all manner of villains, where he lay until 4th July following'. He accuses Dampier of not seeing him properly treated and virtually abandoning him to his fate, though he admits that his commander left him four months' supply of provisions which, however, were 'stolen by the Portuguese'. He was not left alone. His servant, a boy called Robert Raines, was put ashore with him together with one Joseph Busby, who may already have been ill, and who died of disease at Bahia. His other companion, surprisingly, was James Gregson. He emerges in this story as seedy, treacherous and villainous, though an accomplished survivor.

In his letter to the Lords of the Admiralty, Fisher dilates further on his time at Bahia, and drops several dark hints about the company Dampier kept there, though how he could know so much from the confines of his prison cell is questionable; again there are slight contradictions between the journal and the letter. In the letter he writes:

> The third day my captain went ashore to the governor to tell him a pack of lies and to desire him to let him have a prison to put me in . . . I was forced to send for some things ashore that I might sell them to buy me provisions, but my captain at first he would not send my guns nor pistol nor small shot ashore.

Dampier in fact relented, if he had ever refused. But worse was to come:

> He sent . . . me . . . my journal books . . . but first he overhauled my journal and tore out what he pleased. During my captain's stay here he made good his promise in not hurting a hair of Every's men for here he met with some of them and did continually keep them company and did allow his men to do the same . . .

Fisher says he admonished the men from the window of his prison, but they told him they had the captain's permission to fraternize. Fisher rounds off this part of his accusation with the announcement that one of Every's men was John Guy, who 'came to me and told me that he just came from my Captain and he had promised not to harm a hair of his head, and that he [Guy] was the man that cut the cables on board the *Charles* which was the ship that Every run away withal'.

This all seems too good to be true: would Guy have been so obliging as to furnish Fisher with all this information? And would he have used the 'hair of his head' phrase which Fisher himself seems so fond of? The only possible explanation for Guy's behaviour, if Fisher's story is true, is that he was gloating, convinced that Fisher would never make it back to England. Fisher goes on to credit himself with stopping a plan of Dampier's to enlist some of Every's men by threatening to report it to the governor of Bahia. Dampier of course gives a different version of this.

On 4th July Fisher and his servant were put on a Lisbon-bound ship with Gregson. In the letter to the Lords of the Admiralty which I have already quoted from, written on the way, in September 1699, Fisher says of his unwelcome companion:

> He has been a great actor of my misfortune and the only person that was the occasion of a mutiny laid to my charge. I have been forced to be at a great deal of charge in maintaining him and give him a great many good words to get him aboard this ship, but I find it will be to little purpose, for in his passage he has turned his religion and does design to leave me for fear of being brought to justice . . .

Gregson actually tried to convert Fisher and Raines to Roman Catholicism as well.

It is a long, fawning and rambling letter, in which Fisher chiefly begs their Lordships to pay no attention to the letters from the *Roebuck* which will give Dampier's side of the story. He also takes the opportunity to point out every infraction of naval law which Dampier knowingly or unknowingly committed. Needless to say, Fisher was at pains to correct his captain whenever he saw occasion.

Once in Lisbon, he contacted the English consul, John Earle, and was examined before being permitted to leave for England. From Lisbon he sent copies of letters written in his support, some by English residents at Bahia, to the Admiralty, and requested repayment of expenses he was put to during his 'unjust' confinement. From his entire manner at that time, one gets the picture of a man obsessed with the idea of his own ill-usage, and determined to seek redress.

He arrived in England in December 1699. He laid his case before the Lords of the Admiralty, who promised him justice when the *Roebuck* returned; but for some reason Fisher did not remain in the Navy. He entered the merchant service in February 1700, commanding a ship of 120 tons, and returned home in April 1702 to find Dampier back as well. In the meantime, Fisher's wife had renewed his petition for justice. Fisher made another petition, to the Earl of Pembroke, and then another two at least to jog what may have been reluctant memories. In one he gives his credentials. These are impressive: he volunteered for military service in 1688, was made a gunner, and distinguished himself at the relief of Londonderry the following year, after which he transferred to the Navy, and was made third lieutenant in 1690. He was able to produce seven glowing character references from former captains, including one, dated 21st May 1693, from Sir George Rooke, who was to be president of the court-martial.

Fisher's story was borne out by depositions from various crew members. Baptist Watson, a crewman, says that he saw Gregson beaten for saying he would throw the master overboard. James Barnaby testifies that Fisher did not beat him up, but adds that he heard 'a Spaniard who was discharged from their ship say he would kill Mr Fisher for having used him ill, but heard of nobody else concerned in it nor was any mention made of the captain'. So much for Dampier's suborning of Andrew Gastior. There is no mention of Gastior's leaving the ship at Bahia. The surgeon, Walter Borthwick, fails to remember any mention of Every in the discussion about privateers. Captain Barfoot, who met the *Roebuck* at the Cape Verdes, deposes that Fisher seemed a very assiduous and obedient officer, but adds 'I never heard the captain [Dampier] exclaim against his said lieutenant but on the contrary commended him to be a good officer.' An undated letter written on board the *Roebuck* supports Fisher's accusations unreservedly, and bears out his description of how he saved the ship off the Cape Verdes when the master was drunk. It further states that the purser and the clerk were villains and that Dampier was 'altogether governed' by them. It's signed by ten sailors. Topping the list is James Gregson, followed by Baptist Watson who, to judge from other examples of his handwriting, penned the letter. Another letter from the *Roebuck*, dated 8th April 1699 and signed 'JB' (perhaps John Boate), suggests a ship rife with intrigue and adds: 'It is my opinion they want two or three more Mr Watsons on board to swear what they would have him.' Though Watson was, if anything, on Fisher's side. James Gregson wrote a letter dated 14th May to the Admiralty in which he attacks Dampier's and Hughes's poor navigation. Of Dampier he writes: 'I believe it was through ignorance for I have known him some years and did always think I should find him to be a very ignorant man.' Gregson was later to write again in grovelling justification of what appears to have been his desertion of the *Roebuck* at Bahia, making as his dubious defence the case that Dampier was such a bad captain that he might have been obliged to mutiny had he stayed on board.

Dampier had written very fully on the subject of Fisher's behaviour to the Lords of the Admiralty from Bahia on 22nd April 1699. He adds that he has told the governor of Bahia that they are on their way to Bencouli, not wishing to reveal the secret of their true destination. Portugal might be very interested in a voyage to Australia. He also states that he had met three of Every's men at Bahia and adds, 'I would have brought them away with me had it not been for these unhappy differences which made me dread such infectious company.' He admits to caning Fisher and says that he did so in self-defence: 'He grinned at me in his usual manner and I thought he would collar me.'

In his court-martial papers, Dampier defends himself with vigour and anger, though he does not lose his dignity. He first points to Fisher's contempt for him. Already in the Downs Fisher, in speaking of Dampier to Philip Paine, the gunner, had said 'Damn him for an old rogue, he minds nothing.' Paine and Brand also report hearing Fisher speak with contempt of the Lords of the Admiralty, and Dampier says he reproved his lieutenant for this. As for Fisher's row with the boatswain, in Jacob Hughes's log there is an entry which states that on 21st November 1698 Fisher, the boatswain and 'a woman' were to be transferred to the *Messenger* and taken up to Chatham for 'a trial'. Whether the row was over the woman is not clear. Dampier himself did not like the boatswain, and he was dismissed, to be replaced by John Norwood. Fisher never refers to the incident. It is odd that Dampier didn't use it in his defence, especially as Hughes was one of his witnesses, and had equally been libelled and slandered by the lieutenant.

Worse was to come. In one of his depositions, Dampier attests:

The 28th January [1699] the lieutenant was going to put his bed and bedclothes into the pinnace that lay on the booms, and the boatswain told him that the captain had ordered him to suffer no man to go into the boat, nor put anything in her. The lieutenant replied, the captain ought to have acquainted him with it, and ordered his bed to be put into the boat. The captain . . . told the lieutenant that he did expect it from him to show good examples. The lieutenant presently bent his fist and held it to his nose and said he did not care a fart for him, and also told the captain that if ever he saw James Barnaby on the quarterdeck he would kick him off . . .

As for the incident of the broached barrel of beer on 10th March, when the last vestiges of a civilized relationship between them broke down, the account Dampier gives of what happened is graphic:

The captain speaking roughly to the lieutenant for broaching a butt of beer in the night, he called the captain names softly and urged the captain to strike him. Then he loudly called him a great many ill names, as old rogue, old dog, old cheat, and endeavoured to stir up the seamen to mutiny by telling them that the captain knew nothing but was a mere cheat, and when he would not be silent but constantly continued railing on his captain he was at last confined to his cabin.

But it did not end there:

The next day when he continued railing on the captain and calling him as many ill names as he could invent, the captain sent Mr Hughes to desire him to hold his tongue, or else he should be forced to take other measures with him; the lieutenant replied, let the old rogue kiss mine arse, I am a prisoner and I will speak what I please.

Then the water gets a bit murkier. On 18th March, says Dampier, many of the officers advised him to get his bedding on to the quarterdeck, apprehensive of a mutiny fomented by Fisher. Paine secured the gunroom door, and all the small-arms were brought up on to the quarterdeck. The three men chained to the gangway and interrogated in this version were

Beale, Boate, and not Owen Harris but Baptist Watson. According to this version, a 'paper written against the captain' was found on John Boate, who said he'd been ordered to do it by Fisher. If Boate was the 'JB' who wrote the letter referred to above, the *Roebuck* should have been renamed the *Intrigue*! One of James Barnaby's depositions is almost farcical: 'James Barnaby maketh oath that Baptist Watson came to him and told him he would have him tell the captain that somebody had a design upon his life . . . and that Watson named three men to him but he has forgot their names . . .' A likely story!

As for Dampier's fears in Bahia about falling into the hands of the Inquisition, we read here that it was Fisher (possibly aided by Gregson) who turned the priests against him.

In support of his defence, Dampier collected depositions from Paine, Barnaby, Robert Chadwick and John Knight, among others. Alexander Beale 'had gone a voyage and could not be found'. Among the depositions we have two interesting ones regarding the beginning of the fracas on 10th March: 'Lieutenant Fisher acknowledges that in his passion he did call him old rogue, and tell him of his privateering, but that was not till after he had been beaten by him on the deck.' On the other hand: 'Captain Dampier affirms that he called him old rogue and other ill names softly before he struck him, which was the occasion of his doing it.'

The matter of John Norwood is far less well documented and stands very much in the shadow of that of Fisher. It appears to have been something of a put-up job. Norwood's widow Ursula wrote to Prince George of Denmark, consort of Queen Anne and Lord High Admiral of England, on 27th May 1702, that:

> having just reason to suppose both by my husband's letters and papers who was boatswain of the said ship [the *Roebuck*], and also by the report of the officers and sailors that belonged to her that by the barbarous and inhuman usage and confinement for the space of four months and more in his cabin, his door nailed up, and shutters made on purpose to prevent air, was suffocated and died at the islands of Barbados.

This is very sad stuff, but the truth is more prosaic: Norwood was indeed confined by Dampier for a period as a punishment for 'ill practices with the men and endeavouring to discourage the voyage'. Four months is very unlikely. This would have been after Fisher had left the ship, but Dampier is not wrong in suspecting that Fisher might have been behind the charge: 'Captain Dampier . . . declared in court that he had never heard anything of the charge till just against the trial betwixt him and Lieutenant Fisher, and that it was set on foot by the said lieutenant out of ill-will to him.' Dampier had never had the boatswain flogged, or done anything to cause his death. After Norwood had shown himself duly penitent, he was released, as was the custom, and resumed his duties. He remained with the ship until the end, returned home, and did indeed die at Barbados – but by that time he had been at liberty for ten months. Philip Paine testifies that Norwood was a sickly man both before and after his imprisonment, and Borthwick the surgeon tells us that Norwood 'being ill, he did let him blood and found his blood to be putrefied, and that his legs were swelled, but this was after he was set at liberty'. Only Baptist Watson, who was in Fisher's pocket, deposes that 'he heard John Norwood say a little before he died that his confinement had broken his heart'.

The court-martial was held on Monday 8th June 1702 on board HMS *Royal Sovereign*, anchored at Spithead. Sir George Rooke presided, and the other senior judges were Sir Cloudesley Shovell, Vice-Admiral Thomas Hopson and Rear-Admiral Sir Stafford Fairbourne. The great admirals Rooke and Shovell were about the same age as Dampier. Shovell shared a similar humble rural background. It is hard to say how they reached their decision. Perhaps the shadow of Captain Kidd fell over Dampier; perhaps Fisher, as a longstanding professional Navy man, had to be seen to be protected. Perhaps Dampier's defence was not good enough: one cannot imagine him at ease or discharging himself well in such circumstances. Whatever the reasons, though they cleared him in the case of Norwood, they found against him in the case of Fisher, and his punishment was severe:

Captain Dampier has been guilty of very hard and cruel usage towards Lieutenant Fisher in beating him on board the said ship and confining him in irons for a considerable time, and afterwards imprisoning him on shore in a strange country, and it is resolved that it does not appear to the court by the evidence that there has been any grounds for this ill usage of him, and that the said Captain Dampier falls under the 33rd Article for these his irregular proceedings, and the court does adjudge that he be fined all his pay to the Chest at Chatham . . . and it is farther of the opinion that the said Captain Dampier is not a fit person to be employed as commander of any of her Majesty's ships.

So much for Dampier's brush with the Royal Navy.

PART FOUR

The *St George* Venture

CHAPTER SEVENTEEN

An Uncertain Recovery

Several of the early biographies of Dampier leave out the *Roebuck* trial completely. Admiral Smyth, writing in 1837, is no exception, though he does point out one other aspect of Dampier's career at that time which is worth mentioning: all the lists of naval officers, both in manuscript and those published by Admiral Hardy, officially enter Dampier as having drowned in the wreck of the *Roebuck*. It is unlikely that the Navy wanted to bury Dampier's memory so deeply. After all, there are indications that the trial would never have come about had it not been for Fisher's bullying insistence, and possibly the influence of powerful friends of his. This is therefore a very odd error, for not only was the court-martial officially recorded, but Dampier himself published his account of the *Roebuck*'s voyage in the following years. More to the point, the *London Gazette*, Number 3906, gives the following notice: 'Captain William Dampier, being prepared to depart on another voyage to the West Indies, had the honour to kiss her Majesty's hand, being introduced by his Royal Highness the Lord High Admiral. 16 April, 1703.'

From this one sees that Dampier's situation was not as bleak as it might have been. He had not been stripped of his Customs House appointment, and his friends in the Royal Society and elsewhere did not abandon him. Early in 1703, memoranda of the Treasury Chambers of the Customs approve the transfer of the Customs House income to his 'assigns'.

Dampier made a speedy recovery of his fortunes after the *Roebuck* trial. The transfer of his income was made, as we have seen from the *London Gazette*, because he was signed up for another voyage – this time as commander of a privateering expedition to his old hunting grounds off the coast of Peru. This is not all that surprising. He may have been broken as a naval officer, but the Navy was not the whole world, and our mariner's reputation outside it was intact: his knowledge of the South Seas was unique among Englishmen; his contribution to scientific knowledge in the areas of geography, hydrography, natural history and navigation was immense. It would have been insane to deny opportunity to such a man.

The Lord High Admiral who introduced Dampier to Queen Anne was her consort, Prince George of Denmark. On her accession in April 1702, Anne had created him Generalissimo of All Her Forces, Lord Warden of the Cinque-Ports and Captain-General of the London Artillery Company, and Lord High Admiral. He was not a shining light, but 'his temper was mild and gentle', and 'he was free from all vice'. Despite the deaths of all their children, they had a long and happy marriage. Prince George was a member of the Royal Society and took a keen interest in navigation and its related sciences, so it is no wonder that he should have taken Dampier up in defiance of his official connection with the Navy, the more so as he was highly enough placed to be able to ignore any remonstrations from that body. Not that there would have been any. Fisher had had his pound of flesh, and the whole matter could now be forgotten. It must have irked Fisher, however, to see Dampier raised so high again, and in so short a time.

The War of the Spanish Succession had begun in May 1702, bringing with it renewed opportunities to engage in privateering expeditions, with England and Holland ranged against France and Spain. The venture Dampier was to lead was composed of two privateers, the *St George* and the *Fame*, both, according to contemporary documents, with crews of eighty men (the *St George* actually carried 120) and owned by a consortium of businessmen, some of whom had an interest in the *St George*, and others in the *Fame*. Among them were William Price and Michael Mitford, but the principal owner of the *St George* was a young Bristol merchant called Thomas Estcourt. He was a very rich man, and in 1702 he spent £4,000 in fitting her out as a privateer. She had previously been called the *Nazareth*, but was now given a more warlike and patriotic name. She weighed about 200 tons, and was equipped with twenty-six guns, though these were mainly of small calibre. It is hard to say why she was not better armed. Perhaps the owners were looking for ways to save money. If so, it was to prove a very foolish move.

How Dampier and Estcourt met is not certain, but Dampier was the ideal man for the job of captain. One clue concerning the circumstances of their meeting is contained in a remark by Admiral Smyth, who writes:

> We are armed with authority for stating that among the owners were our navigator's friends, Sir Robert Southwell, the President of the Royal Academy, and Edward Southwell, her Majesty's Secretary of State for Ireland, though their names were carefully kept out of view.

Another interested party was Helena Southwell, who wrote to her brother Edward on 21st July 1705: 'I believe I shall very soon have the manteau and petticoat you promised, for I dreamed Captain Dampier was come home with a very good cargo.'

Estcourt may have read Dampier's *A New Voyage*. He may or may not have known about the court-martial; but if he did, he decided that Dampier's advantages outweighed his disadvantages. In any case this was ultimately to be a venture to a part of the world Dampier knew well, where he was known, and feared, by local Spanish governors, and in a business he understood. Dampier, who had no money as usual but still retained his 'golden dreams', must have jumped at the opportunity. He apparently talked persuasively to Estcourt about 'vast profits and advantages to the owner', and described rich Spanish treasure-ships to be found at Buenos Aires – perhaps overstating his case in order to clinch the deal. The expedition was apparently first designed to intercept the Spanish Atlantic treasure-fleet, but Dampier proposed that if it failed to make a substantial enough profit in that ocean, he could sail round the Horn and cruise for the big galleons that plied annually between Manila and Acapulco. Privately, this may have been his intention all along; and he had not forgotten the gold mines at Santa Maria. In any case it must be borne in mind that we depend for most of our information about this voyage on the account of it written by William Funnell, a member of the crew who was in the first place far from reliable and in the second antipathetic to Dampier.

Dampier had certain stipulations attaching to his acceptance of the command. As with the *Roebuck*, he wanted men around him that he knew. This time, again for reasons we can only guess at, few of them can have been available – perhaps many had shipped into the Navy – but he did manage to secure the services of James Barnaby as his second lieutenant.

There was one other old shipmate to hand: Edward Morgan, who had served with Dampier on the *Cygnet* and had been a member of its crew when that ship left our mariner at the Nicobar Islands. Morgan was in prison at the time on a charge which we do not know – probably, to judge from his later behaviour, theft or fraud. Dampier insisted on having him aboard, and the start of the expedition was delayed until Morgan had served his term. Morgan, who became owners' agent on the *St George*, must have been able to give a very plausible account of himself. Perhaps no one knew that his career since the *Cygnet* had sailed from Nicobar had been chequered, to say the least. He had abandoned piracy to become a thief on land; he had converted to Roman Catholicism, and he had been an unofficial secret agent. On one occasion he had been accused of smuggling French prisoners of war out of the country, no doubt for money. Morgan was also appointed purser. In those days, the purser was in charge of the ship's accounts and his office was wide open to corruption. The purser was rarely a popular officer; and Morgan's partnership with Dampier was a murky one.

The mariners received their Commission and their Letter of Marque in April 1703. Articles had already been drawn up the previous October between the owners and the sailors, and signed on the one hand by Estcourt and Price, and on the other by Dampier and Morgan. The sailors were to receive no wage but that deriving from the prizes they took – the old principle of 'no purchase, no pay', which minimized the risk of the owners, but meant that a crew could swiftly become discontented and mutinous if the cruise turned out to be a lean one. Dampier was bound to abide by the Articles, under a penalty of £5,000. A strict note was to be kept of all prizes, and the spoils on return to be divided between the owners and the sailors at the respective rate of two-thirds and one-third. Three other investors in the venture are mentioned in the Articles: Richard Collett, Richard Longford, and John Jacob, aka John Gascoign.

There were difficulties, however, from the outset. Dampier says the owners of the two ships disagreed; William Funnell, the chronicler of the voyage, says that the captains disagreed. The former is more likely; Dampier claims to have been in London at the time the split occurred. Whatever the truth of the matter, Captain John Pulling of the *Fame* retired from the expedition before the ships had even left the Downs, and sailed off towards the Canary Islands on his own account. The *Fame* was blown up at Bermuda in August 1703, owing to the carelessness of one of the purser's servants, who was drawing brandy from a barrel with a lighted candle in his hand. There was no bitterness between Dampier and Pulling – many years later, shortly before his death, Dampier was influential in getting Pulling's son Henry appointed as Lord Orford's principal adviser in setting up the South Sea Company. In a petition to the Privy Council on behalf of his son dated 30th April 1715, just over a month after Dampier's death, Pulling refers to Dampier as 'the famous voyager'.

Leaving Deal Road on 30th April, Dampier made his way to Kinsale, on the south coast of Ireland, in the *St George*, and arrived there on 18th May 1703, to await the arrival of another ship, the *Cinque-Ports* galley, commanded by Captain Charles Pickering. The *Cinque-Ports* was a smaller vessel than the *Fame*, weighing ninety tons, with sixteen guns and a crew of sixty-three, but she was the replacement ship selected to join forces with Dampier. New agreements were drawn up, with Estcourt, Price and Collett representing the *St George*, and Philip Calvert, John Mascall and Charles Pickering representing the *Cinque-Ports*. One of Pickering's crew was a mariner from Fife by the name of Alexander Selkirk. This obscure seaman would become the model for one of the most famous fictional heroes of all time: Robinson Crusoe.

The *St George* was already fully provisioned for her voyage, so it seems strange that she should have put in at Kinsale at all. The fact is that Edward Southwell had more than a little interest there. In time he would develop the place into a major provisioning port. There was an exchange of letters between Southwell and Dampier while Dampier waited for the *Cinque-Ports* and cleaned his ship. Southwell lent Dampier a folio of Spanish charts. Meanwhile there was bickering about money. Price and Collett complained in a letter to Southwell that Dampier was outrageous in his demand for an advance of £450, and recommended that more reliance be placed on Edward Morgan than on the captain. Dampier himself was aware that delays in Kinsale were costing money, and wrote to Southwell on 13th June 1703:

> I shall endeavour to get myself ready to sail as soon as may be, to save expenses, which are daily growing upon us. I have already cleaned the ship . . . and can be ready in four days' time so that I shall afterwards only wait for Captain Pickering's arrival.

Dampier sounds very bullish. He has recruited more men to his crew, which now numbers over 100, and he looks to have 120 before he leaves. He is getting on well with Southwell's agent, Mr Souldin, and Southwell himself is unstinting in the credit he advances to the expedition. But he is still at Kinsale on 10th July, when Price once again writes complainingly to Southwell:

> I observe also that they have spent in about five weeks' time above nine tuns of harbour beer, which is more than a hogshead every day, and everything else seems to be managed with the same sort of husbandry, – and I see the captain gives up the conduct of these matters to others without exercising his own reason, and therefore I wish you would be pleased to take some notice of his improvidence, and enjoin him to look better after things for the future.

Estcourt is getting impatient too, Price adds in the course of his long letter. The good news is that the *Cinque-Ports* is almost ready to sail, having been delayed principally owing to the difficulty of recruiting sufficient and decent men.

Among those recruited is John Smallbone, who, it will be remembered, got the ship out of difficulty when John Cook sailed from Virginia in 1683, when he and Dampier climbed the mizzen mast and opened their coat flaps to the wind. Smallbone is to travel over to Kinsale with Pickering, but Price recommends that he be appointed first lieutenant to Dampier 'in the room of Mr Huxford, whom we look upon to have been the chief occasion of all these extravagancies both at home and abroad'. Dampier, never much of a man for money matters, had clearly delegated financial responsibility to Huxford, who had either abused his trust or was incapable of managing the economic affairs of the *St George*. Quite what Morgan was doing in all this is unclear. At any rate, Huxford was not replaced immediately, and in the end Smallbone does not appear to have held any post of importance.

Huxford wasn't necessarily bad at managing the expedition's finances. Price was overstating his case. A hogshead of beer a day represented half the regulation daily allowance in a Navy man-of-war of similar size to the *St George*. As for other spending, the *St George*, despite all the money Estcourt had spent on her, was still an old, reconditioned ship. In Kinsale she had been in need of further repair. Price, Estcourt and the others may have had a greater stake in the venture than Southwell, but they were cutting corners to maximize their profit. It was a false economy.

On the other hand, there is nothing in Dampier's behaviour to suggest that he was anything other than eager to be gone. He and Morgan wrote a letter to the owners on 13th July:

> Our last was of the 25th June. Since have not received the favour of any yours. We have now to advise you that Esquire Southwell has been aboard our ship with several other gentlemen that came with the Duke of Ormond here; he is mightily well satisfied to find we are so well manned and fitted, of which he assured us he would write to you.

They go on to complain that they need more money, and give detailed justification of their demands. The situation between owners and sailors seemed to have reached a very low ebb. Even Southwell's secretary, William Wogan, reports that the owners 'have conceived so ill an opinion of Captain Dampier's conduct and management, that they begin to despair of the voyage, and give over for lost what they have already laid out'.

Meanwhile, Dampier was arranging through Southwell some sort of financial security for his wife. One is tantalized by his relationship with Judith. They can scarcely have known each other, and yet his solicitude for her is always great. We do not even know for certain when she died, although we can be sure she predeceased him – she is not a beneficiary of his last will, made shortly before his death – and it may be that he never saw her again after this latest sojourn in England. But it would be pessimistic to view the marriage as a complete failure, and wrong to judge a seventeenth-century relationship by our standards. Judith was evidently a woman of great strength of character, as we can judge by hints in the letter Dampier wrote to Southwell on 3rd August:

> it would be expedient for me to send an instrument, signed by me, for disposing of the £200 left in your hands for the use of my wife, which I have accordingly done, and leave it to your management either to get me for it a proportionable share of the ship, or a dividend of what may be got in the voyage. I have not yet written to my wife about it, but shall by next post, and I know it will not please her; however, seeing it must be so, I don't question but she will be satisfied till my return with the salary at the Custom-House, which I hope you will stand her friend to get for her in my absence.

Judith would have been displeased because the £200 Dampier assigns to Southwell appears to represent his entire capital, and the 'instrument' he sends to the latter making the sum over to his management also annuls the clause in his will wherein he leaves the same sum to Judith. As the likelihood of Dampier's dying in the course of the voyage – he was now over fifty – was high, Judith was justified in wondering whether she would ever see the money – or any security – again.

Dampier promises to tell Southwell his precise plans in his next letter. Sadly, this has not come down to us, as it would have confirmed or denied the point made by William Funnell, who wrote the only known account of the voyage, that Dampier's proposal to the owners was to sail to the Rio de la Plata and take Spanish galleons there. Dampier was later to deny that he did, and he would certainly have known best where Spanish booty was to be found. Perhaps the original proposals were an invention of William Funnell, to discredit Dampier.

At long last the *Cinque-Ports* arrived, and the expedition was able to set sail on 11th September 1703.

CHAPTER EIGHTEEN

Disagreement and Disaster

We don't know much about William Funnell. He styles himself 'Mate' on the title page of his book, *A Voyage round the World*, which James Knapton published in 1707, but he never held that rank aboard the *St George*. He was first a steward, and later Dampier promoted him to midshipman. He deliberately sets out to ape Dampier's style, though it may be that this was shaped by an editor employed by Knapton. Subsequently Funnell's book was deliberately associated with Dampier's name in order to sell it more effectively.

Something else is apparent, as has been pointed out by a Victorian biographer of Dampier, W. Clark Russell: 'It is noticeable that, as we progress in Dampier's career, his individuality grows less and less distinguishable. He is vague in Funnell's narrative; he is vaguer still in Woodes Rogers' and then he disappears.' Russell overstates the case. Dampier is a vivid character in Funnell's account, though we see him at one remove, and he is described unsympathetically. But in the two accounts of his final voyage, which I will come to later, it is true that Dampier cuts a minor figure. His commander, Woodes Rogers, mentions him only incidentally in his memoir. It may be that Dampier's bolt was shot by then. By the standards of the time he was an old man and perhaps his memory was failing him in terms of navigation. But I must leave any such speculation until later.

Funnell's tone is set by remarks that occur in his Preface:

The success indeed of our expedition was not such as might at first have been expected from the skill of our commander and the resolution of our men. Disagreements and mismanagements having broken our measures, and defeated our most promising hopes, as they have often been occasions of the miscarriages of the greatest and noblest attempts.

It is wheedling, and attacks Dampier without appearing to; undermining rather than confronting him.

It is Funnell who describes the original plans for the voyage:

Our proposals were to go into the river of Plate, to Buonas Aires [*sic*], to take two or three Spanish galleons which Captain Dampier gives an account are usually there; and if by that expedition we got to the value of £600,000, then to return again without proceeding further: but if we missed of our success there, then to cruise upon the coast of Peru.

The amount he mentions seems fantastic, but he goes on to say that the Manila ships are 'commonly reported' to be worth thirteen or fourteen *million* pieces of eight each. He also explains that they did not go to the Rio de la Plata because they heard at Madeira that the treasure galleons had already arrived at Tenerife. In his *Vindication*, Dampier denies *any* plan to go to the Rio de la Plata, and fulminates unfairly against Funnell's 'reasons' why they did not go there. In fact, Funnell only mentions the £600,000 the Plate galleons were supposed to produce. Dampier took exception to this, which would have been a prodigious sum by any standards.

It is hard to say why Dampier did not publish his own account of this voyage. It is even harder to say why such an inveterate journal-keeper does not seem to have done so on this occasion. But if Dampier wrote anything of substance after the New Holland books, it has disappeared. It may be that as his last two voyages were to a part of the world he had already visited and described in his first great work, he did not think it necessary to repeat the observations made there – though one would have thought that he would be tempted to add to them.

What is of most concern to us is the character presented of him: a poor commander, a coward and a drinker. Even allowing for overstatement and self-justification, there must be some truth in Funnell's implied allegations. What we have from Dampier is a short rebuttal of Funnell's work, which was all he had time to give vent to before sailing away again. It was entitled *Captain Dampier's Vindication of his Voyage to the South Seas in the Ship St George, with Some Small Observations for the Present of Mr Funnell's Chimerical Relation of the Voyage round the World; and Detected in Little, Until He Shall Be Examined More at Large*. It was also published in 1707, but it will come as no surprise that its publisher was not James Knapton. It is a mere eight pages long, but it is packed with pure fury.

Unfortunately for Dampier, there was a rejoinder to this. John Welbe, another midshipman on the *St George*, published *An Answer to Captain Dampier's Vindication*, which supports Funnell's version of events. Oddly enough, in a letter written years later in 1722, Welbe contradicted the assertions he'd made in his pamphlet. Welbe was not a man with great things before him; but he writes well and temperately, and his testimony must be heard.

As with Fisher, one wonders most of all what can have excited such antipathy. Dampier was overbearing and ill-tempered. Bad temper and bullying in a commander are marks of weakness and an inability to keep order. Lack of self-control is also one of the symptoms of alcoholism.

It may be that Dampier was a good commander of his ship, but a bad commander of his men. In battle, he seems to have been a disaster. Welbe, who spares Dampier nothing, makes an interesting comment about Dampier's arrogance, which has been more than hinted at elsewhere:

> He used sometimes to call the officers aft to a council of war. Now, it is usual in a council of war for the youngest officer to give his opinion first; but, to the contrary, Captain Dampier would always give his own opinion first; and then, if any of the officers gave their opinion contrary to his, he would fly out in a passion, and say, if you know better than I do, take you charge of the ship. He was always a man so much self-conceited, that he would never hear any reason.

There are echoes of the estate manager William Whaley in this. Whaley had a very similar opinion of Dampier.

One wants to believe Dampier's version of events; but there are enough mishaps echoing the misfortunes of the *Roebuck* voyage to suggest that the failure of the *St George* expedition must to a great extent be laid at Dampier's door. But the officers who remained with Dampier to the end were key officers, the carpenter and the surgeon among them; Dampier once again did what he could with a poor ship and an unreliable crew; had Dampier become the kind of man Funnell suggests, despite the undeniable failure of the *St George* venture, it is unlikely that he would have been selected almost immediately after his return from it to take part in another expedition, as well planned and executed as the *St George* cruise was not.

The first problem arose as early as 7th October 1703, when the two ships anchored at Porto Praya on the island of St Iago in the Cape Verdes. Funnell writes that here 'being some disagreement between our captain and first lieutenant, our captain turned him ashore with his chest and clothes, and servant, much against both their wills, at twelve at night'. This lieutenant was, of course, Mr Huxford, whom the owners had taken against at Kinsale.

Dampier retorts:

There was no such thing, for it was Mr Morgan, purser and agent, that disagreed with Lieutenant Huxford, *went ashore, and fought*. Upon which a Portuguese officer, a sort of corregidor [magistrate], confined Mr Huxford; and a day or two afterwards, he sent himself for his chest and clothes, which was delivered. But the day before I sailed, I sent for him aboard, and his chest and clothes actually came, so that I had no manner of aversion to him; but Mr Morgan swore, if Mr Huxford sailed with us, he would not go on the voyage.

Dampier goes on to say that he ordered Huxford aboard the *Cinque-Ports*, but that when Pickering's second-in-command, Thomas Stradling, and Huxford were being ferried across from the *St George* to Pickering's galley, they had a row as a result of which Stradling put Huxford aboard a Portuguese merchantman which deposited him on St Iago.

This sounds just about all right as far as it goes, though the latter part of Dampier's explanation is very circumstantial. The main point is that Dampier should have upheld the authority of his first lieutenant;

he did not, and he clearly did not have the force of character to settle things between Huxford and Morgan. Morgan, indeed, seems to have Dampier somehow in his power. Above all, none of his experience on board the *Roebuck* seems to have taught our mariner how to manage a ship and its crew in a proper and orderly manner. He had learnt too many bad habits in his first twelve years as a sailor. One editor of Dampier's works in a compendium of voyages published in 1744 commented succinctly:

> It is very clear, from the several particulars recorded in this voyage, which I take to be as honestly and sincerely written, as any I have ever met with, that there is no mighty force requisite to carry on a privateering war in the South Seas; since, if Dampier's temper would have suffered him to live on such terms as were requisite to preserve the affections of his people, it is most certain that he might have raised an immense fortune for himself and for his owners, in spite of anything the Spaniards did against him.

Midshipman Welbe's opening attack on Dampier is a positive broadside: 'What Captain Dampier writes is all scandalous, false and malicious . . . his ferraginous compendium, full of enthusiasms and improbable stuff, such as no man yet could ever understand; no, not even the courageous author himself.' His version of the Huxford story is much more detailed than Funnell's:

> as for what Captain Dampier says concerning Lieutenant Huxford, it is true, Mr Morgan and he had a small quarrel; but it was in taking Dampier's part, who were, both after and before we left Ireland, at continual variance. Witness the very first night we came to sea, they [presumably Dampier and Huxford] had such high words in the cabin that Captain Dampier called to the master in order to put the ship about, and stand in again for Kinsale, in order to put him ashore.

Welbe says he wouldn't have blamed Dampier for doing that, but to put Huxford ashore at St Iago was appalling: 'Mr Huxford begged of him not to be so barbarous as to turn him ashore amongst a parcel of banditties and Negroes; but desired him to let him lie in the longboat; or he would be contented to go before the mast, rather than go ashore amongst a parcel of heathens.' For good measure, Welbe adds: 'I wonder not at the captain's monstrous barbarity, knowing the like scene of cruelty was acted by him when commander of the *Roebuck*.' Dampier's reputation had evidently gone before him. Welbe further tells us that Huxford died, 'partly with hunger', three months after being put ashore.

Funnell's other comments worth noting while at the Cape Verdes concern the people of St Iago, with whom members of the expedition traded. He describes them as the descendants of Portuguese men – Funnell says convicts – and local black women, though the population now was almost universally black: 'yet they still retained the vices of their progenitors, thieving being more common here than any place I have ever visited, insomuch that they will take a man's hat from his head at noonday, and in the midst of company'.

Having taken in fresh water and supplies, they crossed the Atlantic, making for the coast of Brazil. On the way, they caught various kinds of fish, and Funnell describes some of them: there was a dolphin (probably a dolphin-fish), an old wife, an unspecified kind of shark, and something intriguing: a 'jelly-fish', which he says had sharp teeth, a sparkling eye, a long, extended mouth and a prodigiously high fin on its back. It was fourteen inches long, two inches wide and was of a green, jelly-like substance. Perhaps it was a monkfish or some other kind of deep-sea angler which had somehow found its way into their nets. Elsewhere, Funnell's observations of natural history are dutiful, but sometimes they are very good indeed – here the effort to imitate Dampier is most marked – though they are seldom charged with Dampier's enthusiasm. One cannot convince oneself that Funnell has any real sympathy for the animals and peoples he encounters. The illustrations in his book are so crude that scarcely any animal could be identified from them. His navigational observations are lamentably inaccurate. To add insult to injury, he disparages Dampier's own measurements of longitude and latitude.

They crossed the equator on 2nd November, and soon afterwards arrived at the lush Portuguese island of Grande just off the Brazilian coast. Here, the new first lieutenant, James Barnaby, fell out with Dampier, and went ashore with eight men. Here also Charles Pickering died, and was replaced as commander of the *Cinque-Ports* by his lieutenant, Thomas Stradling. At the same time, Alexander Selkirk was promoted to the rank of quartermaster. Funnell writes of the row with Barnaby, who had sailed to Australia and back with Dampier and had been involved in the court-martial, that he and Dampier had quarrelled. In the *Vindication*, Dampier seethes:

> I take God to witness I never disagreed with him; but finding him a little pert in opinion on a dispute between him and Mr Morgan (again!), I ordered him out of the cabin. Some little time after this, as we rode at the Isle of Grande, he goes on board the *Cinque-Ports*, sent for his things, but I refused them; whereupon he comes aboard after a refractory manner, charges me with a promise; and he, and eight of the men, being rather assisted than hindered by the crew (as Mr Funnell knows) mutinied, to begin *their roguery* they took my boat and went away per force, on a design to board a Portuguese bark that was lying on the other shore . . . Upon which, to acquit myself fairly to all nations, I sent letters to the governor of Rio de Janeiro, to acquaint him with the knavish part of their intent . . . this Mr Morgan can testify.

This is too much. By the time Dampier was writing he had not only patched things up with Morgan himself, but had been involved in some shady deals with him. Portugal was an ally, and to accuse Barnaby of piracy just sounds too good to be true. The only conclusion one can draw is that Barnaby was in some way justified in leaving the ship. John Welbe's account gives us more than a clue:

> He [Dampier] says he never disagreed with him, which is false: for being both drunk together in the cabin, they quarrelled. Mr Morgan being ashore knew nothing of it; upon which Mr Barnaby desired Captain Dampier to give him leave to take his chest and clothes out of the ship, and he would go ashore to the Portuguese; and Captain Dampier told him, he might take his clothes and go where he pleased. Accordingly the next day he would have gone ashore,

but Captain Dampier would not let him, but took him and tied his hands behind him. But towards evening, one of our men cut his hands loose; and about ten at night he and eight more of our men put their chests and clothes in the pinnace, and desired some of the ship's company to go in the boat with them, to bring her back again, which accordingly they did, Captain Dampier being in his cabin quite drunk.

Having refreshed their water and supplies at Grande, they set off again early in December. Out on the open sea, creature comforts began to appreciate in value to an astonishing extent: Funnell notes that when one of the crewmen died and his goods were sold on 14th January 1704, his sea-chest, whose real value was five shillings, went for £3; a pair of shoes, valued at 4s 6d, went for 31s, and a half pound of thread, value 2s, went for 17s 6d.

The two ships were separated in a terrible storm off the Falkland Islands. 'Of all miserable times passed by the early mariner,' writes W. Clark Russell, 'the most miserable and insufferable were those which they spent off Cape Horn.' So ferocious was the storm that Dampier never saw the Horn, but by 20th January 1704, believing he had passed it, he plotted a course north and made his way successfully to Juan Fernandez. Funnell implies that Dampier didn't recognize it when he saw it. One wants to side with Dampier; but the problem is that there seems to be no reason for Funnell to be gratuitously malicious.

Rounding the Horn was always a harsh business, even for an old hand like Dampier, who had been round it now several times. It could take months from the last port of call, and when it was completed the ship could be a mess, soaking and stinking; the supplies could be used up or spoiled to such an extent that the ships' rats would prefer to nibble the toes of the sailors as they slept than eat what was left of the food in the barrels. The sense of solitude was dreadful, and the idea of losing one's masts in the storms that blew here was unendurable, because in that event a ship would be as good as lost.

At Juan Fernandez, where she arrived on 10th February, the *St George* was reunited with the *Cinque-Ports*, which had arrived three days earlier; but here a major disagreement occurred, though this time Dampier was not involved. Captain Stradling fell out so badly with his crew that forty-two of them – about half the complement – elected to stay on the island. The nature of the row is not detailed by anyone, but Funnell is fair-minded enough to give Dampier credit for settling it. Everyone went aboard again. So the suggestion I made earlier that he could command a ship but not men falls open to question. The problem with Dampier is that there is no pinning him down. On the other hand, there may be a simpler explanation: there was a common saying among sailors that they would weather out even an unpopular commander 'if he were the devil himself'. However unpopular Stradling may have been at that point in the voyage, they were round the Horn and in view of their hopes of gain: those hopes they would not jeopardize for the sake of abandoning their ship. Captains of privateers could not be voted out of office as in buccaneer and pirate ships.

The *Cinque-Ports* was no larger than a modern ocean-going yacht. Given the overcrowding, and the wretchedness of coming round the Horn, no wonder there was disaffection once the men could relax at Juan Fernandez. But there were still plenty of goats here, despite Spanish efforts to eradicate them, and the turnips and other vegetables planted here years earlier by Dampier and his buccaneering companions had flourished. Funnell describes sea-lions well and fully; he also reports seals with fur second only to sables, and cats of a 'lovely colour'. That he had little real sympathy for animals, however, is demonstrated by the following description of sea-lion hunting, which even by the standards of the time is brutal:

> They are much afraid of man; and so soon as they see him anywhere near, they will make to the water; for they never go far from it. If they are hard pursued, they will turn about and raise their body up with their fore-fins and face you, standing with their mouth wide open upon their guard: so that when we wanted to kill one, to make oil, we used commonly to clap a pistol just to his mouth, as it stood open, and fire it down his throat; but if we had a mind to have some sport with him, which we called lion baiting; usually six, seven or eight, or more of us, would go with each a half pike in his hand, and prick him to death; which commonly would be a

sport for two or three hours before we could conquer him. And oftentimes he would find us work enough. But he being an unwieldy creature, and we assaulting him both behind, before and all round, we must needs conquer. Yet he often put us to the run; and sometimes he would run himself, but he knew not which way, for we commonly got between the water and him.

This must be one of the cruellest descriptions of blood 'sport' on record.

At the end of February they sighted a French ship, the *St Joseph*, and set off in pursuit. She was strongly armed, with thirty guns, and the two English ships fought her fiercely, 'broadside to broadside', for seven hours, before a light wind in her favour enabled her to steer away from them. Dampier gave the order not to follow, thinking it a waste of resources. The *Cinque-Ports* had early stood off from the fight, being too small to take on the French ship, and so the bulk of the fighting had fallen to the *St George*. Gallingly, they later learned that the Frenchman was so badly damaged that she had been on the point of surrendering. Funnell says that when he called off the attack, Dampier told them that 'he knew where to go and could not fail of taking £500,000 any day in the year'. This seems a fantastic boast; but perhaps Dampier was still thinking of Santa Maria. In the chase, the *St George* had run her pinnace, which she was towing, under water, and had to cut her loose. Similarly, the *Cinque-Ports* lost her boat when the cable broke. In it were 'a man and a dog', who were subsequently picked up by the French.

They returned to Juan Fernandez. In their haste to chase the French ship, they had left their supplies behind, and now they saw waiting for them near the island two more French warships, both too well armed to engage. They were forced to abandon their other boats (and six men left behind when the ships left for the chase, four of whom were later picked up by the French) and sail north. Without boats, they were seriously hampered: they could not tow their ships when there was no wind, and they could not go ashore except where they could anchor very close – in itself a dangerous undertaking, because there was always the risk of grounding if anchored in very shallow water. By the same token, they could not land raiding parties to attack Spanish coastal settlements.

Thus when they reached Arica, the best they could do was wait outside the harbour for a prize. In this they were almost lucky, for two French vessels did emerge – one of them the same that they had fought in vain off Juan Fernandez – but Dampier refused to engage, though Funnell says the crews were eager to do so. While the English ships dithered about whether or not to attack, both French vessels made their way safely into Callao Road. Funnell is very censorious of Dampier for failing to take these two ships, and describes the crew as 'very much discontented'. That the two captains lacked sufficient fighting spirit is borne out by a manuscript account found among the papers of one Thomas Goldney, a leading Quaker merchant of Bristol, who also had an interest in the voyage.

In the *Vindication*, Dampier tries to justify his actions. But however much he blusters, the impression one gets is of a confused and mismanaged ship. First of all, he claims that he wouldn't engage the *St Joseph* because he saw from her hull that she was 'European . . . and not a Spaniard'. But the French were the allies of Spain at that time. He goes on rather to damn himself as a commander at the mercy of the will of his men:

I was not willing to pursue her farther, but the men being (as they pretended) in a desire of engagement, *right or wrong*, I followed her, and next morning early, we came up with her; and when I saw nothing would disengage them from *an insignificant attempt*, I encouraged them all I could.

But in the action:

Ten of my men suffered, nine killed and one wounded; which dismayed my men so much, they actually run down off the deck, and made nothing of it afterwards; so that when I could have boarded her and carried her, the mate, Clipperton [whom Dampier calls Cleppington] by name, cried, The men are all gone; and Bellhatch [whom Dampier calls Bellhash] the master, whose office it was to be always upon deck, was gone also, though this gentleman is now a valiant talker, to my detriment . . . Mr Funnell says the crew was desirous to fight this ship again. Now, since they made nothing of it while in my power, what was to be done afterwards? And as to my telling them (as he says) I could get at any time £500,000, I say, so I could, had I kept my boats which were then lost, or would my people have been ruled.

The point here is that he did replace his boats later, and if his people would not be ruled, then only he could take the blame for that.

Welbe's version of events is quite damning:

> the miscarriage of the voyage depends wholly on the want of courage and conduct in the commander. As for the French ship that we engaged near the island of Juan Fernandez, 'tis true, we chased her all the afternoon, and fetched upon her; but taking her to be a European ship (as Captain Dampier says in his own scandalous *Vindication*), he did not care to engage her (he believing that she had guns on board, to which he always had a natural aversion; and besides, not knowing how to behave himself, or work his ship in time of engagement, as it plainly appeared afterwards) . . . None of our men quitted their posts during the time of the engagement except Captain Dampier himself, who the whole time of the engagement neither encouraged his men nor gave any regular command . . . but stood upon the quarterdeck behind a good barricado, which he had ordered to be made of beds, rugs, pillows, blankets & c. to defend him from the small shot of the enemy; where he stood with his fusee in his hand, and never so much as took care to have the quarterdeck guns and pattareroes fired. And whereas he says he could have boarded her, and carried her, it is probably true; but he was so far from intending it, that he called out to make sail, for fear the enemy should clap us on board and take us . . .

However much Welbe may be exaggerating, he writes with a feeling that cannot be denied, and one feels that there must be at least a germ of truth here. The inferences we can draw from this about the decay of Dampier's character are so obvious as to need no further comment from me.

They continued their voyage north along the coast – though by now their presence must have been known to every enemy outpost – and soon easily took a small Spanish prize of 150 tons, out of which they took a selection of goods: 'snuff, Flanders lace, woollen cloth, wrought and unwrought silk, pitch, tar, tobacco, turtleshell, beeswax, soap, cinnamon, Jamaica pepper, jars of balsam of Peru, a few planks, and a pretty good sum of money'. Then, on 30th March 1704, they let her go, as Dampier said that to keep her would hinder his main objective. Although he is blamed for this, Dampier's action was in line with the practice he knew, and he says he did not have an officer capable of commanding a prize. One wonders if John Smallbone had died, for he was a sailor of unusually great experience. On the other hand, there is a suggestion in the Goldney manuscript that Dampier and Morgan let the prize go without taking too much in return for a bribe from the Spanish.

The English took a further prize, laden with indigo and cochineal, on 31st March, but let it go as well, according to the Goldney manuscript, on the same terms. This time Morgan also purloined a silver dinner service from the captain's cabin, worth 1,000 Spanish dollars. According to Funnell, the crew was dissatisfied that Dampier did not take more from either of these ships, but he does record Dampier's official reason for not doing so: he did not wish to 'cumber up his ship, for that he intended to make a voyage at one stroke upon some rich town, on which he had a speedy design'. From both these prizes, however, the English took the boats.

Dampier's scheme, it now emerged, was to sail to and take Santa Maria, in search once again of his golden dreams. On the way, approaching Gallo Island, they took a small Spanish prize of fifty tons, which they fitted out as a tender. On 17th April, sailing from Gallo, they took another prize, on board which was a Guernseyman, who had been taken prisoner while cutting logwood in the Bay of Campeachy two years earlier. He was delighted to be freed, and now shipped with Dampier. They arrived off Santa Maria on the rainy night of 27th/28th April, and a raiding party made for it in the tender and three captured launches. It was a filthy night and they were soaked to the skin. Welbe says that before they attacked, Stradling wanted Dampier to give each man a dram of brandy to encourage them. 'But Captain Dampier answered, If we take the town, they will get brandy enough; but if we don't take it, I shall want it myself.'

At daylight an Indian canoe approached and hailed them, and Funnell says that Dampier gave the order for it to be fired upon. This must be nonsense. Dampier knew that the Indians here hated the Spaniards, and that he could have relied on their aid. The only possible explanation is that someone let off a shot without an order being given. This is what Dampier says happened, and there is no reason to doubt him. As his biographer Clennell Wilkinson puts it: 'One feels that he would have done better with this crew if he had brought that famous cane of his into action more often.' But interestingly on this voyage there is no mention at all of Dampier drubbing anyone. If Funnell or Welbe had had any excuse to accuse him of physical cruelty, they would have done; but they do not. Their supplies were so low that the ration was reduced to five plantains to every six men per meal. Morale was equally low. Two boats, with twenty-two men in each, went up the river after the Indian canoe, which of course had made away towards the town. The tender followed. It was still dark, but the men on the boats heard dogs barking ashore, and landed, finding themselves in the little settlement of Suchadero, which had been abandoned by its inhabitants. Here at least they were able to gather up some food: potatoes, chickens and maize.

The tender, missing them in the darkness, went up as far as Santa Maria, but, realizing her mistake, came back down again, intercepting on the way a canoe in which a packet of letters was found. They were from Panama to Santa Maria, and in them they found news from the president of Panama to the governor of Santa Maria that a force of 250 Englishmen was in the vicinity, and that he was sending 400 reinforcements to Santa Maria, with more to follow.

They decided to make an immediate attack on the town, but they bungled it. They fell foul of three Spanish ambushes before they gave up the attempt and withdrew to their main ships. In any case the Spanish would have hidden anything of value by now. They made their way from Suchadero on 1st May, and anchored off Punta Garachina on 6th.

At midnight that night their luck changed almost miraculously. A large Spanish trader anchored near them, believing them to be friendly ships. They took her with no trouble at all, and sailed her to the islands of the Bay of Panama, putting Alexander Selkirk aboard to run her, meanwhile sinking the little tender they had used in the attack on Santa Maria. Here they rummaged her between 15th and 18th May.

They found her to be full of flour, sugar, brandy, wine and thirty tons of quince marmalade, together with a variety of dry goods. But even this led to dissension, for Funnell alleges that Dampier let her go without looking properly for 80,000 Spanish dollars hidden in her hold, of which he had had notice.

Dampier may have wanted to cut and run before the Spanish at Santa Maria got their reinforcements or alerted the authorities at Panama to set out after him. He may have suspected that the rumour of a hidden store of money was a deliberate ruse to delay them. He still had his mind on 'greater designs'. Welbe comments drily that as soon as the Spanish captain of the big prize ship knew that Dampier was a privateer with a commission, he told him that he had put the bulk of his money ashore at Trujillo, having heard from the French ships that there were enemy Englishmen in these waters. The captain knew that Dampier would have to take him at his word, on his honour as a privateer. Had Dampier been a pirate, he could have tortured more information out of the Spaniard. Welbe cannot accuse Dampier of any more on this occasion than acting honourably, but he implies that Dampier may have let the Spaniard go in return for another bribe, and according to the Goldney manuscript, this was also the view of the owners later. As for Morgan, he took the opportunity to relieve the ship of another silver dinner service.

Meanwhile they took yet another modest prize.

They made the most of this opportunity to clean their ships and refresh themselves; but here it was, on 19th May 1704, that Dampier and Stradling decided to part company. Liberty was given to the crews to choose their ship, and five men changed from each, Funnell tells us. Funnell adds that the two captains had quarrelled, which would not have been unusual on such voyages, and it may be that tension had been growing between them in the course of this unfortunate venture, though Dampier later denied it fiercely in his *Vindication*.

Stradling now returned immediately to Juan Fernandez, in the hope of recovering the crewmen and supplies left there when the expedition had been obliged to abandon them several months earlier. Two, who had managed to hide from the French, remained to be rescued. The others, and the supplies, had been taken by the ships which had seen off the *St George* and the *Cinque-Ports*.

The *Cinque-Ports* was now in poor condition, and that may have occasioned the quarrel which now arose between Stradling and his quartermaster, Alexander Selkirk. Selkirk volunteered to be left on the island, rather than continue with Stradling. So bitter was the argument that Stradling was happy to oblige. Selkirk was set ashore with bedding and books, provisions, and some powder and shot. We are told that as the boat which set him down pulled away back to the ship, Selkirk changed his mind and called to the men in it to take him back; but Stradling would not have him. This proved to be a lucky thing for Selkirk, as the *Cinque-Ports* later foundered on the coast; only Stradling and half a dozen of his men survived. They were captured by the Spaniards and sent as prisoners to Lima. Several years later, Stradling escaped aboard a French ship and made his way home.

Selkirk was the first Briton to suffer such a marooning, survive, return, and tell the tale. In time his story reached the ears of Daniel Defoe, and in 1719, aged fifty-nine, the journalist, pamphleteer and political maverick, needing money to pay for his daughter's wedding, published his first novel (and one of England's first). Loosely based on Selkirk's experience and that of William, the Moskito Indian, it was called *Robinson Crusoe*.

Meanwhile, Dampier continued his unlucky cruise. He had learnt from another small prize that the Spanish had fitted out two men-of-war to hunt him down. On 22nd July they encountered one of them and fought a hard battle with her, using up a large amount of ammunition, but neither doing nor receiving much damage. Funnell says grandiloquently that the *St George* fired 560 shots to the Spaniards' 115; to which Dampier retorts that not sixty ever hit the Spanish vessel. Given the small bore of the English cannon, Dampier's version is probably the more credible; and yet, if that was the case, why did he waste so much ammunition to so little effect? The wind was adverse, so that he could not cut and run; and he was obliged to put on a brave face, given that his crew was demoralized and on the verge of mutiny. Welbe denies this, and with worrying precision attributes the botching of the fight to simple bad seamanship on Dampier's part. It is hard to accept that Dampier was losing his touch and throwing away his experience. But if he was becoming an alcoholic, the decline is easier to understand.

There may be other, attendant reasons for Dampier's slide downhill. He was over fifty, already a good age for his day. He had spent almost as much time on the deck of a ship as on land; and his body had had to cope with all the rigours of travel to the four corners of the globe, with little or no medication to help it. Dampier may have taken to drink, or he may have aged prematurely. Perhaps both. Whatever the truth is, age was eroding him; but however much it might conquer his powers, it had not yet curbed his spirit.

Nightfall put an end to the conflict, and in the morning they found the sea empty: the Spanish vessel had sailed away. So perhaps after all he was bested. On 28th July, in the Bay of Tacames, they took a fifty-ton bark which they kept, calling her the *Dragon*.

If Dampier is to be believed, though his *Vindication* of the voyage is very intemperate, he was ill-served by a craven crew. Shortly after this encounter, he sent a boat ashore to collect wood and supplies from a village near the shore, but upon one shot being fired from it, the raiding party beat a hasty retreat back to the ship. 'And these are the mighty bravoes that are fit to set people by the ears at home, and make scandal as rife with me as 'tis with them,' he comments acridly. There is no doubt that mutiny was in the air. Dampier was already watching his master, Bellhatch, his mate, John Clipperton, and others as being 'on the watch to overset the voyage'. Added to these problems, the ship was beginning to show serious signs of wear. They had no real profit from their cruise, and everyone was thoroughly fed up with the whole venture. It was now the middle of August.

In this mood they made their way to the islands in the Gulf of Nicoya, to find one where they could careen in safety. This they did, catching fish and turtle to eat; but when the carpenter was able to assess the state of the hull of the *St George*, his report was gloomy. The planking was completely honeycombed, so much so that Funnell says that firm wood was no thicker than a sixpence (the thickness of a modern ten pence piece). He adds: 'We could thrust our thumbs quite through with ease' in some places. Had the case really been that bad, the *St George* would have gone no further, but Funnell writes with less self-discipline with regard to the facts than Dampier ever did in the good days of his writing. Even so, they had no timber to replace rotten planking, and the carpenter — a competent man on this voyage — did his best with nails and oakum. Caulking was done with whatever came to hand *in extremis* in those days: jerked beef, tar, tallow, bits of rope — anything that would keep the water out or, at least, from winning.

The *Dragon* had been fitted out as a consort, and while the *St George* was hauled up on the beach being repaired, all her ammunition and stores had been transferred to the *Dragon* in order to lighten the large vessel. At this moment, on 2nd September 1704, those most discontented with the voyage, twenty-one in all, mutinied under the leadership of the mate, Clipperton, and seized the prize. In it he sailed away under cover of darkness; though he relented before parting company completely and returned a fair proportion of the ammunition and supplies. George Shelvocke, who later sailed with Clipperton, but had no reason to like him, accuses Clipperton of having also stolen Dampier's commission, without which our mariner would have been unable to prove himself other than a pirate. In fact Clipperton did nothing of the sort. Dampier himself says that he had the commission still, after Clipperton's departure, in the middle of a tirade in his *Vindication* against those who were abandoning him:

> I can't forget to tell the world these fellows in their common practice, Bellhatch, Clipperton and the rest, whenever they were upon command, stripped the prisoners, Indians or Spaniards; whereas let them convict me of anything more than the most compassionate Christian usage to all ranks of men, and this I thought was the best way of performing the voyage. Therefore to return to Mr Clipperton, let the world judge if these rogues (whose cruelty is a mask of cowardice) were not upon the watch from time to time, to overset the voyage; for there was Bellhatch the master, Clipperton the mate, Bath the gunner, and about twenty men; with the never-to-be-forgotten Captain Thomas, which I will speak of hereafter . . . As soon as ever the mate Clipperton was gone, then the rest of the crew made a demand to have the money and plate; and what was got, shared amongst them, which I refused to do; and when I found they were in the mutinying vein, I produced the Queen's Orders, and told 'em it was out of my power; but if at the end of the voyage

they would carry the ship into any port of the West Indies or East, I would do justice to my owners and them.

Again, this is all protesting too much. The crew must have been aware of Morgan, the owners' agent, helping himself to booty; and in view of his own plan to defraud the owners, as we shall see, Dampier is guilty here of rank hypocrisy, if no more.

John Clipperton has been represented both as a hero and a villain. In fact he seems to have been a capable seaman, generally well regarded, whose subsequent career was distinguished, though ultimately tragic. Once again, one is faced with the fact that, on balance, such a man would not have mutinied without due cause. But there were still principal officers who remained loyal to Dampier. The truth of the matter remains impossible to assess fairly. It may simply have been that Clipperton and those who went with him were dissatisfied with Dampier's success as a commander. After all, he had apparently promised the moon; but he had delivered next to nothing.

Clipperton made his way along the Gulf of Nicoya, plundering as he went, then crossed the Pacific to the Philippines, and thence to Macao, where his crew divided up and dispersed. Funnell later met some of them at the Cape of Good Hope on his own way home. Clipperton returned to England in 1706 and went on, in 1718–22, to make another privateering voyage round the world, partly in the company of George Shelvocke. It was an ill-fated venture. He and Shelvocke did not get on, and matters were made worse when the ships' owners replaced Shelvocke with Clipperton as overall commander of the venture. Almost as soon as they were at sea, Shelvocke used a storm as an excuse to part company from Clipperton. Shelvocke had all the expedition's liquor aboard, which made matters very difficult for Clipperton in the management of his crew. The two captains did not meet again for two years. In the course of an unlucky voyage, during which he did his duty as well as he could in the circumstances, Clipperton took to drink himself. He returned to Galway in Ireland in June 1722, where he was reunited with his family; but he died within a week of landing.

Dampier rallied his remaining men with the proposal that they now go after the Manila ship, soon due to arrive off the west coast of Mexico.

Quite how he proposed to take such a large and heavily armed vessel with the crazy and battered *St George* is unclear, but he persuaded his crew to it. Dampier by now was desperate for some kind of success; it may be that the proposal was political: he had to hold the crew together at all costs if they were to get home. Whatever the reason, they set off to cruise for her, and on 9th October had the luck to take a prize whose captain was one Christopher Martin, who was a native of the Canary Islands, but had grown up in London and had sailed as a gunner with Captain Eaton many years before. He ran away while Eaton was at Gorgona Island and hid until Eaton had left. Then he made himself a catamaran with two tree-trunks, rigged a mast, made a sail of two shirts, and filled a bag with oysters as his provisions. In this way the resourceful man sailed over to the mainland, a voyage of just over a day and a night.

Martin helped them locate the Manila ship and on 6th December they came in sight of her near the Volcan de Colima. She was the *Rosario*, armed with eighteen- and twenty-four-pounder cannon. The most the *St George* had was five-pounders. Nevertheless she engaged the galleon. Christopher Martin advised that the privateers try to come alongside and board immediately, and that, given the discrepancy of armament, would have been the best course of action. One would have thought that with all his experience Dampier would have seen it for himself. But instead he hesitated, allowing the Spanish to get a broadside or two in, damaging the *St George* so badly – one shot into her rotten timbers at the stern took out two feet of plank near the waterline – that she was obliged to stand off. Funnell describes the action without comment. Welbe accuses Dampier of the rankest cowardice. Indeed, sadly, if Welbe is to be believed, he is describing the actions of a man who has either lost his nerve or who is damagingly drunk. Dampier's own account, saying that the helmsman disobeyed his orders, is scarcely convincing. In the *Vindication* he gives a long, embittered and nautically technical justification of his failure to take the Manila ship. It has to be said that Dampier is so angry that he doesn't appear to have read Funnell's work closely, or failing that, to remember details. Of the fight with the Manila ship, for example, Dampier accuses Funnell of saying that they gave the Spaniard several broadsides before she could run her guns out. Funnell actually says that she got her guns out *before* they could fire on her, the delay being occasioned by an argument about whether or not to get alongside immediately and try to board her.

Welbe's version is the most interesting. After they had sighted the Manila ship, he says:

> She hoisted her Spanish ensign and fired a gun to the leeward, as a friend, believing us to be a Spanish ship. Upon which the officers desired the captain to hoist Spanish colours and answer her with a gun to leeward, but he would not consent to it, but immediately hoisted an English ensign and fired a shot at her.

This may have been very honourable of Dampier, but it was against all the accepted rules of combat, and robbed him of a brilliant advantage. Quite why he did it is unclear. He had raised the red flag of no quarter when engaging the Spanish man-of-war.

Welbe continues:

> She no sooner perceived that we were an enemy, but immediately sprung her luff, and hauled close upon a wind, and so got to windward of us, and got time [to make] a clear ship, and got a tier of guns out from betwixt deck . . . After which we tacked, and run along her side, the men being resolved to clap her on board, but the captain was so much against it that when the boatswain ordered the man at the helm to edge near her, in order to clap her on board, the captain swore he would shoot the man at the helm through the head, if he offered to edge near her. After which, having received several shot under water, one of the men told the captain that our ship was sinking, and that now was the time to clap her on board. But instead . . . the captain cried out, Where is the canoe? Where is the canoe? And was for getting into the boat to save his life, which showed what man of courage and conduct he was.

Having missed their opportunity, they stood off from the Spaniard, 'being exceedingly vexed at the captain's conduct'. This became even odder, and if Welbe is telling the truth, Dampier seems to have been as drunk as a lord: 'Then the captain said, Well, gentlemen, I will not say, as Johnny Armstrong said, I'll lay me down and bleed awhile; but I will lay me down and sleep awhile; but he forgot to wake again, till seven or eight o'clock the next morning.' He left no orders with his officers, but set a sentry at his cabin door to prevent his being disturbed.

Whatever the truth of the matter, lost in recriminations, they failed to take the ship, and thus lost a fortune estimated by Martin at sixteen million pieces of eight.

Nevertheless, Dampier persuaded his men to agree to cruise with him for another six weeks. If by then they had turned up nothing of profit, he said, he would agree to make sail for the East Indies. They did manage to take a brigantine on 26th November, which they fitted up as a consort. In the Bay of Amapalla on 5th January 1705 they managed to catch a vast number of swarming fish, including fifty-eight albacores of fifty to 150 pounds each, and much smaller, sprat-sized fish by the bucketful.

But by the end of January, discontentment led to another 'mutiny', in which thirty-five men, including Funnell, Welbe and Morgan, elected to part company with Dampier, and, taking the latest prize, to sail in her for home via the East Indies. In this latest confrontation, which Dampier describes with great bitterness, though Funnell and Welbe allege that the separation was by agreement, even Edward Morgan turns – if Dampier is to be believed – with violence against his old comrade in arms. However, preparation for departure seems to have been orderly enough. Fresh water was far up a hillside, so that a forty-fathom-long canvas pipe had to be rigged to carry it down to the ship. The ship's doctor advised the men not to throw out the duckweed in the water, as it would help the water retain its freshness.

To read Dampier's account of the split in his *Vindication*, however, is to enter the realms of melodrama. Funnell hinted in his book that one source of discontent was the rumour of a secret deal between Dampier and some of the men. Dampier seizes on this first and then builds to a climax which an unkind person might describe as hysterical:

> We must not omit that Funnell says, that it was concluded between Captain Dampier and thirty of our men, to continue in the South Seas, but upon what terms this agreement was made, was kept a secret.
>
> 'Tis well known I never proposed anything that was otherwise

than honourable and justifiable on our return to England; he [Funnell] knows their villainy, and is really witty in his turning robbery and murder upon me. *Whereas* I would have kept all my men, and begged for any little respite, that they would consider the blackness of their action. So that where Mr Funnell himself was chiefly an undertaker, his fear of being taken up at home, may extort this as well as other follies he is guilty of. For when he would colour over the matter, he says the owners' agent (Mr Morgan, who is beholden to him) appointed and shared the provision; so among them be it. I was no sooner at an anchor at Amapalla, but all hands as one man went to work in getting the bark on board, and took my guns and provision out by force. And that Mr Bellhatch by name, that all men may know him, and how far he is to be entrusted, took me by the throat, and swore if I spoke a word, they would dash my brains out, the rest standing by conniving at the action. So that when we come to repeat that which may be spoken of more at large, they asked for my keys of the powder room and chests of small arms. I denied 'em. Mr Morgan himself said, as to that we have iron crows [crowbars] on board, they are as good keys as we desire, and with that broke 'em open.

Of sixty hands that remained, they left me twenty-seven men after rifling everything. Now I refer myself to all mankind, as they made their brags they left me but one sailor; *so they left me life there*. But would they bereave me of my good name here, and stab my reputation forever? But to make sure play still, they turned my [Spanish] prisoners ashore, and by this method intended to lay such a bar in my way, that as they have reported, I should never come home. It is a miracle in nature how I did. Considering the Spaniards had notice of me before I got upon the coast of Peru, through releasing their prisoners. Now let all mankind judge of the miserable condition I was in . . .'Twould be tedious to insert their impudence; but when that buffoon, Toby Thomas by name, said, Poor Dampier, thy case is like King James', everybody has left thee, I must declare to the world then, as always, the doctor was the only officer that stood by me in all my adversities . . .

The doctor was John Ballet, who was to go on Dampier's last voyage with him. Dampier presents himself as more sinned against than sinning; but the question remains whether or not the crew had a genuine grievance. Was he trying to cheat them? It isn't very likely, but Dampier seems to be covering up for something. As for Morgan's behaviour, it is extraordinary that later in London Dampier should once more have teamed up with him. Why Morgan deserted him is another mystery: he wouldn't have jibbed at turning pirate – if that was indeed Dampier's plan. Might they still in some way have had a hidden partnership? Amidst so many allegations and no proof at all, anything is possible.

Welbe is certain that Dampier's idea was to cheat the owners and sail from now on for his own profit. Of the quarrel with Bellhatch, Welbe says that it was occasioned by Dampier's 'usual treatment to everybody, being Rogue, Rascal, Son-of-a-Bitch, and other such vulgar expressions'.

Those who parted from Dampier here had a hard voyage ahead of them. They had no doctor, medicines or carpenter. Funnell does not say if they had a leader. Perhaps he was the 'Captain Toby Thomas' Dampier refers to so angrily. Their supply of fresh meat was soon used up, and from 3rd February until the end of the month they fed entirely on plantains, two per man per meal, and two meals a day. These lasted until the end of the month. Though they occasionally caught fish, Funnell gives a stark description of their predicament thereafter:

We had then recourse to our flour, of which half a pound was allowed daily to each man, and two ounces every other day of salt beef or pork; but the meat had been so long in salt, that it shrunk one half when boiled, wherefore we concluded it was better to eat it raw, which we did as long as it lasted. By the beginning of April that began to fail, so that we were reduced to flour alone, which was sore spoiled, being full of maggots, spiders and other vermin, so that nothing but the extremity of want could have induced us to eat it. It was surprising to behold this strange alteration in the flour, which only a few days before was white and fine, and was now in a manner all alive, the maggots tumbling over each other in prodigious numbers. On strict enquiry, these maggots seemed to proceed from the eggs of spiders deposited among the flour, out

of which maggots were bred, and then fed voraciously on the flour
... In this manner we spent ten weeks, at the end of which we
were in a very melancholy condition, and nothing but the hope of
seeing land could possibly keep us from despair.

They reached Guam in the Ladrones on 11th April. Early May found
them on the coast of New Guinea, and by the end of the month they
were at the clove-trading centre of Amboyna. There they were interned by
the Dutch, who treated them inhumanly, and their vessel was confiscated.
They were sent home on the next Europe-bound convoy, via Batavia and
the Cape of Good Hope, where Funnell gives us one more disgusted
description of Hottentots, and they arrived in London on 28th August
1706. Morgan left them in Batavia, converted his loot into cash, and
arrived home about a month ahead of Funnell.

Dampier had been left with twenty-seven men. The *St George* continued
to cruise, taking the town of Puna successfully and commandeering a
Spanish ship to replace the by now ruined *St George*, which they abandoned
at Lobos de Mar. In her, Dampier navigated his men across the Pacific
once again, and reached the East Indies, where he and his men were
arrested by the Dutch authorities as pirates – either Clipperton had
really stolen their commission or, as Dampier's last commander, Woodes
Rogers, tells us, they had lost it somehow at Puna – and languished for
some time there before being allowed to return as passengers via South
Africa to England. The Dutch were allies of England, after all.

Back home at the end of 1707, Dampier had nothing to show for his
voyage. Had he even lost the £200 he had invested through Southwell?
There is evidence to suggest from an action brought by some of the
original owners that Dampier was involved with Morgan in a scheme to
defraud them of a portion of the small profit the venture had made. If
true, and it seems very likely, then it is understandable. Dampier wanted
financial security: by now he was approaching sixty. Yet his personality
was such that it was incapable of achieving security except by desperate
and risky means. He probably felt he had to redress the poor luck fate
had dealt him by any means. What rich, bourgeois owners would regard
as a small loss would be a significant gain to him. But he was judging
them by his own financially feckless standards: he failed to recognize

that the fundamental characteristic of the rich is extreme care when it comes to money.

Thomas Estcourt had died in 1704 without an heir, and left everything to his younger sister Elizabeth, then a minor and unmarried. His executors were his relatives Walter Estcourt and Richard Longford. By the time Dampier arrived home and the balance of profit and loss on the expedition had been assessed, Elizabeth had reached her majority and married one Richard Cresswell. These two then sued ten parties interested in the venture for fraud. The defendants included Goldney, Dampier and Morgan, as well as Thomas Stradling and Richard Longford. Goldney was also accused of using Cresswell money to invest in a further privateering venture, in which the Cresswells therefore claimed an interest. This venture, the voyage of the *Duke* and *Dutchess*, also involved Dampier. It was further alleged that Longford, Dampier, Collett, Jacob *alias* Gascoign and others met at the Young Devil Tavern near Temple Bar and at Collett's house, among other places, to conspire to make a division of the spoil without Elizabeth's knowledge. The details are murky and no case was ever proved, but the Cresswells were well informed about the conduct of the voyage by someone who had taken part in it, and their anonymous source bore out the allegations of Funnell and Welbe, and for that reason it is worth mentioning. Incidentally, there is a tradition that Elizabeth was subsequently murdered by her older sister Mary, who wished to inherit her property, and that her ghost walked her house for years. But that, fortunately, is another story. What happened to Dampier's investment of £200 with Southwell we do not know. He probably lost it.

Funnell disappears from view after the publication of his book. Welbe, however, does reappear later. Between 1713 and 1716 he made several vain applications to the authorities to make a voyage to Terra Australis. By 1716 he was in prison for debt. In spring 1720, calling himself Captain John Welbe, he was the 'master of a small ship in the River of Thames', and seems to have been the victim of a fraud. He was also involved in other litigation, including a charge of treason brought by him and two others against the Swedish consul, Nicholas Mandell. But again we are in murky waters, for he writes to the Earl of Newcastle from Old Southampton Buildings, Chancery Lane, on 13th March 1720, to complain of the 'barbarous usage' he has suffered in being arrested himself: 'The officers knocked down my servant, broke open my doors and took me out of my bed and carried me away in an uncommon manner where I remained in custody three days before I could get bail.' This time he seems to have been involved in some kind of marine insurance fraud. A whole series of letters to Lord Newcastle suggest a man suffering from some kind of persecution mania. I can find no trace of him after 1722.

Even though he was broke, and disreputable again, Dampier's talent as a navigator proved to be his best insurance. He may have been too poor to invest in the next venture, and he may have had to borrow money to buy clothes to go on it; but at least he was invited to take part. No longer as commander, to be sure, but he was too old for that, and after the *St George* and the *Roebuck* it is understandable that no one offered him such a job again anyway. The post he was offered gave him some responsibility, but not a disagreeable amount: he was to go as pilot for the South Seas.

PART FIVE

The *Duke* and *Dutchess*

CHAPTER NINETEEN

Familiar Seas, New Beginnings

As the War of the Spanish Succession approached its fifth year, a new law found its way on to the English statute book.

The Cruisers and Convoys Act of 26th March 1708 (6 Anne cap. 13) was designed both to provide reliable protection for English merchant shipping and to encourage well-planned privateering expeditions against the merchant ships of France and Spain. At least forty-three men-of-war were to be deployed to protect the shipping lanes and trade routes, and for 'the better and more effectual encouragement' both of privateers and naval raiders, the Crown waived its long-standing right to a 20 per cent share in the booty derived from prize vessels. Furthermore, the government, if it wanted to use any prize ship, had to buy it from the captors. Booty was subject to duty, but otherwise this regulation made investment in privateering much more attractive.

Privateering itself had become more formal. International rules had been established to control it, and infraction of those rules could result in heavy fines of up to £3,000. Booty was shared at about 60 per cent to the owners, 30 per cent to the sailors, and 10 per cent in duty and Admiralty dues. Crews were permitted to 'pillage' the personal effects of captured crews and passengers, which theoretically had to be collected at the mainmast as 'plunder' and divided by rank. The size of privateering vessels was regulated by an Order in Council of 1695 to be of 200 tons or more, and of no fewer than twenty guns. Because of the great gains to be made, and the better conditions, 50 per cent of the crew had to be 'landmen', to ensure an even spread of experienced seamen through the Royal and Merchant marines.

The great prize – the Eldorado – of the privateers was the Manila ship. The Spanish had colonized the Philippines despite the fact that according to the Treaty of Tordesillas they lay on the Portuguese side of the line. This led to disputes between the two countries, but in the case of the Philippines, possession was nine-tenths of the law. In any case the Portuguese were fully occupied with their already thriving spice trade. The islands were discovered by Magellan in 1521, and named by Ruy López de Villalobos after Philip II twenty-one years later. But it wasn't until 1564 that Miguel López de Legazpi was commissioned to subdue them. This he did so ruthlessly and effectively that within seven years he had founded Manila and established a trade with Mexico.

There was little in the Philippines to trade with, though good hardwood timber for ships grew there and the vessels built in the shipyards were famous for their durability and strength. Woodes Rogers, commander of Dampier's last voyage, wrote: 'These large ships are built with excellent timber, that will not splinter. They have very thick sides, much stronger than we build in Europe.'

Goods for trade with the New World and from there with the Old came from the Orient, which was nearby. From China, India, Japan (in the early days of the trade), Persia and, to some extent, Siam, came silk, both raw and worked, carved ivory, musk, scents, cushions, carpets, velvets, taffetas, tapestries, stockings, brocades, orange and peach preserves, 'very fine capons', spices, clocks, porcelain, songbirds and jewels. In the new moon of March the islands were visited by flotillas of ocean-going Chinese junks, which Dampier saw and described admiringly when he was first in these waters. Manila became a legendary merchant city.

After the trading season, one large galleon, later more usually two, set off across the Pacific late in June, laden with these goods. They would also carry gold, either as bullion or manufactured goods. In the autumn they reached the port of Acapulco, and immediately a market was held, which lasted thirty days. The gains to be made must have been worth the effort, for Acapulco in those days had little else to recommend it. Simon de Anda wrote that Vera Cruz, which was never known for salubrity, was a paradise in comparison with the 'abbreviated inferno' of Acapulco, with 'its heat and its venomous serpents, and the constant trembling of the earth . . . the sepulchre of Mexicans and Filipinos . . . All the treasures of the world could not compensate for the necessity of living there or travelling the road between Acapulco and Mexico.'

The ship returned from Acapulco at the end of March carrying settlers, supplies needed in Manila, and silver – scarce in China – to pay for the next year's trade. The silver mines of Potosí in Peru and Zacatecas in Mexico, both discovered in the mid sixteenth century, were of course another magnet for European freebooters.

The first galleon sailed in 1565, and the last left Acapulco in 1815. It was the longest-running regular maritime service in history. For the first twenty years, as Santiago de Vera wrote: 'As no other ships but ours have been sighted on the voyage, which is through so remote regions, they have always sailed with little or no artillery, and with as little fear from corsairs as if they were on the river of Seville.' But then in 1587 disaster struck, when the young English raider, Thomas Cavendish, took the *Santa Ana*. The success of his action rocked Spain, but it established no precedent. There had been occasional attempts, or projected attempts, on the Manila ship, such as Dampier's in the *Cygnet* and in the *St George*, but she had not been taken since.

Experienced seamen were scarce in Manila and most governors were venal. They sold the offices aboard ship, which brought great opportunities for lining one's pocket, to relatives or friends, or anyone who would pay their price. The galleons were often under-armed because cannon took up space that could be occupied by goods. Even the shipbuilding and maintenance businesses were riddled with corruption and inefficiency. To live in Manila was to make money with no effort at all. A few weeks' frantic activity each year, before the departure of the Manila ship and after the arrival of the Acapulco ship, and the rest of the time was one's own. The Pacific route was secure. People grew soft, greedy and unwary.

But the voyage was a hard one. A fixed route had been charted by Francisco de Gali in 1584, lying to the south of the Hawaiian Islands, which is why the Spanish never discovered them. The journey from Manila to Acapulco was one of the longest and toughest in the world. It lasted six months, and the fate of those aboard was not helped by poor seamanship, overcrowding, and, as the modern chronicler of the Manila ship, William Lytle Schurz, has it, 'criminal improvidence in the matter of supplies'. Raveneau de Lussan remarked: 'All the crew are so sick and moribund, that of 400 men . . . not a quarter are in condition to defend her, for the malady known as scurvy never fails on the way from the Philippines.' The return journey was better: favourable winds halved the time it took, and the passengers and crews could enjoy the citrus fruits grown on the Californian coast specifically for them.

Thirty galleons were wrecked in the course of the 250 years that the ships ran back and forth. In the course of all that time the English took the great prize four times: Cavendish took the *Santa Ana* in 1587; Anson took the *Covadonga* in 1743; Cornish took the *Santissima Trinidad* in 1762. But in 1709 the prize was taken by the privateering expedition led by Captain Woodes Rogers, whose pilot for the South Seas was Captain William Dampier.

Woodes Rogers was probably born in Poole into an old West Country family, whose motto was *Je ferai mon devoir*, in about 1679. His unusual Christian name was the maiden name of his paternal great-grandmother, and the name was given to the first-born son of the Rogers family for three generations; Rogers himself broke the tradition. The family moved to Bristol and there, in 1705, Rogers married Sarah, daughter and heiress of Admiral William Whetstone, a neighbour of theirs. He quickly became a man of stature in Bristol, inheriting the freedom of the city from his father. He had a house in the new and fashionable Queen Square, and his family life was equally fulfilled: he and Sarah produced three children within the first three years of their marriage. He was a heavily built, tall man with a big body and short legs. His face was round, he had dark eyes and a fleshy, aquiline nose, arched eyebrows and a humorous mouth.

Rogers was a successful merchant, and he had invested his modest legacy in a small pottery. He had also spent seven years apprenticed to a sea captain, but when he turned to privateering he was still a relatively inexperienced commander. Privateering suggested itself to him because he wished to make compensation for losses he hints at, but does not give details of, at the hands of the French. His first experiences of privateering had been as a member of a syndicate of owners. It was his steadiness, his sense of duty and his natural talent for leadership which recommended him to the owners, despite his relatively young age, to command the expedition.

The western half of Hispaniola had been ceded to France by Spain at the Treaty of Ryswick in 1697, and the new governor was Jean-Baptiste du Casse. He quickly established a power base and as commander of the French fleet protected Spanish shipping from English attack in the Caribbean after war had broken out again in 1702. Rogers would have been well aware of the situation in the Caribbean through his father-in-law who had recently been commander of the English Caribbean fleet.

The Spanish wanted to encourage their allies in order to keep out the aggressive Dutch and English. In 1698, the French mariner Beauchesne-Gouin rounded the Horn and opened the Pacific to the French. Rogers had read the Frenchman's account of his voyage, as had Daniel Defoe, who in 1701 wrote a pamphlet arguing that England should establish solid interests along the Spanish Pacific coast. Dampier's expedition in the *St George* had been a fiasco. It needed to be followed up, and quickly. Three French ships, the *St Joseph*, which Dampier had attacked but failed to take, together with the *St Esprit* and the *Baron de Breteuil* – the consorts which had chased Dampier and Stradling from Juan Fernandez – had successfully rounded the Horn in 1703. The French should not be allowed to take the initiative away from England. But the French had already realized large profits in the South Seas, and French trade, as Rogers observed, enabled Louis XIV to continue a war which otherwise he could not afford.

Although one source credits Dampier with suggesting the expedition which Woodes Rogers was to lead – Dampier did have a hand in its development – credit for the idea is claimed and must be accorded to Rogers himself. He was in a much stronger position than Dampier to make the arrangements, being a Bristol man, respected, and with a wealth of contacts in the city.

It didn't take Rogers long to attract an impressive list of backers. Thomas Goldney, who'd been involved with the *St George* venture and was obviously undeterred by it, put up a massive £3,726, making him the principal investor. Among the rest were at least three former and future mayors of Bristol, the town clerk, James Rumsay, who put up £1,552 10s, and two sheriffs. One interested party was Alderman John Batchelor, who had twice been Master of the Society of Merchant Venturers, and had great experience in the privateering business. He became a major investor in the scheme, buying sixteen shares at £103 each. Another large stakeholder was Dr Thomas Dover, who put up £3,312.

Dover was no passive investor, but sailed with the expedition as chief medical officer, for which he drew a salary of £423 per year. As his personality was to carry some weight on the voyage, it is worth introducing him in more detail now.

He was born in about 1660 and established himself early at the forefront of practical medicine, along with Thomas Sydenham, Hans Sloane and others, at a time when the subject was still riven with superstition and quackery. At that time the London Pharmacopoeias contained such specifics as blood, fat, bile, bones, viscera, claws, teeth, hoofs, horns, pigs' dung, cats' urine, and so on. Physicians were grandees, dispensing medicine at second hand. The actual administration was done by apothecaries. Dover's main claim to fame was his advocacy of mercury as a universal cure, from which he got his nickname of 'Dr Quicksilver'. He overdid his recommendation of mercury as a panacea: 'The Indians at the Malucco Islands, and the ladies at Smyrna, often take quicksilver as a remedy against barrenness. An ounce may be taken once a day for a month or two, which will prove an extraordinary remedy.' But he was very far from being a stupid man, and in terms of the state of medicine in his day, he was a real pioneer: 'The most offensive, and most dangerous of all species of vermin, are not visible to the naked eye.'

Dover lodged with Sydenham in London but on the latter's death in 1689 went to live in Bristol. The doctor soon became a pillar of the community, and as physician to the poor of the workhouse he gave his services free of charge. Like most eminent doctors of his day, however, he made a fortune. We don't know why he elected to go on the voyage. He certainly didn't need the money. He was the inventor of the famous Dover's Powder, a precursor of aspirin, which was used as a universal cure-all for centuries, and whose opium base ensured that once people started using it, they would find it indispensable – though this was not Dover's primary intention. Perhaps he was bored with his life as a successful physician. At the time of the voyage he was still only about forty-eight years old. What is certain is that his shipmates must have loathed him. He was overweening, pompous, dictatorial, disputatious and vain.

Two ships were fitted out for the voyage at some expense and, supposedly, with great care – though in fact, as we'll see, far from enough care was taken. Both ships were small three-masted frigates, being about eighty feet long and twenty-five in the beam. They were given the names of *Duke* and *Dutchess* in honour of Marlborough, whose recent victories in Flanders had brought him fame, and his wife. Patriotically enough, the *Duke*'s mascot was a bulldog. The *Duke* was larger than her consort, being 320 tons and carrying thirty guns. The *Dutchess* weighed 260 tons and carried twenty-six guns. The largest cannon were six-pounders. Both ships' hulls were double-sheathed against the teredo worm. It appears that the *Duke* was built especially for the voyage. Her hull cost £1,318. The *Dutchess* was bought second-hand for £830 and refitted. No expense was spared: the *Duke* cost £6,880 to fit out, and the *Dutchess* £4,160. The *Duke* was to carry a crew of 183 men, and the *Dutchess* 151. Both ships had commissions from Prince George of Denmark to cruise on the coasts of Peru and Mexico in the South Seas, and to act jointly or separately against the French and the Spanish.

We don't know how Dampier was recruited for the voyage. He was now fifty-six years old, but his thirst for adventure was unquenched. Either that, or he needed work, and the area of the world the expedition was bound to was not only one he knew well, but one where his reputation, despite his failures, struck terror into the hearts of the Spaniards. It's worth remembering that his name had begun to be known on this coast more than a quarter of a century earlier. He had no real dependants. If Judith was still alive by this time, and we do not know for sure that she was, she would scarcely have been able to object – perhaps she would not have wanted to object – to his leaving her yet again.

Dampier had not lost his friends through the failure of the *St George* venture, and they may have made recommendations to the owners of the *Duke* and *Dutchess*. It is also likely that Woodes Rogers, a careful man in all respects and especially in the preparation of a voyage of this nature, had read Dampier's book. As a result, he may have approached Dampier himself. Unfortunately, Dampier tells us nothing of the matter. He seems to have laid down his pen for good. If he wrote any account of this voyage himself, it has been lost. Once again we owe what we know of the expedition to others. Woodes Rogers is the principal historian of this voyage. There is no hint that Dampier minded joining the expedition in a humbler capacity than he'd been used to; it was not unusual for such a thing to happen, though if he had been offered a higher rank, he would doubtless have taken it. However, he had no money to invest in the venture, his last two voyages were regarded as failures, and he may have been perfectly content to confine his work to navigation and the revision of his charts.

The manning of the expedition was exceptional. In order to reduce the risk of mutiny, 'and to secure a succession in the case of deaths', not only was the normal complement of officers doubled, but the whole enterprise was run by committee: every major decision, such as when and where to make an attack, would be decided at a meeting of officers. Each ship had its own committee, and there was a Joint Council for decisions affecting the entire venture. As the biggest shareholder aboard, Thomas Dover was president of this council, and had the right to a double or casting vote in case of a stalemate. This cumbersome arrangement was managed by Woodes Rogers with confidence, skill, and, on the whole, good humour. In its formalism one can discern the beginnings of modern bureaucracy. The eighteenth century was going to create a very different world from the one Dampier was used to. No wonder he kept quiet for much of this voyage. One can easily imagine such an independent man being very unhappy in committee meetings. This was a long way from the manner in which Sharp, Davis and the rest managed their ships. On the other hand, the new system meant that Woodes Rogers would never have to face the problems with officers and men that Dampier had encountered.

To prevent disagreement between the officers, the expedition was governed by a detailed constitution, ratified on 14th July 1708. Each meeting was minuted. The whole operation of the council is best described in its original definition, from which the following quotation is taken:

We . . . require and direct, that all attempts, attacks, and designs upon the enemy, either by sea or land, shall be first consulted and debated, either in the particular council [ship's committee] if separated, or in the general council if together; and as the majority shall conclude how and when to act or do, it shall be indispensably and cheerfully put into execution, and without necessary delay. In case of any discontents, differences or misbehaviours among the officers and men, which may tend to the disturbance of good order and government on board, either the men or persons may appeal to the captain to have a hearing by the council, or the captain shall call a council to have the matter heard or decided, and may prefer or displace any man according to desert. All decisions and judgments of the council shall be finally determined by the majority of voices; and in the case of an equality, Captain Dover is to have a double voice as president, and we do accordingly order and appoint him as president of the council. All matters transacted in this council shall be registered in a book by the clerk appointed for that purpose.

Instructions for the disposal of prizes taken and prize goods follow, and the captains are enjoined:

To take particular care to keep company, and be assisting to each other in all extremities, as much as possible, and both ships' companies to be united, as if but one ship, one supplying the other freely and willingly with what might be wanting, and to preserve concord among all the men and officers aboard both ships.

The owners and organizers of the expedition were determined to learn from the lessons of the past.

Shares of the booty were also strictly apportioned. The following list shows what a selection of officers and men might expect:

CAPTAIN:	24 SHARES
2ND CAPTAIN:	20 SHARES
IST LIEUTENANT:	16 SHARES or £3 wages and 8 shares
MASTER:	10 SHARES or £2 10s and 5 shares
OWNER'S AGENT:	10 SHARES or £2 10s and 5 shares
PILOT:	8 SHARES or £2 10s and 4 shares
BOATSWAIN:	6 SHARES or £2 and 3 shares

From which it will be seen that Dampier's portion was modest enough. An interesting feature of the share-out system is the possibility provided for those below the rank of second captain – in other words, those without their own cash investment in the venture, to opt for a combination of wages and shares. This device ensured a return for each man, and was designed to reduce the risk of discontentment and mutiny. Ordinary sailors were offered two and a half shares or £1 8s and one and a quarter shares; 'landmen' were offered one and a half shares or fourteen shillings and three-quarters of a share. Provision was also made for reparation to any man so severely injured as 'not to get a livelihood'. For ordinary seamen this was calculated as a lump sum of £30. If a man were killed, his widow would be compensated. In addition, bonuses were offered for singular bravery in a fight. The owners would take two-thirds of the overall profits of the voyage, and their agents were enjoined to keep a strict account of what was taken.

The *Duke* was commanded by Woodes Rogers himself. Under him were a second captain; a master, John Bridge; three lieutenants: Robert Frye, Charles Pope and Thomas Glendall; and three mates. Thomas Dover held the rank of 'Doctor of Physick, Second Captain, President of Our Council, and Captain of Marines'. With him was his brother-in-law, Samuel Hopkins, an apothecary, who was his assistant and also 'his lieutenant, if we landed a party anywhere under his command during the voyage'. One wonders at these medical men leading forces into battle. A man called William Hopkins was 'ship's corporal, Captain Dover's sergeant, and cook to the officers'. John Finch, 'late wholesale oilman of London', was chief steward. John Ballet, the surgeon who had stood by Dampier on the *St George* venture, was rated third mate with special medical responsibility. Dampier also shipped with Rogers, though he would not always remain on the *Duke*. The interpreter for the expedition was Alexander White, about whom little more is known than that he had lived in Peru for many years.

The *Dutchess* was commanded by Stephen Courtney. He 'was a man of birth, fortune, and of very amiable qualities'. His second captain was Edward Cooke, who wrote a dry but workmanlike account of the voyage on his return. Cooke had twice lost ships to the French and been made their prisoner; like Rogers, he sought revenge on them and restitution from them, though he writes that when he was their prisoner they treated him with 'extraordinary [and] singular civility'. It is Cooke who credits Dampier with first proposing the voyage, and Cooke also says that when 'any considerable enterprise' was debated in council the advice of Dampier had to be sought. Again there were three lieutenants, including Rogers's younger brother, John, a master, and, for some reason, this being the smaller vessel, five mates. The medical crew was headed by James Wasse, who had studied in Leyden – 'a very honest, useful man' – a physician and surgeon, with two orderlies, Charles May and John Lancy, under him. The owners' interests were represented by Carleton Vanbrugh, younger brother of the architect and playwright, aboard the *Duke*, and William Bath aboard the *Dutchess*. In accordance with Admiralty regulations, however, not all the men aboard were seasoned sailors, and that included some of the officers. Two of the midshipmen on the *Duke*, George Underhill and John Parker, were junior lawyers in search of some adventure before launching on their legal careers. Thomas Dover's complete ignorance of nautical matters, coupled with his arrogance, was to lead to near-disaster later in the voyage. Fortunately, Dover's manner successfully alienated everybody. No one would support him, and that negated the power his double-vote would otherwise have given him.

One result of having such a large medical team on board – six men for a total joint complement of 334 was not a bad proportion – was that mortality through sickness on the voyage was impressively low. As always, scurvy presented the greatest threat. It could take hold within a five-week voyage, and its symptoms – lethargy, loosened teeth, black blotches on the skin, and swollen limbs – were all too easily recognized. It is worth noting that as early as 1636 John Woodall in *The Surgeon's Mate* recommended the daily taking of fruit as an antidote for the sickness, though it was to be 159 years before the Royal Navy officially adopted the remedy. An ounce of citrus juice daily was enough to keep scurvy at bay, though chocolate, fresh green vegetables and fresh meat would also serve. After 1795, it vanished overnight. Meanwhile, about 800,000 seamen had lost their lives through the sickness since Woodall published his findings. Dover himself was far from expert in the treatment of scurvy. He wrote:

> There needs nothing more to be done for the cure of this disease, which has hitherto puzzled physicians in all ages, than to drink a quarter of a pint of allum [*sic*] posset drink [alum is sulphate of

potassium and aluminium; a posset is hot milk curdled by any strong infusion], first and last, made as strong as your stomach will bear it. This I have experienced for thirty-five years, and do not remember that it ever failed.

This opinion was published in 1732, in *The Ancient Physician's Legacy to His Country*, a 'compendium of fifty-eight years' medical practice and experience', written in a dauntingly pompous style. Fortunately Dover's cure for scurvy does not appear to have been used on board either the *Duke* or the *Dutchess*.

When all the preparations had been made, the ships provisioned and the crews recruited, the *Duke* and *Dutchess* made their way down the Bristol Channel from King Road in the afternoon of 1st August 1708. Rogers's journal entry for 2nd August describes both ships as being 'well furnished with all necessaries on board for a distant undertaking', though he was soon to discover that in this belief he was unduly optimistic. The crew was a very mixed bag, reflecting as much as anything poor employment prospects on land and the lure of the great gains to be had on a privateering voyage. Rogers writes:

Above one third were foreigners from most nations; several of her Majesty's subjects on board were tinkers, tailors, haymakers, pedlars, fiddlers & c.; one Negro and about ten boys. With this mixed gang we hoped to be well manned, as soon as they had learnt the use of arms, and got their sea-legs, which we doubted not to teach 'em, and bring them to discipline.

CHAPTER TWENTY

A Better Class of Privateer

Woodes Rogers published his *Cruising Voyage round the World* in 1712, the year following his return, and conscientiously dedicates it to the surviving owners. It's a humorous and lively account which reveals Rogers's determined and generally humane personality. It may well have been polished for the printed page, but there is little to suggest that it is not essentially Rogers's own work.

They set sail from Bristol in convoy with a number of ships of the Royal Navy, three frigates, five galleys and a sloop, their first port of call being Kinsale, which by now had been built up into a provisioning depot. Within two days of their departure, Rogers is lamenting the poor condition of his vessels, which could not keep up with the rest. It is a wonder that he didn't realize how ill equipped he was from the outset. One can either put this down to inexperience, though he shows none in the management of the voyage, or perhaps in his blandly optimistic entry for 2nd August he was merely being dutiful. Owners always wanted to maximize profits, and if that meant cutting corners on equipment, they would. Naturally thrifty, they could never differentiate between genuine and false economy.

He writes on 3rd August:

Our ship and the *Dutchess* did not sail so well as the major part of the galleys, our masts and rigging being all unfit for the sea, or ships out of trim, and everything in disorder, being very indifferently manned. Notwithstanding our number, we had not twenty sailors in the ship, and it's very little better on board the *Dutchess*; which is a discouragement, only we hope to get some good sailors at Cork.

They were already at sea, and whatever their deficiencies, when they sighted a sail, the *Dutchess* gave chase, but lost her prey about 8 o'clock in the evening. Caution was advisable in any case: at Bristol they'd heard that the *Jersey*, a French man-of-war of forty-six guns, was cruising the Bristol Channel; the news 'obliged us to keep hammocks up, and a clear ship for a fight, all night'.

On 5th August they anchored at midday off the two rocks then called the Sovereign's Bollocks (now known simply as the Sovereigns) off Kinsale. The next day they proceeded to Cork, not helped by a useless Kinsale pilot who almost wrecked them, and on 8th August they were joined by a convoy in the company of HMS *Hastings* – one of the warships that had rescued Dampier from Ascension Island after the *Roebuck* had foundered. At Cork a man called Noblett Rogers, no relation of Woodes, but a brother of one of the owners, organized the recruitment of better sailors to replace the most useless of the existing crew as well as early deserters: it was clear by now to all the men that life on board the *Duke* and the *Dutchess* was going to be disciplined, and that this was not to be the kind of free and easy voyage some of them might have assumed.

They made good whatever was lacking in their provision, thanks to the enterprising Noblett Rogers, and superfluous sheet-cable 'and other new store cordage' was sent ashore to make room for the new stores and the new men taken on board – the crews seem to have been augmented here. In a small frigate a quarter of the hold was occupied by spare cable before hemp was replaced by chain.

At Cork, the crew took their last leave of home. Several impetuously married local girls – perhaps both men and women were inspired to hasty matrimony by drinking too much 'flip' – a cocktail of beer and spirits, sweetened with sugar and drunk hot. One crewman, a Dane who had as few words of English as his new wife had of Danish (she may only have spoken Erse), became especially tearful at parting. Perhaps it was just because they were both drunk.

On 30th August, HMS *Hastings* issued a splendid list of signals to be used to keep company. Here are two of them:

SIGNALS BY DAY:

When I would have the fleet to weigh, I will hale home my main topsail yards, and fire a gun.

SIGNALS BY NIGHT:

Springing a leak: you are to fire five guns, and show lights, as many as you think fit, and in the most convenient places to be seen.

The *Duke* and the *Dutchess* made similar arrangements of signals and rendezvous between them so that they would not lose each other's company on the long voyage ahead of them. On 31st August they were ready to depart, and the next day they sailed in a convoy of about twenty merchant ships, watched over by the *Hastings*. Evidently they were now in much better trim, for on 2nd September Rogers reports:

We and our consort stood out of the fleet to chase a sail we saw to windward. Our ships sailed as well as any in the fleet, not excepting the men-of-war; so that we began to hope we should find our heels, since we go so well, though deep laden and pestered [encumbered]. We found the chase to be a small vessel coming into the fleet from Baltimore [in Eire].

It seems odd that they should be going to work quite so early in the enterprise, but no doubt Rogers wanted to see how the men worked together, and to keep them on their toes, and stimulated. On 4th September they accepted gifts from Captain John Paul of the *Hastings* of 'scrubbers, scrapers, and a speaking trumpet' and other essential items which they still lacked.

Captain Paul, evidently impressed, proposed cruising together with Rogers and his two ships off Finisterre, once the convoy duties of the *Hastings* were over – which is some indication of how autonomous was the captain of the naval vessel in those days of slow, remote and difficult communication. Rogers, however, turned the offer down, 'our ships being very full, and our consort being unwilling to lose time so near home'. They parted company with the *Hastings* amicably. Only now, on the verge of the Atlantic crossing, was the crew apprised of the true purpose of the voyage. This, after all, was the last chance to put malcontents off into the *Hastings*.

But I found no complaint aboard the *Duke*, except for one fellow who expected to have been tithing-man that year in his parish, and said his wife would be obliged to pay forty shillings in his absence: but seeing all the rest willing, he was easily quieted, and all hands drank to a good voyage.

They parted company with the *Hastings* on 6th September and sent a letter to their owners with her. They were now almost alone. Only the *Crown* galley, bound for Madeira, kept them company.

They were still not as well supplied as might have been expected. Three days later, they held their first committee meeting, to decide whether or not to put in to Madeira, to bolster their 'slender' stocks of liquor – 'good liquor to sailors is preferable to clothing'. Rogers notes that his men are 'meanly clad', so provision would have to be made for that too, as they would be facing cold and hardship in rounding the Horn. The committee was made up of all the senior officers aboard, including Dampier, to whose experience deference was shown.

On 11th September they chased and took a Swedish ship. Sweden was a Protestant nation and no part of the conflict; the slim excuse for arresting her was that the English suspected her of carrying contraband goods. However, they 'found it difficult to prove she was a prize', and so they 'let her go without the least embezzlement'. The encounter was very cordial. The Swedish commander gave Rogers two hams, and some 'rufft dried beef'. Rogers gave him 'a dozen bottles of red streak cider'. They saluted each other with cannon fire at parting.

But letting the Swede go did not please a number of the crew, who promptly mutinied aboard the *Duke* under the leadership of the boatswain, Giles Cash. There were murmurings amongst the crew of the *Dutchess*, too. No doubt they were waiting to see how the wind would blow aboard the *Duke*.

It is interesting that Rogers had to bend over backwards to reason with his crew; but he managed to defuse the situation by reasoning. 'I laboured to convince them of the necessity of our making dispatch, and that if we could make her a prize, it would unman our ships too much to send her into any port . . . which pacified the major part.' Alexander Wynter was made boatswain in place of Cash. Cash was put aboard the *Crown* in irons and sent with her to Madeira.

I did not at his first confinement think of sending him off; but this day [14th September entry: the journal for each day was kept from noon to noon] a sailor came aft to the steerage door, with near half the ship's company of sailors following him, and demanded the boatswain [Cash] out of irons. I desired him to speak with me by himself on the quarterdeck, which he did, where the officers assisted me, seized him, and made one of his chief comrades whip him. This method I thought best for breaking any unlawful friendship amongst themselves, which, with different correction to other offenders, allayed the tumult . . .

On 15th September they parted company with the *Crown*, sending letters home with her, and on 16th Alexander Wynter was replaced as boatswain by John Pilar after only one day in office. The other mutineers, showing themselves duly penitent, were pardoned and restored to duty.

The *Duke* and *Dutchess* made for the Canary Islands, 'it being little wind . . . and to prevent loss of time', to cruise there for their missing supplies, and for liquor. Dampier had praised the wine of the Canaries in his writings, but they were in any case well known in England. They sighted Tenerife on 18th September and on the same day took a Spanish vessel of twenty-five tons bound from Oratava to Fuerteventura. There were forty-five passengers aboard, who 'rejoiced when they found us English, because they feared we were Turks'. Amongst the prisoners were four friars. One of them was the Padre Guardian for Fuerteventura, 'a good, honest old fellow'. He and the officers of the *Duke* got tight together, drinking the health of Charles III – that is, the Archduke Charles of Austria, whom England and its allies had in 1703 proposed to make king of Spain. The rest of the friars, Rogers comments darkly, 'were of the wrong sort'.

It was at Tenerife that Carleton Vanbrugh first proved himself to be more of a liability to the expedition than an asset. Against Rogers's better judgement, he insisted on going ashore with some of the prisoners to negotiate the ransom of the bark, whose cargo, two butts of wine and a hogshead of brandy, 'we designed for our own use in both ships, the agents of each being to take an account of it at the first opportunity'. Reckonings were clearly going to be very precise on this voyage.

Vanbrugh was promptly taken prisoner himself by the Spanish authorities, and they were supported by the English merchants at Tenerife. It will be remembered that the Canary Islands, because of their economic importance as wine traders to England, were deemed neutral in wartime. Trade was offered, but, as the English merchants put it, 'you will make restitution of the said bark, otherwise Mr Vanbrugh will not be permitted to go off, and there will be extravagant reprisals made upon our estates and persons'.

Rogers and Courtney replied on the same day, 20th September: 'It was Mr Vanbrugh's misfortune to go ashore; and if he is detained, we can't help it . . . If Mr Vanbrugh is unjustly detained, we'll carry the prisoners we have on board to the port we are bound to, let the consequence be what it will.' Their contention was that the prize had been taken on the high seas. Rogers notes a day later: 'We were angry at their tediousness and our ill-treatment, our time being precious.' No doubt Dampier was warning him about delaying too long before rounding the Horn. The same day, however, at 8 p.m., the Spanish gave in and sent a boat with supplies and Carleton Vanbrugh in it. Vanbrugh was clearly not only unrepentant but in a combative mood, for a few days later there was a committee meeting to deal with complaints from him about alleged ill-treatment from Rogers. Rogers's frustration can be imagined: Vanbrugh was an irresponsible and arrogant man, a hindrance to the smooth running of the venture. The complaint was referred to the full council, which sided with Rogers and censured Vanbrugh. But Vanbrugh's personality was one that would not learn and would not be chastened.

They left the Canary Islands and made their way southwards, their next planned landfall being the Cape Verdes. On the way they crossed the Tropic of Cancer, and as it was the custom in those days to celebrate not only the crossing of the equator but the two tropics as well, those who had never passed it before were duly initiated by ducking. On 25th September, Rogers observes: 'This proved of great use to our fresh-water sailors, to recover the colour of their skins, which were grown very black and nasty' – thereby revealing a practical origin for the ceremony. The ceremony itself is described in a contemporary journal:

Five of our men, not being willing to pay a bottle of brandy and a pound of sugar, were ducked according to custom, it being the first time they had passed [the line]. The manner of ducking is this: there is a block made fast to the main yardarm, through which is reeved a long rope, one end whereof comes down on the quarterdeck, the other to the water, at which end is made fast a stick about a foot and a half long thwartways, on which the person sits across, holding fast with his hands the rope as it goes up, having a running knot about him; when being ready he is hoisted up close to the yardarm by the people on the quarterdeck, and at once let run. His own weight from that height plunges him under the water as low as the ship's keel; then they run him up again as fast as they can and so serve him three times; then he is free and may drink with the others that paid.

Woodes Rogers himself thought the ritual 'too heathen', though he had to allow it. Dampier must have seen it a dozen times. He knew all too well the importance of the arcana of the sailors' life: the bonds forged from the technical argot, amounting to a foreign language to the ears of the uninitiated; from the constant presence of the threat of death; from the isolation from women and normal society; from the boredom and the lack of privacy. To be a hardened mariner was to belong to a kind of survivors' club: a freemasonry of the seas; and the pride associated with membership had the psychological benefit of compensating for and obscuring the sense of the sacrifices made in order to get it.

At the end of the month they reached the Cape Verdes and anchored in the Bay of St Vincent. Edward Cooke writes that they saw an abundance of flying fish, and that one of them fell on to the deck of the *Dutchess*. Rogers says that there was no one aboard either ship that knew the islands; but why he made such a statement with Dampier as his pilot is a mystery. Dampier is referred to rarely in his work, and although such references are respectful, they are not admiring. Although Cooke acknowledges Dampier's experience when he cites him, he does so briefly and from his books rather than from any conversations he might have had. Why this should be is a mystery. As we shall see, Dampier's memory seems to be failing him when it comes to the location of places with which he had been very familiar all his travelling life. Did this apply to his recollection of the Cape Verdes? One wants to hope not.

They took in supplies at Sao Antonio: limes, tobacco, oranges, fowls, potatoes, hogs, 'bonanoes', musk and water-melons, as well as two cows, which they managed to buy 'cheap enough'. The islanders were poor, and would drive whatever bargain they could. Here, however, a 'linguist', or interpreter, Joseph Alexander, deserted them. In the woods Edward Cooke saw some large spiders, 'as big as a small walnut', whose webs made the way through the trees difficult, 'being as strong as ordinary thread, and very many of them'.

The men remained restive. They had never reconciled themselves to the loss of the 'small Canary prize', and now, as they sailed on, it looked as if another mutiny threatened. The bone of contention now was how plunder – that part of the booty which fell directly to the sailors – was to be defined: 'They all insisted there was never any privateer's crew hindered from plunder.' Rogers and Courtney had waived the right to 'cabin plunder', but that did not mollify the men, despite the fact that, as a result of the captains' concession, 'the officers and men did voluntarily allow' the captains '5 per cent each out of the value of all plunder'. Rogers argues that 5 per cent was much less than their due, but they would have happily waived it all, if only they could keep the men contented, and concentrate on the main design of the voyage. Cooke reports in detail a discussion held in committee aboard the *Dutchess* on 7th October regarding plunder, and the nine Articles they drew up to cover its definition and distribution.

The greater the distance from home, the more volatile the situation aboard became. In order to instil both discipline and a sense of civilization and proportion, Rogers introduced the custom of morning and evening prayer daily from 28th October. This may have been triggered by an altercation on the *Dutchess* on 22nd October between one William Page, who had been promoted from fifth to second mate, and Edward Cooke. Page had been insubordinate to Cooke, and Cooke had struck him. Page had then hit back and there had been a fight. After that, Page went aboard the *Duke*, and John Ballet replaced him on the *Dutchess*. To cool off, Page was clapped into the bilboes – two bars of iron, with sliding shackles, to which a malefactor was attached in a sitting position, as if in the stocks.

On 19th November, the ships arrived at Isla Grande. Dampier was sent ahead in a well-manned pinnace to reconnoitre, and returned at 10 o'clock at night to confirm that they had indeed arrived at their next port of call. On the following day, Dampier was sent to 'sound all the way to our watering place and see if no enemy lay there'. In the meantime it rained remorselessly.

The Portuguese gave them a friendly welcome and here two Irishmen – James Brown and Michael Jones – deserted, but after a night in the jungle they gave themselves up, frightened by the howling of the wild beasts – probably only monkeys. A few days later, Carleton Vanbrugh was in trouble again over the shooting of an Indian in a canoe belonging to a Portuguese friar. But these matters did not disrupt the good relations between the privateers and the local population. On 27th November Rogers and his men were invited to Angre de Reyes for the feast of the Conception. The governor, Rafael de Silva Lagos, made them very welcome. Rogers's own description of what happened then is most lively:

> He asked us if we would see the convent and the procession. We told him our religion differed very much from his. He answered we were welcome to see it, without partaking in the ceremony. We waited on him in a body, being ten of us, with two trumpets and a hautboy, which he desired might play us to church, where our music did the office of an organ, but separate from the singing, which was by the friars well performed. Our music played *Hey Boys up go we!* and all manner of paltry tunes; and after service our musicians, who were by that time more than half drunk, marched at the head of the company, next to them an old father and two friars carrying lamps of incense with the Host, next came the Virgin Mary on a bier carried on four men's shoulders, and dressed with flowers and wax candles & c.

The ceremony lasted two hours, after which the English were 'splendidly entertained by the Fathers of the Convent, and then by the governor . . .' *Hey Boys up go we!* was an interesting choice: it was a popular comic song during the Commonwealth, which discusses Puritan taste. The revelry continued next day on board, where the privateers treated the 'gentlemen of the town' to drinks. The good-humoured religious rivalry continued:

They were very merry, and in their cups proposed the Pope's health to us; but we were quits with 'em, by toasting that of the Archbishop of Canterbury. To keep up the humour, we also proposed William Penn's to them, and they liked the liquor so well that they refused neither.

There remained the serious business of shooting the Indian to settle. The Indian had since died. Vanbrugh hadn't fired himself, but he had given the order to fire while in the ship's pinnace. He was acting entirely on his own authority, and at the committee meeting held to inquire into the matter, Rogers stressed the need to keep strict discipline, and asked for and got a vote of confidence from his officers in his own authority to command. Vanbrugh was transferred to the *Dutchess* and replaced on board the *Duke* by William Bath. Neither agent was up to much: Vanbrugh was a coxcomb, and Bath was an idle drunk.

They sailed from Isla Grande at the beginning of December, refreshed and ready for the long and difficult haul round Cape Horn. On 23rd December they passed the Falkland Islands. Over Christmas, they sighted a sail and gave chase. The wind being poor, they lowered their boats and towed their ships after the potential prize, but they lost her on 26th.

Rogers allowed a generous ration of punch for the men to toast the New Year. As the weather grew colder, they prepared for it:

Clothes and liquor were now an excellent commodity amongst our ship's company, who are but meanly stored: we had six tailors at work for several weeks to make them clothing, and pretty well supplied their wants by the spare blankets and red clothes belonging to the owners, and what every officer could spare was altered for the men's use.

They were not ready before time. On Wednesday, 5th January 1709 they met a tremendous storm. Edward Cooke, a conscientious man, clearly more used to keeping a log than writing a full account, here turns his businesslike but graphic style to good use. Of the two ships, the *Dutchess* was much the worse hit:

This day we had a violent gale of wind at NW and very bad weather; at two in the afternoon reefed both courses, then lowered our foreyard, and lay by till five; at which time our waist was filled with water, and we expecting the ship would sink every minute, got down our foreyard as well as we could and loosed the spritsail to wear the ship, which at last we did, but in wearing, we thought she would have foundered with the weight of water that was in her, by reason that she had so deep a waist. Thus we scudded before the wind, the *Duke* following, and at nine shipped a sea at the poop, as we were in the cabin going to eat; it beat in all the cabin windows and bulkhead, and hove the first lieutenant [William Stretton] halfway between the decks, with several muskets and pistols that hung there, darting a sword that was against the bulkhead of the cabin through my man's hammock and rug, which hung against the bulkhead of the steerage, and had not the bulkhead of the great cabin given way, all we who were there must inevitably have been drowned before the water could have been vented. Our yawl was staved on deck, and it was a wonder that many were not killed with the shutters, the bulkhead and the arms which were drove with a prodigious force; but God in his mercy delivered us from this and many other dangers. Only one man or two were hurt, and some bruised, but not one rag of dry clothes left us, our chests, hammocks and bedding being all soaked in water.

On 6th January Rogers and Dampier took the yawl and went over to the *Dutchess*. They found the crew 'in a very orderly pickle, with all their clothes drying, the ship and rigging covered with them from the deck to the maintop'; but as the month progressed, the crews began to suffer from colds and scurvy – the *Dutchess* being worse off than the *Duke*. But they had come round the Horn in one piece, and on 31st January at seven in the morning they reached Juan Fernandez. A few days beforehand, Rogers had written in his log:

We are very uncertain of the latitude and longitude of Juan Fernandez, the books laying 'em down so differently that not one chart agrees with another, and being but a small island, we are in some doubts of striking it, so design to hale in for the mainland to direct us.

It is interesting that Dampier, who had been here several times and would have corrected his own charts, and whose proper job on this voyage would now have started, seems to have had so much difficulty. Rogers comments:

> Even Captain Dampier was much at a loss, though he had been there so often, and had as it were a map of the island in his head, which exactly agreed with it as we came there. This ought to induce sea-officers to prefer their own proper business to amusement, since, with all this knowledge, we were forced to make the main land of Chile, in order to find this island, and did not strike it at the last without considerable difficulty.

Waiting for them on the island, after a solitary stay of four years, was Alexander Selkirk. Edward Cooke spends little time on him in his first volume, though in his second, which is an expansion of certain aspects of the first, he gives the world's most famous castaway a great deal more space – as if he had been advised that the man's story was a good selling point. In both volumes Cooke gives exhaustive detail of prizes taken and their crews and cargoes. In his second volume, he devotes his fifth chapter to 'how a day is gained or lost in sailing round the globe'. Did he discuss this at least with Dampier? He does not tell us.

Selkirk's 'rescue' is one of the best-known events in English maritime history. Rogers gives his story in detail. Adverse winds made it difficult to come into Juan Fernandez at first, and so Dover was sent ahead to cover the last four leagues in the pinnace, his crew rowing against the wind, so that they did not get in until dusk. But they saw a fire ashore and did not land for fear of the presence of Spaniards. The following day, Rogers sent in the yawl, which remained away longer than expected, so that he sent the pinnace, well armed, after it. 'The pinnace returned immediately from the shore, and brought abundance of crawfish, with a man clothed in goatskins, who looked more wild than the first owners of them. He had been on the island four years and four months . . .' Rogers goes on to say that Dampier told him Selkirk was the best man in the *Cinque-Ports* galley. Selkirk had lit the fire on the beach because he had seen the frigates off the island and guessed them to be English from the way they were sailed.

Selkirk had been left with a musket, a hatchet, a knife and a cooking pot. He had managed to come to terms with his solitude after the first eight months. When his gunpowder was used up, he caught goats by running after them, and became very fast and sure-footed. For vegetables he had those that Dampier and his companions had planted years earlier, and other fruits grew naturally on the island. Apart from goats, the other European animals left here by various ships were cats and rats, which had multiplied enormously. The rats gave Selkirk a great deal of trouble, nibbling his feet as he slept, until he tamed a very large number of the cats by feeding them goats' flesh. They then slept around him and kept the rats at bay. He is also said to have trained some of them, and some young goats, to dance with him. He retained his knowledge of human speech by reading the Bible aloud regularly; and busied himself with building two huts, one for sleeping and one•for cooking. Lieutenant Robert Frye accompanied him to his 'habitation', which he had built well out of the way in order to avoid being found by any visiting Spaniards, but no one else accompanied him, as the track was 'hidden and uncouth'. The men nicknamed him the governor of Juan Fernandez.

Selkirk, recommended by Dampier, was offered the job of second mate aboard the *Duke*, but he could not at first be so easily persuaded to go along with them. Edward Cooke makes the fascinating remark:

It was with some difficulty that he was persuaded to go on board, on account of a certain officer that he heard was there, yet upon promise of being restored to his former dwelling, if not satisfied, he at length complied, and found such entertainment as made him not long for his solitary retreat.

It has been suggested that the 'certain officer' was Dampier himself. It is much more likely that Selkirk would have felt strong antipathy towards Stradling, and yet, although Cooke does not mention the 'certain officer' by name, it is inconceivable that Selkirk would not have named the man for whom he bore such dislike. All we can conjecture is that Selkirk, although he did not sail on the *St George* with Dampier, had developed such a low opinion of him as a commander that he did not wish to sail with him again in any circumstances – though to go to the length of refusing to be taken off Juan Fernandez seems to border on madness. It follows that Selkirk's mind may have been temporarily disturbed by the shock of his rescue after so long in solitude, and that this reaction was a manifestation of that. In any event, the two men seem to have got on well enough after Selkirk joined the expedition. Selkirk himself was thirty years old when they took him off the island, and in the peak of fitness. It took him some time to get used to conversing with his fellow men again and before he could touch alcohol or eat the ship's food. He remained with the expedition until it returned to England in 1711, and in London he enjoyed a certain notoriety. Richard Steele dedicated an entire issue of *The Englishman* (Number 26, 3rd December 1713) to him, using the interview, which is very good, as a springboard for moral reflection. Selkirk told Steele that 'I am now worth £800, but shall never be so happy, as when I was not worth a farthing.' Steele's own portrait of Selkirk is interesting:

> When I first saw him, I thought, if I had not been let into his character and story, I could have discerned that he had been much separated from company, from his aspect and gesture; there was a strong but cheerful seriousness in his look, and a certain disregard to the ordinary things about him, as if he had been sunk in thought. When the ship, which brought him off the island, came in, he received them with the greatest indifference, with relation to the prospect of going off with them, but with great satisfaction in an opportunity to refresh and help them; the man frequently bewailed his return to the world, which could not, he said, with all its enjoyments, restore to him the tranquillity of his solitude. Though I had frequently conversed with him, after a few months' absence, he met me in the street; and though he spoke to me, I could not recollect that I had seen him: familiar converse in this town had taken off the loneliness of his aspect, and quite altered the air of his face.

His story being well covered by Cooke, Rogers and Steele, no one could accuse Defoe of having cheated Selkirk out of his story. Left to himself, Selkirk would never have written it. He was dead by 1721, having returned to the sea, and survived or eluded two court charges, one of bigamy and the other of assault.

They spent until 10th February cleaning the ships and fetching in wood and water. Their other priority was to cure the scurvy with a balanced diet of fresh goat meat and green vegetables. There were plenty of goats. Selkirk had marked some of them by slitting their ears, and one such 'of most venerable aspect, dignified with an exceeding majestic beard' was found on the island by Lord Anson when he touched there in 1741. Dover does not seem to have insisted on treating the scurvy sufferers with an alum posset, and for a moment an air of idyllic calm reigns:

'Twas very pleasant ashore among the green piemento trees, which cast a refreshing smell. Our house was made by putting a sail round four of 'em, and covering it atop with another sail; so that Captain Dover and I both thought it a very agreeable seat, the weather being neither too hot nor too cold . . .

They cut down coconut and cabbage palms to get the fruit, and they boiled up eighty gallons of sea-lion oil to refine it for use as lamp and cooking fuel. Some of the men made a meal of young seals, and declared the meat to be as good as English lamb. 'For my own part I should have been glad of such an exchange,' writes Rogers, unconvinced.

On 13th February a council decision was made to make for the Lobos Islands. In order that the two consorts might not lose each other on the way, directives for signalling in every conceivable circumstance were laid down. On arrival at Lobos:

Either ship arriving . . . and not finding his consort there, he is immediately to set up two crosses, one at the landing-place nearest the farther end of the starboard great island going in, with a glass bottle hid underground twenty yards directly north from each cross, with intelligence of what has happened since parting, and what their further designs are. This is to be done and in readiness, that if they give chase, or be forced out by the enemy, the missing ship may not want intelligence from her consort.

Vanbrugh came back aboard the *Duke*, and Bath was sent back to the *Dutchess*. 'I hope for the best,' writes Rogers, rather gloomily. On 17th, four managers of plunder from each ship were appointed – two officers and two men – one pair of each to go aboard the other's ship, so that there could be no question of unfairness in the distribution of plunder. A water ration was introduced as a safety device, in case they should find themselves a long time at sea.

By mid March they had taken no prizes, and there is a worried note in Rogers's journal: 'Our men begin to repine, that though come so far, we have met with no prize in these seas.' Luckily, three days later, on 16th, they took a little sixteen-tonner out of Paita bound for Cheripe to load flour. The Spanish sailors aboard said that no enemies had been seen in these waters since Dampier's last visit, and gave them news of the fate of Captain Stradling and his ship. They commandeered the little flour bark, renamed her the *Beginning*, and took her to Lobos with them to fit her out as a privateer.

They arrived at Lobos the next day and had restructured the bark within two more days. Edward Cooke was put in command of her. It was necessary to clean both the frigates again. The hulls were encrusted with barnacles almost as big as mussels – 'a ship grows foul very fast in these seas'.

They took a fifty-ton prize, the *San José*, but she carried nothing of value. They kept her, however, as their hospital ship, and renamed her the *Increase*. Selkirk was put aboard as master. Edward Cooke went shooting for turkey, but made an unpleasant error:

Here's abundance of vultures, alias carrion-crows, which looked so like turkeys, that one of our officers at landing blessed himself at the sight and hoped to fare deliciously here. He was so eager, that he would not stay till the boat could put him ashore, but leaped into the water with his gun, and getting near to a parcel [group], let fly at 'em; but when he came to take up his game, it stunk insufferably, and made us merry at his mistake.

Less amusing was an exploit of Carleton Vanbrugh, who remained a thoroughly unpleasant piece of work:

Mr Vanbrugh threatening to shoot one of our men at Lobos, only for refusing to carry some carrion-crows that he shot, and having lately abused Captain Dover . . . the latter desired a committee might be called to examine into Mr Vanbrugh's conduct, and we came to the following issue: that Mr Vanbrugh had committed sundry misdemeanours, and according to our orders, we not believing him a fit person to be one of the committee, had chosen Mr Samuel Hopkins in his stead.

Vanbrugh later tried to regain his place on the committee by secretly offering always to support Rogers in a vote. Rogers turned him down.

Apart from security from the Spanish, there was little to recommend this inhospitable place. Rogers pointed out the danger of eating seals' livers – perhaps because of a superfluity of Vitamin A. One Spanish crewman died after eating some, but the meat may have been bad. Rogers further complained that the seals' smell gave him a headache. Dampier may have spent some time reflecting on his last voyage: for it was at these islands that he had abandoned the ill-fated *St George*.

They sailed from Lobos on 30th March. On 2nd April the water was turned blood-red by great shoals of plankton, and on the same day Lieutenant Robert Frye, in the *Duke*'s pinnace, took a large prize, the *Ascensión del Señor*, of four or five hundred tons, commanded by José and Juan Morel. The next day the *Beginning* took a bark of thirty-five tons. The expedition suddenly looked much more promising. The prisoners taken from the *Ascensión* told the privateers that a local bishop should have been aboard their ship, but as she had sprung a leak at Panama, he had transferred to a French-built ship which had been following them and which would stop at Paita to recruit. The privateers resolved to try to take her. They also decided that they would attempt Guayaquil, still one of the most important ports, and the only shipyard on the whole Spanish Pacific coast. In anticipation of success, a hugely complicated and detailed memorandum of what constituted plunder was drawn up and signed by Rogers, Dover and Courtney. There would be no room for any loose interpretations on this voyage: everything was to be done by the book. And there can be no doubt that the method was, by and large, effective.

Their run of luck did not change. On 15th April they took the French-built vessel, the *Havre de Grâce*, which had come over as a supply ship and been sold by the French to the Spanish for four times her original value. The Spaniards may have renamed her the *Jesu Maria*. She was a good prize, but the bishop was no longer aboard, having landed with all his attendants and treasure at Punta St Helena, with the intention of staying at Guayaquil. The *Havre* was taken at a cost, for in the battle Rogers's younger brother John was killed, aged twenty. In his journal, Rogers wrote:

> As I began this voyage with a resolution to go through it, and the greatest misfortune shall not deter me, I'll as much as possible avoid being thoughtful and afflicting myself for what can't be recalled, but indefatigably pursue the concerns of the voyage, which has hitherto allowed little respite.

There was to be no respite now. A week later, in uncomfortably hot weather, bitten half to death by mosquitoes in the mangrove swamps, guided by Dampier and one of the captured Spanish captains, they prepared to attack Guayaquil. As so often happened, the port got wind of the presence of the privateers before they could take advantage of surprising it. Once the English knew the alarm had been raised, Rogers, Dover and Courtney wasted another hour debating whether or not to make a landing. Rogers was for pressing home an attack before Guayaquil had time to organize its defences; but when Dampier was consulted, he told Rogers that the buccaneers never 'attacked any large place after it was alarmed'.

After several setbacks, they did manage to take the city, but found, as they expected, little of value left in it. They sacked it of what there was, but carrying the goods to the water proved hard work: the weather remained hot and humid, and there had been pestilence in the town recently. The men suspected that the Spanish might have concealed some of their treasure under the floor of the church, but Rogers would not let them look there, since the church was full of new graves where infection could very easily have lurked.

Edward Cooke gives a concise description of Guayaquil, which is worth repeating:

> It is divided into two, called the old and new towns, both of them together consisting of about 500 houses, joined by a long wooden

bridge for people to pass over a-foot, above half-a-mile in length
. . . The situation is low boggy ground, so dirty in winter that
without this bridge there would be scarce any going from one house
to another . . . This morass ground was full of the largest toads I
ever saw, some of them as big as an English twopenny loaf . . .

The sacking of the town was conducted in an orderly, even military
fashion, and though few stones were left unturned, there were no atrocities
either.

The houses up the river were full of women, and particularly at
one place there were above a dozen handsome genteel young women
well dressed, where our men got several gold chains and earrings,
but were otherwise so civil to them, that the ladies offered to dress
'em victuals, and brought 'em a cask of good liquor. Some of their
largest gold chains were concealed, and wound about their middles,
legs and thighs & c. But the gentlewomen in these hot climes being
very thin clad with silk and fine linen, and their hair dressed with
ribbons very neatly, our men by pressing felt the chains & c. with
their hands on the outside of the ladies' apparel, and by their linguist
modestly desired the gentlewomen to take 'em off and surrender
'em. This I mention as a proof of our sailors' modesty, and in respect
to Mr Connelly and Mr Selkirk . . . who commanded the party . . .

Although this sounds too good to be true, it really does seem that
no outrages occurred during the entire exercise. There were very few
casualties – one Portuguese crewman was blown up when a shell split
immediately upon being fired from a Coehorn mortar. As for looting, a
Dutchman called John Gabriel, who found a cask of brandy in a house
he was ransacking and drank himself senseless, was returned to the
privateers by the owner of the house when he came to himself, no doubt
nursing a massive hangover. There was no other serious drunkenness
during the taking of the town.

Selkirk and Connelly netted £1,000-worth of jewellery from the women,
but far more eluded them on the backs of the townspeople who managed
to get away. The privateers started to negotiate a ransom for the city
and for the ships they had taken in the harbour. As usual discussions

dragged on, and the Spaniards initially failed to come up even with the 30,000 pieces of eight eventually agreed on – though this was a far lower sum than that originally demanded. At last, on 27th April, the privateers withdrew, in haste because they feared that the Spaniards would by now have had time to summon reinforcements. Much booty had to be left behind because there was neither time nor space to load it. The withdrawal itself was a miserable business. Rogers writes:

> I marched on the rear with a few men, and picked up pistols, cutlasses and poleaxes, which showed our men were grown very careless, weak and weary of being soldiers . . . The hardest work we had was to get the guns [cannon] down to the water, the earth being so soft that they who helped to carry them sank half a leg deep . . .

Altogether, the taking of Guayaquil had been a qualified success. Making a note of their departure on the morning of 28th April, Rogers comments that the privateers

> at parting made what show and noise we could with our drums, trumpets and guns, and thus took our leave of the Spaniards very cheerfully, but not half so well pleased as we should have been, had we taken 'em by surprise: for I was well assured from all hands that at least we should have got above 200,000 pieces of eight in money . . . and a greater plenty of necessities [than] we now found . . .

They still hadn't received all the ransom money. The expedition anchored at Punta Arena. On 2nd May the Spaniards paid 22,000 pieces of eight, and on 7th another 3,500 in plate. With that the English had to be contented, and they discharged most of their hostages the following day. Rogers had developed a poor opinion of the local Spaniards, whom he found effete and pox-ridden. He wondered if they could prevent the local Indians from reclaiming the lands that had formerly been theirs without the help of the large numbers of mixed-race people who sided with the colonizers.

The *Duke* and *Dutchess* then made sail with their prizes to the Galapagos Islands to rest. Many of the men now fell sick, having caught the pestilence which had been rife at Guayaquil. On the way, they saw great schools of albacore pursuing flying fish, and one of the big tuna leapt into a ship's boat. At 6 p.m. on 15th May, Dover's brother-in-law Samuel Hopkins died. 'He read prayers once a day ever since we passed the equinox,' Rogers wrote. 'He was a very good-tempered, sober man, and very well beloved by the whole ship's company.'

This was not a good time to lose their apothecary. Originally, twenty men had fallen ill, but the numbers quickly increased to sixty aboard the *Duke*, and eighty aboard the *Dutchess*. Meanwhile, Dover and the medical team did what they could to treat the disease. It is to their credit that only about a dozen men died. Dover's stock went up, but so did his high opinion of himself. In his own inflated account of the matter, he begins by saying: 'When I took by storm the twin cities of Guayaquil . . .'

On the way to the Galapagos the expedition lost track of a third mate, Simon Hatley, one of the plunder managers, who disappeared in small prize bark with a crew of ten. All attempts to find them were vain.

They moved on to Gorgona to careen and refit their ships – perhaps they felt the island was more secure than the Galapagos – and there they spent much of the summer, despite the rain and the many snakes that made the place less hospitable than it might have been. They overhauled the *Havre de Grâce* and rechristened her the *Marquiss*. They had high hopes of her, but she sailed so heavily that if Rogers had not been overruled by Courtney and Dover he would have abandoned her. He referred to her as their 'clog'. Her cargo had been 500 bales of papal bulls. Most of these the English threw into the sea, but they kept back some to burn the pitch off their ships' bottoms during careening. Rogers was always tolerant of Catholic worship among his Spanish prisoners, but scornful of what he regarded as their superstitious beliefs, especially in the miraculous qualities of images of the Virgin.

The other task they were faced with was the appraisal of the plunder. This was a troublesome task to Rogers and it wasn't made any easier when another mutiny threatened early in August, since the crew believed that they were being cheated of their fair share. They were appeased by 'making some abatements on Mr White's, Mr Bath's, and Mr Vanbrugh's shares'. Rogers's patience was by now sorely tried. It is rare that he shows the degree of frustration and irritation that he must often have felt; but he does so now:

> Sailors usually exceed all measures when left to themselves, and account it a privilege in privateers to do themselves justice on those occasions, though in everything else I must own they have been more obedient than any ship's crews engaged in the like undertaking that I ever heard of. Yet we have not wanted sufficient trial of our patience and industry in other things; so that if any sea officer thinks himself endowed with these two virtues, let him command in a privateer, and discharge his office well in a distant voyage, and I'll engage he shall not want opportunities to improve, if not to exhaust, all his stock.

If Rogers, with all the advantages he had on this cruise, could feel so angry, we may find it easier to understand Dampier's apparent shortcomings on the two voyages he commanded. But whether Rogers consulted the older man or took him into his confidence is uncertain, and probably unlikely. As we have seen, Dampier on this voyage is a shadowy figure, often unsure of his bearings, though he must have done his job at least adequately well, for there is never a breath of complaint against him. At Gorgona, however, there is another hint that our mariner might not have been as expert as Rogers might have hoped: 'Captain Dampier has been here several times, but never rode where we did, which is the best and only Road in the island.'

They were still taking prizes. The ninety-ton *San Tomás de Villanueva y San Demas* had been taken on 6th June by the *Dutchess*. On board were a gentlewoman and her family, including a newly married daughter of eighteen and her husband. They were assigned the great cabin on one of the prizes, the *Ascensión*, and kept prisoner there. As the young husband was jealous of his wife – 'the Spaniard's epidemic disease,' remarks Rogers – their guard was Third Lieutenant Thomas Glendall: 'Alone having charge of the galleon and prisoners: for being above fifty years of age, he appeared to be the most secure guardian to females that had the least charm, though all our young men have hitherto appeared modest beyond example among privateers . . .'

At least Rogers had something to be grateful for; and if the management of the expedition left him biting his lip from time to time, he also had moments of leisure in which his observations of natural history can rival Dampier's:

> We caught an ugly creature here, which I suppose may be of the monkey kind, because it looked like one of the middling sort, but with this difference; his hair was thicker and longer, his face, eyes and nose less, and more wrinkled and deformed; his head of the same shape, but his ears not so large; his teeth longer and sharper, his hinder parts more clumsy, and his body thicker in proportion, with a very short tail, and instead of five claws like fingers as a monkey has, he had only three on each paw, with the claws longer and sharper. We let one of 'em go at the lower part of the mizzen shrouds, and it was about two hours getting to the masthead, which a monkey would have performed in less than half a minute. He moved as if he had walked by art, keeping an equal and slow pace, as if all his movements had been directed by clockwork within him. The Spaniards call it a sloth, and not improperly; they say it feeds on the leaves of a certain lofty tree, and when it has cleared one, before it can get down and walk a little way to find another, would grow lean and be almost starved.

Dampier recommended the monkeys 'and baboons' of these parts as good eating, but could persuade none of the *Duke*'s officers to try them, 'provisions being not yet scarce enough'.

They continued to work on their ships during August. Some of the *Dutchess*'s cannon were jettisoned – they were less valuable than cargo – to make her stiffer, and so sail better. They had also picked up a number of slaves as part of their booty. These Rogers found hard to manage, and had no market to sell them; but a free black man from Jamaica called Michael Kendall joined the privateers at Gorgona, having escaped Spanish captivity. Rogers now had the idea of forming the thirty-odd male black slaves he had aboard into a platoon under Kendall. If they fought on the side of the privateers against the French and Spanish, he would give them their freedom. He gave them bolts of material to make themselves uniforms.

About the middle of the month, they took another prize whose crew told them that Queen Anne's consort, Prince George of Denmark, had died – 'which we were not willing to believe, but drank his health at night, which can do him no hurt if he is dead'. In fact, Prince George had died on 28th October the previous year, which is some indication of how slowly news could travel in those days.

On 20th August, Rogers arranged a mock battle between the two frigates to exercise the men, keep boredom at bay, and put his new black platoon through its paces. The exercise, complete with fake blood, was a huge success – though one Welsh crew member became so carried away that he took pretence for reality, loaded his musket with shot, and would have used it if he hadn't been detected and restrained in time.

They wanted to trade with local Indians on the mainland at Tacames. The Indians were hostile at first, but the privateers' interpreter, Alexander White, and a Spanish prisoner managed to persuade them that they were meant no harm. The Indians, who were Christian converts, fetched their missionary padre, and a priest who was a prisoner on board wrote to him to say that the privateers could be trusted – though at the same time he left his colleague in no doubt about their power to loot and burn if they so chose. Trade soon began, and as the *Ascensión* had amongst its cargo some holy relics and statues of saints, a few of the latter were given to the Indians for their little church. At the end of the month, Cooke and Frye were rewarded with a black slave boy apiece – their names were Dublin and Emanuel – as a reward for their exceptional bravery in taking the *Marquiss*. At Tacames, they let their prisoner priest go, rewarding him, in response to his own request, with:

> the prettiest young female Negro we had in the prize, with some baize, linen and other things for his good services in helping to promote our trade for provisions here . . . The young padre parted from us extremely pleased, and leering under his hood upon his black female angel, we doubt he will crack a commandment with her, and wipe off the sin with the Church's indulgence.

They also put ashore the captain of the *San Tomás*, together with a selection of goods and some 'useless' black slaves, for all of which he promised to pay 3,500 pieces of eight, which were to be remitted by way of Portobello with the English trading sloops from Jamaica. Rogers tells

us that he and Courtney trusted the man implicitly, which they must
have done, to take such a risk: but business was often done this way
between enemies, and it worked, surprising though that may seem today.
Here too they released most of their remaining prisoners, and discharged
the *Ascensión* and the *San Tomás*.

At the beginning of September they made for the Galapagos Islands
once again, and we get another glimpse of Dampier. It is not reassuring.
Dampier has moved from the *Duke* by now, but no reason is given. Rogers
writes:

> This day [8th September] I had Captain Courtney, Captain Cooke
> and Captain Dampier aboard, who dined with us. Captain Cooke
> complained of his ship being crank [sailing lightly], and that we
> need not have tacked so near the shore, since we might easily fetch
> the Galapagos without tacking. All agree to this except our pilot,
> who is very positive of seeing other islands about 100 or 110 leagues
> from the Main under the equinox. He tells us he was at them
> formerly when he was a buccaneer, and has described 'em . . .

But as the islands Dampier described at that dinner would have lain
between them and the Galapagos, they would have seen them. The others
concluded that Dampier was mistaken, and that he was really thinking
of the Galapagos group all along. It is a hard thing to consider that
Dampier's memory may have been failing him; but the possibility must
be faced.

At the Galapagos, the men rested and refreshed themselves. Rogers
gives us a delightful description of the giant tortoises – 'with a shell
black as jet, not unlike the top of an old hackney coach' – though he
dislikes the 'meat' of both tortoise and turtle. The sailors rode on the
backs of the tortoises. Rogers had an unfortunate encounter with a sea
lion which attacked him, but he fought it off with his pike.

A renewed and vain search was made for Simon Hatley. It may be
worth recounting his fate here. Finding himself alone, and with only two
days' supply of water, Hatley decided to run for the mainland. The
voyage took two weeks. How he achieved it with the loss of only one
man is a miracle, but when he landed he and his men fell into the hands
of the Spanish and were sent as prisoners to Lima, where they remained

until the Treaty of Utrecht was signed in 1713, bringing enmity between England and Spain to an end. Hatley made his way home, but shipped again with George Shelvocke as second captain on his privateering expedition a few years later. Off Cape Horn with him in 1719, Hatley shot and killed a 'black albatross' that had been flying behind the ship. This action, described by Shelvocke in his published account of the voyage, would later inspire Coleridge's *Rime of the Ancient Mariner*.

The beginning of October saw them cruising off the coast of Mexico. The squadron was now slimmed down to the *Duke*, the *Dutchess*, the *Marquiss*, and one small prize bark, used as a tender. Rogers had Courtney, Cooke and Dampier come aboard. He was worried that the men were weakening on their diet of tortoise and turtle, of which they obviously had plenty. The fresh meat kept scurvy at bay, but it was 'but a faintly food,' thought Rogers, and needed augmenting with bread or flour, which, however, was now severely rationed to a quarter of a pound per man per day. From the pattern of the voyage so far, it is clear that the main routes were planned by Dampier. He may have been cheated forever of his mines at Santa Maria, but now they were going after the biggest prize of all: the Manila ship.

On 8th October they reached the middle island of the Tres Marias, where there was good water. They found no sign of life, but a human skull lay on the ground: 'Which we suppose to have been one of the two Indians Captain Dampier tells us were left here by Captain Swan about twenty-three years ago; for victuals being scarce with these buccaneers they would not carry the poor Indians any farther, but, after they had served their turns, left them to make a miserable end on a desolate island,' comments Rogers soberly. One wonders what he thought of Dampier as a man. Here they held a council meeting to confirm their plan to cruise for the Manila ship, and here Thomas Dover transferred to the *Dutchess*. Rogers does not give a reason; but it is likely that tension between the two men was becoming intolerable.

Rogers was still paying enough attention to natural history to get his men to make observations on the egg-laying habits of the turtle population; but on board he had to sort out fecundity of another kind: one of the black girls on board gave birth to a baby girl 'of tawny colour'. James Wasse acted as midwife, giving the girl thick strong Peruvian wine to ease the pain. She hadn't been aboard more than six months, but nevertheless she was severely admonished to be good thereafter. Here Rogers is at his most puritanical:

> One of the *Dutchess*'s black nymphs having transgressed in this way, was lately whipped at the capstan. This I mention to satisfy the censorious, that we don't countenance lewdness, and that we took these women aboard only because they spoke English, and begged to be admitted for laundresses, cooks and seamstresses.

He wasn't so fastidious when handing over the black girl slave to the priest; but emotional entanglements on board were quite another matter, and could be very disruptive.

They were now cruising in earnest for the Manila ship. In his journal entry for Friday, 29th October 1709, Edward Cooke writes: 'We agreed to spread ourselves, for fear the Manila ship should pass by unseen. The *Duke* to cruise about two leagues to the southward of the *Dutchess*, the *Dutchess* in the middle and the *Marquiss* two leagues to the northward of her.'

There was further trouble as the cruise continued into November and the men began to grow fractious again. A man called Peter Clark was clapped in irons for saying that he wished himself aboard a pirate ship, or that a pirate would come along and overpower them. On 19th, Cooke had two of his men 'whipped and pickled' for stealing water 'and other offences'. Pickling was the action of rubbing salt or vinegar into the wounds caused by a flogging. Yet another agreement about the division of plunder was drawn up, and gambling was forbidden – though as some of the men had already lost all but their shirts, this seemed a little like locking the stable door after the horse had bolted. As stores were running seriously low, when it was discovered that someone had broken into the lazaretto (storehouse), a serious investigation took place. The steward had taken the precaution of tying the storehouse key to his genitals while he slept; but the thief had managed to remove it without disturbing him. He was found out, however, and flogged. His messmate and accomplice was let off – Rogers confessing blandly that 'knowing his friends in Bristol, I was unwilling to punish him'.

By 20th December they were off Cape St Lucas in California. There was still no sign of the Manila ship, and their bread ration was only good for another seventy days. The plan now was to make for Guam, and Rogers was busy calculating where and how they were to get extra provisions before starting the crossing. They had abandoned all hope of the Manila ship by now; but on the following day 'to our great and joyful surprise, about 9 o'clock the man at the masthead cried out he saw a sail'. What he had sighted was the *Nuestra Señora de la Encarnacion Desengaño*, the smaller of the two Manila ships that had sailed that year.

Having no alcohol to give the men, Rogers had a large cauldron of chocolate boiled. Then the crews prayed before giving battle, but their devotions were interrupted by an opening salvo from the Manila ship. She had barrels hanging from each yard-arm to make boarding difficult, and she had twenty big guns and a crew of 193, but after a fierce battle the privateers took her on 22nd December. The Spaniards had nine killed and ten wounded. The English suffered two casualties: an Irishman called Will Powell was slightly wounded in the buttock, and Rogers himself was badly hit:

> I was shot through the left cheek, the bullet struck away great part of my upper jaw, and several of my teeth, part of which dropped down upon the deck, where I fell . . . I was forced to write what I would say, to prevent the loss of blood, and because of the pain I suffered by speaking.

Christmas Eve saw them safely at anchor with their great prize in Puerto Segura. Her hold was crammed with riches – gold, precious stones, spices, porcelain and, above all, silks. There were 4,310 pairs of silk stockings, 28,502 pounds of raw silk, and 24,289 'pieces of divers sorts of chintz'. They were 'much overjoyed' at their unexpected good fortune, and in addition the commander of the *Nuestra Señora de la Encarnacion Desengaño*, John Pichberty, a Frenchman and a brother-in-law of du Casse, had agreed to give them bills of exchange worth 6,000 Spanish dollars – more than the ransom money – payable in London for the release of his own men and the remaining Guayaquil hostages. Rogers was still in agony:

> In the night I felt something clog my throat, which I swallowed with much pain, and suppose it's a part of my jawbone, or the shot,

which we can't yet give an account of. I soon recovered myself, but my throat and head being very much swelled, have much ado to swallow any sort of liquids for sustenance.

On Christmas Day, two lookouts were posted on a hilltop by the shore to keep an eye open for the larger Manila ship, the *Nuestra Señora de Begoña*. They sighted her the following day and the privateers set out to take her, leaving the *Encarnacion* with Dover in charge of a skeleton crew to guard both her and the prisoners. Despite his injuries, Rogers insisted on accompanying the attack. The battle lasted most of Boxing Day: a netting deck hampered boarding attempts, and the ship was simply too strong for them, despite all their efforts, and despite the early advantage they'd had when she'd mistaken the *Duke* for her consort, the *Encarnacion*. The privateers began to run low on ammunition, and had their masts and rigging shot away. The enemy threw a fireball on to the *Duke*'s quarterdeck, which blew up a chest of loaded arms and musket-cartridge boxes, as well as several powder cartridges. Carleton Vanbrugh and a Dutch crewman were badly burnt, and a flying splinter caught Rogers in the left heel, smashing it to pieces. Although Rogers estimated that they fired over 500 six-pound balls into the Manila ship, she was so strongly built that they had no effect. In addition, she was fiercely defended, for she had aboard a number of English and Irish freebooters who were travelling home with their own private cargoes of loot. On 27th, they reluctantly agreed to call off the attack and cut their losses. 'We might as well have fought a castle of fifty guns as this ship,' wrote Cooke.

They still had the *Encarnacion*, which they now renamed the *Batchelor*, in honour of Alderman John Batchelor, who it will be remembered was one of the expedition's senior backers. A dispute now broke out between the officers. Some supported Dover as commander of the *Batchelor*. Woodes Rogers opposed his appointment strenuously, on the grounds that he didn't have nearly enough experience to manage such a ship. Dampier, surprisingly, supported the Dover faction. Rogers refused to be browbeaten, though he regretted that after having won such an important prize they should start the new year by falling out among themselves in a 'paper war'.

A compromise had to be reached, however, and on 9th January 1710 Rogers, 'being very weak and in much pain . . . not able to stir', sent his opinion of the matter in writing, which effectively was that Dover should be in charge of the cargo, but that experienced officers be put aboard to sail her, and that these officers should not be under Dover's command. In the end the council appointed Lieutenants Robert Frye and William Stretton as joint second captains in charge of navigation, and put Alexander Selkirk aboard as master. Pichberty and the Spanish prisoners were given the tender and provisions enough to take them to Acapulco, and were let go. Pichberty also took letters directed home for the privateers, which despite the war were duly delivered over to the Spanish Atlantic fleet, and arrived at their destination. Rogers had behaved honourably, and Pichberty had no reason to behave otherwise.

On 11th January they set sail for Guam, which they reached two months later after a 'long and tedious passage'. Their provisions for the journey were slender, but even so Rogers was unjustifiably tight with his rationing, and moreover ordered that less be issued to the blacks aboard than to the whites – despite the fact that his black platoon had discharged itself well in the recent fighting, and that he had promised the men their freedom. There had already been desertions from among the blacks before the *Duke* and *Dutchess* left for Guam, and such unfair treatment as this may have been to blame.

At Guam they had a cordial reception, and were able to recuperate briefly before leaving again on 22nd March. Rogers took a native proa home for a souvenir, in the hope of sailing it 'for a curiosity on the canal at St James's Park'. By 29th April, their provisions were running very low. Cooke tells us that the men were trading rats among themselves for sixpence apiece, 'and eat them very savourly'.

Dampier advised that their best hope was to make for Ternate or Tula, for they would get no supplies on the coast of New Guinea. They shaped a course for Ternate, but on 15th May had the luck to discover a good store of rice aboard the *Batchelor*. On 21st Rogers sighted what he thought was Ceram, and sent to Dampier, then aboard the *Dutchess*, to confirm. By now the *Duke* had developed a bad leak, and their fresh water stocks were low. They therefore decided to make for Bouton (Butung). Dampier continued to be vague: 'Our pilot . . . says he has been formerly through the straits, and in his book tells us of a town near the south part of 'em, where the king resided, but he knew nothing of it now, except the bare story.' Dampier indeed visited Butung in 1687, and he is specific enough about the island in his *New Voyage*. It is fair to bear in mind that it was now more than twenty years since that visit; but it seems odd that there was no copy of *A New Voyage* aboard the *Duke*.

But at last, at the end of June, they reached Batavia. Here, six months after he had sustained the wound, Rogers was operated on, and the musket shot cut out of his mouth. 'I also had several pieces of my foot and heel-bone taken out, but God be thanked am now in a fair way to have the use of my foot, and to recover my health. The hole the shot made in my face is now scarce discernible.' The sailors made merry on cheap arrack (eightpence a gallon), and the officers held committee meetings. Dampier and Thomas Glendall, who must have been the two oldest officers on the expedition, were appointed judges of plunder aboard the *Batchelor*. The cargoes of booty were repacked where necessary and re-stowed.

They set about provisioning themselves for the journey home, but the Dutch, though friendly, caused long delays before the privateers could get their ships careened. The *Marquiss* was by now so eaten away with worm that they decided to sell her as salvage, and she was bought by a Captain Opey for $575, which was considered to be quite a bargain. Finally they left Batavia on 12th October 1710, reaching the Cape of Good Hope on 29th December. A day earlier their surgeon, James Wasse, had died. Also to die here about five weeks later was Carleton Vanbrugh. Cooke, who had become his friend and had been appointed his executor, arranged his funeral; 'the ships firing guns every half minute as is customary on these occasions'. It is interesting that the steady Cooke should have befriended Vanbrugh. Had Vanbrugh changed? How seriously injured had he been in the attack on the *Begoña*?

From here they sailed home on 6th April in the company of a Dutch convoy under the command of Admiral Pieter Vos. Their route took them 'north about', sailing around the north of Scotland in order to avoid possible encounters with French or Spanish cruisers, and anchoring at Texel on 23rd July 1711. In the same year, the South Sea Company was 'erected' in England. It is not too fanciful to think that Dampier entertained hopes of being involved in it.

In their accounts, both Rogers and Cooke give long descriptions, though not always first-hand ones, of the countries they touch at. As we have seen, this was important at the time, for much of the information they were giving was new at home. However, some of the second-hand accounts contain errors which Cooke and Rogers could have corrected if they had taken due care, and neither gives the sense of bound-breaking that Dampier's books do. Dampier deals almost exclusively with first-hand experience.

But there is another element too: Woodes Rogers and Edward Cooke were sane, steady men. Dampier, both blessedly and accursedly, was neither of these things. By the time Admiral Burney was writing his account of Dampier's voyages, in 1816, Dampier's books, whose contents by then were largely superseded, were out of print and virtually unobtainable.

Regretting this, Burney writes of him:

This voyage is the last in which William Dampier is known to have been engaged. Many years spent in a laborious and almost unremitting exercise of his profession, added to disappointment that his endeavours were not attended with better success, must have much worn his constitution at the time he sailed with Woodes Rogers . . . It is not easy to name another voyager or traveller who has given more useful information to the world; to whom the merchant and the mariner are so much indebted . . .

CHAPTER TWENTY-ONE

The Return of the Wanderer

Rogers had brought his ships round the world intact – the first time such a feat had been achieved and recorded by an English mariner for well over a century. He had also brought back over 80 per cent of his crew – another major accomplishment. But the problems of the venture were not over yet.

In 1711, as we have seen, the South Sea Company was founded. It was the brainchild of the leading Tory, Robert Harley, and he was abetted and advised by Daniel Defoe. Defoe may have helped Rogers prepare his book for the press, and may have had a hand in the politically aggressive Introduction. The East India Company, allied to the Bank of England and sympathetic to the Whigs, was therefore especially sensitive at that time to any threat of competition, albeit in another part of the world. When it got wind of Rogers's return home via the East Indies (it had its own spies in Batavia), it would not accept that the minimal amount of necessary trading for provisions he had done in those waters did not constitute an infraction of its own monopoly. While threats of arrest were made in London, Rogers and his ships hoped to ride out the storm in Dutch waters, where they were unassailable; but they could not stay there for ever. The ships were in poor condition and the crews, so close to home after so long, were impatient to be back, and impatient to get their share of the considerable booty they had brought back with them.

News of their arrival and successful voyage was, of course, all over the English capital by now, and the government, aware of the unusually high value of the goods on which it could charge duty now riding in the Zuider Zee, had a keen interest in its safe return. It therefore sent out a strong escort of men-of-war from the Nore: the *Essex*, of seventy guns; the *Canterbury* and *Medway*, each of sixty guns, and the sixth-rate *Dunwich*, of twenty-four. The convoy left Dutch waters on 22nd September but was delayed by adverse winds. New sails were purchased for the *Batchelor*, which of course was the ship everybody wanted to see, and they set off again, arriving in the Downs on 2nd October. The newspapers were full of it. Sadly, Admiral Whetstone had died the previous April and so could not rejoice in his son-in-law's success; and poor Alderman Batchelor did not live to reap the benefits of his investment, as he died within weeks of the arrival of the ship named in his honour. Rogers's little fleet dropped anchor at last at Erith on 14th October.

Negotiations with the East India Company dragged on for months, but finally, in early 1712, it settled for a flat payment of £6,000, and relations with the owners thereafter were friendly. Nevertheless, £6,000 was a considerable sum, and legal costs had also eaten into the profits of the venture.

Litigation was far from over. An enormous amount of Byzantine legal and financial haggling dragged on through 1712 and well into 1713. After so long and so demanding a voyage, the ships only fetched £935; the total grossed from the sale of all goods, ransom bills and payments derived from the venture was the princely sum of £147,975 12s 4d. The owners took two-thirds of this, but half of their share went in legal expenses, bribes, customs duties, storage fees, sundry expenses and offsets against the original investment. Even so, the investors did not do so badly: Thomas Dover, if one counts the salary he drew as an officer of the expedition, made a profit of £2,755. The Quaker merchant, Goldney, made about £3,100. The sailors had inflated their expectations in their own minds to millions of pounds; but the officers and men of the expedition had to be content with just under £50,000 between them. Few ordinary seamen got more than £50 each. We know from his interview with Steele that Selkirk got £800. Rogers himself netted only just over £1,500, and that was immediately absorbed by his creditors: such debts had piled up during his three year absence (the house in Queen Square and a wife and three children) that on his homecoming he was declared bankrupt.

His later life, despite grave setbacks, confirms one's view of him as a steady, conscientious and mildly ambitious man. He had bounced back enough by 1713 to propose a colonization of Madagascar, and although that came to nothing, four years later he was able to purchase a twenty-one-year lease on the Bahamas, of which he became governor. Here he was instrumental in stamping out piracy and establishing a solid economy based on plantations. Remembering Dampier's behaviour in punishing Fisher, it is interesting to note that while at the Bahamas Rogers himself pistol-whipped an officer, the commander of the *Rose* frigate, for insubordination. Rogers's improvement of the Bahamas was not plain sailing. The islands were neglected, the locals shiftless, and the only source of revenue when he arrived came from piracy. He had soon bankrupted himself again in efforts to reform the economy of the place, and the government and the Lords Proprietors would not bale him out. He returned to England in 1721 and languished in a debtors' prison for several years, in the course of which, it has been suggested, his wife abandoned him, before the authorities finally recognized their own debt of gratitude to him. The Crown granted him a modest pension and restored his governorship. He returned to the Bahamas in 1728, where he continued his work of improvement. Worn out by it, he died in 1732, and lies in a forgotten grave. He had lived out his family motto to the letter: *Je ferai mon devoir*: I will do my duty. His old shipmate and rival author, Edward Cooke, was drowned at sea at about the same time.

The moral and political victories of the voyage were huge. Rogers and his officers were lauded as heroes in London and Bristol, and their achievement served as a great advertisement for opening up the possibilities of the Pacific coast of South America for England. Cooke and Rogers immediately set to work on working up their journals for publication – Cooke just beating Rogers to it, but getting his first volume out so fast that it had to be followed by a second to fill out the gaps. Both men knew the news value of Selkirk's rescue: it is mentioned on the title-page of Rogers's book and, picking up the cue, on the title-page of Cooke's second volume, where, as we have seen, he devotes far more space to Crusoe's prototype than he did in his first. There is plenty of evidence in both books of extensive reading of other accounts and compendiums. On balance, Rogers's book is better than Cooke's, but Cooke's eye for detail is almost as keen as Dampier's, as is his enthusiasm for natural history. No doubt both men, and their officers, as well as Selkirk, were interviewed by government officials and by the press, with Defoe and Steele well to the fore.

As for Dampier, he was engaged in complicated litigation in order to get his share for the rest of his life. He maintained that his expectation from the voyage was £2,000. He had been advanced about £200 drawn before and during the voyage, and £1,150 on his return, but the balance seems never to have been paid. It is unlikely however that he spent the last three years of his life in poverty, since he would have been able to borrow on expectation.

Dampier was far from the only crew member involved in litigation. Almost everybody was in the same position. Various lawyers had scented money and one, Stephen Creagh, had thought it worth his while to go over to Holland and persuade 209 of the sailors, including Dampier, to engage him to look after their interests at 5 per cent of their receipts.

A suit in Chancery had been started by the crew and no division of the spoils that fell to their share was possible until it had been resolved. A complicated statement has survived from Dampier's cousin and sole executor, Grace Mercer, made to the Master in Chancery, Mr Mellor, and contained in a report by him dated 9th May 1719. In it she claims that the owners should have paid interest on Dampier's shares in the venture from the time they originally calculated the dividend. She claims that Dampier was owed eleven shares, though Cooke's list assigns only eight to the pilot. Dampier also claimed a one-sixteenth share of the net profits of the venture. But as if this were not complicated enough, Dampier seems to have offered the surgeon, John Ballet, three of his shares if he would join the expedition, and though no paper exists to prove this, the Master in Chancery allowed Ballet's claim. As eight plus three is eleven, this would explain Grace Mercer's claim. At the same time he disallowed a bid for a 5 per cent cut from Creagh. In 1717, according to Bertram Rogers, who researched Dampier's finances in detail in the mid 1920s, the Master had paid Grace Mercer £1,050 17s 10d as the balance due to her. In the end, together with the money paid to Dampier in his lifetime – about £1,350 – the total Dampier or his heirs received as a result of his participation in the voyage seems to have been around £2,450. Of course, the £1,350 was an advance which would have to be paid back, and Grace Mercer never got the full value of the shares and the one-sixteenth interest in the net profits which she claimed for – which would have been about £2,200. But Dampier's accounts are even more complex than his life. At one stage the owners offered a once-and-for-all settlement of £500, which our mariner refused, believing, not without justification, that he was being shortchanged, and holding out for £1,000. As a result the deal fell by the board. Grace may have lived to regret her cousin's obstinacy, and she probably ended up inheriting nothing. But it is likely that any debts he died owing were written off. In addition, his Customs House salary seems to have been paid right up until the end. It is possible, too, that he derived some revenue from royalties on his books, which continued to sell well.

By the end of 1714, Dampier knew that he had not long to live. The years and years living in harsh conditions and inhospitable climates had taken their toll, and he had become, in the words of his will, 'weak and diseased' in body, though 'of sound and perfect mind'. He signed his will on 29th November 1714. In it he leaves one-tenth of his estate to his brother George, and the remainder to Grace Mercer, who appears to have lived with him as his housekeeper for the last few years of his life, which were spent in Coleman Street, near Old Jewry in the parish of St Stephen, in the City of London. No mention is made of Judith, so we must assume that she had already died, since it would have been out of character for Dampier not to have remembered her now.

As we know so little about Judith, so we know little more of Grace. She may have been the daughter of Henry Mercer, Dampier's mother's brother. She was baptized about 24th October 1686, and in March 1718 may have married one Elisha Mallett in London. She must have been a persistent woman, to pursue Dampier's case so vigorously after his death – but that is all we can tell of her.

The will was proven on 23rd March 1715, but the exact date of Dampier's death is unknown. Equally unknown is where he lies buried, for no records have come to light to help us. There are memorials. Two can be found in the parish church of St Michael in East Coker, Dampier's birthplace. One was erected by the government of Western Australia to commemorate the tricentenary of our mariner's birth. At the same time there was a plan to dismantle his alleged birthplace in the village and rebuild it in Western Australia, following the example of 'Cook's cottage' in Melbourne; but the idea came to nothing for financial reasons. When Queen Elizabeth II visited Western Australia in 1955, Boans Ltd of Perth presented a Dampier window display which had been set up in their firm to the West Australian Museum. There is a town named after our mariner in Western Australia: Dampier was founded in the 1860s and is now the port outlet for Hamersley Iron Pty Ltd, which has mining rights to 5,000 million tonnes of iron ore in the town's hinterland. It is also the home of Dampier Salt Ltd. The town of Broome has a Dampier monument in the form of a stone sea-chest, placed in a park overlooking Roebuck Bay. A Royal Navy survey ship, the first of its kind to be commissioned after the Second World War, was named after him. In the 1960s Dampier was used in a newspaper advertising campaign by Thames Board Mills Ltd.

It is the second memorial to Dampier in East Coker Church that one sees first, since it is on the south wall opposite the entrance. It is not beautiful. It was erected following an initiative by a remote descendant and namesake of Dampier, the scientific historian Sir William Dampier, FRS. A subscription of £36 9s was got up, and the plaque was unveiled on Tuesday 19th May 1908 at 2.30 p.m. It did not make its appearance without controversy, for the then vicar, Charles Powell, described by Sir William's sister Bessy as having 'a very good opinion of his own abilities', and who had written a short biographical monograph about our mariner in 1907, objected to the use on the memorial of the word 'buccaneer'. In a letter to Sir William of 4th October 1907, he writes:

> With regard to 'buccaneer': why should we mention that part of Dampier's life which he distinctly says he repented of? The word will be probably misleading and suggest a bloodthirsty pirate. Mr G. T. Chafyn-Grove [a local worthy] has spoken of him in reference to the revival of interest in him as 'a pirate ruffian that ought to have been hung'. I should not be surprised if he opposed the erection of the tablet or called for its removal on that very account.

But Sir William got his way, and on the plaque Dampier is described as a 'buccaneer, explorer, hydrographer and sometime Captain of the ship *Roebuck* in the Royal Navy of King William the Third'.

His real monument is his work. He was not only a pioneer of navigation, leaving observations and directions to be followed, corrected and improved upon by those who sailed in his wake, such as George Anson and Philip Carteret (who rectifies several errors); but an inspiration to all eighteenth- and early-nineteenth-century explorers of the seas. He was a writer and scientist whose enthusiasm for his subjects knew no bounds. He was also a freebooter and at times a villain, and he never abandoned his hopes of riches. Perhaps at the end he was aware that the riches he had found and made known to the rest of us were as great as any gold. I hope so. He deserves to have gone to his grave content. Though he never went to sea again after 1711, and probably never left London, I am certain that he would not have been able to keep away from the River Thames, and that his eyes never lost their habit of scanning the water.

On the west wall of St Michael's is another plaque, to the poet T. S. Eliot, who traced his own family back to East Coker and is buried there. Dampier would have appreciated the lines that precede the words which appear on his monument, and it is good to end with them:

> Old men ought to be explorers
> Here or there does not matter
> We must be still and still moving
> Into another intensity
> For a further union, a deeper communion
> Through the dark cold and the empty desolation,
> The wave cry, the wind cry, the vast waters
> Of the petrel and the porpoise. In my end is my beginning.

SEVENTEENTH- AND
TWENTIETH-CENTURY PLACE NAMES

17th Century	*20th Century*
Achamack	Accomac
Achin	Banda Aceh
Alcoranes	Alacran Cluster (north of Yucatán)
Allegrance	Alegranze
Amapalla Gulf	Gulf of Fonseca
Amapalla Island	Tiger Island
Amboyna	Ambon
Anabao, Anamabao	? Semau
Antego	Antigua
Anthony Cave's Island	Anthony Caen's Island
Aynam	Hainan
Bahia	Salvador
Bande Island	Banda Island
Bashee Islands	Batan Group
Batavia	Jakarta
Bayedore	Bojadore
Beef Island	Carmen Island
Bencalis	Bengkalis
Bencola, Bencouli	Bengkulu, Benkulen
Bird Island	Manu
Blanco Island	Isla Blanca (Hermanos Group)
Boca del Toro	Bocas del Toro
Bonao Island	Boano Island

Bouro Island	Buru Island
Bouton Island	Butung Island
Buonas Aires	Buenos Aires
Cachao	? Hanoi
Cacuses	Caicos Sands (off NW Hispaniola)
California, Lake of	Gulf of California
Callasusung	Kalin Susu
Cambodia River	Mekong River
Cambusses Islands	Kombuys Islands
Campeachy	Campeche
Celebes	Sulawesi
Ceram	Seram
Chambongo	Zamboanga
Checapeque River	Chiltepec River
Chuche	? Senova
Cobaya, Quibo	Coiba
Cocos Island (12°S,98°E)	Keeling Island
Collima	Colima (19°20'N,103°40'W)
Comana	Cumana
Concordia	Kupang (Timor)
Condecedo Cape	Point Piedras
Coolacan River	Culiacan River
Copang Bay	Kupan Bay
Crockadore	Krakatoa
Don Mascarin	Mauritius
Duke of Grafton's Island	Batan Island
Duke of Monmouth's Island	Sabtan Island
Ende Island	Flores Island (near Timor)
Estapa	Istapa
Fetter Island	Kambing Island
Fort St George	Madras
Garret Dennis Island	Gerard de Nys Island
Gilolo Island	Halmahera Island
Groyne, the	Corunna
Guasickwalp	Coatzocoalcos
Halpo	Jalpa

Jihore	Johor
Keyhoocha	Acayuca
Key Monbrack	Cayma Brac
Kosiway Island	Kasiwooi Island
Ladrones	Marianas
Lambana Island	Lomblen Island
Lancerota	Lanzerote
La Vell Cape	Cabo de Vela
Logos Cape	Lopez Cape
Luconia	Luzon
Mabo Cape	? Selee Cape
Macassar	Ujung Padang (Sulawesi)
Malacca	Melaka
Mansheters Island	Menscheneters Island
Merga	Mergui
Mericaia	Maracaibo
Meschasipi River	Mississippi River
Mindora	Mindoro
Misacomby, Omba Island	Ombai Island
Oleta River	? Canas River, ? San Pedro River
Oratavia	Orotava
Palimbam	Palembang
Pallacat	Pulicat
Palmas	? Tupilco
Panuk River	Panuco River
Passange Jonca	Passanjan (Sumatra)
Pernambuco	Recife
Petaplan	Petatlan
Pines Island	? Isla de la Juventad
Pintare Island	Pantar Island
Ponticheri	Pondicherry
Port Marquis	San Marcos
Pracel	Paracel
Pulo Condore	? Con Son (situated off the mouths of the Mekong River)
St Iago, St Jago	Santiago, Sao Tiago

St Jago River	Rio Grande de Santiago
St Martin's Land	Punta Morillo
SS Peter and Paul River	Rio San Pedro (Campeche)
Salinas	Real de las Salinas
Sallegua	? Manzanillas Bay, ? Puerto Navidad
Sall Island	Sal Island (Cape Verdes)
Sal River	Mazatlan River
Samballas Islands	San Blas Archipelago
Sambo River	Sambre River
Santa Maria River	? Chucunaque River
Tabago	Taboga
Tabogilla	Tabaguilla
Teguantapecque	Tehuantepec
Ternate Island	? Kepulauan Sula
Tispo	Tuxpan
Tompeck	Tampico
Tondelo	Tonala
Tranzambar	Tranquebar
Valderas	Banderas
Venta Cruz	Cruces
Watela	Watubella
Wishart's Island	? St Matthias Island

BIBLIOGRAPHY

Editions of Dampier's Works Consulted (Including Some Works Appearing in Anthologies) in the British Library

1697 (*A New Voyage*, 3 copies)

1698

1699 (3 copies)

1699 *A SHORT ACCOUNT FROM, AND DESCRIPTION OF, THE ISTHMUS OF DARIEN, WHERE THE SCOTS COLONY ARE SETTLED – according to our late News, and Mr Dampier and Mr Wafer* (Vallange, Edinburgh)

1700

1703 (fifth edition)

1703 (*New Holland*, 2 copies)

1705

1707 *Captain Dampier's VINDICATION OF HIS VOYAGE TO THE SOUTH SEAS IN THE SHIP ST. GEORGE, with some observations for the present of Mr Funnell's chimerical relation of the VOYAGE ROUND THE WORLD; and detected in little, until he shall be examin'd more at large* (Mary Edwards, London)

1709 (*A Continuation*, 2 copies)

1729 (*Voyages round the World*, 3 volumes, 3 copies)

1756 (in *A Compendium of Voyages*, volume 6)

1766 (in *A Compendium of Voyages*, volume 6)

1767 (in *A New Collection of Voyages*, volume 3)

1774 (in *An Historical Account of All the Voyages round the World*, volume 1)

1776 (*Voyages*, 2 volumes)

1893 (*A New Voyage*)

1906 *Dampier's Voyages*, 2 volumes, edited by John Masefield (E. Grant Richards, London; limited edition of 1,000). The only complete modern edition, and the best.

1927 *A New Voyage round the World*, with an introduction by Sir Albert Gray (Argonaut Press, London)

1931 *Voyages and Discoveries*, with an introduction by Clennell Wilkinson (Argonaut Press, London)

1937 (*A New Voyage*)

1939 (*New Holland*)

1994 *William Dampier — Buccaneer Explorer*, abridged, edited and with an introduction by Gerald Norris (Folio Society, London)

Biographies and Biographical Material

Anon, *Life and Adventures of William Dampier, with a History of the Buccaneers of America* (Blackie, London, 1895)

Anon, *Naval Biography; or, the History and Lives of Distinguished Characters in the British Navy* (Baynes, London, 1809)

Baer, Joel, H., *William Dampier at the Crossroads: New Light on the 'Missing Years', 1691–1697* (in the *International Journal of Maritime History*, VIII, no. 2, December 1996, pp. 97–117)

Bennett, J. H., *William Dampier, Buccaneer and Planter* (in *History Today*, XIV, no. 7, July 1964, pp. 469–77)

Bingley, William, *Biographical Conversations on the Most Eminent Voyagers etc.* (John Sharpe, London, 1818)

Bonner, Willard Hallam, *Captain William Dampier, Buccaneer-Author* (Stamford University Press, California, 1934). Concentrates on Dampier's influence as a writer.

Burney, James, *A Chronological History of the Voyages and Discoveries in the South Seas or Pacific Ocean*, volume 4 (Nicol; Payne and Foss; Longman, Hurst, Rees, Orme and Brown; Cadell and Davis; Nornaville and Fell; John Murray, London, 1816). A beautifully produced and superbly written account.

—*History of the Buccaneers of America*, abridged edition with an introduction by Malcolm Barnes (Allen and Unwin, London, 1950)

Cockburn, Elizabeth O., *William Dampier, Buccaneer-Explorer-Hydrographer* (Shelleys, Sherborne, 1987)

Lloyd, Christopher, *William Dampier* (Faber and Faber, London, 1966)

Marchant, Leslie R., *An Island Unto Itself: William Dampier and New Holland* (Hesperian, Western Australia, 1988). Concentrates on Dampier's visits to Australia.

Rogers, Bertram M. H., *Dampier's Voyage of 1703* (in the *Mariner's Mirror*, X, 1924, pp. 366–81)

—*Woodes Rogers' Privateering Voyage of 1708–1711* (in the *Mariner's Mirror*, XIX, 1933, pp. 196–211)

—*Dampier's Debts* (in *Notes and Queries*)

Russell, W. Clark, *William Dampier* (Macmillan, London, 1889)

Shipman, Joseph C., *William Dampier, Seaman-Scientist* (Lawrence, Kansas, 1962)

Smyth, W. H., *A Biographical Sketch of Captain Dampier* (in *The United Service Journal and Naval and Military Magazine*, nos. 1, 2, 3, 4, 5; July–November 1837) (Henry Colburn, London)

Wilkinson, Clennell, *William Dampier* (Bodley Head, London, 1929)

Buccaneers, Pirates and Privateers

Black, Clinton V., *Pirates of the West Indies* (Cambridge University Press, 1989)

Botting, Douglas, *The Pirates* (Time-Life, Amsterdam, 1979)

Cordingly, David, *Life among the Pirates* (Little Brown, London, 1995)

Cordingly, David, and John Falconer, *Pirates, Fact and Fiction* (Collins and Brown, London, 1992)

Esquemeling, John, *The Buccaneers of America*, edited by William Swan Stallybrass (Routledge, London, 1923). This is a complete edition and contains Basil Ringrose's account as Part IV. Part III Chapter XII is 'A brief account of Captain Sharp and other his companions', not by Ringrose.

Exquemelin, A. O., *The Buccaneers of America*, with an introduction by

Jack Beeching (Penguin, Harmondsworth, 1969). This edition does not contain Ringrose's account.

Feder, Joshua B., *Pirates* (Mallard, New York, 1992)

Gosse, Philip, *The History of Piracy* (Longmans, Green and Co., London, 1932)

Grant, Neil, *Buccaneers* (Angus and Robertson, London, 1976)

Johnson, Captain Charles, *A General History of the Robberies and Murders of the Most Notorious Pirates*, edited by Arthur L. Hayward (Routledge, London, 1926). Other editions consulted were those of 1724 (first edition), 1726, 1765, 1788 and 1850.

Lucie-Smith, Edward, *Outcasts of the Sea* (Paddington, London and New York, 1978)

McIntyre, Captain Donald, *The Privateers* (Paul Elek, London, 1975)

Mitchell, David, *Pirates* (Thames and Hudson, London, 1976)

Norris, Gerald, *West Country Pirates and Buccaneers* (Dovecote, Dorset, 1990)

Platt, Richard, *Pirate* (Dorling Kindersley, London, New York, Stuttgart, 1995)

Senior, C. M., *A Nation of Pirates: English Piracy in its Heyday* (David and Charles, London, 1976)

Starkey, David J., *British Privateering Enterprise in the Eighteenth Century* (Exeter University Press, 1990)

Villar, Roger, *Piracy Today* (Conway Maritime, London, 1985)

Wright, Rachel, *Pirates* (Franklin Watts, London, 1991)

Wycherley, George, *Buccaneers of the Pacific* (Rich and Cowan, London, 1935)

General Bibliography

Anson, George, *A Voyage round the World in the Years 1740–1744* (SPCK, undated Victorian edition)

Barclay, Patrick, *The Universal Traveller* (Purser and Read, London, 1735)

Barlow, Edward, *Barlow's Journal of his Life at Sea in King's Ships, East and West Indiamen and Other Merchantmen from 1659 to 1703*, transcribed from the original manuscript by Basil Lubbock, two volumes (Hurst and Blackett, London, 1934)

Bowley, R. L., *The Fortunate Islands* (Bowley, Berkshire, 1968)

Callander (ed.), *Terra Australis Incognita*, volume 2 (Donaldson, London and Edinburgh, 1768)

Chappell, Edwin, *Samuel Pepys as a Naval Administrator* (Cambridge University Press, 1933)

—*Samuel Pepys* (privately printed, 1937)

Charnock, John, *Biographia Navalis*, volume 3 (Faulder, London, 1795)

Clark, Sir George, *The Oxford History of England 1660–1714* (Oxford University Press, 1955)

Clipperton, John, *Clipperton's Voyage*, in *Terra Australis Incognita*, volume 3 (1766 edition)

Clipperton, John (and William Ambrosia Cowley), *The Voyage round the World*, in *Navigantium Atque Iterantium* (1744 edition)

—*Voyages of Clipperton and Shelvocke*, in *Voyages and Travels*, volume 1 (? 1785 edition)

Clowes, William Laird, *The Royal Navy* (Samson Low, Marston, London, 1898)

Cooke, Captain Edward, *A Voyage to the South Sea and round the World, Perform'd in the Years 1708–1711* (Lintot and Gosling *et al.*, London, 1712)

Davis, Ralph, *The Rise of the English Shipping Industry in the Seventeenth and Eighteenth Centuries* (Macmillan, London, 1962)

Defoe, Daniel, *Robinson Crusoe* (first edition 1719)

—*The Life, Adventures and Piracies of the Famous Captain Singleton* (first edition 1720)

—*A New Voyage round the World* (first edition 1724)

Description of a Mappemonde by Juan Vespucci and of a Buccaneer's Atlas by William Hack in the possession of Bernard Quaritch (Catalogue issued July 1914, and in BL Tracts 011903/d1)

Dictionary of National Biography: entries for Albermarle (Monck), Carlisle (Howard), Dampier, Defoe, Prince George of Denmark, Orford, Rooke, Shelvocke, Spragge.

Dover, Thomas, *The Ancient Physician's Legacy to his Country* (Hitch, London, 1742)

Encyclopaedia Britannica: entry for Tasman.

Evelyn, John, *Diary and Correspondence of John Evelyn, FRS*, volume 2 (Bohn, London, 1859)

Foreman, John, *The Philippines* (Filipiniana Book Guild, Manila, 1980)

Frith, C. H. (ed.), *Naval Songs and Ballads* (Navy Records Society, London, 1908)

Funnell, William, *A Voyage round the World* (James Knapton, London, 1707)

Hack, William (ed.), *A Collection of Original Voyages*, volume 4 (John Knapton, London, 1729). This contains the accounts of Cowley and Sharp.

Hakluyt, Richard, *The Tudor Venturers*, edited by John Hampden (Folio Society, London, 1970)

Hamilton, Alexander, *A New Account of the East Indies*, edited by Sir William Foster, two volumes (first published 1727, Argonaut Press, London, 1930)

Harris, John (ed.), *Navigantium Atque Itinerantium Bibliotheca*, Woodward, Ward *et al.*, two volumes (London, 1744). This great work in huge volumes covers nearly everyone. Kerr (see below) leans heavily on Harris. In this edition only volume 1 is relevant, especially pp. 77–184: Cowley, Dampier, Funnell, Woodes Rogers.

Hawkesworth, John (ed.), *An Account of the Voyages Undertaken by the Order of his Present Majesty for Making Discoveries in the Southern Hemisphere*, three volumes (Strahan, London, 1773). Contains an account of Captain Carteret's voyage, and is illustrated with beautiful charts.

Johnson, Charles, *The Successful Pyrate* (Bernard Lintott, London, 1713)

Kenny, C. E., *The Quadrant and the Quill* (privately printed, London, 1944). An account of Samuel Sturmy.

Kerr, Robert (ed.), *A General History and Collection of Voyages and Travels*, Blackwood *et al.*, volume 10 (Edinburgh, 1814). Accounts of Clipperton, John Cook, Cowley, Dampier, Funnell, Woodes Rogers and Shelvocke, pp. 208–484.

Leadam, I. S., *The Political History of England 1702–1760* (Longmans, London, 1909)

Leslie, Robert C. (ed.), *Life Aboard a British Privateer in the Time of Queen Anne, Being the Journal of Captain Woodes Rogers, Master Mariner* (Chapman and Hall, London, 1889)

Little, Bryan, *Crusoe's Captain* (Odhams, London, 1960)

Lodge, Richard, *The Political History of England 1660–1702* (Longmans, London, 1910) de Lussan, Raveneau, *Journal of a Voyage into the South Seas in 1684 and Three Following Years with the Filibusters*, translated and edited by Marguerite Eyer Wilbur (Arthur H. Clark, Cleveland, 1930)

Manwayring, Sir Henry, *The Sea-Man's Dictionary, or, an Exposition and Demonstration of all the Parts and Things Belonging to a Ship. Together with an Explanation of All the Terms and Phrases Used in the Practick of Navigation* (Benjamin Hurlock, London, 1644)

Marx, Robert F., *Pirate Port* (Pelham, London, 1968)

Moore, John Hamilton (ed.), *A New and Complete Collection of Voyages and Travels* (London, ? 1785)

Moorehead, Alan, *The Fatal Impact* (Hamish Hamilton, London, 1966)

Morris, Roland, *Island Treasure: the Search for Sir Cloudesley Shovell's Flagship 'Association'* (Hutchinson, London, 1969)

Rediker, Marcus, *Between the Devil and the Deep Blue Sea* (Cambridge University Press, 1987)

Richman, Irving, *California Under Spain and Mexico 1535–1847* (Houghton Mifflin, New York, 1911)

Ringrose, Basil, see Part IV, pp. 289–475, of the 1923 edition of Esquemeling noted above.

Ritchie, Robert C., *Captain Kidd and the War Against the Pirates* (Harvard University Press, 1986)

Roberts, W. Adolphe, *Sir Henry Morgan, Buccaneer and Governor* (Pioneer Press, Kingston, Jamaica, 1952)

Robinson, Charles Napier, *The British Tar in Fact and Fiction* (Harper, London, 1909)

Rogers, Woodes, *A Cruising Voyage round the World*, edited by G. E. Manwaring (The Seafarers' Library, Cassell, London, 1928)

Schurz, William Lytle, *The Manila Galleon* (Historical Conservation Society, Manila, 1985)

Shelvocke, George, *Voyage round the World* (London, 1930 edition)

Smollett, Tobias, *Roderick Random* (first edition 1748)

Stapleton, Marjorie, *Make the Things Sailors Made* (Studio Vista, London, 1975)

Steele, Richard, *The Englishman*, no. 26, 3rd December 1713

Stevenson, Robert Louis, *Treasure Island* (first edition 1883)

Strong, L. A. G., *Dr Quicksilver: the Life and Times of Thomas Dover, MD* (Andrew Melrose, London, 1955)

Swift, Jonathan, *Gulliver's Travels* (first edition 1726)

Wafer, Lionel, *A New Description of the Isthmus of Darien*, edited and with an introduction by L. E. Elliott Joyce (Oxford University Press for the Hakluyt Society, 1934). This book has an excellent introduction and bibliography.

Welbe, John, *An Answer to Captain Dampier's Vindication* (Bragge, London, no date but *c.* 1707)

Williams, Basil, *The Oxford History of England 1714–1760*, 2nd edition revised by C. H. Stuart (Oxford University Press, 1960)

Williams, Eric, *From Columbus to Castro: the History of the Caribbean 1492–1969* (André Deutsch, London, 1970)

Winston, Alexander, *No Purchase, No Pay* (Eyre and Spottiswoode, London, 1970)

Wycherley, William, *The Plain Dealer* (first published 1676)

OTHER SOURCES

Somerset Record Office

A/APO, 1: Family trees of Dampiers of Blackford, Bruton, Colinshayes etc.

DD/BR/by C/1229: Nineteenth-century wills and indentures relating to a Dampier family, with a family tree.

DD/SAS: Deeds. Dampiers of Blackford. 1637–1765.

DD/WHh: Helyar Archive. Dampier's letters from Jamaica. Jamaica Papers.

DD/X/DMP 1N/III: Scroll of pedigree.

DD/X/HVY 1H/441: Commentary on Dampier's family tree.

D/P/cok.e 2/1/1: East Coker parish records.

D/P/cok.e 2/9/1 L/M: East Coker parish records.

East Coker Parish Church

Helyar Court Rolls.

Papers relating to the 1908 plaque in the church.

Papers relating to the celebrations in 1951 to mark the tricentenary of Dampier's birth.

The Public Record Office

ADM 1/5262 i,ii,iii: Accounts of the loss of the *Roebuck*. Papers relating to that voyage and to Dampier's court-martial.

ADM 52/94: The log of the *Roebuck* by Jacob Hughes.

Calendar of State Papers, Colonial Series, America and West Indies: Vols. 1675–6; 1677–80; 1681–5; 1685–8.

Calendar of State Papers, Domestic: Admiralty List 1700–1702.

CO/1/34–65

CO/5

CO/5/1

SP9465–72 (Chancery Lane): Letters to the Secretary of State from British ambassadors; some in code.

Dampier's will.

The Manuscript Students' Room at the British Library

Additional

5414 and 5415: Map collections

12410: Long's collections for the history of Jamaica.

12423: Journal of Edward d'Oyley 1655–62. D'Oyley was commander-in-chief 'of all his Highness' forces in America'.

12429: Collection of tracts relating to Jamaica volume 1 1505–1693.

12430: Collection of tracts relating to Jamaica volume 2 1655–1702.

13965: Spanish reports about Maracaibo, 1676.

13975: De Indias volume 2.

13977: Papeles Varios de Indias.

13992: Spanish papers relating to the West Indies and the Philippines.

22676: Miscellaneous papers relating to the Island of Jamaica 1662–1765.

28189: A very early Spanish manuscript 'rutter' marked 15th April 1583.

33054: Newcastle papers volume CCCLXIX – relating to Welbe.

Harley

4034: Hack: Charts of the Pacific coast of South America.

Sloane

44: Hack's version of the drafts taken by Sharp from the *Rosario* and worked up as a presentation volume for Charles II.

45: Hack: Maps of the South American coastline, the Galapagos, with Cowley's names for them, 'Pepys' Island' and some Caribbean islands.

46a and b: Sharp's journal.

48: Ringrose's journal edited by Hack. See 3820.

49: John Cox's journal.

54: William Ambrosia Cowley's journal.

239: The original drafts taken by Sharp from the *Rosario*.

1709: Miscellaneous papers.

2292: A collection of 'rutters'.

2724: Papers of the Earl of Carlisle relating to Jamaica.

2752: Fauconberg's observations – the second part of this volume contains an anonymous manuscript account of the first Darien expedition in 1680.

3236: Dampier's journal, containing his transcription of part of Wafer's journal.

3295: John Strong's journal.

3820: Ringrose's original unadulterated journal.

28079: Tracts relating to trade – contains among other things Wafer's report to Thomas, Duke of Leeds, about trading in the South Seas.

INDEX

Note: WD = William Dampier; *D&D* = *Duke* and *Dutchess*

383